Communications in Computer and Information Science 500

More information about this series at http://www.springer.com/series/7899

Anna-Lena Lamprecht · Tiziana Margaria (Eds.)

Process Design for Natural Scientists

An Agile Model-Driven Approach

Editors
Anna-Lena Lamprecht
Chair Service and Software Engineering
Institute of Computer Science
University of Potsdam
Potsdam
Germany

Tiziana Margaria
Chair Software Engineering
Computer Science and Information Systems Department
University of Limerick

and

Lero, The Irish Software Research Center
Limerick
Ireland

ISSN 1865-0929 ISSN 1865-0937 (electronic)
ISBN 978-3-662-45005-5 ISBN 978-3-662-45006-2 (eBook)
DOI 978-3-662-45006-2

Library of Congress Control Number: 2014950464

Springer Heidelberg New York Dordrecht London

Printed on acid-free paper

Springer is part of Springer Science+Business Media (www.springer.com)

Preface I

In contrast with our seemingly endless ability to generate more biological data, faster, and at lower cost, there are increasingly worrisome observations of human limitations with respect to managing and manipulating these massive and highly complex datasets. With data at this scale, mistakes are easily made, and as Baggerly noted "the most common errors are simple... the most simple errors are common" when it comes to biological data management. Many, possibly most, biological researchers lack the skills to programmatically manipulate large datasets, and therefore continue to use inappropriate tools to manage the "big data" that even a modestly resourced laboratory can now create. Serious errors introduced during data management and manipulation are difficult to detect by the researcher and, because they go unrecorded, are nearly impossible to trace during peer-review.

Beyond data manipulation errors, the statistical expertise required to correctly analyze high-throughput data is rare, and biological researchers—even those who are extremely competent in rigorously executing the data-generating "omics" experiments—are seldom adequately trained in appropriate statistical analysis of the output. As such, inappropriate approaches, including trial-and-error, may be applied until a "sensible" answer is found. Finally, because manually driven analyses of high-throughput data can be extremely time-consuming and monotonous, researchers will sometimes inappropriately use a hypothesis-guided approach—examining only possibilities that they already believe are likely based on their interpretation of prior biological knowledge, or personal bias towards where they believe the answer should be. Thus, the scientific literature becomes contaminated with errors resulting from "fishing for significance," from research bias, and even from outright errors.

These problems are becoming pervasive in omics-scale science. The affordability and accessibility of high-throughput technologies is such that now even small groups and individual laboratories can generate datasets that far exceed their capacity, computationally and statistically, to adequately manage and correctly analyze. The end result is a glut of non-reproducible science making its way into the primary literature and databases. Recent "forensic audits" of the scientific literature, such as those executed by Begley and Elles, have shown that a large proportion of bioinformatics research cannot be replicated independently, with numbers ranging from a low of 25% up to a staggering 89% of non-replicable research in a recent study of oncology publications from 2001 to 2011.

While an independent study by Baggerly into the accuracy and quality of published high-throughput analyses triggered retractions (and even a scientific misconduct investigation!) a study by Ioannidis revealed that, even in the prestigious Nature Genetics, more than half of the peer-reviewed, high-throughput studies cannot be replicated. Yet, ostensibly, these studies have all passed "rigorous peer review." The failure of peer-review to detect non-reproducible research is, at least in part, because the analytical methodology is not adequately described, but perhaps equally because the reviewers find these analyses as challenging as the original investigator did; even if the original data were made available to them, together with a clear and comprehensive description of the analytical methodology (as we would hope are present in the Materials and Methods section of a manuscript), it still might not be reasonable to expect a reviewer to rigorously evaluate the study because the analytical infrastructure is difficult to envision or replicate from a textual description alone.

In recognition of these limitations, the Institute of Medicine in 2012 published several recommendations relating to proper conduct of high-throughput analyses. These include: rigorously described, annotated, and followed data management procedures; "locking down" the computational analysis pipeline once it has been selected; and publishing the workflow of this analytical pipeline in a formal manner, together with the full starting and result datasets. These recommendations help ensure that (a) errors are not introduced through manual data manipulation, (b) there can be no human intervention in the data as it passes through the analytical process, and (c) that third parties can properly evaluate the data, the analytical methodology, and the result at the time of peer-review, even to the point of re-running the analysis for validation purposes.

Formal workflow technologies have proved effective at resolving many of these issues, and in fact, beyond just transparency and reproducibility, they even provide opportunities for time-saving and convenience. For example, the use of formal workflows provides an excellent opportunity to automate the collection of provenance information (purpose, source, data used, date, algorithms, interfaces, versions, name of data publisher, etc.), far beyond what is commonly captured by even the most attentive biological researcher. It is perhaps surprising, therefore, that integration of formal workflows into the scientific "culture" is lagging, and ad hoc. Nevertheless, as regulatory and funding agencies become increasingly concerned and dubious about the quality of the research they are supporting, the pressure to improve the way we "do science" grows. It is clear that the only path forward involves mechanization of much of the scientific analysis process.

It is for all the reasons above that I am so pleased to see this book on scientific workflows, directly aimed at the bench researcher as its target audience. The broad scope of research questions covered in these chapters will speak to the full breadth of researchers who, until now, have been reluctant to consider adopting these powerful new approaches to data management and analysis. Having a few key exemplars such as these—formal workflows solving real scientific problems—will hopefully "blaze the trail" for other researchers to follow. At the same time, reading these use cases will no doubt spur those of us who study scientific workflow technologies to produce even better tools that make life easier for the biologists whose data we care so much about.

May 2014

Mark D. Wilkinson
Isaac Peral Distinguished Researcher
Center for Plant Biotechnology and Genomics, UPM, Madrid, Spain

Preface II

At present, 95% of all digital data are estimated to have a geospatial reference (Hamilton, in Perkins, 2010). Geospatial reference is the definition of the absolute or relative position of objects or geographical phenomena. This is determined, in the first case, by coordinates, and, in the latter case, by spatial relations or neighborhood of geospatial objects. For centuries, spatial data have been processed to generate maps or map-like cartographic representations. In doing so, cartographers made use of the fact that maps are the only visual representations of geographic space simultaneously showing both the absolute and the relative positions of spatial objects. In addition, they have served as an effective data storage well beyond the advent of ICT in cartography in the late 1960s.

Unlike remote sensing imagery, maps are not images but graphical models of geospatial reality. Map models are generated in a systematic process by transforming non-graphic spatial data of the real world into spatially related graphic symbols. Selection and processing of the geospatial source data are subject to the specific thematic and/or geographical requirements of a given application. The data-to-symbol transformation is controlled by a sequence of processes implementing a set of cartographic representation methods and other cartographic regulations. This regulatory framework determines the thematic as well as the scale-related modeling and symbolization of the preprocessed geospatial data. It is, in fact, this processed-based, application-oriented transformation of graphic-free geodata into graphic map data that accounts for the professional cartographic quality of the maps produced.

To generate quality cartographic representations or, in more modern terms, geovisualizations, expertise in both methods and techniques is required on how to process non-graphic geospatial data into proper graphic maps. This expertise has, for centuries, been passed on personally from master to apprentice. Hence, different "schools" of geodata processing into maps can easily be distinguished. Around the turn of the nineteenth to twentieth centuries the process of map-making has been codified and formalized in early textbooks on cartography. It is obvious that the written description of the transformation process of geospatial data into maps required strict formalization beforehand of the processing steps involved for interpersonal application. Only this will put a trained person into a position to produce quality maps by applying the mapping processes to a geospatial dataset. Depending on the data, map purpose, application, and scale, a finite number of processes is required to generate the respective map types. To make sure the application of the relevant processes to similar datasets will yield identical map representations, the range of individual processes has been formalized in about a dozen so-called cartographic representation methods. The representation methods describe the processes involved in transforming specific geodata and their features into precisely matching map models or map types.

Hence, cartographic representation methods can be considered a set of formalized processing rules sets applied to visualize geodata expressively and effectively.

Today, almost without exception, geodata are handled and processed with ICT systems more or less dedicated to this purpose. Thus, the methodical need for the formalization of geovisual processes is complemented by the technical requirements of formalization when it comes to implementing geovisualization processes in a software environment. Software engineering, in particular, has a distinctive history and substantial record of modeling processes. Accordingly, it deals with developing as well as implementing software solutions, which can be dedicated or generic, proprietary, or open-source. Formalization requirements both from a methodical and a technical perspective can thus be considered a common ground of geoinformation processing and software engineering. It goes without saying that geoinformation processing will benefit from software systems facilitating the formalization and implementation of data-to-map transformations in an intuitive, easy-to-comprehend way. One such software environment is the open-source jABC framework used in the range of applications collected in this volume. Systems like jABC help to code a set of processing rules into a formalized technical framework that can be implemented in ICT systems for geoinformation processing.

The use cases presented demonstrate both the potential of jABC as well as the benefits the implementation of this framework holds for the applications in question. From a geoinformation perspective it furthermore shows the added value a fruitful collaboration of the two disciplines will hold for geoinformation applications as well as for geoinformation scientists.

June 2014

Hartmut Asche
Professor of Geoinformation Science
Department of Geography, University of Potsdam, Germany

Contents

Framework

Bioinformatics Applications

Geovisualization Applications

Scientific Workflows and XMDD

Anna-Lena Lamprecht and Tiziana Margaria

Chair for Service and Software Engineering, Potsdam University,
Potsdam, D-14482, Germany
{lamprecht,margaria}@cs.uni-potsdam.de

Abstract. A major part of the scientific experiments that are carried out today requires thorough computational support. While database and algorithm providers face the problem of bundling resources to create and sustain powerful computation nodes, the users have to deal with combining sets of (remote) services into specific data analysis and transformation processes. Today's attention to "big data" amplifies the issues of size, heterogeneity, and process-level diversity/integration. In the last decade, especially workflow-based approaches to deal with these processes have enjoyed great popularity. This book concerns a particularly agile and model-driven approach to manage scientific workflows that is based on the XMDD paradigm. In this chapter we explain the scope and purpose of the book, briefly describe the concepts and technologies of the XMDD paradigm, explain the principal differences to related approaches, and outline the structure of the book.

Keywords: scientific workflows, workflow management systems, model-driven design, XMDD.

1 Introduction

Scientific algorithms, tools, and databases have assisted researchers of all disciplines in different phases of their data analyses for over two decades now. These tools and databases are usually not installed locally, because handling the large amounts of data, possibly together with high time and space complexities of the underlying algorithms, requires the software to be run on supercomputers or appropriate clusters. Grid computing, the precursor of the cloud for collective scientific computing facilities, has been an outcome of this need. Tool providers offer interfaces to execute their service programs remotely, often as web interfaces or web services.

Working with a large set of different services needed for an analysis process and coordinating the use of computational tools and information repositories distributed throughout the world is a cumbersome and error-prone task when the individual steps are carried out manually. Challenging data analysis tasks typically require complex processes and specific care in combining, monitoring, and documenting the single analysis steps. Therefore, frameworks that provide the means for automating complex analysis processes involving a number of

A.-L. Lamprecht et al. (Eds.): Process Design for Natural Scientists, CCIS 500, pp. 1–13, 2014.
DOI: 10.1007/978-3-662-45006-2_1

heterogeneous services enjoy great popularity. In particular, workflow modeling techniques of all flavors are increasingly successful. Essentially, they aim at simplifying access to the services, so that scientists with little programming experience, but with well-founded knowledge about the domain and the specific process, can orchestrate cohorts of services easily in order to achieve their goals.

Services and service collections providing access to remote data repositories or to computational tools form the basic components from which workflows are built. Workflow management systems then provide composition interfaces where users can select and combine services into workflows. The assembly often happens graphically by placing service "proxies" as building blocks on a canvas, and connecting them either according to the flow of control or according to the flow of data [1]. Usually these systems also provide the means for direct execution of the workflow model, and several more features that add convenience for the users in different ways.

A principal question regarding workflow management systems concerns their scope of applicability: In which application areas can they be used most fruitfully, in comparison to direct programming or scripting? The ROI of workflow modeling systems depends on the levels of complexity, reuse, quality, assurance and more. Certainly, data analyses or analysis steps that are completely fixed and can be repeated or reused without any change could rather be implemented conventionally, and then used as individual software programs or reused as atomic services within larger workflows. However, whenever there exist (at least potential) variants of a computational experiment, the workflow approach is beneficial due to its agile, modular assembly and composition style. In fact, understanding how much this facilitates an easier understanding and change of the analysis processes also by users that are not specially trained in programming was one of the major motivations for the study underlying this book.

This book introduces its readers to the field of *model-driven design and management of scientific workflows* in a case study-based fashion. It collects the outcomes of the practical project work carried out within the one-semester course "Process modeling in natural sciences". We started teaching this course in 2007, predominantly to Master students of the "Bioinformatics" and "Geoinformation and Geovisualization" programs at the University of Potsdam, gradually transforming into a project-oriented class that applies a "learn by doing approach". The course addresses processes and workflow management concepts and applies them in the project reality, acknowledging the fact that the notions of service-orientation and workflow modeling are increasingly relevant and widely adopted in the scientific community. Still, to our knowledge this approach to teaching informatics-heavy process science to experimental scientists in an individual and hands-on applied fashion is so far unique.

In This Book

The heart of the process part of the course is the practical project work carried out by the students. They design and implement workflows for self-defined applications stemming from their respective areas of expertise. A collection of projects developed in the summer term 2012 forms the basis for this book. This collection of scientific workflow applications provides insights and experience about the modeling of scientific workflows from the users' point of view as well as from the computer-science perspective.

Besides documenting the impact high-level that workflow modeling might have on the work of natural scientists, this book serves three major purposes:

1. It acts as a **primer for practitioners** who are interested to learn how to think in terms of services and workflows when facing domain-specific scientific processes.
2. It provides interesting **material for readers** already familiar with this kind of tools, because it introduces systematically both the technologies used in each case study and the basic concepts behind them.
3. As the addressed thematic field becomes increasingly relevant for lectures in both computer science and experimental sciences, it also provides helpful **material for teachers** that plan similar courses.

To the best of our knowledge, no other book currently available serves these purposes.

In "Workflows for e-Science – Scientific Workflows for Grids" [2], Taylor et al. present a comprehensive and heterogeneous collection of applications from different scientific disciplines that use a variety of different methods and technologies. Considering our book as a primer, this is a nice complement providing a wider survey of the field to readers already familiar with workflow technologies and process- and service-oriented thinking.

In "Scientific Workflows - Programming, Optimization, and Synthesis with ASKALON and AWDL" [3], Qin and Fahringer provide a well-elaborated and comprehensive introduction to basic and advanced topics of scientific workflow management in general and to the ASKALON framework and its extensions in particular. For practitioners not trained in computer science and new to the field of workflows, it may again be a nice second step, being more technical and "heavyweight" and providing a very limited number of concrete examples aimed at illustrating specific technical capabilities of the specific framework.

This book is also different from the available literature on graphical programming systems like, e.g., LabView [1]. In these systems, workflows are used as visual program representations, but they still require a deep technical knowledge of the programming issues, without actually lifting the level of abstraction in handling the technology to render it accessible by users that are not specially trained in IT or programming. Enabling the non-IT experts to proficiently work with workflows without undergoing a prior deep technical training is, on the contrary, the principal focus of the service-oriented methods that we apply in our workflow modeling concepts and that we demonstrate in this collection of case studies.

Our book focuses on what is needed to be a primer to the field of scientific workflows. We start with a systematic but technically simplified introduction to our methods and technologies for process management and workflow design.

[1] `http://www.ni.com/labview/`

They are then consistently applied by all the case studies. All the applications are presented in a uniformly structured fashion in order to facilitate the reader's understanding and conceptualization. As such, the book can be used as a text book for similar courses for students of experimental sciences, but it does also provide helpful additional material for anybody dealing with workflow modeling for other reasons.

In the following we introduce our specific approach to scientific workflow modeling (Section 2) and some selected applications (Section 3), give a brief survey of related approaches (Section 4) and outline the structure of the book (Section 5).

2 Extreme Model-Driven Design of Scientific Workflows

XMDD (eXtreme Model-Driven Design), introduced in [4] and refined in [5–9], is a methodology aimed at the easy uptake by practitioners that wish a fast but high-quality and high-assurance service assembly. Simplicity [7] is here the key guiding principle. According to the motto "*easy for the many, difficult for the few*", XMDD is an approach that systematically reinforces the intuition of the users when dealing with a graphical workflow design framework that eases service composition, and at the same time it provides the high-assurance level of quality that is usually based on formal description languages and formal methods, that are however normally inaccessible to non-IT experts, and challenging even for the average programmer and software engineer. The simplicity tradeoff we adopt foresees the use of *embedded* formal descriptions and formal methods (the "difficult" part), whereby due to the embedding, users do not need to be aware of these traits and capabilities that are for them kept under the hood of the tool they use, thereby achieving a simplicity effect.

Extreme Model Driven Design (XMDD) leverages this approach of separation of concerns by combining the decisive traits of several modern software engineering schools into a coherent paradigm that efficiently and effectively leverages their characteristic contributions. XMDD builds on ideas taken from

- eXtreme programming [10], for providing immediate feedback through requirement and design validation by means of model tracing, simulation and early testing, virtualizing the implementation of functionality,
- service orientation [11], for virtualizing the implementation of functionality,
- aspect orientation [12], for treating crosscutting as well as role specific concerns modularly, and
- model-driven design [13], for controlling the overall development at the modeling level.

For the process definition and management according to the XMDD paradigm we use a multi-purpose domain-independent modeling framework: the Java Application Building Center (jABC) [14]. Thank to a rich set of associated embedded technologies and plugins, it provides a comprehensive yet intuitive graphical framework that users use to integrate services, build workflows (in the form of directed graphs) from the components that result from the integration, analyze and execute them, and finally deploy and provision them in the form of applications or services. It is based on well-established software technology, as described above, and has been used successfully in different application domains.

The aim of this software framework is to support in their daily work and boost the productivity of application experts without specific IT knowledge. Such users use the jABC environment to model and design workflows in a service-oriented fashion and the jETI service integration technology [15, 16] to execute remote tools and services as if they were locally available. These are the two central technologies used in this book.

3 Our Experience So Far

With jABC and jETI we participated in different conferences and initiatives in the area of scientific workflows, such as the NETTAB 2007 workshop session "From Components to Processes in Bioinformatics" [17], the SWAT4LS Workshops [18–20] and the 2010 Biohackathon [21]. The exchange of experiences with other researchers from the scientific workflow community and the work on several case studies during the last years has taught us how to best proceed to service-enable different subdomains of scientific processes and workflows and how to use our technology to orchestrate complex analyses of experimental data. Some of our previous case studies are particularly useful for a comparison with the cases presented in this book as well as for in-depth further study:

- Our first case study in the bioinformatics application domain concerned a distributed workflow for validation of orthologous gene structures among a selection of higher organisms [22]. This study demonstrates how to model hierarchical bioinformatics workflows in the jABC framework, based on external tools and resources in the same fashion as described in [23].
- The study described in [24] deals with the preprocessing and statistical analysis of liquid chromatography/mass spectrometry (LC/MS) data using the statistics language GNU R [25] and in particular the XCMS package [26]. In this application, the required R functionality is integrated using the jETI technology, while the jABC again serves as workflow definition environment.
- GeneFisher-P [27] is a service-oriented and workflow-based re-implementation of the GeneFisher [28, 29] web application for PCR primer design, realized using jABC and jETI. It makes it possible to run the primer design process in a batch processing manner, and thus to design primers for large amounts of input sequences automatically. Furthermore, it facilitates the user-level definition of workflow variants, useful for customizing workflows by including alternative services for the individual steps of the design process. This has been done, for instance, by the biologist Janus Borner in his Diploma thesis at the university of Hamburg [30]: he integrated specific scripts for the backtranslation steps and used them to build his specific variants of the original workflow.

- Woven around workflows for multiple sequence alignment - a commonly known computation that is in fact part of many analyses in genomics, proteomics and transcriptomics - the study described in [31] focuses on illustrating how the framework enables end users that are not IT experts to define, analyze, execute, modify, and interactively develop bioinformatics analysis processes. These workflows are at the same time particularly suited to demonstrate the flexibility and agility that analyses gain in the framework, especially in contrast to the completely predefined service programs that are widely spread in the scientific domain.
- Flux-P [32] is an approach to automate and standardize ^{13}C-based metabolic flux analysis [33] using jABC and jETI. Flux-P is currently exemplarily based on the FiatFlux software [34]. It demonstrates how to create services that carry out the different analysis steps autonomously and how to subsequently assemble them into software workflows that perform automated, high-throughput intracellular flux analysis of high quality and reproducibility. Besides significant acceleration and standardization of the data analysis, the agile workflow-based realization supports flexible changes of the analysis workflows on the user level, making it easy to perform custom analyses.
- The Climate Impacts: Global and Regional Adaptation Support Platform (ci:grasp) [35][2] is a web-based climate information service for exploring climate change related information in its geographical context. The project described in [36] uses the jABC workflow modeling and execution framework to make flexibilized versions of the processes implemented in ci:grasp available to the scientific community, enabling users to flexibly define and adapt the workflows according to their specific needs.

An essential characteristic of scientific workflows, including the case studies listed above, is their being subject to frequent changes. This demands for workflow systems that enable a flexible workflow development style, where exchanging services and building variations of workflows is easy for the user. Our experiences with students and project partners using jABC and jETI provide evidence that an accessible level of abstraction has indeed been reached, and that it enables an agile handling of workflows. For instance, the GeneFisher-P and FiatFlux-P workflows were frequently adapted by their users (biology diploma and bio-engineering PhD students without specific computer science education) according to changing experimental setups. What is more, similar workflows were built by (computer science and other) students autonomously in the scope of different lectures and projects.

While the majority of the the applications listed above stem from the bioinformatics domain (note there is also a domain-specific incarnation of the normally domain-independent jABC and jETI frameworks in the bioinformatics area that is called Bio-jETI [37]), this book comprises a greater share of workflows from the geovisualization and image processing domains. This demonstrates that the framework is easily applicable also in other scientific domains.

[2] http://www.cigrasp.org

4 Relationship to Other Scientific Workflow Systems

After almost two decades of research and development in the field of scientific workflows, several workflow design and management environments with different characteristics are available for scientific applications. This section briefly surveys some other existing approaches to scientific workflow management and compares them with regard to some aspects that are important in the scope of this book with the XMDD-based approach followed in the jABC framework. More elaborate comparisons and discussions are available, for example, in [1, 38].

Kepler [39], Taverna [40–43], Triana [44] and Pegasus [45], for example, are popular scientific workflow systems born on top of distributed computing projects (such as Grids and Clusters). They offer successful workflow design environments and workflow enactment engines. Kepler, for example, is internally based on Ptolemy II [46], an actor-based environment for embedded system design, and its native actors concern basic data management operations on a grid. Accordingly, its workflow definition component is targeted towards a grid management level, which is finer granular and more technical than the services that jABC and jETI address. In fact, which jABC/jETI we explicitly strive for an adequate end-user-level granularity, and for maintaining the full power of general-purpose model-driven design when adapting the framework to a particular scientific domain. This enables a very high level of agility in the workflow design process, which is still an uncommon characteristic for the state-of-the-art scientific workflow management tools.

In contrast to the jABC, the provenance of most scientific workflow frameworks is neither from a software engineering/programming environment background, nor from a process model semantics or formal verification culture. The traditional Scientific Data Management community from which these tools arose is in fact historically data-oriented, and more interested in data distribution issues than on clean semantics of the behavioral aspects of a workflow.

The frameworks listed above are in fact inherently data flow-oriented workflow systems. This is indeed the most substantial difference to our framework, where the models define the control flow of a workflow. Both approaches are usually considered to be capable of expressing the same processes. In practice, however, when using the data-flow approach there are limitations with respect to the inclusion of elaborate control structures (cf., e.g. [38]). In the jABC a set of different common control structures is already available and shared among its different application domains. They make it easy to model sophisticated processes, for instance with different execution traces depending on the kind of input data, or with iterations or recursions over sets of data. The data itself is managed within an execution context of the model, and uses identifiers similar to variables to refer to particular data items. In our experience, the control flow-oriented environment for service design and analysis is an evolution step as scientific workflows become increasingly networked, parallel, conditional, event-driven, recursive, and asynchronous. This is the kind of complexity sources whose control is at the core of the jABC's strengths.

Additionally to the agile XMDD-based workflow development approach described and illustrated in this book, our framework comprises many more features and capabilities that deal with the application of (especially constraint-based) formal methods to support the design of scientific workflows [38, 47–49]. In fact, the jABC has been built with a focus on formal verification capability (cf. [50–52]). A clear formal semantics of the models and of the notion of composition provide the basis for the formal analysis and verification of properties of the designed workflows based on (automatic) mathematical proofs. To the best of our knowledge, the additional benefits offered by the jABC plugins for verification, synthesis and code generation are so far still unique among scientific workflow systems. In their intention they are related to approaches for semantics-based service discovery like in BioMoby [53–55], or for automatic workflow composition like in jORCA [56, 57], SADI/SHARE [55, 58, 59], Wings [60] or ASKALON [3]. Comprehensive case studies on these topics are currently being carried out, bound to become the subject of a separate volume.

5 Outline of the Book

This book combines an introduction to service- and process-oriented thinking for scientific workflows, of the corresponding technology, and a gallery of applications that have been developed using these means. Thus, it can be used as a collection of examples and case studies of scientific workflows, and also serve as an introduction to the technical aspects of domain-specific modeling with the jABC framework.

The book is organized in three major parts:

- Part I (Framework, comprising [61–64]) introduces the methodologies and technologies that we use. It also clarifies the concrete setup available during the course and discusses lessons learned and future perspectives.
- Part II (Bioinformatics Applications, comprising [65–70]) contains the reports on the 6 student projects concerning applications from the bioinformatics domain.
- Part III (Geovisualization Applications, comprising [71–79]) is composed from the reports on the 9 applications from the geoinformation and visualization domain.

Each of the articles in Part II and III is supplemented with a small "identikit" box, which is placed between the conclusion section and the references. In order to make the individual article accessible for readers who do not work through the whole book, it briefly summarizes the context of the study, gives a basic profile of the described project and points to further related work.

References

1. Lamprecht, A.L., Margaria, T., Steffen, B.: Bioinformatics: Processes and Workflows. In: Laplante, P.A. (ed.) Encyclopedia of Software Engineering, pp. 118–130. Taylor & Francis (November 2010)

2. Taylor, I.J., Deelman, E., Gannon, D.B., Shields, M.: Workflows for E-Science: Scientific Workflows for Grids. Springer (2007)
3. Qin, J., Fahringer, T.: Scientific Workflows - Programming, Optimization, and Synthesis with ASKALON and AWDL. Springer, Heidelberg (2012)
4. Margaria, T., Steffen, B.: Agile IT: Thinking in User-Centric Models. In: Margaria, T., Steffen, B. (eds.) Leveraging Applications of Formal Methods, Verification and Validation. CCIS, vol. 17, pp. 490–502. Springer, Heidelberg (2009)
5. Margaria, T., Steffen, B.: Business Process Modelling in the jABC: The One-Thing-Approach. In: Cardoso, J., van der Aalst, W. (eds.) Handbook of Research on Business Process Modeling. IGI Global (2009)
6. Margaria, T., Steffen, B.: Continuous Model-Driven Engineering. IEEE Computer 42(10), 106–109 (2009)
7. Margaria, T., Steffen, B.: Simplicity as a Driver for Agile Innovation. Computer 43(6), 90–92 (2010)
8. Steffen, B., Margaria, T., Wagner, C.: 94. In: Round-Trip Engineering, pp. 1044–1055. Taylor & Francis (2010)
9. Margaria, T., Steffen, B.: Service-Orientation: Conquering Complexity with XMDD. In: Hinchey, M., Coyle, L. (eds.) Conquering Complexity, pp. 217–236. Springer, London (2012)
10. Beck, K., Andres, C.: Extreme programming explained: embrace change. Addison-Wesley Professional (2004)
11. Margaria, T., Steffen, B., Reitenspiess, M.: Service-Oriented Design: The Roots. In: Benatallah, B., Casati, F., Traverso, P. (eds.) ICSOC 2005. LNCS, vol. 3826, pp. 450–464. Springer, Heidelberg (2005)
12. Kiczales, G., Lamping, J., Mendhekar, A., Maeda, C., Lopes, C., Loingtier, J.M., Irwin, J.: Aspect-oriented programming. In: Akit, M., Matsuoka, S. (eds.) ECOOP 1997. LNCS, vol. 1241, pp. 220–242. Springer, Heidelberg (1997)
13. Schmidt, D.C.: Guest Editor's Introduction: Model-Driven Engineering. IEEE Computer 39(2), 25–31 (2006)
14. Steffen, B., Margaria, T., Nagel, R., Jörges, S., Kubczak, C.: Model-Driven Development with the jABC. In: Bin, E., Ziv, A., Ur, S. (eds.) HVC 2006. LNCS, vol. 4383, pp. 92–108. Springer, Heidelberg (2007)
15. Steffen, B., Margaria, T., Braun, V.: The Electronic Tool Integration platform: concepts and design. International Journal on Software Tools for Technology Transfer (STTT) 1(1-2), 9–30 (1997)
16. Margaria, T., Nagel, R., Steffen, B.: jETI: A Tool for Remote Tool Integration. In: Halbwachs, N., Zuck, L.D. (eds.) TACAS 2005. LNCS, vol. 3440, pp. 557–562. Springer, Heidelberg (2005)
17. Romano, P., Schrder, M., Cannata, N., Signore, O. (eds.): Proceedings of the 7th International Workshop NETTAB 2007: A Semantic Web for Bioinformatics - Goals, Tools, Systems, Applications (June 2007)
18. Burger, A., Paschke, A., Romano, P., Splendiani, A.: Semantic Web Applications and Tools for Life Sciences 2008. In: Proc. of 1st Workshop SWAT4LS 2008. CEUR Workshop Proceedings, Edinburgh (November 2008)
19. Marshall, M.S., Burger, A., Romano, P., Paschke, A., Splendiani, A.: Semantic Web Applications and Tools for Life Sciences 2009. In: Proc. of 2nd Workshop SWAT4LS 2009. CEUR Workshop Proceedings, Amsterdam, The Netherlands (November 2009)
20. Burger, A., Marshall, M., Romano, P., Paschke, A.: Proceedings of 3rd Workshop on Semantic Web Applications and Tools for Life Sciences (SWAT4LS 2010). In: CEUR Workshop Proceedings, Berlin, Germany (December 2010)

21. Katayama, T., Wilkinson, M., Micklem, G., Kawashima, S., Yamaguchi, A., Nakao, M., Yamamoto, Y., Okamoto, S., Oouchida, K., Chun, H.W., Aerts, J., Afzal, H., Antezana, E., Arakawa, K., Aranda, B., Belleau, F., Bolleman, J., Bonnal, R., Chapman, B., Cock, P., Eriksson, T., Gordon, P., Goto, N., Hayashi, K., Horn, H., Ishiwata, R., Kaminuma, E., Kasprzyk, A., Kawaji, H., Kido, N., Kim, Y., Kinjo, A., Konishi, F., Kwon, K.H., Labarga, A., Lamprecht, A.L., Lin, Y., Lindenbaum, P., McCarthy, L., Morita, H., Murakami, K., Nagao, K., Nishida, K., Nishimura, K., Nishizawa, T., Ogishima, S., Ono, K., Oshita, K., Park, K.J., Prins, P., Saito, T., Samwald, M., Satagopam, V., Shigemoto, Y., Smith, R., Splendiani, A., Sugawara, H., Taylor, J., Vos, R., Withers, D., Yamasaki, C., Zmasek, C., Kawamoto, S., Okubo, K., Asai, K., Takagi, T.: Lamprecht: The 3rd DBCLS BioHackathon: improving life science data integration with Semantic Web technologies. Journal of Biomedical Semantics 4(1) (2013)
22. Margaria, T., Kubczak, C., Njoku, M., Steffen, B.: Model-based Design of Distributed Collaborative Bioinformatics Processes in the jABC. In: Proceedings of the 11th IEEE International Conference on Engineering of Complex Computer Systems (ICECCS 2006), pp. 169–176. IEEE Computer Society, Los Alamitos (August 2006)
23. Steffen, B., Margaria, T., Braun, V., Kalt, N.: Hierarchical Service Definition. Annual Review of Communications of the ACM 51, 847–856 (1997)
24. Kubczak, C., Margaria, T., Fritsch, A., Steffen, B.: Biological LC/MS Preprocessing and Analysis with jABC, jETI and xcms. In: Proceedings of the 2nd International Symposium on Leveraging Applications of Formal Methods, Verification and Validation (ISoLA 2006), pp. 308–313. IEEE Computer Society, Paphos (2006)
25. The R Project for Statistical Computing, `http://www.r-project.org/` (Online; last accessed May 5, 2013)
26. Smith, C.A., Want, E.J., O'Maille, G., Abagyan, R., Siuzdak, G.: XCMS: Processing Mass Spectrometry Data for Metabolite Profiling Using Nonlinear Peak Alignment, Matching, and Identification. Analytical Chemistry 78(3), 779–787 (2006); PMID: 16448051
27. Lamprecht, A.L., Margaria, T., Steffen, B., Sczyrba, A., Hartmeier, S., Giegerich, R.: GeneFisher-P: variations of GeneFisher as processes in Bio-jETI. BMC Bioinformatics 9(suppl. 4), S13 (2008)
28. Giegerich, R., Meyer, F., Schleiermacher, C.: GeneFisher – software support for the detection of postulated genes. In: Proceedings of the International Conference on Intelligent Systems for Molecular Biology (ISMB), vol. 4, pp. 68–77 (1996)
29. Hagemeier, D.: GeneFisher2 - an AJAX based implementation of GeneFisher-P. Bachelor's thesis, University Bielefeld, Faculty of Technology (December 2006)
30. Borner, J.: A molecular approach to chelicerate phylogeny. Diploma thesis, Universität Hamburg (2010)
31. Lamprecht, A.-L., Margaria, T., Steffen, B.: Seven Variations of an Alignment Workflow - An Illustration of Agile Process Design and Management in Bio-jETI. In: Măndoiu, I., Wang, S.-L., Zelikovsky, A. (eds.) ISBRA 2008. LNCS (LNBI), vol. 4983, pp. 445–456. Springer, Heidelberg (2008)
32. Ebert, B.E., Lamprecht, A.L., Steffen, B., Blank, L.M.: Flux-P: Automating Metabolic Flux Analysis. Metabolites 2(4), 872–890 (2012)
33. Wiechert, W.: 13C metabolic flux analysis. Metabolic Engineering 3(3), 195–206 (2001)
34. Zamboni, N., Fischer, E., Sauer, U.: FiatFlux a software for metabolic flux analysis from 13C-glucose experiments. BMC Bioinformatics 6, 209 (2005)

35. Wrobel, M., Bisaro, A., Reusser, D., Kropp, J.P.: Novel Approaches for Web-Based Access to Climate Change Adaptation Information MEDIATION Adaptation Platform and ci:grasp-2. In: Hřebíček, J., Schimak, G., Kubásek, M., Rizzoli, A.E. (eds.) ISESS 2013. IFIP AICT, vol. 413, pp. 489–499. Springer, Heidelberg (2013)
36. Al-areqi, S., Kriewald, S., Lamprecht, A.L., Reusser, D., Wrobel, M., Margaria, T.: Agile Workflows for Climate Impact Risk Assessment based on the ci:grasp Platform and the jABC Modeling Framework. In: International Environmental Modelling and Software Society (iEMSs) 7th Intl. Congress on Env. Modelling and Software (accepted, 2014)
37. Margaria, T., Kubczak, C., Steffen, B.: Bio-jETI: A service integration, design, and provisioning platform for orchestrated bioinformatics processes. BMC Bioinformatics 9(suppl. 4), S12 (2008)
38. Lamprecht, A.-L.: User-Level Workflow Design. LNCS, vol. 8311. Springer, Heidelberg (2013)
39. Altintas, I., Berkley, C., Jaeger, E., Jones, M., Ludscher, B., Mock, S.: Kepler: An Extensible System for Design and Execution of Scientific Workflows. In: Proceedings of the 16th International Conference on Scientific and Statistical Database Management (SSDBM 2004), pp. 21–23. IEEE Computer Society (June 2004)
40. Oinn, T., Addis, M., Ferris, J., Marvin, D., Senger, M., Greenwood, M., Carver, T., Glover, K., Pocock, M.R., Wipat, A., Li, P.: Taverna: A tool for the composition and enactment of bioinformatics workflows. Bioinformatics 20(17), 3045–3054 (2004)
41. Hull, D., Wolstencroft, K., Stevens, R., Goble, C., Pocock, M.R., Li, P., Oinn, T.: Taverna: A tool for building and running workflows of services. Nucleic Acids Research 34(Web Server), W729–W732 (2006)
42. Missier, P., Soiland-Reyes, S., Owen, S., Tan, W., Nenadic, A., Dunlop, I., Williams, A., Oinn, T., Goble, C.: Taverna, reloaded. In: Gertz, M., Ludäscher, B. (eds.) SSDBM 2010. LNCS, vol. 6187, pp. 471–481. Springer, Heidelberg (2010)
43. Wolstencroft, K., Hainès, R., Fellows, D., Williams, A., Withers, D., Owen, S., Soiland-Reyes, S., Dunlop, I., Nenadic, A., Fisher, P., Bhagat, J., Belhajjame, K., Bacall, F., Hardisty, A., Nieva de la Hidalga, A., Balcazar Vargas, M.P., Sufi, S., Goble, C.: The Taverna workflow suite: designing and executing workflows of Web Services on the desktop, web or in the cloud. Nucleic Acids Research 41(W1), W557–W561 (2013)
44. Taylor, I., Shields, M., Wang, I., Harrison, A.: The Triana Workflow Environment: Architecture and Applications. In: Workflows for e-Science, pp. 320–339. Springer, New York (2007)
45. Deelman, E., Singh, G., Hui Su, M., Blythe, J., Gil, A., Kesselman, C., Mehta, G., Vahi, K., Berriman, G.B., Good, J., Laity, A., Jacob, J.C., Katz, D.S.: Pegasus: A framework for mapping complex scientific workflows onto distributed systems. Scientific Programming Journal 13, 219–237 (2005)
46. Eker, J., Janneck, J., Lee, E., Liu, J., Liu, X., Ludvig, J., Neuendorffer, S., Sachs, S., Xiong, Y.: Taming heterogeneity - the Ptolemy approach. Proceedings of the IEEE 91(1), 127–144 (2003)
47. Lamprecht, A.L., Margaria, T., Steffen, B.: Bio-jETI: A framework for semantics-based service composition. BMC Bioinformatics 10(suppl. 10), 8 (2009)
48. Lamprecht, A.L., Naujokat, S., Margaria, T., Steffen, B.: Semantics-based composition of EMBOSS services. Journal of Biomedical Semantics 2(suppl. 1), S5 (2011)

49. Lamprecht, A.L., Naujokat, S., Steffen, B., Margaria, T.: Constraint-Guided Workflow Composition Based on the EDAM Ontology. In: Burger, A., Marshall, M.S., Romano, P., Paschke, A., Splendiani, A. (eds.) Proceedings of the 3rd International Workshop on Semantic Web Applications and Tools for Life Sciences (SWAT4LS 2010), vol. 698. CEUR Workshop Proceedings (December 2010)
50. Steffen, B., Margaria, T., Claßen, A., Braun, V.: Incremental Formalization: A Key to Industrial Success. Software - Concepts and Tools 17(2), 78–95 (1996)
51. Jonsson, B., Margaria, T., Naeser, G., Nyström, J., Steffen, B.: Incremental requirement specification for evolving systems. Nordic J. of Computing 8, 65–87 (2001)
52. Steffen, B., Margaria, T., von der Beeck, M.: Automatic synthesis of linear process models from temporal constraints: An incremental approach. In: ACM/SIGPLAN International Workshop on Automated Analysis of Software, AAS 1997 (1997)
53. Wilkinson, M.D., Links, M.: BioMOBY: An open source biological web services proposal. Briefings in Bioinformatics 3(4), 331–341 (2002)
54. DiBernardo, M., Pottinger, R., Wilkinson, M.: Semi-automatic web service composition for the life sciences using the BioMoby semantic web framework. Journal of Biomedical Informatics 41(5), 837–847 (2008)
55. Withers, D., Kawas, E., McCarthy, L., Vandervalk, B., Wilkinson, M.: Semantically-guided workflow construction in Taverna: the SADI and BioMoby plug-ins. In: Margaria, T., Steffen, B. (eds.) ISoLA 2010, Part I. LNCS, vol. 6415, pp. 301–312. Springer, Heidelberg (2010)
56. Karlsson, J., Martín-Requena, V., Ríos, J., Trelles, O.: Workflow composition and enactment using jORCA. In: Margaria, T., Steffen, B. (eds.) ISoLA 2010, Part I. LNCS, vol. 6415, pp. 328–339. Springer, Heidelberg (2010)
57. Martín-Requena, V., Ríos, J., García, M., Ramírez, S., Trelles, O.: jORCA: easily integrating bioinformatics Web Services. Bioinformatics 26(4), 553–559 (2010)
58. Wilkinson, M.D., Vandervalk, B., McCarthy, L.: SADI Semantic Web Services - 'cause you can't always GET what you want! In: Proceedings of the IEEE Services Computing Conference, APSCC 2009, December 7-11, pp. 13–18. IEEE Asia-Pacific, Singapore (2009)
59. Wilkinson, M.D., Vandervalk, B., McCarthy, L.: The Semantic Automated Discovery and Integration (SADI) Web service Design-Pattern, API and Reference Implementation. Journal of Biomedical Semantics 2(1), 8 (2011)
60. Gil, Y., Ratnakar, V., Deelman, E., Mehta, G., Kim, J.: Wings for Pegasus: creating large-scale scientific applications using semantic representations of computational workflows. In: Proceedings of the 19th National Conference on Innovative Applications of Artificial Intelligence, vol. 2, pp. 1767–1774. AAAI Press (2007)
61. Lamprecht, A.L., Margaria, T.: Scientific Workflows and XMDD. In: Lamprecht, A.-L., Margaria, T. (eds.) Process Design for Natural Scientists. CCIS, vol. 500, pp. 1–13. Springer, Heidelberg (2014)
62. Lamprecht, A.L., Margaria, T., Steffen, B.: Modeling and Execution of Scientific Workflows in the jABC Framework. In: Lamprecht, A.-L., Margaria, T. (eds.) Process Design for Natural Scientists. CCIS, vol. 500, pp. 14–29. Springer, Heidelberg (2014)
63. Lamprecht, A.L., Wickert, A.: The Course's SIB Libraries. In: Lamprecht, A.-L., Margaria, T. (eds.) Process Design for Natural Scientists. CCIS, vol. 500, pp. 30–44. Springer, Heidelberg (2014)
64. Lamprecht, A.L., Wickert, A., Margaria, T.: Lessons Learned. In: Lamprecht, A.-L., Margaria, T. (eds.) Process Design for Natural Scientists. CCIS, vol. 500, pp. 45–64. Springer, Heidelberg (2014)

65. Reso, J.: Protein Classification Workflow. In: Lamprecht, A.-L., Margaria, T. (eds.) Process Design for Natural Scientists. CCIS, vol. 500, pp. 65–72. Springer, Heidelberg (2014)
66. Blaese, L.: Data Mining for Unidentified Protein Sequences. In: Lamprecht, A.-L., Margaria, T. (eds.) Process Design for Natural Scientists. CCIS, vol. 500, pp. 73–87. Springer, Heidelberg (2014)
67. Schulze, G.: Workflow for Rapid Metagenome Analysis. In: Lamprecht, A.-L., Margaria, T. (eds.) Process Design for Natural Scientists. CCIS, vol. 500, pp. 88–100. Springer, Heidelberg (2014)
68. Lis, M.: Constructing a Phylogenetic Tree. In: Lamprecht, A.-L., Margaria, T. (eds.) Process Design for Natural Scientists. CCIS, vol. 500, pp. 101–109. Springer, Heidelberg (2014)
69. Vierheller, J.: Exploratory Data Analysis. In: Lamprecht, A.-L., Margaria, T. (eds.) Process Design for Natural Scientists. CCIS, vol. 500, pp. 110–126. Springer, Heidelberg (2014)
70. Schtt, C.: Identification of Differentially Expressed Genes. In: Lamprecht, A.-L., Margaria, T. (eds.) Process Design for Natural Scientists. CCIS, vol. 500, pp. 127–139. Springer, Heidelberg (2014)
71. Kuntzsch, C.: Visualization of Data Transfer Paths. In: Lamprecht, A.-L., Margaria, T. (eds.) Process Design for Natural Scientists. CCIS, vol. 500, pp. 140–148. Springer, Heidelberg (2014)
72. Hibbe, M.: Spotlocator Project Documentation. In: Lamprecht, A.-L., Margaria, T. (eds.) Process Design for Natural Scientists. CCIS, vol. 500, pp. 149–158. Springer, Heidelberg (2014)
73. Teske, D.: Geocoder Accuracy Ranking. In: Lamprecht, A.-L., Margaria, T. (eds.) Process Design for Natural Scientists. CCIS, vol. 500, pp. 159–170. Springer, Heidelberg (2014)
74. Sens, H.: Web-Based Map Generalization Tools Put to the Test: A jABC Workflow. In: Lamprecht, A.-L., Margaria, T. (eds.) Process Design for Natural Scientists. CCIS, vol. 500, pp. 171–181. Springer, Heidelberg (2014)
75. Noack, F.: CREADED: Coloured-Relief Application for Digital Elevation Data. In: Lamprecht, A.-L., Margaria, T. (eds.) Process Design for Natural Scientists. CCIS, vol. 500, pp. 182–195. Springer, Heidelberg (2014)
76. Respondeck, T.: A workflow for computing potential areas for wind turbines. In: Lamprecht, A.-L., Margaria, T. (eds.) Process Design for Natural Scientists. CCIS, vol. 500, pp. 196–211. Springer, Heidelberg (2014)
77. Scheele, L.: Location Analysis for Placing Artificial Reefs. In: Lamprecht, A.-L., Margaria, T. (eds.) Process Design for Natural Scientists. CCIS, vol. 500, pp. 212–224. Springer, Heidelberg (2014)
78. Kind, J.: Creation of Topographic Maps. In: Lamprecht, A.-L., Margaria, T. (eds.) Process Design for Natural Scientists. CCIS, vol. 500, pp. 225–234. Springer, Heidelberg (2014)
79. Holler, R.: GraffDok: A Graffiti Documentation Application. In: Lamprecht, A.-L., Margaria, T. (eds.) Process Design for Natural Scientists. CCIS, vol. 500, pp. 235–247. Springer, Heidelberg (2014)

Modeling and Execution of Scientific Workflows with the jABC Framework

Anna-Lena Lamprecht[1], Tiziana Margaria[1], and Bernhard Steffen[2]

[1] Chair for Service and Software Engineering, Potsdam University, Potsdam, D-14482, Germany
{lamprecht,margaria}@cs.uni-potsdam.de

[2] Chair for Programming Systems, Dortmund University of Technology, Dortmund, D-44227, Germany
bernhard.steffen@cs.tu-dortmund.de

Abstract. We summarize here the main characteristics and features of the jABC framework, used in the case studies as a graphical tool for modeling scientific processes and workflows. As a comprehensive environment for service-oriented modeling and design according to the XMDD (eXtreme Model-Driven Design) paradigm, the jABC offers much more than the pure modeling capability. Associated technologies and plugins provide in fact means for a rich variety of supporting functionality, such as remote service integration, taxonomical service classification, model execution, model verification, model synthesis, and model compilation. We describe here in short both the essential jABC features and the service integration philosophy followed in the environment. In our work over the last years we have seen that this kind of service definition and provisioning platform has the potential to become a core technology in interdisciplinary service orchestration and technology transfer: Domain experts, like scientists not specially trained in computer science, directly define complex service orchestrations as process models and use efficient and complex domain-specific tools in a simple and intuitive way.

Keywords: scientific processes and workflows, service integration, service orchestration, model-driven development, XMDD, jABC, jETI.

1 Introduction

As a general-purpose modeling framework for graphical process coordination and verification, the jABC [48] fully implements the concepts of service oriented computing [13]. It is a meanwhile mature service engineering environment that follows the eXtreme Model-Driven Development (XMDD) paradigm [37] and it has been used over the past two decades for business process and service logic modeling in several application domains, including telecommunications [43], supply chain management [14], e-commerce [20], and collaborative decision support systems [30,41], as well as scientific domains like bioinformatics [23].

The jABC uniformly supports all abstraction levels, ranging from the requirements analysis and conceptual design with non-IT experts (like in the requirements

A.-L. Lamprecht et al. (Eds.): Process Design for Natural Scientists, CCIS 500, pp. 14–29, 2014.
DOI: 10.1007/978-3-662-45006-2_2

and specification case study in Supply Chain Management described in [14]), over user-level design of scientific workflows [25,23] and the application to the construction of a family of retargetable compilers in Genesys [18,16], a framework for the high-level engineering of code generators in XMDD fashion [34], to the application design in the SWS Challenge Mediation Scenario [20] and middleware-level configurations in the MaTRICS [4,5] for the remote configuration and fault tolerance of the Online Conference Service [30].

From an end-user point of view, all the user interaction happens within an intuitive graphical environment, hardly requiring any classical programming skills. Users are able to model their analysis processes based on libraries of basic services in a graphical and intuitive way, combining functionality of services of different providers, and even from different application domains to solve complex problems that a single tool never would be able to tackle. Orchestration of services happens on the basis of the processes they realize in the respective application domain. These processes embody the business logic, and are expressed themselves as (executable) process models. The orchestrated processes can be hierarchical, allowing an easy reuse of subprocesses. Users are enabled to design and execute the orchestrated services, verify logical specifications using an embedded model checker or even generate stand-alone source code for the independent and repeating execution of a process. Services can also be grouped and classified according to domain-specific criteria, using taxonomies and ontologies.

Largely a rewrite and synthesis of [31,24,22,19,23], but also referring to some other articles on the addressed topics [48,32], the following introduces the principles of process and workflow modeling with the jABC in a hands-on fashion, from the point of view of a jABC user, not of a developer (Section 2), and briefly addresses the integration of domain-specific (remote) services into the framework (Section 3).

2 Process and Workflow Modeling in the jABC

The jABC [48,35] is a framework for service-oriented design and development that allows users to develop services and applications easily by composing reusable building blocks into (flow-) graph-like structures that are both formally sound and easy to read and to build. These building blocks are called *Service Independent Building Blocks* (SIBs) in analogy to the telecommunication terminology [43], and in the spirit of the Service-oriented Computing paradigm [38,28]. Their user-oriented nature is central for the *One-Thing Approach* [36], an evolution of the model-based lightweight coordination approach of [34] specifically applied to services. The SIBs are parameterizable, so that their behavior can be adapted depending on the current context of use. Furthermore, each SIB has one or more outgoing branches, which specify the successor(s) of the SIB. Which branch of the SIB is used is determined at runtime.

On the basis of a large library of such SIBs, the user builds models for the desired system in terms of hierarchical graphs called *Service Logic Graphs* (SLGs) [45]. In an SLG a SIB may represent a single functionality or a whole subgraph (i.e., another SLG), thus serving as a macro that hides more detailed

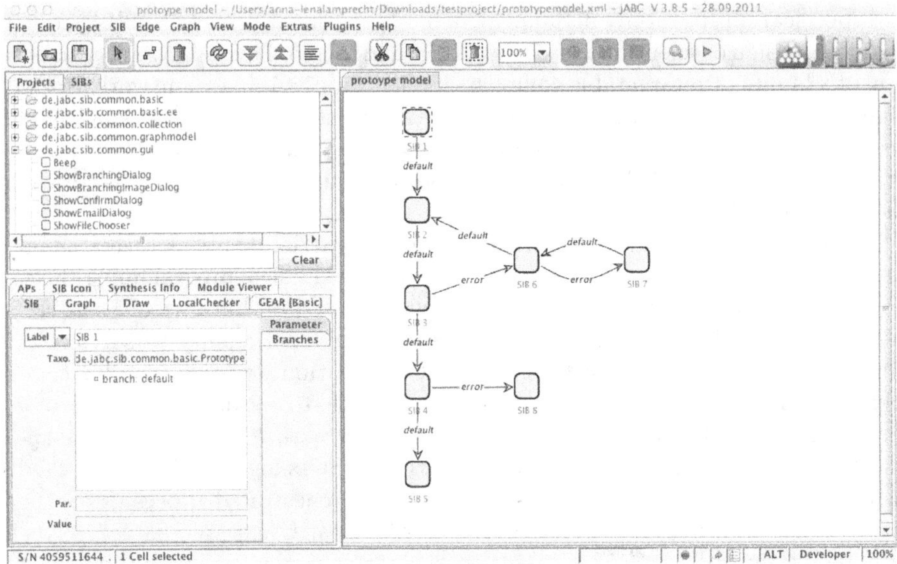

Fig. 1. Workflow modeling GUI of the jABC framework

process models. This feature grants a high reusability not only of components, but also of whole (sub-)models, within larger applications.

Figure 1 gives an impression of the user interface of the jABC framework: it provides a graphical high-level programming layer where no classical programming skills are required for workflow modeling. The available SIBs are listed in a browser (upper left), from where they can be dragged onto the drawing area (right), where the construction of the service compositions in terms of SLGs takes place. SIBs are connected by directed edges, which carry one or more labels (branches) to define the flow of control: the execution of a SIB determines which branch has to be taken to continue the computation at runtime. Data exchange between the individual SIBs is done via the so-called "ExecutionContext", a kind of shared memory where the SIBs can put and access data objects. Different inspectors (lower left) can be used for the detailed configuration of component and model parameters.

Semantically, SLGs are control flow graphs with fork/join parallelism, internally interpreted as Kripke Transition Systems [39]. The advantages of the SLG representation are in fact manifold: being a control-flow-oriented service definition formalism, it is adequate to support complex control structures as primitives. For example, iterations over lists or matrices are provided as SIBs in the environment. At the same time the data dependencies (which are secondary to the control flow) do not clog the representation: even large processes with complex data flows are still easily readable. Moreover, SLGs are at the same time mathematically analyzable objects: they are directed graphs, whose nodes (the SIBs) represent basic services and whose edges (their branches) define the flow of control. They are thus amenable to the sophisticated formal analysis methods provided by modern computer science, like model checking [9,39,46] and model synthesis [33,47,49].

As such, the SLGs also provide a sound semantical basis for the representation of other workflow description formalisms (like, e.g., BPMN, BPEL, UML activity diagrams, or data flow graphs) and constitutes a lingua franca adequate for workflow design, analysis and verification. In fact, alternative formalisms are considered to be just different syntactic (visual) means for representing jABC models tailored for specific communities of users. In this context, we chose to privilege the abstract semantic view of the executable models over 'syntactic' sugar, and therefore use only the jABC notation.

The remainder of this section introduces different features of the jABC more concretely. Section 2.1 describes the "CommonSIBs", a set of SIBs for frequently occurring workflow steps that are provided with every jABC installation. The basic jABC is furthermore equipped with several plugins that exploit different semantic interpretations of the SLGs. Most useful when working with scientific processes and workflows (cf. [23]) are the plugins for definition of custom SIB taxonomies (Section 2.2), workflow execution (Section 2.3), the validation and verification of models (Section 2.4), and the model compilation and deployment (Section 2.5). The jETI plugin, which provides specific functionality for the integration and execution of remote services, is described in the next Section 3.

2.1 Common SIBs

The *Common SIBs* provide a collection of SIBs implementing functionality that is frequently needed during workflow development. This comprises, for instance, data handling, file management, basic user interaction, and different means for coordinating activities. Features like these are highly generic and thus provided by default in each jABC installation.

The following four CommonSIB subcollections are particularly relevant for the case studies of this book:

- *Basic SIBs* help work with the execution context, jABC's mechanism for data passing and communication between SIBs. SIBs for putting objects into the execution context, for accessing objects from the contexts, for evaluating conditions and for basic operations on character sequences are examples of commonly used Basic SIBs.
- *Collection SIBs* help deal with arrays, collections and maps. In addition to adding and removing objects from different kinds of collections, this library offers, for instance, SIBs that iterate over a collection object or perform specific operations like sorting a list.
- *GUI SIBs* support the user communication at runtime, e.g. showing dialogs for user interaction. This library contains predefined common dialogs for user interactions, such as displaying a message, selecting a file, and the input of login data.

– *IO SIBs* help perform file-related tasks. Reading and writing files are probably the most important and most frequently used functions in this library. Additionally, it provides functionality for browsing directories, executing console commands, and zipping and un-zipping files.

For concrete applications, it is typically necessary to have further SIBs that provide functionality required for the specific domain. Section 3 describes how to achieve this.

2.2 SIB Taxonomies

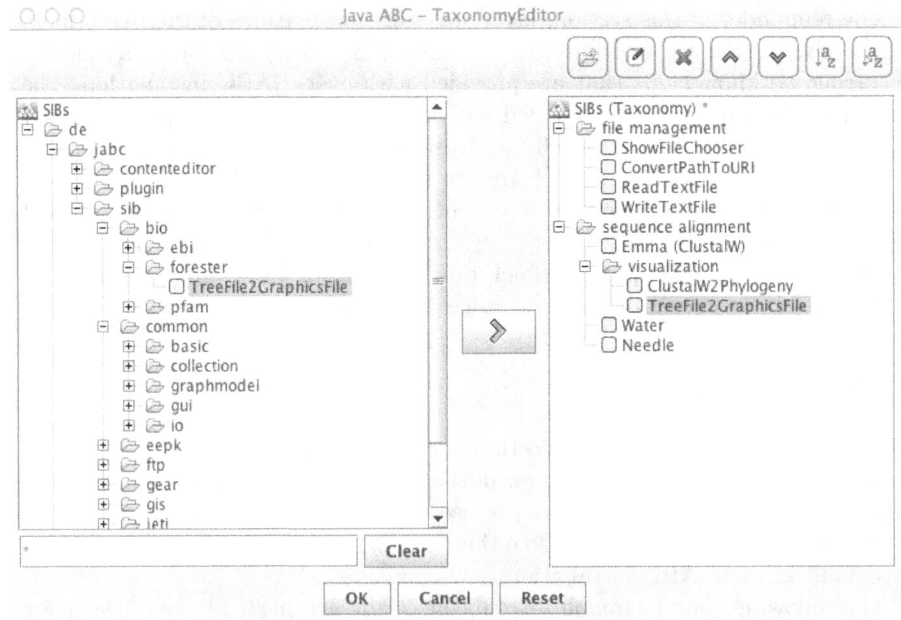

Fig. 2. Categorization of SIBs with the Taxonomy Editor

By default, the SIBs displayed in the SIB browser are sorted according to their location in the file system. The user can choose between a hierarchichal layout view (i.e. with the complete folder structure) and a flat layout view i.e. a package view). With the *Taxonomy Editor* plugin, a collection of SIBs can be (re-) arranged in arbitrary hierarchical categories. The users can introduce their own specific categories, for instance classifying them according to the area of functionality, and associate SIBs with these categories. This is exemplarily shown in Figure 2 for a group of file management and bioinformatics (sequence alignment) services. A SIB can potentially appear at various places in the taxonomy in case it belongs to different categories. Furthermore it does not have to be assigned with its real class name, but can get self-defined aliases.

2.3 SLG Execution

SLGs in the jABC are immediately executable when they consist of SIBs that implement the interfaces of the jABC's *ExecutionEnvironment*, which provides an API for starting, observing, and controlling the execution of models. It also provides *ExecutionContexts*, i.e. areas of shared memory which hold the data that is produced and consumed by the SIBs. The *Tracer* plugin is a comfortable graphical user interface to the ExecutionEnvironment, for instance offering means for model enactment and step-wise execution within the jABC.

As most workflow models are composed of Common SIBs (that are fully implemented and thus executable) plus a few extra SIBs that use algorithms or external available services, we informally talk about SLGs as "living models", because they most often can be directly executed after their composition.

Technically, the Tracer plugin is an interpreter for SLGs that uses the ExecutionEnvironment for enactment and the execution contexts as a means to implement the communication of data and information between the SIBs.

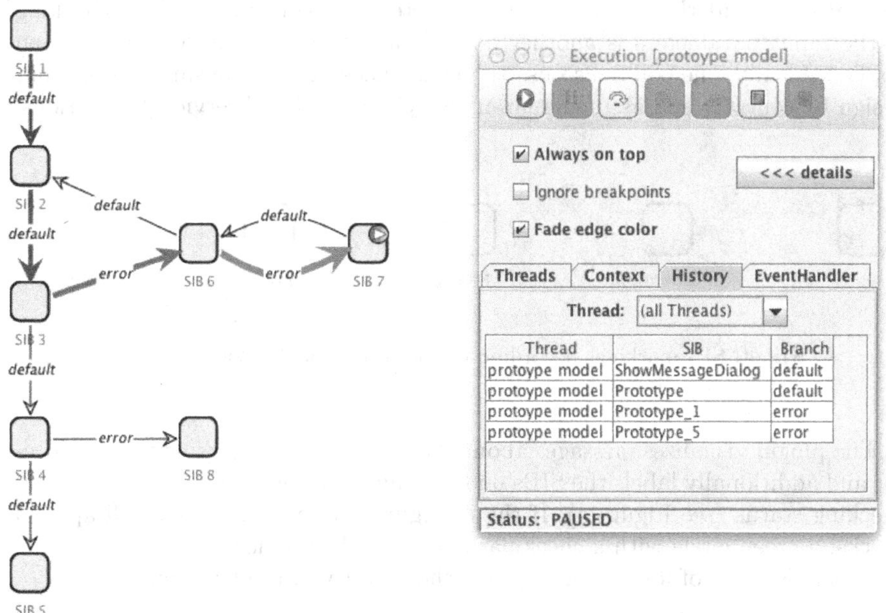

Fig. 3. Model Execution with the Tracer Plugin

Figure 3 shows an example model execution. It is steered by the buttons on the upper side of the Tracer window. The Tracer plugin allows for the overall or step-wise execution of the workflow, the latter being useful especially for debugging (breakpoints can also be set). The three tabs at the lower side of the Tracer window provide further information about the running threads, about the data in the execution context, and, as shown in the figure, about the SIBs and branches visited so far in the current execution run.

2.4 SLG Validation and Verification

The *LocalChecker* and the *ModelChecker* verify constraints on single SIBs and on the whole model, respectively. Constraints embody knowledge about the application domain, the specific process under design, as well as well-formedness conditions. We talk here of incremental modeling of knowledge, as new properties or restrictions can be identified at any time, and added to the knowledge base of the verification environment (cf. [46,15]). Both local and model checking can be applied to the model continuously, enabling the process developer to recognize mistakes immediately, without need of model execution or code-level testing.

The LocalChecker plugin is responsible for testing the local well-formedness of SIBs. What is actually checked depends on the concrete implementation of the individual SIB. The standard checks provided by the plugin mainly deal with the configuration of the SIBs, such as that all the required branches must be present and labelled, and that all required parameters are configured. Type checking of the input parameters is another possible and useful extension that is often applied. Ideally, one could also use the local checking mechanism to implement design by contract and assume-guarantee styles of SIB and service descriptions.

Fig. 4. SIB markings according to the results of the LocalChecker

The plugin visualizes messages about the results of the checking in an inspector and additionally labels the SIBs on the canvas with icons indicating the local checking status (see Figure 4). If the configuration of a SIB passes all applied checks, a green circle with a checkmark is overlaid to its icon.

Otherwise, one of four labels denotes the severity of the problem:

- *informations* (blue circle with exclamation mark) denote that something might deviate from the normal usage, e.g., when no incoming branch is available and the SIB is not properly included into the process,
- *warnings* (yellow triangle with exclamation mark) refer to possible misconfigurations like unused branches,
- *errors* (red circle with a cross) can be caused by SIB configuration errors, like branches that have no target or required parameters that are not set,
- *fatal errors* (red circle with a green bar) are due to exceptions that occur in the SIB's implementation and cannot be handled by the user.

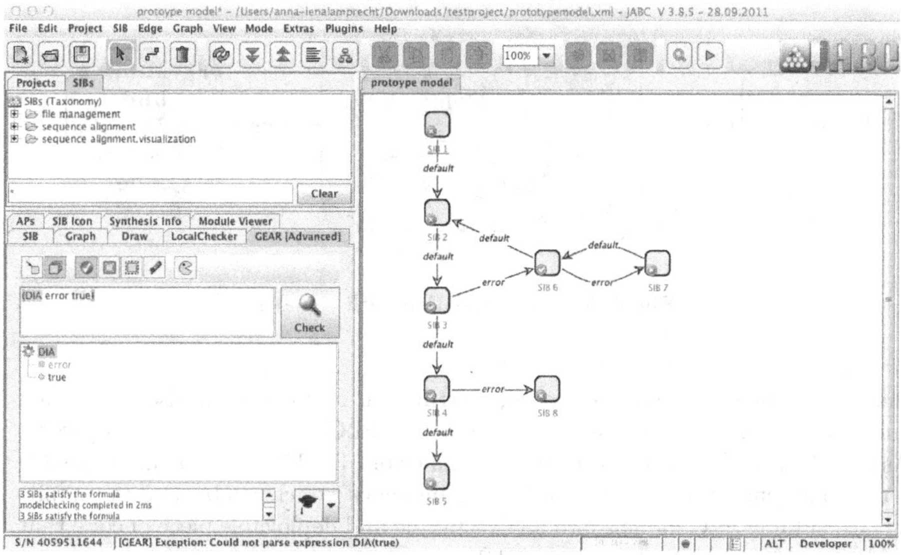

Fig. 5. Global Verification with the GEAR Model Checking Plugin

Complementary to the SIB-level checks of the LocalChecker, the *GEAR* model checking plugin [6,7] is used for the formal verification of global properties of an entire SLG. When the GEAR plugin is loaded, two additional tabs appear in the inspector pane (lower left corner of the GUI) where the properties of the SIBs and the constraints for the model, respectively, are created and managed. The constraints concern the correctness and well-formedness of the workflows. They are expressed as temporal formulae of one of several temporal logics, most frequently in CTL [9, Chapter 4] or the modal μ-calculus [9, Chapter 7]. Users can specify sets of rules that the workflow has to obey, and may concern policies, or best practices, or constraints. When a formula is checked, the satisfying SIBs in the SLG are marked with a green checkmark, the others with red crosses (exemplarily shown in Figure 5).

Frequently, model constraints are safety properties that should invariantly hold for the whole process, that is, which should be satisfied at all SIBs. In these cases every unsatisfying SIB indicates a constraint violation, that is, a situation, where the model must usually be corrected/improved. However, there are often also cases in which the model is correct and the constraints need some refinement or some reformulation, in order to better reflect the knowledge about the specifics of the application and its domain [46,15].

2.5 SLG Compilation and Deployment

The jABC is conceived not only as a process modeling tool, but as a complete software development framework, hence it provides different means for model compilation to program code or to a variety of other representations. This way,

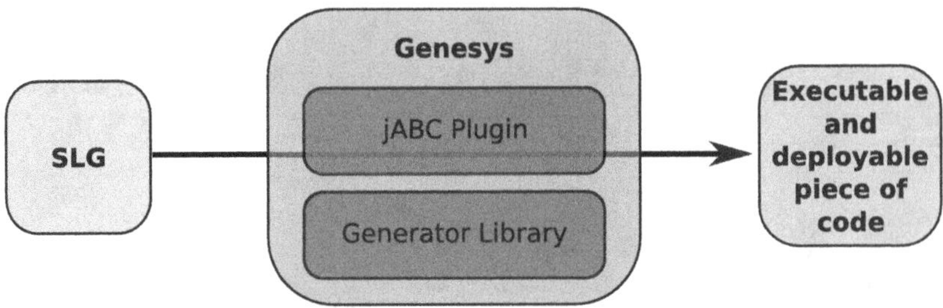

Fig. 6. Model compilation with Genesys

the created processes can be stored, distributed, and executed also in formats and environments independent from the actual SLGs and the jABC framework. As sketched in Figure 6, the *Genesys* Framework [19,17,16] offers an extensible set of code generators for different target languages, which can be used to compile any executable SLG models into an executable and deployable piece of code that can be run independently of the jABC.

Currently, the Genesys code generator library contains predefined generators for Java, Java HTTP Servlets, and complex domain-specific SIBs. The predefined code generators are themselves available both as compiled Java classes and in the form of SLGs, since they have been assembled from an appropriate set of code generation SIBs provided by the library themselves. In this spirit, specialized code generators for further target formats can easily be defined by building appropriate jABC models, mostly starting with a preexisting one and modifying and enhancing it to suit the new needs. The Genesys plugin to the jABC then manages the access to the underlying code generation library by providing inspectors and dialogs for using and creating code generators within the jABC.

3 Service Integration: jETI, REST and Web Services

While the basic jABC, the Common SIBs and the plugins introduced in the previous section essentially provide domain-independent functionality, domain-specific workflow building blocks are typically required when realizing concrete processes. Tailoring the framework to a particular domain involves in fact the integration of (remote) specialist services that are required in the course of the particular processes and workflows. Obviously, the extent and richness of the tool repository plays a crucial role in the success of the platform: the benefit gained from our experimentation and coordination facilities grows with the amount and variety of integrated algorithms, services, and software tools.

While the case studies reported in this book concern scientific workflows, the jABC framework is not limited to this particular application domain: by providing an appropriate set of building blocks, any application domain can be covered. Examples are the user-level definition of telephony services [43], model-based code generation [19,17,16], and the automated completion of model sketches [26,40]. Thus easy and powerful integration facilities are essential to the capability of jABC to cover a large selection of domains.

In the context of the jABC framework, integration of services mostly means to provide SIBs that encapsulate the (remote) invocation of a particular service or the access to a specific resource. Technically, SIBs use just a few lines of Java code to encapsulate the desired functionality. This functionality can either be available locally, such as in case of access to local services (in the easiest case in the form of Java APIs) as well as be provided by remote tools, for instance via web services. In many cases, appropriate web service interfaces are already available and can be used by the components as described in Section 3.1. Often, however, tool developers lack the time or technical knowledge to set up proper web services for their programs. In many of these cases, the jETI technology described in Section 3.2 can help to integrate them as services into the jABC.

3.1 Integrating Web Services

Web services [8], as defined by the World Wide Web Consortium (W3C), provide programmatic interfaces for application-to-application communication via the internet. Technically, web services are a platform- and language-independent technology for distributed computation useful to create client-server applications. This contrasts other RPC technologies (like CORBA, Java RMI, or EJB) that were not platform- and language-independent.

In the classical web service architecture, the application interfaces are characterized by means of an XML-based language, the *Web Service Description Language (WSDL)*, which provides elements for describing functions, data, data types and protocols of a web service. Essentially, the remotely accessible operations are defined along with their parameters and return values. From these WSDL documents, so-called *stubs* can be automatically generated for different target languages for both the client and the service provider side.

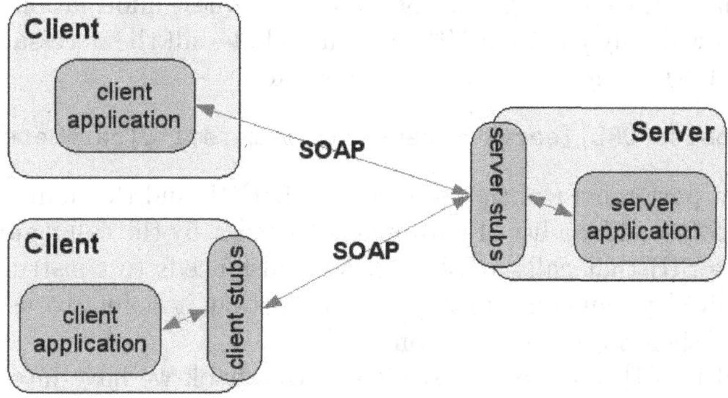

Fig. 7. Schema of client-server interaction using SOAP-based web services

As illustrated in Figure 7, server-side stubs are responsible at the provider's side for the communication with the clients via the network. Client applications usually send requests and receive responses in the form of SOAP messages that are transmitted via HTTP. For web services with simple input data types, these messages can be built directly by the client. In case of services with more complex input data types, as common in many scientific application domains, it is more convenient to generate client-side stubs from the WSDL description and let the client make use of these pre-defined communication interfaces.

Consequently, when creating clients for existing web services, the first step is usually the generation of the client-side stubs from the WSDL document. This can be done in many ways, for instance by the `wsimport` program included in current JDKs. This tool generates a source code package containing Java classes for all required data types and operations specified in the given WSDL document.

The next step is then to implement the client application itself. In the case of the jABC, the clients are the jABC's process building blocks, the SIBs. Different from other common service handling frameworks, the SIBs have an invocation-level granularity [29]. They encapsulate a certain functionality, which in this case is the invocation of a single web service operation. True to our philosophy of behavioral, workflow-oriented service consumption, no matter how complex the service itself is, with the SIBs we access it invocation by invocation. If we need different operations, we create different SIBs, one for each type of specific operation invocation. Therefore, the SIB's execution code simply has to:

1. initialize a connection to the web service by defining a new service object,
2. build the request object including all parameters,
3. call the service with the set parameters,
4. save the response in the execution environment.

As detailed in [27], for the case studies of this book we have integrated this way a number of external web service resources, namely from the EBI (European Bioinformatics Institute) [42,21,12] and from the the CSISS (Center for Spatial Information Science and Systems)[1].

In the last years, REST-style web services [10] have become increasingly popular. They enable the client application to easily request information and access functionality by simply calling a URL which includes all the necessary parameters. Such an URL typically looks something like:

```
http://[website-URL][service-name]?[parameter1]&[parameter2][...]
```

where the first part consist of the website's basic URL and the name of the concrete service, followed by a list of parameters to be set by the calling application. Accordingly, a SIB that calls a REST service just needs to construct an URL with the required parameters, retrieve the data that it points to using HTTP GET, and put them into the execution context.

As detailed in [27], for the case studies of this book we have integrated this way a number of external REST resources: the Pfam services [11], the GeoPlugin services [3] and the Gisgraphy services [2]. Furthermore (also described in [27]), we provided a small collection of generic REST SIBs which can be configured to access arbitrary REST services simply by providing the complete URL.

3.2 Electronic Tool Integration

The jETI (Electronic Tool Integration) platform [44,32] provides means for making file-based Java or command line applications accessible via the internet. In contrast to other remote integration techniques, jETI has only few system requirements and is easy to set up. No further coding is needed for the integration, since all configurations can be done via the HTML interface of the jETI Tool Configurator. Integration of services by means of jETI is convenient especially in the case of legacy applications and whenever else the setup of a classical web or REST service is not adequate or feasible.

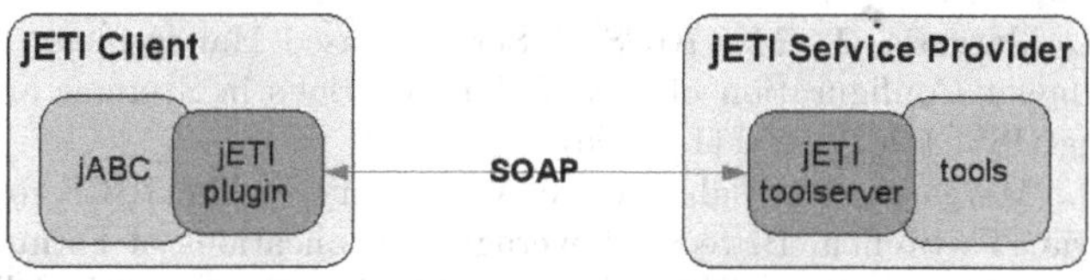

Fig. 8. Schema of Client-Server Interaction Using the ETI Technology

In jETI, as sketched in Figure 8, the service provider maintains a server that accesses (a collection of) applications on the one side, and on the other it provides an interface to the internet. At runtime, the server receives service requests from a client (in our case an SLG) and forwards them to the actual tools, then collects the results, builds adequate response messages and sends them back to the client. Similar to web services' WSDL descriptions, relevant request parameters as well as the actual calls used by the jETI server to execute the tools are defined in an XML file. This information is also used by the jETI server to automatically generate the SIBs for the defined services.

As detailed in [27], for the case studies of this book we have integrated this way the Generic Mapping Tools (GMT) [51,50].

4 Conclusion

In this chapter, we have described the main features of the jABC framework for its use as a graphical tool for modeling scientific processes and workflows. Associated technologies and plugins provide means for a rich variety of supporting functionality, such as remote service integration, taxonomic service classification, model execution, model verification, and model compilation. As such, the jABC is a comprehensive environment for service-oriented modeling and design according to the XMDD (eXtreme Model-Driven Design) paradigm. With the sophisticated execution context and hierarchy concepts, the graphical process definition in the jABC is in fact as powerful as application development in a classical programming language. Its way of "orchestration without programming" is, however, directly accessible by non-IT experts, unlike the scripting or programming-based approaches to workflow management that are still most common today.

References

1. CSISS/GMU Geospatial Web Services, `http://geobrain.laits.gmu.edu/grassweb/manuals/index.html` (last accessed September 9, 2013)
2. Free opensource geocoder and webservices for geonames and openstreetmap data, `http://www.gisgraphy.com/` (last accessed September 9, 2013)
3. geoPlugin to geolocate your visitors, `http://www.geoplugin.com/` (last accessed September 9, 2013)
4. Bajohr, M., Margaria, T.: MaTRICS: A Service-Based Management Tool for Remote Intelligent Configuration of Systems. Innovations in Systems and Software Engineering (ISSE) 2(2), 99–111 (2005)
5. Bajohr, M., Margaria, T.: High Service Availability in MaTRICS for the OCS. In: Margaria, T., Steffen, B. (eds.) Leveraging Applications of Formal Methods, Verification and Validation. CCIS, vol. 17, pp. 572–586. Springer, Heidelberg (2008)
6. Bakera, M., Margaria, T., Renner, C., Steffen, B.: Verification, Diagnosis and Adaptation: Tool-supported enhancement of the model-driven verification process. In: Revue des Nouvelles Technologies de l'Information (RNTI-SM-1), pp. 85–98 (December 2007)
7. Bakera, M., Margaria, T., Renner, C., Steffen, B.: Tool-supported enhancement of diagnosis in model-driven verification. Innovations in Systems and Software Engineering 5, 211–228 (2009)
8. Booth, D., Haas, H., McCabe, F., Newcomer, E., Champion, M., Ferris, C., Orchard, D.: Web Services Architecture. W3C Working Group Note (February 2004), `http://www.w3.org/TR/ws-arch/` (last accessed May 5, 2013)
9. Clarke, E.M., Grumberg, O., Peled, D.A.: Model Checking. The MIT Press, Cambridge (1999)
10. Fielding, R.T.: Architectural Styles and the Design of Network-based Software Architectures. PhD thesis, University of California, Irvine (2000)
11. Finn, R.D., Mistry, J., Tate, J., Coggill, P., Heger, A., Pollington, J.E., Gavin, O.L., Gunasekaran, P., Ceric, G., Forslund, K., Holm, L., Sonnhammer, E.L.L., Eddy, S.R., Bateman, A.: The Pfam protein families database. Nucleic Acids Research 38(suppl 1), D211–D222 (2010)
12. Goujon, M., McWilliam, H., Li, W., Valentin, F., Squizzato, S., Paern, J., Lopez, R.: A new bioinformatics analysis tools framework at EMBL-EBI. Nucleic Acids Research 38(Web Server issue), W695–W699 (2010)
13. Huhns, M.N., Singh, M.P.: Service-Oriented Computing: Key Concepts and Principles. IEEE Internet Computing 9, 75–81 (2005)
14. Hörmann, M., Margaria, T., Mender, T., Nagel, R., Steffen, B., Trinh, H.: The jABC Approach to Rigorous Collaborative Development of SCM Applications. In: Margaria, T., Steffen, B. (eds.) Leveraging Applications of Formal Methods, Verification and Validation. CCIS, vol. 17, pp. 724–737. Springer, Heidelberg (2008)

15. Jonsson, B., Margaria, T., Naeser, G., Nyström, J., Steffen, B.: Incremental requirement specification for evolving systems. Nordic J. of Computing 8, 65–87 (2001)
16. Jörges, S.: Construction and Evolution of Code Generators. LNCS, vol. 7747. Springer, Heidelberg (2013)
17. Jörges, S., Lamprecht, A.-L., Margaria, T., Schaefer, I., Steffen, B.: A Constraint-based Variability Modeling Framework. International Journal on Software Tools for Technology Transfer (STTT) 14(5), 511–530 (2012)
18. Jörges, S., Margaria, T., Steffen, B.: Genesys: service-oriented construction of property conform code generators. Innovations in Systems and Software Engineering 4(4), 361–384 (2008)
19. Jörges, S., Steffen, B., Margaria, T.: Building code generators with genesys: A tutorial introduction. In: Fernandes, J.M., Lämmel, R., Visser, J., Saraiva, J. (eds.) Generative and Transformational Techniques in Software Engineering III. LNCS, vol. 6491, pp. 364–385. Springer, Heidelberg (2011)
20. Kubczak, C., Margaria, T., Steffen, B., Nagel, R.: Service-oriented Mediation with jABC/jETI (2008)
21. Labarga, A., Valentin, F., Anderson, M., Lopez, R.: Web services at the European bioinformatics institute. Nucleic Acids Research 35(Web Server issue), W6–W11 (2007)
22. Lamprecht, A.: Orchestration of Heterogeneous Bioinformatics Processes in Bio-jETI as a Service Integration, Design, and Provisioning Platform. Master's thesis, Georg-August-Universität Göttingen (August 2007)
23. Lamprecht, A.-L.: User-Level Workflow Design. LNCS, vol. 8311. Springer, Heidelberg (2013)
24. Lamprecht, A.-L., Margaria, T., Steffen, B.: Seven variations of an alignment workflow - an illustration of agile process design and management in bio-jETI. In: Măndoiu, I., Wang, S.-L., Zelikovsky, A. (eds.) ISBRA 2008. LNCS (LNBI), vol. 4983, pp. 445–456. Springer, Heidelberg (2008)
25. Lamprecht, A.-L., Margaria, T., Steffen, B.: Bio-jETI: a framework for semantics-based service composition. BMC Bioinformatics 10(Suppl 10), S8 (2009)
26. Lamprecht, A.-L., Naujokat, S., Margaria, T., Steffen, B.: Synthesis-Based Loose Programming. In: Proc. of the 7th Int. Conf. on the Quality of Information and Communications Technology (QUATIC 2010), Porto, Portugal, pp. 262–267 (September 2010)
27. Lamprecht, A.-L., Wickert, A.: The Course's SIB Libraries. In: Lamprecht, A.-L., Margaria, T. (eds.) Process Design for Natural Scientists. CCIS, vol. 500, pp. 30–44. Springer, Heidelberg (2014)
28. Margaria, T.: Service is in the Eyes of the Beholder. IEEE Computer (November 2007)
29. Margaria, T., Boßelmann, S., Doedt, M., Floyd, B.D., Steffen, B.: Customer-Oriented Business Process Management: Visions and Obstacles. In: Hinchey, M., Coyle, L. (eds.) Conquering Complexity, pp. 407–429. Springer, London (2012)
30. Margaria, T., Karusseit, M.: Community Usage of the Online Conference Service: an Experience Report from three CS Conferences. In: Proceedings of the IFIP Conference on Towards The Knowledge Society: E-Commerce, E-Business, E-Government, Deventer, The Netherlands, pp. 497–511. Kluwer, B.V (2002)
31. Margaria, T., Kubczak, C., Steffen, B.: Bio-jETI: a service integration, design, and provisioning platform for orchestrated bioinformatics processes. BMC Bioinformatics 9(Suppl 4), S12 (2008)

32. Margaria, T., Nagel, R., Steffen, B.: jETI: A tool for remote tool integration. In: Halbwachs, N., Zuck, L.D. (eds.) TACAS 2005. LNCS, vol. 3440, pp. 557–562. Springer, Heidelberg (2005)
33. Margaria, T., Steffen, B.: Backtracking-free design planning by automatic synthesis in *M*ETA*Frame*. In: Astesiano, E. (ed.) ETAPS 1998 and FASE 1998. LNCS, vol. 1382, pp. 188–204. Springer, Heidelberg (1998)
34. Margaria, T., Steffen, B.: Lightweight coarse-grained coordination: a scalable system-level approach. Software Tools for Technology Transfer 5(2-3), 107–123 (2004)
35. Margaria, T., Steffen, B.: Agile IT: Thinking in User-Centric Models. In: Margaria, T., Steffen, B. (eds.) Leveraging Applications of Formal Methods, Verification and Validation. CCIS, vol. 17, pp. 490–502. Springer, Berlin (2009)
36. Margaria, T., Steffen, B.: Business Process Modelling in the jABC: The One-Thing-Approach. In: Cardoso, J., van der Aalst, W. (eds.) Handbook of Research on Business Process Modeling. IGI Global (2009)
37. Margaria, T., Steffen, B.: Service-Orientation: Conquering Complexity with XMDD. In: Hinchey, M., Coyle, L. (eds.) Conquering Complexity, pp. 217–236. Springer, London (2012)
38. Margaria, T., Steffen, B., Reitenspieß, M.: Service-oriented design: The roots. In: Benatallah, B., Casati, F., Traverso, P. (eds.) ICSOC 2005. LNCS, vol. 3826, pp. 450–464. Springer, Heidelberg (2005)
39. Müller-Olm, M., Schmidt, D., Steffen, B.: Model-Checking - A Tutorial Introduction. In: Proceedings of the 6th International Symposium on Static Analysis (SAS 1999), pp. 330–354 (1999)
40. Naujokat, S., Lamprecht, A.-L., Steffen, B.: Loose programming with PROPHETS. In: de Lara, J., Zisman, A. (eds.) Fundamental Approaches to Software Engineering. LNCS, vol. 7212, pp. 94–98. Springer, Heidelberg (2012)
41. Neubauer, J., Margaria, T., Steffen, B.: Design for Verifiability: The OCS Case Study. In: Formal Methods for Industrial Critical Systems: A Survey of Applications, ch. 8, pp. 153–178. Wiley-IEEE Computer Society Press (March 2013)
42. Pillai, S., Silventoinen, V., Kallio, K., Senger, M., Sobhany, S., Tate, J., Velankar, S., Golovin, A., Henrick, K., Rice, P., Stoehr, P., Lopez, R.: SOAP-based services provided by the European Bioinformatics Institute. Nucleic Acids Research 33(Web Server issue), W25–W28 (2005)
43. Steffen, B., Margaria, T.: META*Frame* in practice: Design of intelligent network services. In: Olderog, E.-R., Steffen, B. (eds.) Correct System Design. LNCS, vol. 1710, pp. 390–415. Springer, Heidelberg (1999)
44. Steffen, B., Margaria, T., Braun, V.: The Electronic Tool Integration platform: concepts and design. International Journal on Software Tools for Technology Transfer (STTT) 1(1-2), 9–30 (1997)
45. Steffen, B., Margaria, T., Braun, V., Kalt, N.: Hierarchical Service Definition. Annual Review of Communications of the ACM 51, 847–856 (1997)
46. Steffen, B., Margaria, T., Claßen, A., Braun, V.: Incremental Formalization: A Key to Industrial Success. Software - Concepts and Tools 17(2), 78–95 (1996)
47. Steffen, B., Margaria, T., Freitag, B.: Module Configuration by Minimal Model Construction. Technical report, Fakultät für Mathematik und Informatik, Universität Passau (1993)
48. Steffen, B., Margaria, T., Nagel, R., Jörges, S., Kubczak, C.: Model-driven development with the jABC. In: Bin, E., Ziv, A., Ur, S. (eds.) HVC 2006. LNCS, vol. 4383, pp. 92–108. Springer, Heidelberg (2007)

49. Steffen, B., Margaria, T., von der Beeck, M.: Automatic synthesis of linear process models from temporal constraints: An incremental approach. In: ACM/SIGPLAN International Workshop on Automated Analysis of Software, AAS 1997 (1997)
50. Wessel, P.: The GMT Home Page, `http://gmt.soest.hawaii.edu` (last accessed January 3, 2013)
51. Wessel, P., Smith, W.H.F.: Free software helps map and display data. EOS Trans. Amer. Geophys. U. 72(41) (1991)

The Course's SIB Libraries

Anna-Lena Lamprecht and Alexander Wickert

Chair for Service and Software Engineering, Potsdam University,
Potsdam, D-14482, Germany
{lamprecht,awickert}@cs.uni-potsdam.de

Abstract. This chapter gives a detailed description of the service framework underlying all the example projects that form the foundation of this book. It describes the different SIB libraries that we made available for the course "Process modeling in the natural sciences" to provide the functionality that was required for the envisaged applications. The students used these SIB libraries to realize their projects.

Keywords: scientific workflows, web services, bioinformatics, geoinformation, geovisualization.

1 Introduction and Overview

The domain-independent symbiosis of jABC [37] and jETI [27] introduced in the previous chapter [24] becomes a scientific workflow design, management, and execution system when it is enhanced by adequate domain-specific SIB libraries for the workflow's application domains. The jABC comes with a large collection of SIBs for common, frequently needed, domain-independent workflow functionality. These Common SIBs [10] are useful also for working with scientific workflows, but not sufficient. The students' projects in the scope of our course mostly concerned workflows for specific bioinformatics and geo-visualization applications, and hence required additional domain-specific SIBs. This chapter gives an overview of the services that we as the advisers of the course integrated into the jABC framework and provided as SIBs. With the created SIB repository the students were then able to model the SLGs that realize the workflow scenarios they envisioned. Note that some students also integrated the required services themselves, as described in their individual chapters.

Table 1 surveys the repository of SIBs made available for the course. It comprises existing SIB libraries from previous projects as well as new libraries that have been implemented by us during the course. The table entries are the names of the different SIB collections followed by a number in brackets that corresponds to the number of SIBs contained in the respective library. In total, more than 275 SIBs were finally made available. As the different rows show, the repository covers science-oriented bioinformatics and geoinformatics functionality, but also a number of SIBs that provide additional, more general functionality that can be useful in different domains. The columns of the table categorize the SIBs according to the technologies used for the implementation of the underlying services, which determines the way how the respective services are integrated into

A.-L. Lamprecht et al. (Eds.): Process Design for Natural Scientists, CCIS 500, pp. 30–44, 2014.
DOI: 10.1007/978-3-662-45006-2_3

Table 1. Overview of the Course's SIB Libraries

<table>
<tr><th rowspan="2">domain</th><th colspan="3">remote services</th><th rowspan="2">API-based (161)</th></tr>
<tr><th>jETI-based (7)</th><th>WSDL-based (85)</th><th>REST-based (46)</th></tr>
<tr><td rowspan="2">bioinformatics (25)</td><td rowspan="2"></td><td></td><td>pfam-sibs (6)</td><td rowspan="2">forester-sibs (1)</td></tr>
<tr><td colspan="2">ebi-sibs (18)</td></tr>
<tr><td>geoinformatics (93)</td><td>gmt-sibs (7)</td><td>csiss-sibs (67)</td><td>geoplugin-sibs (4)
gisgraphy-sibs (6)
lbm-sibs (9)</td><td></td></tr>
<tr><td rowspan="2">both (general) (160)</td><td rowspan="2"></td><td rowspan="2"></td><td></td><td>ftp-sibs (2)
common-sibs (119)
jeti-helper-sibs (9)
openoffice-sibs (21)
rest-sibs (5)
twitter-sibs (1)</td></tr>
<tr><td colspan="2">qrcode-sibs (3)</td></tr>
</table>

the jABC framework to become SIBs. As can be seen from the columns, four major kinds of services are used here:

- jETI-based remote services, which are especially suitable for integrating file-based command line tools,
- WSDL-based web services, for which SIBs can easily be implemented making use of client-side code generated from the WSDL documents,
- REST-based web services, for which SIBs can easily be implemented using standard JRE functionality (`java.net` package), and
- different kinds of (Java) APIs, which can naturally be called from SIBs.

Some SIB library names appear in more than one column when the respective SIB collections comprise services of different technologies. Details of what this means for the respective integration processes are given in the previous chapter of this volume [24], which introduces the principles of modeling and executing scientific workflows in the jABC. The SIBs abstract from these implementation details, so that in the following we focus only on their functionality when we describe in more detail the SIB repository available for the course.

Section 2 describes the available bioinformatics-specific SIBs, Section 3 deals with the geoinformatics-specific SIBs, and finally Section 4 presents the SIBs for the other, more general services. Apart from the gmt-sibs, which are directly generated from our jETI server on request, and the Common SIBs, which are included in the jABC standard distribution, all SIBs listed here are available at the web site of the jabc-sibs community project at `https://projekte.itmc.tu-dortmund.de/projects/jabc-sibs` (registration required).

2 The Bioinformatics SIBs Collections

In this section we describe the SIBs for access to specific bioinformatics services and libraries that were used in students' projects. These libraries had been available in a smaller version already before the course and were used in previous projects. They were now extended on-demand according to the upcoming requirements.

2.1 ebi-sibs Library (18): SIBs for EBI Web Services

The main mission of the European Bioinformatics Institute (EBI) is to build, maintain and provide biological databases and information services. Via a steadily growing number of web and web service interfaces the EBI provides access to several of its data resources (for instance the EMBL Nucleotide Database, UniProt, Ensembl, and IntAct), to a plethora of analysis tools, including the EMBOSS suite [32], and specific tools for similarity searches, multiple alignment, structural analysis and for exploring literature and ontologies [29,23,18].

For the students' projects, we implemented SIBs for 18 of the EBI's SOAP web services, covering different bioinformatics areas. As there is no specific taxonomic organization, we list them alphabetically:

- `ArrayExpressExperiments` searches the ArrayExpress database (a database of functional genomics experiments) for experiments.
- `ArrayExpressFiles` searches ArrayExpress for files.
- `ClustalW2Phylogeny` creates neighbor-joining or UPGMA phylogenic trees based on ClustalW sequence alignments.
- `Emma` computes a multiple sequence alignment using ClustalW.
- `Garnier` predicts secondary structures of proteins.
- `Getorf` finds and extracts open reading frames (ORFs).
- `Makenucseq` creates random nucleotide sequences.
- `Makeprotseq` creates random protein sequences.
- `NCBIBlast` searches sequence databases using the NCBI BLAST algorithm.
- `Needle` computes a Needleman-Wunsch global sequence alignment.
- `Pepinfo` plots amino acid properties.
- `PsiSearch` combines the Smith-Waterman search algorithm with the PSI Blast profile construction strategy to find distantly related proteins.
- `Scopparse` generates a DCF file from raw SCOP files.
- `Ssematch` searches a DCF file for secondary structure matches.
- `Transeq` translates nucleotide sequence into the corresponding peptide sequences.
- `WSDBFetch` fetches database entries based on IDs or accession numbers.
- `Water` computes a Smith-Waterman local alignment.
- `WUBlast` searches sequence databases using the WU BLAST algorithm.

SIBs from the ebi-sibs library were used in the following student projects:

- Protein classification workflow (Judith Reso) [30]
- Workflow for rapid metagenome analysis (Gunnar Schulze) [34]
- Workflow for phylogenetic tree construction (Monika Lis) [25]

Note that also Leif Blaese used EBI web services in his project "Data mining for unidentified protein sequences" [16], but accessed them by using a command line client via the ExecuteCommand SIB from the Common SIBs library. While this introduces undesirable platform dependency, it makes it possible to influence the order in which the numerous web service queries in this workflow are submitted and the results collected (which is not possible with the predefined ebi-sibs), possibly leading to a faster overall workflow execution time.

2.2 pfam-sibs Library (6): SIBs for Pfam Web Services

The Pfam protein families database [17] provides a number of REST-style web services for data retrieval and database searches [11]. The following SIBs have been implemented for use in a project on functional annotation of protein sequences:

- `Accession2Id` converts a Pfam accession number into a Pfam ID.
- `Id2Accession` converts a Pfam ID into a Pfam accession number.
- `PfamAAnnotations` retrieves the annotations from a Pfam-A family page.
- `PfamAFamilyList` retrieves a list of all Pfam-A families in the latest Pfam release.
- `ProteinSequenceData` retrieves the protein sequence data from a Pfam-A family page.
- `SequenceSearch` searches for Pfam domains matching the input protein sequence.

SIBs from the pfam-sibs library were used in the following student projects:

- Protein classification workflow (Judith Reso) [30]
- Workflow for rapid metagenome analysis (Gunnar Schulze) [34]

2.3 forester-sibs Library (1): SIBs for the Forester API

The forester libraries provide a rich collection of functionality for phylogenomics and and evolutionary biology research [41]. They are, for instance, the basis for the Archaeopteryx phylogenic tree viewer (formerly ATV [42]). The forester-sibs use the Java library of the Archaeopteryx project to create graphical representations (e.g. PNGs) from textual phylogenetic tree formats. While there is potential for more, currently the forester-sibs library consists only of one SIB:

- `TreeFile2GraphicsFile` creates a graphics file from a phylogenetic tree file.

This SIB was used by Monika Lis in her project "Workflow for phylogenetic tree construction" [25] for the visualization of the created phylogenetic tree.

3 The Geoinformatics SIBs Collections

In this section we describe the SIBs to access specific geoinformatics services and libraries that were used in students' projects. Only the lbm-sibs library had been available before the course and used in previous projects. All the other SIBs have come into being in the scope of our course.

3.1 gmt-sibs Library (7): SIBs for the Generic Mapping Tools (GMT)

The Generic Mapping Tools (GMT) [40,39] are "an open source collection of 65 tools for manipulating geographic and Cartesian data sets (including filtering, trend fitting, gridding, projecting, etc.) and producing Encapsulated PostScript File (EPS) illustrations ranging from simple x-y plots via contour maps to artificially illuminated surfaces and 3-D perspective views"[39]. Being file-based command line tools, they were most easily integrated into the jABC framework using the **jETI technology** (cf. previous chapter).

We did not integrate the entire GMT with all possible arguments, but only those that were required for the students' projects. Concretely, the following GMT-SIBs have been created (see [39] for comprehensive documentation):

- `grd2xyz` converts one or more 2D grid files to ASCII or binary format.
- `grdclip` clips the range of data values in a 2D grid file.
- `ps2raster` converts one or more postscript files to raster format.
- `pscoast` plots land masses, water masses, coastlines, borders and rivers of a given region into a postscript file.
- `psscale` plots a grey scale or a color scale on a map in postscript format.
- `pstext` plots text on a map in postscript format.
- `psxyz` plots 3D lines, polygons and symbols in a postscript file.

SIBs from the gmt-sibs library were used in the following student projects:

- Location Analysis for Placing Artifical Reefs (Lasse Scheele) [33]
- Creation of Topographic Maps (Josephine Kind) [21]

With the jETI server up and running and the experiences with the GMT that we have obtained during the project work, integrating more of these tools is now a straightforward process and can be done on demand when the need arises in the scope of future projects.

3.2 csiss-sibs Library (67): SIBs for the CSISS Web Services

The geospatial web services of the Center for Spatial Information Science and Systems (CSISS) [3] "have been developed to provide geospatial processing and analysis based on existing software or geosciences modules" [3]. Based on the open source Geographic Resources Analysis Support System (GRASS) [8] and some existing web services and geoscience analysis modules, the CSISS web services provide functionality for working with raster, vector and satellite image data. The 67 SIBs implemented for this collection cover all six categories of services (for more elaborate documentation please refer to the CSISS web site [3]):

1. Geospatial web services for satellite image processing (12):
   - `Raster_EdgeDetection` finds the edges in an image.
   - `Raster_FFT` processes the image based on the FFT algorithm.
   - `Raster_FusionBrovey` performs a Brovey transformation.
   - `Raster_HIS2RGB` transforms an HIS image to RGB color space.
   - `Raster_IFFT` transforms the output of `Raster_FFT` into a normal image.
   - `Raster_Mosaic` mosaics adjacent images.
   - `Raster_OIF` calculates the optimal index factor.
   - `Raster_PCA` performs a principal components analysis (PCA).
   - `Raster_RGB2HIS` transforms and RGB image to HIS color space.
   - `Raster_SupervisedClassifcationService` can be used to reclassify multispectral satellite data with supervised classification methods.
   - `Raster_TasseledCap` performs Tasseled Cap (Kauth Thomas) transformation.
   - `Raster_UnsupervisedClassifcationService` can be used to reclassify multispectral satellite data with unsupervised classification methods.
2. Geospatial web services for raster map processing (28):
   - `Raster_Aspect` generates a raster map layer of aspect derivates.
   - `Raster_BBoxClip` clips a raster map by a bounding box.
   - `Raster_Buffer` creates buffer zones in a map.
   - `Raster_ChangeColortable_Copy`, `Raster_ChangeColortable_Predefined` and `Raster_ChangeColortable_Userdefined` change the color table of an image by copying a table from another image, or by using predefined or user-defined tables, respectively.
   - `Raster_CreateContour` produces a contour map.
   - `Raster_GeoparameterCalculation` extracts terrain parameters.
   - `Raster_GreyScale` converts the map to greyscale.
   - `Raster_ImageAlgebra` performs arithmetics on raster map layers.
   - `Raster_LatLonBBoxClip` clips a raster map by a bounding box.
   - `Raster_MatrixFilter` applies a matrix filter.
   - `Raster_NDVI` calculates the normalized differenced vegetation index.
   - `Raster_PatchMultiBand` mosaics RGB channels of adjacent images.
   - `Raster_PatchSingleBand` patches together adjacent map layers.
   - `Raster_PolygonClip` clips a raster map by a polygon.
   - `Raster_Profile` identifies raster map values on user-defined lines.
   - `Raster_ProfileCurvature` computes profile curvatures.
   - `Raster_Rescale` changes the image scale.
   - `Raster_RGBcomposite` combines RGB map layers into a color image.
   - `Raster_RGBextract` extracts the RGB components.
   - `Raster_Slope` computes slopes.
   - `Raster_SurfaceGeneration` creates a raster elevation map.
   - `Raster_SurfaceInterpolation` performs raster data interpolation.
   - `Raster_TangentialCurvature` computes tangential curvature.

  - `Raster_TopographicIndex` creates a topographic index.
  - `Raster_TopographicShading` creates a shaded relief map.
  - `Raster_Vectorization` converts a raster map to vector format.
3. Geospatial web services for raster map statistics (6):
  - `Raster_AreaStatistics` creates a histogram of the training areas.
  - `Raster_ClassificationStatistics` calculates classification statistics for the cells of the map.
  - `Raster_CovarianceCorrelation` gives a covariation/correlation matrix.
  - `Raster_DefinedIntervalStatistics`, `Raster_EqualIntervalStatistics` and `Raster_ManualIntervalStatistics` compute equal interval classification statistics based on the specified interval size, class numbers and class ranges, respectively.
4. Geospatial web services for vector map processing (15):
  - `Vector_AttributeColumn` prints the types and names of the attributes.
  - `Vector_Buffer` creates a buffer around selected features.
  - `Vector_BuildPolylines` builds polylines from lines or boundaries.
  - `Vector_BuildTopology` creates topologies.
  - `Vector_CleanTopology` automatically fixes vector topologies.
  - `Vector_FeatureExtraction` extracts vector objects for selected features.
  - `Vector_FeatureSelection` supports selection of features from a vector.
  - `Vector_GML2SHP` converts GML to shape file format.
  - `Vector_Overlay` overlay two vector maps.
  - `Vector_Patch` patches together several map layers.
  - `Vector_QueryInformation` reports basic information about the map.
  - `Vector_Rasterization` transforms a vector map layer to raster format.
  - `Vector_SHP2GML` converts shape files to GML format.
  - `Vector_ShortestPath` performs shortest-path analysis.
  - `Vector_ValueExtraction` extracts raster values.
5. Web services for hydrological analysis based on raster maps (5):
  - `Raster_DrainageBasin` computes drainage directions and watershed basins.
  - `Raster_FlowAccumulation` computes flow accumulations.
  - `Raster_FlowDirection` computes flow direction.
  - `Raster_StreamExtraction` computes stream networks.
  - `Raster_OpennessCalculation` computes surface openness.
6. Web service for fire-spread simulation (1):
  - `Fire_SpreadSimulation` simulates the spread of wildfires.

SIBs from the csiss-sibs library were used in the following student projects:

- Web-based Map Generalization Tools Put to the Test (Henriette Sens) [35]
- CREADED: Coloured-Relief Application for Digital Elevation Data (Franziska Noack) [28]
- Location Analysis for Potential Areas for Wind Turbines (Tobias Respondeck) [31]

3.3 geoplugin-sibs Library (4): SIBs for the Geoplugin Web Services

GeoPlugin [6] is a REST-style web service that provides operations to determine the location of an IP address and retrieves additional information for a given geolocation. The geoplugin-sibs library comprise four SIBs:

- `Geolocation` returns information (such as city, region, countryName, ...) for a given IP address.
- `Location` returns the closest location (if possible) for a given latitude-longitude pair.
- `NearbyPlaces` returns nearby places for a given latitude-longitude pair.
- `Postalcode` returns the postal code for a given latitude-longitude pair.

SIBs from the geoplugin-sibs library were used in the following student projects:

- Visualization of Data Transfer Paths (Christian Kuntzsch) [22]

3.4 gisgraphy-sibs Library (6): SIBs for the Gisgraphy Web Services

Gisgraphy introduces itself as "a free, open source framework that offers the possibility to do geolocalisation and geocoding via Java APIs or REST webservices" [4]. The gisgraphy-sibs cover all six web services that gisgraphy provides:

- `AddressParser` parses a text address and returns its components (street name, house number, street type, etc.).
- `Fulltext search` does a fulltext search and returns all associated information of the found item.
- `Geocoding` returns information (such as city, zipCode, country, ...) for a given address with country code.
- `Geolocalisation` finds nearby places, streets, etc. of a given latitude-longitude pair and a radius.
- `Reverse geocoding` returns street name and other information of a given latitude-longitude pair.
- `Street search` returns information of a given street.

SIBs from the gisgraphy-sibs library were used in the following student project:

- GraffDok: A Graffiti Documentation Application (Robin Holler) [20]

3.5 lbm-sibs Library (9): SIBs for Location-Based Mapping Services

The lbm-sibs have originally been implemented for projects preceding our course, but were updated to be useful again. Making use of different location-based mapping services (OpenStreetMap API [2], Google Maps API [7], InstaMapper [9] and Wikipedia's GeoNames database [5]), they comprise the following SIBs:

- `AddWaypoint` draws a waypoint for a given location into a map using the OpenStreetMap API.

- `CenterMap` centers the map around a given location using the OpenStreetMap API.
- `GetLocationFromGoogle` retrieves a geoposition matching a given search string using the Google Maps API.
- `GetLocationFromInstaMapper` gets the most recent geolocation for a given device using InstaMapper GPS tracking.
- `GetLocationFromGeonamesByPostalCode` retrieves a list of geolocations for a given postal code using the GeoNames database.
- `GetLoactionsFromInstaMapper` gets the last $amount geolocations for a given device using InstaMapper GPS tracking.
- `GetSurroundingLocationsFromGeonames` gets a list of surrounding geolocations for a given geolocations using the GeoNames database.
- `SetZoomLevel` sets a new zoom level for the given map using the OpenStreetMap API.
- `ShowOpenStreetMap` initializes and opens a new map window with OpenStreetMap's rendered tiles.

While these SIBs had been used for tutorial exercises preceding the project work, they have not appeared in any of the final projects. Instead, the students used services with similar but more application-specific functionality, like the latest functions provided the Google Maps API, or the geoplugin and gisgraphy SIBs described above.

4 SIBs Collections for Other Functionality

In this section we describe the SIBs to access general, domain-independent services and libraries that we prepared for the students' projects. Although not all these libraries were actually used in the projects, for instance when more suitable alternatives were finally found, these libraries provide useful functionality and are likely to be used in other projects, so we include them here.

4.1 ftp-sibs Library (2): SIBs for FTP Operations

The ftp-sibs provide basic file transfer services:

- `FtpDownload` downloads a file from a remote FTP server.
- `FtpUpload` uploads a file to a remote FTP server.

In addition to the local and remote paths, user name and password must be specified in order to establish the connection to the server. Note that no external library was necessary for the implementation of these SIBs, the standard Java libraries provide all required functionality.

SIBs from the ftp-sibs library were used in the following student projects:

- CREADED: Coloured-Relief Application for Digital Elevation Data (Franziska Noack) [28]
- Location Analysis for Potential Areas for Wind Turbines (Tobias Respondeck) [31]

4.2 jeti-helper-sibs Library (9): SIBs for Working with jETI Services

The jeti-helper-sibs come with the jETI plugin for the jABC framework. As jETI works with a separate execution context, the so-called TransferHandler that transparently manages the transfer of data between client and server(s), all data that is to be transferred to/from a jETI service has to go via this context. The jeti-helper-sibs provide different ways for preparing data to be used by jETI services, and to process data that is returned from jETI service executions:

- `ETIErrorSIB` displays jETI error messages.
- `ReadFile` loads the specified file to the TransferHandler.
- `ReadFromContext` loads a file name from the context and loads the corresponding file to the TransferHandler.
- `ReadFromURL` reads a file name from an URL and loads the corresponding file to the TransferHandler.
- `Viewer` shows a file from the TransferHandler in a specified program.
- `ViewerWin32` is the same as `Viewer`, but for Windows platforms.
- `WriteFile` writes a file from the TransferHandler to the specified file.
- `WriteFileToURL` writes a file from the TransferHandler to a specified URL.
- `WriteFileToContext` copies a file from the TransferHandler to the temporary directory and writes the file name into the jABC's standard execution context.

SIBs from the jeti-helper-sibs library were used in the following student projects, which are exactly those that also used the jETI-based gmt-sibs library:

- Location Analysis for Placing Artifical Reefs (Lasse Scheele) [33]
- Creation of Topographic Maps (Josephine Kind) [21]

4.3 openoffice-sibs Library (21): SIBs for Accessing OpenOffice Functionality

The openoffice-sibs have also been created in the scope of a previous project [10] to make OpenOffice [1] functionality available for use within jABC workflows. With these SIBs, it is possible to create basic OpenOffice documents (like simple text files and spreadsheets), and to perform basic manipulation operations on them. Some selected examples from this SIB collection are given in the following:

- `CalculateColumnSum` calculates the sum of a table column.
- `CloseDocument` closes the active document.
- `InsertNewSheet` inserted a new sheet (tab) into the spreadsheet container.
- `InsertTable` inserts a table into a text document.
- `MoveCursor` moves the cursor within the current text document
- `NewDocument` creates a new document or opens an existing one.
- `PrintDocument` prints the active document.
- `ReplaceText` replaces all occurrences of a specific text phrase in the the document by another text.

- `SaveDocument` saves the current document to a file.
- `SetCellValue` sets the value/formula/text of a specific cell in a spreadsheet.
- `SetCursorProperties` sets properties of the cursor (like, e.g., font and color) in the text document.
- `SetCurrentSheet` activates a sheet in the spreadsheet container.
- `WriteText` writes a text to the active text document at the current cursor position.

SIBs from the openoffice-sibs library had initially been used to generate report files in the "GraffDok" project of Robin Holler [20], which are assembled from the textual and graphical data that is collected about the graffiti. They were however later replaced by LaTeX commands (executed by the `ExecuteCommand` SIB), simply because the use of LaTeX templates allowed for a better customization of the document layout.

4.4 rest-sibs Library (5): SIBs for General REST Web Service Access

Unlike some of the SIBs described above, which provide access to specific REST-style web services (like, e.g., the pfam-sibs or the gisgraphy-sibs), the rest-sibs are designed to act as generic REST service clients: they simply read the content from a given URL. This way, they can be used to access arbitrary REST services. As the concrete requirements of workflow and the service interfaces vary, we have finally implemented different versions of REST-accessing SIBs:

- `FetchDataURL2File` fetches the data behind the given URL as it is and writes it into a file.
- `FetchImageURL2BufferedImage` fetches the data behind the given URL, interprets it as image and puts it into the ExecutionContext.
- `FetchImageURL2File` fetches the data behind the given URL, interprets it as image and writes it into a file.
- `FetchTextualURL` fetches the data behind the given URL, interprets it as text and puts in into the ExecutionContext.
- `FetchTextualURL2File` fetches the data behind the given URL, interprets it as text and writes it into a file.

SIBs from the rest-sibs library were used in the following student projects:

- Visualization of Data Transfer Paths (Christian Kuntzsch) [22]
- Geocoder Accuracy Ranking (Daniel Teske) [38]
- CREADED: Coloured-Relief Application for Digital Elevation Data (Franziska Noack) [28]
- Location Analysis for Potential Areas for Wind Turbines (Tobias Respondeck) [31]
- Spotlocator - Guess where the Photo was taken! (Marcel Hibbe) [19]

4.5 twitter-sibs Library (1): SIBs for Accessing Twitter

The twitter-sibs library currently contains only one SIB for sending ("tweeting") a message via Twitter [13]:

- `TwitterText` tweets a text message.

The SIB needs to be pointed to an existing Twitter account, which also has to be set up for that functionality. The implementation has been done using the Twitter4J-Library [14], an unofficial but convenient Java library for the original Twitter API. The SIB was used in the "Spotlocator" project of Marcel Hibbe[19].

4.6 qrcode-sibs Library (3): SIBs for Reading and Writing QR Codes

Finally, we have provided the students with SIBs for reading and creating Quick Response (QR) codes:

- `CreateQRCode` creates a QR code from the provided data.
- `DecodeQRCodeFromBufferedImage` decodes a QR code that is available as buffered image.
- `DecodeQRCodeFromURL` decodes the QR code located at the given URL.

In the overview table, this SIB collection is classified both as REST-based and as API-based implementation. This is because creating the QR codes is done via the REST-based web service of the QR-Server API [12], while reading the codes is done via the Java library ZXing [15]. Note that the creation of QR codes allows many configuration options, such as the color of the data squares, the color of the background squares, the border width, and the size of the whole QR code. Although developed according to some specific project ideas, this SIB library has finally not been used in any of the projects.

5 Conclusion

More than 275 SIBs have finally been made available for the student projects. We created around half of them during the course, to a large extent specifically according to the upcoming requirements of the projects. A large part of them was also used in the next editions of the course in the following years, where the SIB libraries were again extended according to the concrete projects' requirements. Although the technical details of individual tools, services and APIs are sometimes challenging, this is generally a swift and easy business. As described in [26], a single component or service does typically offer a number of functionalities. In the *servification* process, the useful functionalities are identified (often ad-hoc for the current use) and transformed into a SIB collection. Further functionalities can be added later on, in a form of *incremental* formalization [36] of the domain. In fact, several of the SIB libraries do still not yet cover the full range of functionality provided by the underlying services, but it will be a straightforward process to extend them accordingly if there is need in the future.

References

1. Apache OpenOffice -The Free and Open Productivity Suite, http://www.openoffice.org/de/ (last accessed September 10, 2013)
2. API - OpenStreetMap Wiki, http://wiki.openstreetmap.org/wiki/API (last accessed September 9, 2013)
3. CSISS/GMU Geospatial Web Services, http://geobrain.laits.gmu.edu/grassweb/manuals/index.html (last accessed September 9, 2013)
4. Free opensource geocoder and webservices for geonames and openstreetmap data, http://www.gisgraphy.com/ (last accessed September 9, 2013)
5. GeoNames, http://www.geonames.org (last accessed September 9, 2013)
6. geoPlugin to geolocate your visitors, http://www.geoplugin.com/ (last accessed September 9, 2013)
7. Google Maps API - Google Developers, https://developers.google.com/maps/ (last accessed March 21, 2013)
8. GRASS GIS - The world's leading Free GIS software, http://grass.osgeo.org (last accessed September 9, 2013)
9. InstaMapper, http://www.instamapper.com (shut down on December 13, 2012)
10. jABC SIBs - Introduction, http://jabc.cs.tu-dortmund.de/sib/ (last accessed September 10, 2013)
11. Pfam: RESTful interface, http://pfam.sanger.ac.uk/help#tabview=tab10 (last accessed September 9, 2013)
12. QR-Code-API - Documentation, command "create-qr-code" - QR-Server, http://qrserver.com/en-us/api/documentation/create-qr-code/ (last accessed September 10, 2013)
13. Twitter, https://twitter.com (last accessed September 10, 2013)
14. Twitter4J - A Java Library for the Twitter API, http://twitter4j.org/ (last accessed September 10, 2013)
15. zxing - Multi-format 1D/2D barcode image processing library with clients for Android, Java, http://code.google.com/p/zxing/ (last accessed September 10, 2013)
16. Blaese, L.: Data Mining for Unidentified Protein Sequences. In: Lamprecht, A.-L., Margaria, T. (eds.) Process Design for Natural Scientists. CCIS, vol. 500, pp. 73–87. Springer, Heidelberg (2014)
17. Finn, R.D., Mistry, J., Tate, J., Coggill, P., Heger, A., Pollington, J.E., Gavin, O.L., Gunasekaran, P., Ceric, G., Forslund, K., Holm, L., Sonnhammer, E.L.L., Eddy, S.R., Bateman, A.: The Pfam protein families database. Nucleic Acids Research 38(suppl 1), D211–D222 (2010)
18. Goujon, M., McWilliam, H., Li, W., Valentin, F., Squizzato, S., Paern, J., Lopez, R.: A new bioinformatics analysis tools framework at EMBL-EBI. Nucleic Acids Research 38(Web Server issue), W695–W699 (2010)
19. Hibbe, M.: Spotlocator Project Documentation. In: Lamprecht, A.-L., Margaria, T. (eds.) Process Design for Natural Scientists. CCIS, vol. 500, pp. 149–158. Springer, Heidelberg (2014)
20. Holler, R.: GraffDok: A Graffiti Documentation Application. In: Lamprecht, A.-L., Margaria, T. (eds.) Process Design for Natural Scientists. CCIS, vol. 500, pp. 235–247. Springer, Heidelberg (2014)
21. Kind, J.: Creation of Topographic Maps. In: Lamprecht, A.-L., Margaria, T. (eds.) Process Design for Natural Scientists. CCIS, vol. 500, pp. 225–234. Springer, Heidelberg (2014)

22. Kuntzsch, C.: Visualization of Data Transfer Paths. In: Lamprecht, A.-L., Margaria, T. (eds.) Process Design for Natural Scientists. CCIS, vol. 500, pp. 140–148. Springer, Heidelberg (2014)
23. Labarga, A., Valentin, F., Anderson, M., Lopez, R.: Web services at the European bioinformatics institute. Nucleic Acids Research 35(Web Server issue), W6–W11 (2007)
24. Lamprecht, A.-L., Margaria, T., Steffen, B.: Modeling and Execution of Scientific Workflows in the jABC Framework. In: Lamprecht, A.-L., Margaria, T. (eds.) Process Design for Natural Scientists. CCIS, vol. 500, pp. 14–29. Springer, Heidelberg (2014)
25. Lis, M.: Constructing a Phylogenetic Tree. In: Lamprecht, A.-L., Margaria, T. (eds.) Process Design for Natural Scientists. CCIS, vol. 500, pp. 101–109. Springer, Heidelberg (2014)
26. Margaria, T., Boßelmann, S., Doedt, M., Floyd, B.D., Steffen, B.: Customer-Oriented Business Process Management: Visions and Obstacles. In: Hinchey, M., Coyle, L. (eds.) Conquering Complexity, pp. 407–429. Springer, London (2012)
27. Margaria, T., Nagel, R., Steffen, B.: jETI: A tool for remote tool integration. In: Halbwachs, N., Zuck, L.D. (eds.) TACAS 2005. LNCS, vol. 3440, pp. 557–562. Springer, Heidelberg (2005)
28. Noack, F.: CREADED: Coloured-Relief Application for Digital Elevation Data. In: Lamprecht, A.-L., Margaria, T. (eds.) Process Design for Natural Scientists. CCIS, vol. 500, pp. 182–195. Springer, Heidelberg (2014)
29. Pillai, S., Silventoinen, V., Kallio, K., Senger, M., Sobhany, S., Tate, J., Velankar, S., Golovin, A., Henrick, K., Rice, P., Stoehr, P., Lopez, R.: SOAP-based services provided by the European Bioinformatics Institute. Nucleic Acids Research 33(Web Server issue), W25–W28 (2005)
30. Reso, J.: Protein Classification Workflow. In: Lamprecht, A.-L., Margaria, T. (eds.) Process Design for Natural Scientists. CCIS, vol. 500, pp. 65–72. Springer, Heidelberg (2014)
31. Respondeck, T.: A Workflow for Computing Potential Areas for Wind Turbines. In: Lamprecht, A.-L., Margaria, T. (eds.) Process Design for Natural Scientists. CCIS, vol. 500, pp. 196–211. Springer, Heidelberg (2014)
32. Rice, P., Longden, I., Bleasby, A.: EMBOSS: the European Molecular Biology Open Software Suite. Trends in Genetics 16(6), 276–277 (2000)
33. Scheele, L.: Location Analysis for Placing Artificial Reefs. In: Lamprecht, A.-L., Margaria, T. (eds.) Process Design for Natural Scientists. CCIS, vol. 500, pp. 222–234. Springer, Heidelberg (2014)
34. Schulze, G.: Workflow for Rapid Metagenome Analysis. In: Lamprecht, A.-L., Margaria, T. (eds.) Process Design for Natural Scientists. CCIS, vol. 500, pp. 88–100. Springer, Heidelberg (2014)
35. Sens, H.: Web-Based Map Generalization Tools Put to the Test: A jABC Workflow. In: Lamprecht, A.-L., Margaria, T. (eds.) Process Design for Natural Scientists. CCIS, vol. 500, pp. 171–181. Springer, Heidelberg (2014)
36. Steffen, B., Margaria, T., Claßen, A., Braun, V.: Incremental Formalization: A Key to Industrial Success. Software - Concepts and Tools 17(2), 78–95 (1996)
37. Steffen, B., Margaria, T., Nagel, R., Jörges, S., Kubczak, C.: Model-driven development with the jABC. In: Bin, E., Ziv, A., Ur, S. (eds.) HVC 2006. LNCS, vol. 4383, pp. 92–108. Springer, Heidelberg (2007)
38. Teske, D.: Geocoder Accuracy Ranking. In: Lamprecht, A.-L., Margaria, T. (eds.) Process Design for Natural Scientists. CCIS, vol. 500, pp. 159–170. Springer, Heidelberg (2014)

39. Wessel, P.: The GMT Home Page, http://gmt.soest.hawaii.edu (last accessed January 3, 2013)
40. Wessel, P., Smith, W.H.F.: Free software helps map and display data. EOS Trans. Amer. Geophys. U. 72(41) (1991)
41. Zmasek, C.M.: forester | software libraries for evolutionary biology and comparative genomics research (November 2012), http://www.phylosoft.org/forester/ (last accessed December 6, 2012)
42. Zmasek, C.M., Eddy, S.R.: ATV: display and manipulation of annotated phylogenetic trees. Bioinformatics (Oxford, England) 17(4), 383–384 (2001)

Lessons Learned

Anna-Lena Lamprecht, Alexander Wickert, and Tiziana Margaria

Chair for Service and Software Engineering, Potsdam University,
Potsdam, D-14482, Germany
{lamprecht,awickert,margaria}@cs.uni-potsdam.de

Abstract. This chapter summarizes the experience and the lessons we learned concerning the application of the jABC as a framework for design and execution of scientific workflows. It reports experiences from the domain modeling (especially service integration) and workflow design phases and evaluates the resulting models statistically with respect to the SIB library and hierarchy levels.

Keywords: domain modeling, service integration, workflow design, service usage statistics.

1 Introduction

The gallery of scientific workflow applications in this book is so far the largest project where non-IT users (in this case Master students with biology and geography backgrounds) autonomously designed complete running workflows for their particular purposes with the jABC. The workflows in previous studies, also predominantly in the bioinformatics and geoinformatics domains (such as [36,19,29,27,12,8]), were in contrast discussed and modeled together with project partners from the field of application. These partners provided valuable input and knowledge, but hardly took part in the actual implementation. For instance, GeneFisher-P [29] and Flux-P [12] have been developed in close collaboration with their later users and strongly according to their needs, resulting in a set of readily configured workflows for the identified processes. The users sometimes built variants of existing workflows, but usually did not design entirely new workflows on their own, as it is the case for the projects presented here.

In general, we can distinguish three roles when working with scientific workflows:

1. The **domain modeler** prepares the initially domain-independent workflow framework for use in a particular application domain. Mostly this concerns the definition of the domain-specific workflow building blocks, deciding which service libraries should be integrated, which SIBs should be available, and how they should be integrated and organized within the jABC's SIB palettes.
2. The **service integrator** actually provides the defined SIBs by integrating the corresponding services into the framework. The service integrator can be the same person as the domain modeler, but also someone else. Service integration is a quite technical task, often requiring a good amount of programming skills, so that we recommend this role to be filled by a person with correspondingly solid IT expertise.

A.-L. Lamprecht et al. (Eds.): Process Design for Natural Scientists, CCIS 500, pp. 45–64, 2014.
DOI: 10.1007/978-3-662-45006-2_4

3. The **workflow designer** then works with the prepared domain-specific workflow framework and designs the workflows for his needs. This is mainly done by selecting, configuring and connecting adequate workflow building blocks so that they perform the intended computations. This kind of workflow design requires extensive knowledge about the application domain, but no classical programming skills, so that this role is filled by the application experts, in our case the students.

In fact, we observed this clear separation between domain modeling, service integration and workflow design in the scope of the course:

1. In the beginning, the **domain modeling** was performed as a joint effort by lecturers and students of the course. While the lecturers provided ("pushed") a number of SIBs from previous projects and services they considered useful also for the new projects, the students analyzed the functional requirements of their projects and asked ("pulled") for new SIB libraries.
2. The lecturers and tutors of the course took then care of **integrating** the identified services and functionality, and provided the missing SIBs. The few students who actually had the required technical expertise integrated the services they needed themselves.
3. The SIB libraries could then simply be used by **workflow designers**, i.e. the students. They realized their workflows without having to deal with the technical details of the underlying services implementations.

Following the above distinction of roles and phases, in Sections 2, 3 and 4 this chapter reports on lessons learned and experiences gained during the domain modeling, service integration and workflow design in the scope of this course, respectively. Focusing on the actual results of the project work, Section 5 evaluates the created workflow applications of this book in terms of some usage metrics (used SIBs, reused services) and workflow structures. Finally, Section 6 concludes this chapter and also the introductory part of this book.

2 Domain Modeling

In the context of the applications described in this book, domain modeling comprises the choice and integration of domain-specific services into the jABC framework in order to prepare it for being used for workflow design. We start with a closer look at two challenges the domain modeler typically faces: finding services providing the required functionality, and finding services suitable for being accessed from a workflow environment.

2.1 Shopping for Service Functionality

Finding tools and services that provide the "right" functionality required for realizing the intended workflows is a sometimes quite time-consuming research task, which is typically performed by web search and literature study. Sometimes one comes across curated service directories for particular scientific areas (like, e.g., the BioCatalogue [10] for life science web services), but they cover only a small part of the actually available functionality, so that other sources of information need to be considered to find adequate services. Accordingly, web search and literature study to find services with functionality adequate for the envisaged applications was a major research task in the beginning of the students' project work.

2.2 Service Access

In addition to finding services with adequate functionality, finding services that are also technically suitable for workflow integration means in the first place to find services that allow for some kind of programmatic access to their functionality. This can be a web service interface, an application programming interface (API), or command line options that execute a tool in "headless" operation mode (i.e. without requiring user interaction via a graphical or other user interface). Many available tools and programs, however, do not fulfill this crucial requirement. Desktop programs and web applications are unfortunately often implemented to require interaction with a human user for their execution. Usually this means that there is no (easy) way to strip the GUI and use them as embedded services in a workflow.

For example, Henriette Sens, author of "Web-Based Map Generalization Tools Put to the Test" [55], was searching for a map generalization tool to include as a service in her workflow, but could not find a single one that could be operated in headless mode as described above. The Flash-based "Mapshaper" web application[1] that she finally used can be started in a browser from the command line (and thus with the `ExecuteCommand` SIB), but is from then on interactive, so that the user can only produce and store a result manually, and then resume the automatic workflow at the respective point.

In general, also licensing issues and availability constraints can be relevant here. That is, services might only be available after signing particular agreements, if using the resources for particular purposes, after paying some access fee, or if being member of a particular organization. While we have experienced obstacles in this regard in other courses, they were fortunately not present for the services used in the projects described in this book.

3 Service Integration

The service integration is done by someone with adequate technical and programming skills. It concerns implementing the access to services, their encapsulation into SIBs and their basic testing, while the development of more complex applications is subsequently done by the application experts that design the actual

[1] `http://www.mapshaper.org`

workflows. Major issues here are usually the technicalities of the service interface, the lack of proper service documentation, and changing service interfaces, as explained and illustrated in Sections 3.1, 3.2 and 3.3, respectively.

3.1 Service Interfaces

Unfortunately, even services which principally allow for programmatic access as described in Section 2.2 cannot always easily be integrated (cf., e.g. [21,20,34]). Different technical obstacles may be identified by the SIB programmer when working on the integration. Then it has to be decided whether the problems can be solved and if solving them is worth the effort, or if an alternative service is available. For example, when we created the twitter-sibs (for sending Twitter [5] messages), we first tried to use the Twitter REST-API [6] directly. After spending much time unsuccessfully trying to handle its authentication protocol, we dropped this plan and decided to use instead the simpler Twitter4J [7] library, although this meant to have no image upload functionality available in our SIBs.

More common is, however, that the programmer simply faces difficult-to-use service interfaces. For instance, the EBI web services [48,23] define several own, complex data types that have to be used by the client application, and furthermore operate most services in asynchronous mode, which requires active polling of the service results. The CSISS services [1] use URLs instead of standard file names for defining input and output data. This makes data transfer difficult, as all involved data has to be accessible by the URLs. All these examples do not prevent the service from being accessed by a SIB, but hamper the actually straightforward integration process.

3.2 Incomplete or Missing Documentation

When working with services of all kinds, one soon realizes that exact descriptions of parameters are very important. If one has incomplete lists of possible values of parameters and comprehensible explanations, it is usually difficult for an external user to integrate an unknown service (cf. also [34]). In the first place, the lack of proper documentation makes life difficult for the programmer who creates the SIBs. However, it is often a problem also for the workflow designer, who usually reads pieces of documentation that are propagated from the underlying levels. Typically, the programmer does not write new domain-specific documentation.

Among the SIB collections created for the students' projects, the CSISS and EBI web services (used in [55,47,50] and [49,11,53,33], respectively) are two examples of service collections with documentation in need of improvement. In fact, we often executed these services with different test data sets (which in the case of CSISS were provided by the providers on request) in order to learn from experience how they actually work, since this was not completely evident from the available documentation alone.

3.3 Changing Interfaces

As discussed elaborately in [25], scientific application domains are characterized by the long-term availability of their basic computational components. At the same time their concrete service interfaces are subject to frequent changes. While it is clear that this is a typical and unavoidable phenomenon when working with public third-party services, it is still a recurring source of interruption during workflow execution and requires code repairs.

For instance, currently many major service providers in bioinformatics are abandoning their SOAP-based web service interfaces and follow the general trend towards using REST-style interfaces. Consequently, SIBs that have been implemented for accessing, e.g., the DDBJ and EBI web services [2,48,23] have to be changed accordingly at some point, to follow the technology shift on the provider's side. Similarly, we experienced different changes of the Google Maps API for location-based mapping [3], so that the corresponding SIBs have been already updated several times. Luckily, as also discussed in detail in [25], the SIB interfaces typically do not change during these updates, so that on the workflow level this change of underlying technology is usually not perceptible at all.

More severe is the case where services simply stop operating. An example here are the EBI's SoapLab [4] services. They used to provide web service access to the tools of the EMBOSS [51] suite, but were terminated in February 2013. For several of the EMBOSS tools, alternative services are provided in the "standard" EBI web service collection [48,23], but do not cover the entire functionality previously available. Another example from the bioinformatics domain is the DDBJ Web API [2], which used to provide access to a number of molecular biology databases and standard query and analysis tools. Its operation has been "temporarily suspended" in February 2012, and not been resumed since then. Consequently, contrary to what was anticipated when we prepared the course, the DDBJ services could not be used in the students' projects and alternatives had to be identified.

4 Workflow Design: The jABC Framework

The experiences with the students from our course and also with project partners using the jABC framework, suggest that it provides an adequate level of abstraction from classical programming: after only a short introduction, non-IT users are quickly able to use it to design and manage scientific workflows according to their needs. In fact, the workflows presented in this book were built by the students mostly autonomously with only little support by the lecturers. As for other examples, the GeneFisher-P [29] and FiatFlux-P [12] workflows have been frequently adapted by their users (biology diploma and bio-engineering PhD students without specific computer science education) according to changing experimental setups.

The feedback on the jABC framework provided by some students gave us more detailed insights about the user's perception of working with the platform. First and foremost, it confirmed our expectation and impression that handling the jABC as a tool is or quickly becomes intuitive. Exemplarily, Christine Schütt, author of "Identification of differentially expressed genes" [54], reports: *"At the beginning it took some time to become familiar with its operating principle. This was of course not such a big surprise for it takes always a bit of work to learn the principles of a program or programming language. [...] Apart from this point no real difficulties occurred during the implementation. [...]"*

In fact, our experience with new jABC users shows that the graphical workflow modeling as such hardly requires any explanation. Dragging and dropping SIBs from the SIB browser to the canvas, and connecting them with labeled branches according to the flow of control, as well as the configuration of simple parameters and the adaptation of existing workflows can usually be learned in less than 30 minutes. We have seen this many times in 45-minute workshops for high school students that we gave at open days at our universities, where the students were shown how to use jABC models to develop strategies for the well-known Connect-Four game [9]. Similarly, enriching the models with custom SIB icons and draw elements and making use of plugins like the LocalChecker and the Tracer can be typically be learned within another hour of instruction.

Some particular concepts and plugins have to be explained and practiced more elaborately before they become useful. This concerns the ExecutionContext with its different scopes and the ContextKeys and ContextExpressions that are required for controlling the flow of data. For instance, Judith Reso, author of "Protein classification workflow" [49], reports in this regard that: *"[...] In the beginning it was difficult to find out how to access local variables and use them as input for another tool. [...]"*. As another example, to make proper use of the model checking plugin, the users need to have at least a basic idea about propositions and logics before they can formulate constraints and use these capabilities of the framework.

The feedback by the students also shows that intuition is subjective: some features that appear intuitive to one user can be quite confusing for another. For instance, with regard to debugging with the Tracer plugin, users' opinions differed considerably. Christine Schütt, for instance, thinks that *"A real good feature of jABC is the animated execution of the workflow model with theTracer plugin. With this it is possible to follow each single step in a debugging style, to see what single SIBs do and to find potential sources of errors even faster."*

Similarly, Monika Lis, author of "Workflow for phylogenetic tree construction" [33], notes on the Tracer: *"A very good option is the Tracer and its execution controller, which enables you to go through your workflow stepwise and look if every single step of your workflow works well and which results it provides."*, but then adds: *"However, the more SIBs have been executed, the more confusing the status overviews including the error messages. That is, in my opinion, the major disadvantage of jABC: The error messages which are, especially for beginners, not easy to interpret. [...]"*.

Problems like this are common, however not caused the by actual jABC framework, but rather by SIBs that are poorly documented or erroneous, or simply due to not knowing which SIBs are available. For instance, Monika Lis describes problems similar to those sketched in Section 3.2 (Incomplete or missing documentation) that she experienced when trying to use new SIBs in her workflow: *"In my case there have been some difficulties while constructing the workflow. First, it was not always possible to use all parameters, because some of them seemed to be faulty and led to breaking up the workflow. Sometimes it was necessary to mess around the parameters if one wanted to see which of them causes in errors, because this was not always clear."*

Janine Vierheller, author of "Exploratory data analysis" [60] describes problems with finding adequate SIBs for a workflow: *"The implementation of the workflow with jABC was not always intuitive, because you start with the functions you already know, which are some Common SIBs. If you search for a specific SIB of which you think it might exist, you have to have a clear idea how this could be named."*

The last two comments point to a common problem that users of workflow management systems face: while the graphical workflow modeling facilities make it *syntactically* easy for the user to design the application, they do not help the user *semantically*. That is, the user is still responsible for identifying services with adequate functionality, and for understanding the technical details of the inputs and outputs so that he/she can connect them correctly. Semantics-based approaches to service discovery that make use of domain-specific ontologies for the description of services and data types, can help in this regard by reducing the gap between the domain language of the user and the technical language of the service infrastructure.

In fact the jABC provides technologies for using such methods, for instance with the plugin for semantically supported service selection described by [61] and with the PROPHETS plugin for semantically supported (semi-) automatic service composition [30,39]. Since their application crucially depends on adequate domain models (consisting of domain-specific ontologies, service and type descriptions in terms of these ontologies, and possibly also different kinds of constraints), which were not available and which could not be built in the time we had, we did not use them in the course. We plan, however, to include this topic in future editions of this course.

Finally, some comments pointed to usage details that sometimes cause confusion in the beginning and can be quite annoying, but are not related to the modeling approach of the jABC and are actually caused by details of the current implementation. For example, Monika Lis reports: *"In general, jABC is a good tool for connecting different services, but the use of jABC takes some getting used to. For example it is strange to need to press enter, if you want to change parameters. You need to forget it a hundred times, until you remember to press it. [...]"*

The overall impression of the jABC as a modeling tool was very positive. The students were able to get productive within hours and did not need to acquire classical programming skills, yet were successful in creating running workflows of medium complexity largely on their own. The encountered difficulties had mostly to do with the more programming-like characteristics, e.g. the management of variables, the use of the context and context expressions, and the issue of poor documentation of the inside error messages delivered by services and routines they used as SIBs. The idea of a typed variable as a placeholder for a value, that can be put there and subsequently looked up is hard to eliminate or simplify further. However, the other two issues can be tackled, although at different levels. The new jABC4 [41] already used in a workflow project in the field of Cachexia research [35] and the jABC5 [40,42] that is in preparation include an integrated and much simplified handling of data, not requiring an explicit management of the context anymore. The poor documentation and error treatment will gradually improve with the more widespread reuse of such components and routines as services, under the pressure of the crowd of workflow developers.

5 Workflow Metrics

In this book, we present 15 scientific workflow projects. 6 in the area of bioinformatics and 9 in the area of geovisualization. To evaluate the scientific jABC workflow models of these students' projects, we created *jABCstats*, a library of jABC workflows that computes metrics of jABC workflows. It is completely modeled with the Common SIBs that come with every jABC distribution. For a detailed explanation of jABCstats the reader is referred to [62]. In the following, Section 5.1 explains briefly the analyses carried out by jABCstats, before Section 5.2 discusses the actual findings for the projects presented in this book.

5.1 jABCstats: Empirical Analysis of jABC Workflows

jABCstats currently provides functionality for the analysis of jABC workflow models with regard to workflow and project sizes, hierarchy levels, control-flow workflow patterns and service usage. For the workflow and project sizes jABCstats simply counts the total number of SIBs in the workflows and the number of workflow files in the projects, respectively. To determine the number of hierarchy levels it uses a simple recursive counting mechanism. For the analysis of the modeling patterns used in the workflows, jABCstats evaluates the control-flow model structure of the workflows and counts the sequence, conditional branching, simple merge, fork, join and loop structures (as described in [59]).

For assessing the service usage, jABCstats analyzes the models with regard to the occurrences of individual SIBs and for each hierarchical level of its complete namespace, extracting this information from the XML file that stores the jABC model. For example, let the namespace be `de.jabc.ExampleSIB`. For this specific SIB the counters for `de.jabc.ExampleSIB`, `de.jabc.*`, `de.*`, and `#allSIBs` are increased by one. This happens for every SIB in the model. The result can be displayed on the screen and/or saved as a CSV file. As shown exemplarily in Figure 1, the resulting CSV file consists of two rows. The first row is labeled with the complete SIB names and all partial namespaces of them. The second row records its occurrences.

The service usage analysis can be applied to single models or to whole directories containing several files. In addition to that, it is also possible to sum

Table 1. Exemplary SIB usage numbers

#allSIBs	de.*	de.jabc.*	de.jabc.ExampleSIB	de.jabc.OtherSIB	...
10	10	6	1	2	...

the SIB counters from different CSV files into one single CSV file and to merge the metrics of different models into one single CSV file, achieving a project-level statistics aggregation.

5.2 Results

Here we describe and discuss the most interesting outcomes that we obtained by applying jABCstats to the 15 workflow projects of this book.

Workflow and Project Sizes: Designed and developed in the scope of a one-semester course, most of the projects are in fact quite small. Most of them (12) comprise only one model, one comprises two, and two projects comprise eight models. The models themselves also vary considerably in their size, being composed from 6 to 156 SIBs, with an average of 26.8 and a median of 18.5 (standard deviation 29.4).

Workflow Hierarchy: As indicated above, 12 of 15 projects only used one main model and are hence only working with one level of hierarchy. The three projects that used more models [11,47,52] have one main model with several submodels (but no further hierarchical cascade), which means that they make use of two levels of hierarchy.

Workflow Patterns: We let jABCstats count the most relevant control-flow workflow patterns in all workflow models of our sample. As Figure 1 shows, the sequence pattern (simple sequential execution of two services) is by far the most-used control structure, with 571 occurrences in the analyzed workflows. Exclusive choices (conditional branchings), simple merges (convergence of branches) and loops (repetitive behavior) also occur quite often, while parallel executions (fork/join) do in fact only play a minor role. Although these are only results for a very small sample of workflows, this substantiates our observation that conditional branchings and loops are required and used quite frequently. Hence it is important that workflow modeling systems provide the possibility to include them in their models.

SIB Usage: Using jABCstats, we created individual SIB usage statistics for all students' projects and merged them into one single CSV file. Then we used a spreadsheet software and GNU R to compute aggregated values and some charts for analyzed workflows. Tables 2, 3 and 4 summarize the created SIB usage

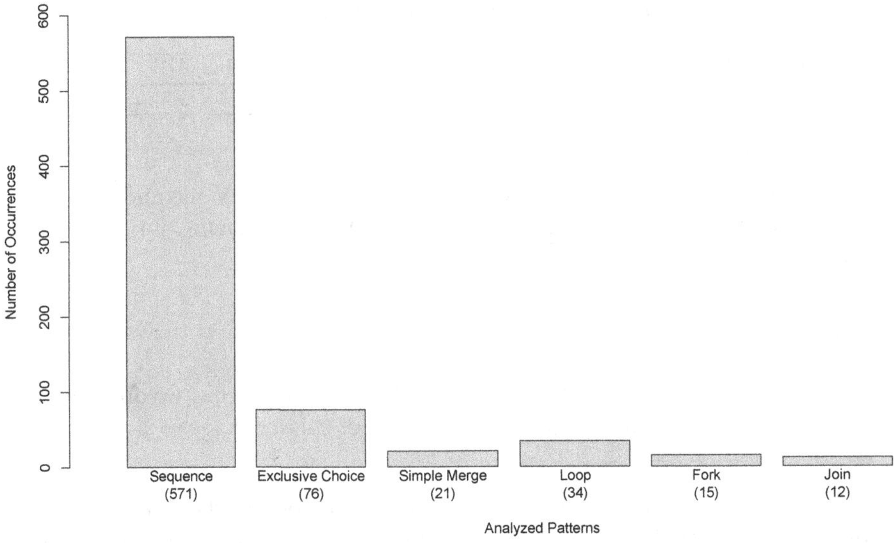

Fig. 1. Usage of workflow patterns

statistics with regard to all available SIBs, the SIBs provided by the jABC and the jABC's Common SIBs in particular, respectively. The upper parts of the tables contain the individual numbers for each project, while the lower parts report aggregated values for all analyzed workflows, namely:

1. the sum (total number) of SIBs from the package used in the projects,
2. the number of projects that used SIBs from the package,
3. the percentage of projects that used SIBs from the package,
4. the minimum number of SIBs from the package used in a project,
5. the average number of SIBs from the package used in the projects, and
6. the maximum number of SIBs from the package used in a project.

We were in particular interested in the distribution of the SIB usage, that is, how many of the individual SIBs were used in the workflows, and how much of the workflows use the individual SIBs. In Tables 2, 3 and 4 we give the numbers for selected hierarchy levels of the namespaces in order to be able to compare the usage of the most relevant groups of SIBs. Below each table, a pie chart additionally visualizes the distribution of the SIB packages used in the workflows, that is, the values contained in aggregation line 1.

Starting with the general overview of the SIB usage (see Table 2), we see, most interestingly, that more than 75% of the SIBs used by the students are included in every jABC distribution. Only about 23% of all SIBs used were created on demand by the lecturers and tutors of the course. This comprises, for instance, the REST SIBs, the FTP SIBs and the different bioinformatics and geovisualization SIBs described in [32]. They have been used by 12 projects (80%). 6 SIBs were created by the geovisualization student Daniel Teske [58]. He created some

Table 2. SIB usage overview

category		all SIBs	jABC SIBs	SIBs created for the students	SIBs created by the students
workflow analysis results per project	Christian Kuntzsch [22]	21	18	3	0
	Christine Schuett [54]	13	13	0	0
	Daniel Teske [58]	18	11	1	6
	Franziska Noack [47]	119	96	23	0
	Gunnar Schulze [53]	40	38	2	0
	Henriette Sens [55]	9	8	1	0
	Janine Vierheller [60]	28	28	0	0
	Josephine Kind [18]	67	48	19	0
	Judith Reso [49]	13	6	7	0
	Lasse Scheele [52]	142	76	66	0
	Leif Blaese [11]	38	38	0	0
	Marcel Hibbe [15]	79	77	2	0
	Monika Lis [33]	14	10	4	0
	Robin Holler [16]	46	45	1	0
	Tobias Respondek [50]	156	104	52	0
aggregation	1. total # of SIBs from package:	803	616	181	6
	2. # of projects using package:	15	15	12	1
	3. % of projects using package:	100	100	80	6.7
	4. min # SIBs from package:	9	6	0	0
	5. average # SIBs from package:	54	41	12	0.4
	6. max # SIBs from package:	156	104	66	6

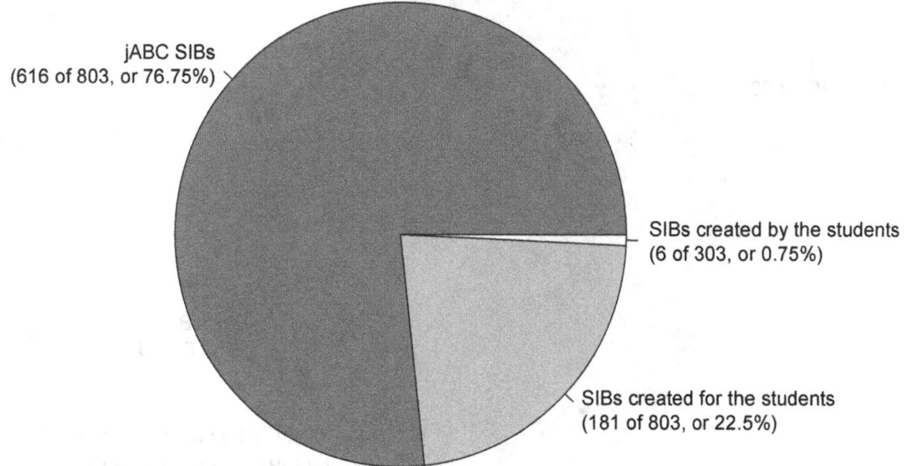

Table 3. Usage statistics of the SIBs provided by the jABC

category		jABC SIBs	Common SIBs	jETI SIBs	Control SIBs	Macro SIBs
workflow analysis results per project	Christian Kuntzsch [22]	18	18	0	0	0
	Christine Schuett [54]	13	10	0	3	0
	Daniel Teske [58]	11	7	0	4	0
	Franziska Noack [47]	96	89	0	0	7
	Gunnar Schulze [53]	38	35	0	3	0
	Henriette Sens [55]	8	8	0	0	0
	Janine Vierheller [60]	28	28	0	0	0
	Josephine Kind [18]	48	16	32	0	0
	Judith Reso [49]	6	6	0	0	0
	Lasse Scheele [52]	76	22	47	0	7
	Leif Blaese [11]	38	33	0	4	1
	Marcel Hibbe [15]	77	77	0	0	0
	Monika Lis [33]	10	10	0	0	0
	Robin Holler [16]	45	43	0	2	0
	Tobias Respondek [50]	104	93	0	11	0
aggregation	1. total # of SIBs from package:	616	495	79	27	15
	2. # of projects using package:	15	15	2	6	3
	3. % of projects using package:	100	100	13	40	20
	4. min # SIBs from package:	6	6	0	0	0
	5. average # SIBs from package:	41	33	5	1.8	1
	6. max # SIBs from package:	104	93	47	11	7

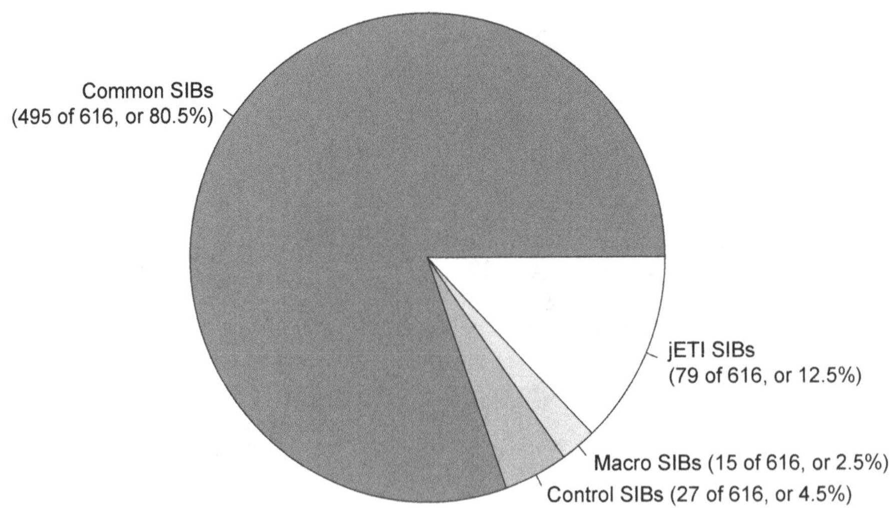

Table 4. Usage statistics of the Common SIBs

package		de.jabc. sib. common.*	de.jabc. sib. common. basic.*	de.jabc. sib. common. collection.*	de.jabc. sib. common. gui.*	de.jabc. sib. common. io.*
workflow analysis results per project	Christian Kuntzsch [22]	18	11	1	3	3
	Christine Schuett [54]	10	0	0	5	5
	Daniel Teske [58]	7	1	0	6	0
	Franziska Noack [47]	89	23	0	60	6
	Gunnar Schulze [53]	35	1	1	14	19
	Henriette Sens [55]	8	0	0	4	4
	Janine Vierheller [60]	28	0	0	19	9
	Josephine Kind [18]	16	16	0	0	0
	Judith Reso [49]	6	0	0	6	0
	Lasse Scheele [52]	22	7	0	15	0
	Leif Blaese [11]	33	13	0	6	14
	Marcel Hibbe [15]	77	49	2	15	11
	Monika Lis [33]	10	5	0	3	2
	Robin Holler [16]	43	13	0	15	15
	Tobias Respondek [50]	93	69	4	0	20
aggregation	1. total # of SIBs from package:	495	208	8	171	108
	2. # of projects using package:	15	11	4	13	11
	3. % of projects using package:	100	73	27	87	73
	4. min # SIBs from package:	6	0	0	0	0
	5. average # SIBs from package:	33	14	0.5	11	7
	6. max # SIBs from package:	93	69	4	60	20

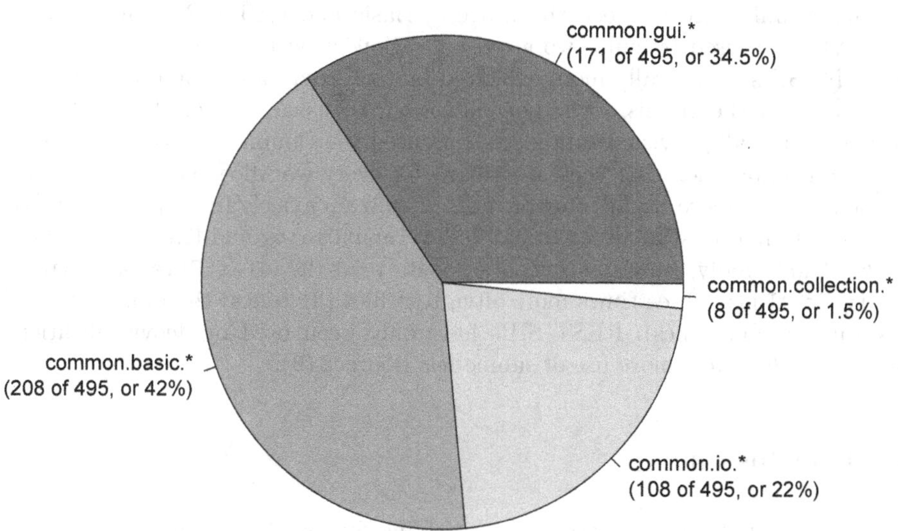

SIBs on his own because he already had background knowledge in Java programming, thus it was easy for him to implement his own SIBs. Not visible from the statistics shown in the tables, the `common.io.ExecuteCommand` SIB is also used quite often to integrate external functionality in the workflows. In fact, 8 projects (53%) made use of this SIB for executing some functionality, such as own scripts, on the local machine.

Going top-down in the namespace hierarchy and having a closer look at the distribution of the jABC SIBs used (see Table 3), we see that the Common SIBs are by far the most-used SIBs from those provided by the jABC (with a share of around 80%). In fact, each project makes use of the Common SIBs. As described in [32], they are necessary for defining values on the context (Basic SIBs), working with collections (Collection SIBs), retrieving some input from the user of the application and showing results (GUI SIBs), and for reading and writing files on the file system (IO SIBs). 13 students (87%) used GUI SIBs and 11 students (73%) used basic and IO SIBs. The outcome of 11 project workflows (73%) depended on some user input (`common.gui.ShowInputDialog`), and 8 projects (53%) used SIBs to read from and write to text files.

Table 4 details further on the usage of the Common SIBs. It shows that most of the Common SIBs used in the projects are from the `common.basic.*` (42%) and `common.gui.*` (34.5%) packages. The IO SIBs make up for 22%, while the Collection SIBs do only account for 1.5% of the Common SIBs that were used in the projects.

Small Comparison of the Bioinformatics and Geovisualization Projects: The total amount of SIBs used by geovisualization students is considerably higher than by the students with bioinformatics-related workflows. Especially the usage difference between the usage of Basic and GUI SIBs is noticeable. jETI SIBs are used by only two geovisualization projects. The diversity of the available SIBs is generally more exploited by the geovisualization projects.

Looking at the details of the percentage of SIB usage, we see that all bioinformatics and all geovisualization students used the Common SIBs, which reinforces our impression that they are a basis for every workflow. Geovisualization students made more use of `common.gui.ShowBranching[/Image]Dialog` SIBs and bioinformatics students used more `ShowInputDialog` and `ExecuteCommand` SIBs. Additionally, geovisualization students read (`ReadTextFile`) and wrote (`WriteTextFile`) three times more often text files (31 times) than bioinformatics students (11 times). REST SIBs have only been used by geovisualization students, who made more use of submodels (`MacroSIB`).

6 Conclusion

The results of this course were very satisfying for us. We had previously used the jABC in many courses in Computer Science (Software Engineering, Formal Methods in System Design, Service-Oriented Architectures, Foundations of

Service Engineering, and many more), but not so systematically with non-IT students. The student feedback provided in this course and meanwhile also in similar courses gives a good impression of the wide usability of the jABC framework. The experiences with student users showed that the framework is syntactically easy to handle, but the central remaining challenge concerns how to make the services more easily accessible. A systematic usability study is subject of future work. Features that would improve the handling and are already available in jABC, or jABC4, but were not used in the students' workflows concern design for simplicity, processes as data, and variability and evolution.

Design for Simplicity

Design for Simplicity aims at fighting the often unexpectedly high longer-term costs for maintenance, adaptation, migration, etc.. Guided by the questions, 'what is really required', 'what is provided in terms of standards solutions', and 'which parts really need to be newly developed' (cf. [37,38]), a number of projects have been realized which comprise, for instance, a plug-in framework enhancing the functionality of the jABC framework [41], a synthesis-based approach solution to service-oriented programming [30], and a learning-based testing approach [57].

Processes as Data

A graphical and dynamic framework for binding and execution of (business) process models has been developed that is tailored to integrate

- ad hoc processes modelled graphically,
- third party services discovered in the (Inter)net, and
- (dynamically) synthesized process chains that solve situation-specific tasks, with the synthesis taking place not only at design time, but also at runtime.

Key to this approach [44,45,46,43] is the introduction of type-safe stacked second-order execution contexts that allow for higher-order process modeling. Tamed by our underlying strict service-oriented notion of abstraction, this approach is tailored also to be used by application experts with little technical knowledge: users can select, modify, construct and then pass (component) processes during process execution as if they were data. The most advanced feature of this framework is the combination of online synthesis with the integration of the synthesized process into the running application [46]. This ability leads to a particularly flexible way of implementing self-adaption, and to a particularly concise and powerful way of achieving variability not only at design time, but also at runtime.

Variability and Evolution

Constraint-based variability modeling is a flexible, declarative approach to managing solution-space variability [17,31]. Product variants are defined in a top-down manner by successively restricting the admissible combinations of product artifacts until a specific product variant is determined. Methods range from applying model checking to manually designed variants to applying synthesis technology [56,13,14] for the fully automatic generation of product variants that satisfy all given constraints [26]. This technology underlies the the loose programming approach, where incomplete specifications are turned into running programs via synthesis [30]. Moreover, it can be even combined with the above mentioned concept of higher-orderedness to realize a very flexible form of runtime adaptability [46].

We see therefore the current basis as an excellent foundation for further studies, for instance more empirical analyses with jABCstats, as shown in [62], but also with regard to the automated synthesis of such workflows based on knowledge nuggets as made possible by the PROPHETS plugin [39]. While the domain models get more precise, and more work is needed to properly describe semantics, constraints, relations concerning services, their data and their embedded functionalities and quality of service, the subsequent workflow design requires less knowledge and less work due to (semi-) automatic composition and conformity to constraints by construction [28,26,25,24]. In this sense, in the further practical investigation we intend to include more semantics, and raise the availability and use of the domain knowledge during the workflow composition.

References

1. CSISS/GMU Geospatial Web Services, `http://geobrain.laits.gmu.edu/grassweb/manuals/index.html` (last accessed September 9, 2013)
2. DDBJ Web API for Biology, `http://xml.nig.ac.jp/workflow/` (temporarily suspended since February 15, 2012)
3. Google Maps, A.P.I.: - Google Developers, `https://developers.google.com/maps/` (last accessed March 21, 2013)
4. Soaplab, `http://soaplab.sourceforge.net/soaplab1/` (last accessed May 5, 2013)
5. Twitter, `https://twitter.com` (last accessed September 10, 2013)
6. Twitter Developers, `https://dev.twitter.com` (last accessed September 11, 2013)
7. Twitter4J - A Java Library for the Twitter API. `http://twitter4j.org/` (last accessed September 10, 2013)
8. Al-areqi, S., Kriewald, S., Lamprecht, A.-L., Reusser, D., Wrobel, M., Margaria, T.: Agile Workflows for Climate Impact Risk Assessment based on the ci:grasp Platform and the jABC Modeling Framework. In: International Environmental Modelling and Software Society (iEMSs) 7th Intl. Congress on Env. Modelling and Software (accepted, 2014)
9. Bakera, M., Jörges, S., Margaria, T.: Test your Strategy: Graphical Construction of Strategies for Connect-Four. In: Proceedings of the 2009 14th IEEE International Conference on Engineering of Complex Computer Systems, ICECCS 2009, pp. 172–181. IEEE Computer Society, Washington, DC (2009)
10. Bhagat, J., Tanoh, F., Nzuobontane, E., Laurent, T., Orlowski, J., Roos, M., Wolstencroft, K., Aleksejevs, S., Stevens, R., Pettifer, S., Lopez, R., Goble, C.A.: BioCatalogue: a universal catalogue of web services for the life sciences. Nucleic Acids Research 38(suppl. 2), 689–694 (2010)

11. Blaese, L.: Data Mining for Unidentified Protein Sequences. In: Lamprecht, A.-L., Margaria, T. (eds.) Process Design for Natural Scientists. CCIS, vol. 500, pp. 73–87. Springer, Heidelberg (2014)
12. Ebert, B.E., Lamprecht, A.-L., Steffen, B., Blank, L.M.: Flux-P: Automating Metabolic Flux Analysis. Metabolites 2(4), 872–890 (2012)
13. Freitag, B., Margaria, T., Steffen, B.: A Pragmatic Approach to Software Synthesis. In: Workshop on Interface Definition Languages, pp. 46–58 (1994)
14. Freitag, B., Steffen, B., Margaria, T., Zukowski, U.: An Approach to Intelligent Software Library Management. In: Proceedings of the 4th International Conference on Database Systems for Advanced Applications (DASFAA), pp. 71–78. World Scientific Press (1995)
15. Hibbe, M.: Spotlocator Project Documentation. In: Lamprecht, A.-L., Margaria, T. (eds.) Process Design for Natural Scientists. CCIS, vol. 500, pp. 149–158. Springer, Heidelberg (2014)
16. Holler, R.: GraffDok: A Graffiti Documentation Application. In: Lamprecht, A.-L., Margaria, T. (eds.) Process Design for Natural Scientists. CCIS, vol. 500, pp. 235–247. Springer, Heidelberg (2014)
17. Jörges, S., Lamprecht, A.-L., Margaria, T., Schaefer, I., Steffen, B.: A Constraint-based Variability Modeling Framework. International Journal on Software Tools for Technology Transfer (STTT) 14(5), 511–530 (2012)
18. Kind, J.: Creation of Topographic Maps. In: Lamprecht, A.-L., Margaria, T. (eds.) Process Design for Natural Scientists. CCIS, vol. 500, pp. 225–234. Springer, Heidelberg (2014)
19. Kubczak, C., Margaria, T., Fritsch, A., Steffen, B.: Biological LC/MS Preprocessing and Analysis with jABC, jETI and xcms. In: Proceedings of the 2nd International Symposium on Leveraging Applications of Formal Methods, Verification and Validation (ISoLA 2006), Paphos, Cyprus, November 15-19, pp. 308–313. IEEE Computer Society (2006)
20. Kubczak, C., Margaria, T., Steffen, B., Nagel, R.: Service-oriented Mediation with jABC/jETI (2008)
21. Kubczak, C., Margaria, T., Steffen, B., Naujokat, S.: Service-oriented Mediation with jETI/jABC: Verification and Export. In: Proceedings of the 2007 IEEE/WIC/ACM International Conference on Web Intelligence and Intelligent Agent Technology, WI-IAT Workshop, Silicon Valley, California, USA, pp. 144–147. IEEE Computer Society Press (November 2007)
22. Kuntzsch, C.: Visualization of Data Transfer Paths. In: Lamprecht, A.-L., Margaria, T. (eds.) Process Design for Natural Scientists. CCIS, vol. 500, pp. 140–148. Springer, Heidelberg (2014)
23. Labarga, A., Valentin, F., Anderson, M., Lopez, R.: Web services at the European bioinformatics institute. Nucleic Acids Research 35(Web Server issue), W6–W11 (2007)
24. Lamprecht, A.-L.: User-Level Workflow Design. LNCS, vol. 8311. Springer, Heidelberg (2013)
25. Lamprecht, A.-L., Margaria, T.: Scientific workflows: Eternal components, changing interfaces, varying compositions. In: Margaria, T., Steffen, B. (eds.) ISoLA 2012, Part I. LNCS, vol. 7609, pp. 47–63. Springer, Heidelberg (2012)
26. Lamprecht, A.-L., Margaria, T., Schaefer, I., Steffen, B.: Synthesis-based variability control: Correctness by construction. In: Beckert, B., Damiani, F., de Boer, F.S., Bonsangue, M.M. (eds.) FMCO 2011. LNCS, vol. 7542, pp. 69–88. Springer, Heidelberg (2012)

27. Lamprecht, A.-L., Margaria, T., Steffen, B.: Seven variations of an alignment workflow - an illustration of agile process design and management in bio-jETI. In: Măndoiu, I., Wang, S.-L., Zelikovsky, A. (eds.) ISBRA 2008. LNCS (LNBI), vol. 4983, pp. 445–456. Springer, Heidelberg (2008)
28. Lamprecht, A.-L., Margaria, T., Steffen, B.: Bio-jETI: a framework for semantics-based service composition. BMC Bioinformatics 10(Suppl 10), S8 (2009)
29. Lamprecht, A.-L., Margaria, T., Steffen, B., Sczyrba, A., Hartmeier, S., Giegerich, R.: GeneFisher-P: variations of GeneFisher as processes in Bio-jETI. BMC Bioinformatics 9(Suppl 4), S13 (2008)
30. Lamprecht, A.-L., Naujokat, S., Margaria, T., Steffen, B.: Synthesis-Based Loose Programming. In: Proc. of the 7th Int. Conf. on the Quality of Information and Communications Technology (QUATIC 2010), Porto, Portugal, pp. 262–267 (September 2010)
31. Lamprecht, A.-L., Naujokat, S., Schaefer, I.: Variability Management Beyond Feature Models. IEEE Computer 46(11), 48–54 (2013)
32. Lamprecht, A.-L., Wickert, A.: The Course's SIB Libraries. In: Lamprecht, A.-L., Margaria, T. (eds.) Process Design for Natural Scientists. CCIS, vol. 500, pp. 30–44. Springer, Heidelberg (2014)
33. Lis, M.: Constructing a Phylogenetic Tree. In: Lamprecht, A.-L., Margaria, T. (eds.) Process Design for Natural Scientists. CCIS, vol. 500, pp. 101–109. Springer, Heidelberg (2014)
34. Margaria, T., Boßelmann, S., Doedt, M., Floyd, B.D., Steffen, B.: Customer-Oriented Business Process Management: Visions and Obstacles. In: Hinchey, M., Coyle, L. (eds.) Conquering Complexity, pp. 407–429. Springer, London (2012)
35. Margaria, T., Floyd, B., Lamprecht, A.-L., Camargo, R.G., Neubauer, J., Seelaender, M.: Simple Management of High Assurance Data in Long-lived Interdisciplinary Healthcare Research: A Proposal. In: ISoLA 2014. LNCS, Springer, Heidelberg (to appear, 2014)
36. Margaria, T., Kubczak, C., Njoku, M., Steffen, B.: Model-based Design of Distributed Collaborative Bioinformatics Processes in the jABC. In: Proceedings of the 11th IEEE International Conference on Engineering of Complex Computer Systems (ICECCS 2006), Los Alamitos, CA, USA, pp. 169–176. IEEE Computer Society (August 2006)
37. Margaria, T., Steffen, B.: Simplicity as a Driver for Agile Innovation. Computer 43(6), 90–92 (2010)
38. Merten, M., Steffen, B.: Simplicity driven application development. Journal of Integrated Design and Process Science (SDPS) 16 (2013)
39. Naujokat, S., Lamprecht, A.-L., Steffen, B.: Loose Programming with PROPHETS. In: de Lara, J., Zisman, A. (eds.) Fundamental Approaches to Software Engineering. LNCS, vol. 7212, pp. 94–98. Springer, Heidelberg (2012)
40. Naujokat, S., Lybecait, M., Steffen, B., Kopetzki, D., Margaria, T.: Full Generation of Domain-Specific Graphical Modeling Tools: A Meta^{2}modeling Approach (under submission, 2014)
41. Naujokat, S., Neubauer, J., Lamprecht, A.-L., Steffen, B., Jürges, S., Margaria, T.: Simplicity-First Model-Based Plug-In Development. Software: Practice and Experience 44(3), 277–297 (2013) (first published online)
42. Naujokat, S., Traonouez, L.-M., Isberner, M., Steffen, B., Legay, A.: Custom Graphical Specification of Multi-Faceted Concurrent Systems: A Metamodeling Approach. In: Proc. of the 12th Int. Conf. on Software Engineering and Formal Methods (SEFM 2014) (2014) (under submission)

43. Neubauer, J.: Higher-Order Process Engineering. Phd thesis, Technische Universitüt Dortmund (2014)
44. Neubauer, J., Steffen, B.: Plug-and-Play Higher-Order Process Integration. IEEE Computer 46(11), 56–62 (2013)
45. Neubauer, J., Steffen, B.: Second-order servification. In: Herzwurm, G., Margaria, T. (eds.) ICSOB 2013. LNBIP, vol. 150, pp. 13–25. Springer, Heidelberg (2013)
46. Neubauer, J., Steffen, B., Margaria, T.: Higher-Order Process Modeling: Product-Lining, Variability Modeling and Beyond. Electronic Proceedings in Theoretical Computer Science 129, 259–283 (2013)
47. Noack, F.: CREADED: Coloured-Relief Application for Digital Elevation Data. In: Lamprecht, A.-L., Margaria, T. (eds.) Process Design for Natural Scientists. CCIS, vol. 500, pp. 182–195. Springer, Heidelberg (2014)
48. Pillai, S., Silventoinen, V., Kallio, K., Senger, M., Sobhany, S., Tate, J., Velankar, S., Golovin, A., Henrick, K., Rice, P., Stoehr, P., Lopez, R.: SOAP-based services provided by the European Bioinformatics Institute. Nucleic Acids Research 33(Web Server issue), W25–W28 (2005)
49. Reso, J.: Protein Classification Workflow. In: Lamprecht, A.-L., Margaria, T. (eds.) Process Design for Natural Scientists. CCIS, vol. 500, pp. 65–72. Springer, Heidelberg (2014)
50. Respondeck, T.: A Workflow for Computing Potential Areas for Wind Turbines. In: Lamprecht, A.-L., Margaria, T. (eds.) Process Design for Natural Scientists. CCIS, vol. 500, pp. 196–211. Springer, Heidelberg (2014)
51. Rice, P., Longden, I., Bleasby, A.: EMBOSS: the European Molecular Biology Open Software Suite. Trends in Genetics 16(6), 276–277 (2000)
52. Scheele, L.: Location Analysis for Placing Artificial Reefs. In: Lamprecht, A.-L., Margaria, T. (eds.) Process Design for Natural Scientists. CCIS, vol. 500, pp. 212–224. Springer, Heidelberg (2014)
53. Schulze, G.: Workflow for Rapid Metagenome Analysis. In: Lamprecht, A.-L., Margaria, T. (eds.) Process Design for Natural Scientists. CCIS, vol. 500, pp. 88–100. Springer, Heidelberg (2014)
54. Schütt, C.: Identification of Differentially Expressed Genes. In: Lamprecht, A.-L., Margaria, T. (eds.) Process Design for Natural Scientists. CCIS, vol. 500, pp. 127–139. Springer, Heidelberg (2014)
55. Sens, H.: Web-Based Map Generalization Tools Put to the Test: A jABC Workflow. In: Lamprecht, A.-L., Margaria, T. (eds.) Process Design for Natural Scientists. CCIS, vol. 500, pp. 171–181. Springer, Heidelberg (2014)
56. Steffen, B., Margaria, T., Freitag, B.: Module Configuration by Minimal Model Construction. Technical report, Fakultät für Mathematik und Informatik, Universität Passau (1993)
57. Steffen, B., Neubauer, J.: Simplified Validation of Emergent Systems through Automata Learning-Based Testing. In: 2011 34th IEEE Software Engineering Workshop (SEW), pp. 84–91 (June 2011)
58. Teske, D.: Geocoder Accuracy Ranking. In: Lamprecht, A.-L., Margaria, T. (eds.) Process Design for Natural Scientists. CCIS, vol. 500, pp. 159–170. Springer, Heidelberg (2014)
59. van der Aalst, W.M.P., ter Hofstede, A.H.M., Kiepuszewski, B., Barros, A.P.: Workflow Patterns. Distributed and Parallel Databases 14(1), 5–51 (2003)
60. Vierheller, J.: Exploratory Data Analysis. In: Lamprecht, A.-L., Margaria, T. (eds.) Process Design for Natural Scientists. CCIS, vol. 500, pp. 110–126. Springer, Heidelberg (2014)

61. Wickert, A.: Semantische Dienstselektion für modellgetriebene Geschäftsprozesse in jABC: Analyse, Integration und Evaluation. Diploma thesis, Universität Potsdam (2010)
62. Wickert, A., Lamprecht, A.-L.: jABCstats: An Extensible Process Library for the Empirical Analysis of jABC Workflows. In: ISoLA 2014. LNCS. Springer (to appear, 2014)

Protein Classification Workflow

Judith Reso

Potsdam University, Potsdam, D-14482, Germany
reso@uni-potsdam.de

Abstract. The protein classification workflow described in this report enables users to get information about a novel protein sequence automatically. The information is derived by different bioinformatic analysis tools which calculate or predict features of a protein sequence. Also, databases are used to compare the novel sequence with known proteins.

Keywords: bioinformatics, sequence analysis, amino acid properties, homology modeling, protein structures, protein structure prediction, clustering.

1 Introduction: Workflow Scenario

Imagine you have a cell culture with some features you did not observe before. You want to know which proteins the cells contain because there might be something special. After cleaning up the cells and extracting proteins you need to get their sequences. This will be done by an external company and you get back the protein sequences as amino acid sequences. You query them against a protein database, for example PDB [4], and recognize that there is no entry. Congratulations! You might have discovered a new protein. This is the point where the workflow starts.

One would create pairwise alignments which means that the sequence is queried against known sequences stored in databases to find similar structures by comparing the sequence of amino acids. Structure similarity could give hints about proteins sharing a common ancestor (homologs) or having similar functions due to divergent evolution. Another possibility is to calculate amino acid propensities. Amino acid propensities are for example hydropathy, charge and polarity. These features are essential for protein folding. A protein is not only a linear strand of continuous amino acids. Depending on their features they interact to each other which means that bridges could be build between residues by e.g. hydrogen and sulfide bonds, Van-der-Waals forces and electrostatic interactions. There are several tools available which use those properties to predict the fold of a protein structure. This is called the secondary structure.

The secondary structures could be also aligned to known structures to determine the family the protein might belong to. Aligning structures means that it is checked whether there are the same motifs (structural elements with a specific pattern) in the same order and of the same length. There exist databases like SCOP [5] and CATH [1] which separate proteins depending on their composition

A.-L. Lamprecht et al. (Eds.): Process Design for Natural Scientists, CCIS 500, pp. 65–72, 2014.
DOI: 10.1007/978-3-662-45006-2_5

of motifs and domains (helices, β-sheets, loops) into families which could also help to get a functional annotation.

Interactions also occur between secondary structure elements which builds the tertiary and quaternary structure. These structures are important for the function of the protein and determine its catalytic effects and binding to other molecules. Multiple sequence alignments could be generated to cluster a set of more similar structures corresponding to the protein. This results in a phylogenetic tree which is similar to a dendrogram. Because we know the species where the protein is derived from this phylogeny could give hints about the evolutionary context of the protein.

The jABC workflow created in this project takes this novel amino acid sequence as FASTA format (which is a typical text like format in bioinformatics to describe structures) and will search and generate some of the introduced features automatically using web services from EBI [2] and PFAM [3]. The process includes calculation of amino acid propensities, browsing databases for homologous sequences by calculation of alignments and prediction of secondary structure. Domains which are important for protein function will be extracted by comparison with the PFAM-database and a phylogenetic tree will be computed also. The task of the workflow is to give a coarse overview about the novel sequence by automatically calling the preselected tools. This overview can give suggestions for further research on the protein itself and also the workflow could be extended for other functions.

2 Service Analysis

To realize the workflow services were needed which are able to do the introduced tasks. Because this workflow is about the analysis of a novel protein sequence, such a sequence has to be provided initially. Therefore one could create amino acids manually by using the basic SIB 'PutString' and converting it into a FASTA file. Another way is to use 'Makeprotseq' which is a web service provided by the EBI [2]. These platform interacts with several bioinformatic databases and gives access to web tools without needing any licenses. To make these web tools usable within jABC, they have been implemented as SIBs [15]. To work with those SIBs a connection to the internet is required but nothing else needs to be installed.

After getting the random sequence by 'Makeprotseq', it has to be analyzed. 'Pepinfo' is a service which enables to calculate and plot amino acid propensities. The services 'WuBlast' and 'PsiSearch' use different alignment algorithms to search for similar sequences in a specified database, e.g. PDB (Protein Data Base). 'WuBlast' is optimized for queries with novel structures as input on databases which are specially formatted. In addition 'PsiSearch' is using an iterative alignment algorithm called Psi-Blast which computes multiple local alignments between proteins. The secondary structure of the novel protein is predicted using 'Garnier' which uses the GOR-Algorithm (for further information see [8]). All of the previous services are derived from the platform EMBL-EBI.

To get an idea about the functional regions of the sequence the service 'SequenceSearch' from the protein family database PFAM [3] is used. This is also a tool which uses multiple alignments to assign a function to a sequence by comparing it to other known sequences and detecting similar motifs and domains between the structures. The results are evaluated using Hidden Markov Models (HMMs).

3 Workflow Realization

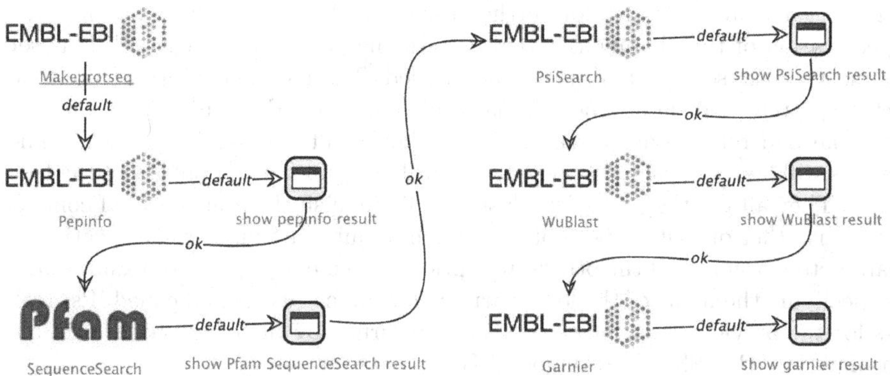

Fig. 1. Protein classification workflow

Figure 1 shows a possible workflow for protein classification based on the services described in the previous section. The SIB where the workflow begins is the 'Makeprotseq'-SIB. This one is declared as 'Start'-SIB. There one can specify how long the novel protein sequence should be. For this workflow, 150 amino acids is set with the parameter 'Length'. The parameter 'Amount' specifies how many sequences should be created and is set to 1. The output of this SIB, i.e. the created sequence, is called 'sequence' and can be used as input by the following services in their ${sequence} parameters.

To get information about amino acid propensities 'PepInfo' takes the created sequence as input and calculates the propensities. This tool requires an email address, the parameter 'Sequence' is used to choose the input sequence (${sequence}) a 'Title' can be specified and the parameter 'result' is used to specify the name of the local variable resulting as output. This result is then shown to the user in a pop-up text dialog using the 'ShowTextDialog' SIB.

The next step uses a Pfam service called 'SequenceSearch'. This SIB takes as input the sequence created by 'Makeprotseq'. The sequence is then queried against the entries in the protein family database 'PFAM' for motifs and domains having a specific structure or function. The return specified with the parameter 'results' consists of Pfam identifiers for domains which are similar to those included in the novel sequence. This result is again simply shown to the user by the 'ShowTextDialog' SIB.

Multiple structural alignments are then calculated with the services 'WuBlast' and 'PsiSearch'. As described before, both tools use different methods so the results of the alignments don't have to be identical. Both tools take the sequence derived from 'Makeprotseq' as input for the parameter 'Sequence'. A further parameter which needs to be specified is the 'Email'-address and the parameter 'Database' which is specifying the database to query. This parameter is set to 'pdb' to search trough the protein data base PDB. Both tools have the option to specify the number of alignments in the output. Here the default is used. 'WuBlast' also allows to specify the alignment output format with the parameter 'align'. This can be useful for further usage of MSAs. 'WuBlast' requires the specification of the alignment program with the parameter 'program'. It is set to blastp because a protein has to be aligned. The parameter 'Stype' must be set to protein and determines the type of sequence. All other parameters are optional and refer to advanced settings. They don't need to be specified. The results will be given as database(pdb)-identifiers, xml-file and output of the tool itself. They all get the prefix 'wublast_' to distinguish them in the local context from the other outputs. The tool 'PsiSearch' requires no further specification of parameters because all the others are optional. The name given to 'resultJobID' is specifying the name of the local variable for further usage and called 'Psi_res'. As for the previous steps, also the results returned by these services are simply displayed by the 'ShowTextDialog' SIB.

Finally, to predict the secondary structure of a protein the web service 'Garnier' is used. It takes as input parameter 'Sequence' the local variable of the sequence and the result which could be named with the parameter 'results' is called 'secondary'. The output of this tool is text like containing the amino acid structure itself and the predicted structural elements at the corresponding position as annotated letters which are repeated as long as a part of the sequence is assumed to build this structure, e.g. a helix will be annotated by 'H'. Also this result is simply shown to the user by the 'ShowTextDialog' SIB.

4 Conclusion

The previous section described a workflow where a sequence is randomly created and used to calculate amino acid propensities, multiple sequence alignments and predict protein secondary structures. Built from SIBs which access publicly available web services, it is fully executable and can be used "as is" as long as only a randomly created sequence is used to initialize the process. If one wants to read in a real novel sequence the SIB 'Makeprotseq' has to be replaced by a SIB which enables to choose a file or the SIB 'PutString' is used as Start-SIB which allows to Copy-Paste a sequence manually. Then the next SIB must be a SIB which converts this string into FASTA-format for further usage by the analysis tools. Similarly, if optional parameters, e.g. for advanced alignments should be set, the corresponding parameters of the SIBs needs to be changed accordingly.

In the present version of the workflow all the web services are simply called one after another, and the (default) results are simply visualized by a pop-up text message. To exploit the distributed nature of the remote services, the workflow could execute in parallel all SIBs which take the same initial protein sequence as input. Instead of just showing the different results in a message box once during execution, they could also written into files and stored on the hard disk for future use. Similarly, the workflow could create a log file where the tools could write their errors for easier traceback.

With regard to further analyses, this workflow could be extended for tertiary structure prediction and structure alignment to check whether there are functional similar proteins evolved by different species which might not be not or only far related to this species. This could illustrate the evolutional context. This tertiary structure could be also checked for interactions with other molecules. There are several tools to predict for example ligand binding.

The workflow could also be extended to automatically check the consistency of developed tools. In bioinformatics it is a big problem to evaluate results biologically correct. This is also shown with this first implementation: A randomly built sequence is used as input for all the web services and results are outputted. One should assume that a non-biological sequence should give no results. But at the moment most of the implemented algorithms are not able to distinguish between biological correct and 'only' mathematically correct. So those workflows could be used to easier optimize services by checking them more automatically.

Also one could implement a SIB or workflow which enables to provide a real novel protein sequence automatically to a database. But then one should ensure that this sequence is really a new one and not only a mutation of a known protein. Therefore one has to check how similar the results of a sequence alignment are.

Regarding the technical details of the workflow realization, using the EBI web services was often difficult for me, as often the documentation of the web services is not clear. Often I tried to find out the valid inputs for the parameters of the EBI SIBs, but the website with the web services of EBI-EMBL [2] is not documented very well. There only the services in SoapLab documented valid values for input (e.g. how to specify the name of the database to query, namely PDB in lower-case letters, pdb).

In the beginning it was also planned to query the input sequence against the SCOP database to classify the protein also by a database tool which is optimized to classify proteins depending on their structure within one step and to annotate the family where the protein sequence could belong to. This was not possible because the SIB 'Scopparse' requires a raw scop file for classification, which was not available in the present setting. A similar idea was to compare the predicted secondary structure to other secondary structures to detect the higher conserved/functional regions of the secondary structure which could also give hints to the protein function. Therefore the SIB 'Ssematch' had been implemented, but could not be used because it requires a DCF-file as input, which was not available.

To calculate a multiple sequence alignment using ClustalW which might be usable by the 'ClustalW2Phylogeny'-SIB the tool 'Emma' should be used in the beginning. But this web service only runs on a multiple input of sequences. It is not querying a sequence against a database. So if there is only one sequence the return value of 'Emma' is empty. I assume that the 'ClustalW2Phylogeny' might need the result of 'Emma' or another multiple sequence alignment as an input. First I thought that a multiple alignments would be computed by PsiSearch, which could then be used to calculate a phylogenetic tree by clustering the sequences depending on their similarity with the service 'ClustalW2Phylogeny'. However, this is apparently not the case, and so the results of 'PsiSearch' can not be processed by this service.

This article is part of a larger evaluation [10], which aimed at illustrating the power of simplicity-oriented development [20] by validating the claim that process modeling can indeed be handed over to the domain experts by providing them with a graphical modeling framework [26] that covers low-level details in a service-oriented fashion [22], integrates high-level modeling in the overall development process in a way that user-level models become directly executable [21,18], and supports ad-hoc adaptations and evolution [17,19].

The project described in this article can be characterized as follows:

- Scientific domain: bioinformatics
- Number of models: 1
- Number of hierarchy levels: 1
- Total number of SIBs: 11
- SIB libraries used (cf. [15]): common-sibs (5), ebi-sibs (5), pfam-sibs (1)
- Service technologies used: SOAP web services, REST web services

The bioinformatics part of this volume contains five other articles on workflow applications in this domain [6,16,25,24,27]. Further examples of workflow projects with he bioinformatics-specific incarnation of the jABC framework, called Bio-jETI [12], have been described, for example, in [11,13,7]. As shown in [12,14,9], bioinformatics is also a suitable field for the application of semantics-based (semi-) automatic workflow composition techniques (as provided by, e.g., [23]) to support the workflow design process.

References

1. CATH: Protein Structure Classification Database at UCL, `http://www.cathdb.info` (Online; last accessed December 10, 2012)
2. EBI Web Services, `http://www.ebi.ac.uk/Tools/webservices/` (Online; last accessed December 10, 2012)
3. Pfam: Home page, `http://pfam.sanger.ac.uk/` (Online; last accessed December 06, 2012)
4. RCSB Protein Data Bank - RCSB PDB, `http://www.rcsb.org/pdb/home/home.do` (Online; last accessed December 06, 2012)

5. SCOP: Structural Classification of Proteins, `http://scop.mrc-lmb.cam.ac.uk/scop/` (Online; last accessed December 10, 2012)
6. Blaese, L.: Data Mining for Unidentified Protein Sequences. In: Lamprecht, A.-L., Margaria, T. (eds.) Process Design for Natural Scientists. CCIS, vol. 500, pp. 73–87. Springer, Heidelberg (2014)
7. Ebert, B.E., Lamprecht, A.-L., Steffen, B., Blank, L.M.: Flux-P: Automating Metabolic Flux Analysis. Metabolites 2(4), 872–890 (2012)
8. Garnier, J., Gibrat, J.-F., Robson, B.: GOR method for predicting protein secondary structure from amino acid sequence. In: Doolittle, R.F. (ed.) Computer Methods for Macromolecular Sequence Analysis. Methods in Enzymology, vol. 266, pp. 540–553. Academic Press (1996)
9. Lamprecht, A.-L. (ed.): User-Level Workflow Design. LNCS, vol. 8311. Springer, Heidelberg (2013)
10. Lamprecht, A.-L., Margaria, T.: Scientific Workflows and XMDD. In: Lamprecht, A.-L., Margaria, T. (eds.) Process Design for Natural Scientists. CCIS, vol. 500, pp. 1–13. Springer, Heidelberg (2014)
11. Lamprecht, A.-L., Margaria, T., Steffen, B.: Seven Variations of an Alignment Workflow - An Illustration of Agile Process Design and Management in Bio-jETI. In: Măndoiu, I., Wang, S.-L., Zelikovsky, A. (eds.) ISBRA 2008. LNCS (LNBI), vol. 4983, pp. 445–456. Springer, Heidelberg (2008)
12. Lamprecht, A.-L., Margaria, T., Steffen, B.: Bio-jETI: A framework for semantics-based service composition. BMC Bioinformatics 10(suppl. 10), S8 (2009)
13. Lamprecht, A.-L., Margaria, T., Steffen, B., Sczyrba, A., Hartmeier, S., Giegerich, R.: GeneFisher-P: variations of GeneFisher as processes in Bio-jETI. BMC Bioinformatics 9 (suppl. 4), S13 (2008)
14. Lamprecht, A.-L., Naujokat, S., Margaria, T., Steffen, B.: Semantics-based composition of EMBOSS services. Journal of Biomedical Semantics 2(suppl. 1), S5 (2011)
15. Lamprecht, A.-L., Wickert, A.: The Course's SIB Libraries. In: Lamprecht, A.-L., Margaria, T. (eds.) Process Design for Natural Scientists. CCIS, vol. 500, pp. 30–44. Springer, Heidelberg (2014)
16. Lis, M.: Constructing a Phylogenetic Tree. In: Lamprecht, A.-L., Margaria, T. (eds.) Process Design for Natural Scientists. CCIS, vol. 500, pp. 101–109. Springer, Heidelberg (2014)
17. Margaria, T., Steffen, B.: Agile IT: Thinking in User-Centric Models. In: Margaria, T., Steffen, B. (eds.) ISoLA 2008. CCIS, vol. 17, pp. 490–502. Springer, Heidelberg (2009)
18. Margaria, T., Steffen, B.: Business Process Modelling in the jABC: The One-Thing-Approach. In: Cardoso, J., van der Aalst, W. (eds.) Handbook of Research on Business Process Modeling. IGI Global (2009)
19. Margaria, T., Steffen, B.: Continuous Model-Driven Engineering. IEEE Computer 42(10), 106–109 (2009)
20. Margaria, T., Steffen, B.: Simplicity as a Driver for Agile Innovation. Computer 43(6), 90–92 (2010)
21. Margaria, T., Steffen, B.: Service-Orientation: Conquering Complexity with XMDD. In: Hinchey, M., Coyle, L. (eds.) Conquering Complexity, pp. 217–236. Springer, London (2012)
22. Margaria, T., Steffen, B., Reitenspieß, M.: Service-Oriented Design: The Roots. In: Benatallah, B., Casati, F., Traverso, P. (eds.) ICSOC 2005. LNCS, vol. 3826, pp. 450–464. Springer, Heidelberg (2005)

23. Naujokat, S., Lamprecht, A.-L., Steffen, B.: Loose Programming with PROPHETS. In: de Lara, J., Zisman, A. (eds.) Fundamental Approaches to Software Engineering. LNCS, vol. 7212, pp. 94–98. Springer, Heidelberg (2012)
24. Schütt, C.: Identification of Differentially Expressed Genes. In: Lamprecht, A.-L., Margaria, T. (eds.) Process Design for Natural Scientists. CCIS, vol. 500, pp. 127–139. Springer, Heidelberg (2014)
25. Schulze, G.: Workflow for Rapid Metagenome Analysis. In: Lamprecht, A.-L., Margaria, T. (eds.) Process Design for Natural Scientists. CCIS, vol. 500, pp. 88–100. Springer, Heidelberg (2014)
26. Steffen, B., Margaria, T., Nagel, R., Jörges, S., Kubczak, C.: Model-Driven Development with the jABC. In: Bin, E., Ziv, A., Ur, S. (eds.) HVC 2006. LNCS, vol. 4383, pp. 92–108. Springer, Heidelberg (2007)
27. Vierheller, J.: Exploratory Data Analysis. In: Lamprecht, A.-L., Margaria, T. (eds.) Process Design for Natural Scientists. CCIS, vol. 500, pp. 110–126. Springer, Heidelberg (2014)

Data Mining for Unidentified Protein Sequences

Leif Blaese

Potsdam University, Potsdam, D-14482, Germany
blaese@uni-potsdam.de

Abstract. Through the use of next generation sequencing (NGS) technology, a lot of newly sequenced organisms are now available. Annotating those genes is one of the most challenging tasks in sequence biology. Here, we present an automated workflow to find homologue proteins, annotate sequences according to function and create a three-dimensional model.

1 Introduction

The advance in DNA sequencing technology over the last years has enormously increased the number of newly sequenced genes. With the advent of the '-omics' technologies as genomics, metagenomics, proteomics, bioinformatics has discovered a number of problems to deal with - one of the most important to effectively manage these data and create biological context for them by creating links between known and unknown data to infer (e.g. in case of protein sequences) evolutionary history, function or even structure of the unknown proteins.

Sequences are usually stored in international Databases, for example GenBank [4], the Nucleic Acid Database of the National Institute of Health (NIH). It has more than 135 million sequence records (as of July 2012). In contrast, the PDB [6], the RCSB Protein Data Bank that stores known structure of proteins, has only about 81 thousand structures (as of July 2012). This shows the imbalance between known sequences and the amount of information *known about* these sequences.

The workflow presented here tries to address this problem. It can be used to automatically mine for information about an unknown protein sequence. Consider for example a metagenomics experiment, where the complete genomic content of an environment sample is analyzed to examine the proteins present (for the sake of this example) [44]. After preprocessing of the data one has a number of protein sequences that have to be assigned a biological context - where they are from, what their function is, etc.

2 Service Analysis

This section introduces the methods and the tools that have been used for the workflow. Note that only online services providing their functionality have been used for the actual realization. The reason for that is, that online services provide lots of computational power while keeping the cost of running for the user small.

A.-L. Lamprecht et al. (Eds.): Process Design for Natural Scientists, CCIS 500, pp. 73–87, 2014.
DOI: 10.1007/978-3-662-45006-2_6

Blast, MaFFT and InterProScan are available at the EBI [16], Phyre is available at the website of the structural bioinformatics group of the Imperial College London [14]. The EBI provides RESTful as well as SOAP-Services. Here, only the REST-services are used.

Technically, the services are accessed from jABC via an *ExecuteCommand*-SIBs that executes cURL within a shell script. The results are downloaded and stored on the user's PC. As shell scripts are used, the user has to run Linux with cURL already installed. cURL is open-source and available at `http://curl.haxx.se/download.html`. The shell scripts should be copied to a folder called 'nat2' in your jABC-directory. In general, the online shell scripts use the default settings of the respective tool. This should give good results in general, but users should be advised that changing these options in the scripts may improve them further. The default values can be found on the web-pages of the EBI. Phyre does not give the option to change the default values.

2.1 Sequence Alignments

Two sequences are homologous, if they are derived from a common (sequence) ancestor. They are further called orthologs, if they share their ancestry due to a speciation event or paralogs if they share it due to gene duplication. These homologous sequences provide lots of information about the unknown gene or protein at hand. The idea is that the genetic code changes over time and the parts of the code that stay the same must hold some valuable information. Consider a speciation event, where two new species emerge from a common ancestor. At first their set of genes will be similar, but after a while (on an evolutionary time scale) their genetic code will drift apart due to accumulation of mutations. Most of those mutations do not occur in protein coding regions and even if they do, they have a certain probability of not changing the protein sequence due to the degeneracy of the genetic code. The protein sequences are thus in general more similar than the gene sequences. Furthermore, a lot of mutations will not change the form or function of the protein (at least not by much) insertions or deletions for example are often in loop regions whereas the core region of a protein or its secondary structure is more conserved. Also, amino acids that have a special role in the proteins function (e.g. binding sites for substrates in enzymes or docking sites for cofactors) are usually highly conserved, they cannot be changed without disturbing the function of the protein. If you have an unknown protein sequence you can infer the structure and function from its homologous' proteins provided those are known. Because of the higher conservation of the amino acids one generally compares proteins on the amino acid-level instead of the gene level. When mentioning sequences, here I refer to protein sequence unless mentioned otherwise.

2.2 Optimal Pairwise Alignment

Homologous sequences are usually found by a pair wise comparison (alignment) between the sequences. They are scored and if the score is above a certain threshold and the finding is statistically significant, the genes are said to be homolog. There are various tools to achieve a pairwise sequence alignment, the probably best known tool are based on the Needleman-Wunsch algorithm [34], which produces an optimal global alignment of two proteins, and on the BLAST algorithm [2], which is usually faster but relies on heuristics.

The Needleman-Wunsch algorithm was developed in 1970 by S. Needleman and C. Wunsch. It uses a dynamic programming approach to find an optimal global alignment of two proteins. The algorithm consists of three main parts: Creating the dynamic programming table, filling it and backtracking to find the optimal alignment. The dynamic programming table is a two-dimensional matrix of the size $m + 1 \times n + 1$ with m, n being the length of the sequences. The value of a field (i, j) in this matrix is computed as the maximum of either $(i-1, j-1)$ plus some weight w, $(i-1, j)$ or $(i, j-1)$. The values are thus computed from the top left to the bottom right field of the table. On Backtracking, the Needleman-Wunsch starts in the bottom right field and goes the other way back to the upper left field of the table; always choosing the path that maximizes the overall achieved score. The chosen path then represents the alignment of the two sequences. If there are multiple equal paths possible, all those alignments are equal.

2.3 Substitution Matrices and Gap Penalties

The weight w that is added is determined by a substitution matrix, for example the BLOSUM or the PAM matrix. Those substitution matrices score the probability of a mutation of one amino acid to another. Due to the different shape and chemical nature of the amino acids not all mutations are even likely. Glycine for example is the smallest amino acid; its side chain consists of only one hydrogen atom. It is very agile and often found in loop regions on the outside of a protein, for example between two alpha helices. Phenylalanine on the other hand is a considerably large amino acid that has a benzene-derivate as side chain. A mutation that would lead to a change from glycine to phenylalanine would have dramatic impacts on the structure of a protein. However, because of the different nature of the two amino acids, this mutation is very unlikely and has a low score in the substitution matrix. The BLOSUM-Matrix (Blocks of Amino Acid Substitution Matrix) calculates the scores as the logarithmic ratio of the probability of the two amino acids appearing in a protein together and the probability of either of the amino acids appearing in the proteins alone. There are different BLOSUM matrices labeled by the percentage of identity of the sequences used to create the matrix. The default value for a lot of programs and services is the BLOSUM62 matrix, which was computed from proteins having at least 68% sequence identity.

The PAM matrix (Point Mutation Accepted, accepted mutations per 100 residues) is a similar substitution matrix, but it was created differently. Here, a phylogenetic tree was build using highly related sequences. The ratio of the number of changes of each type of amino acid to the total number of occurrences of that amino acid in the set of sequence is used as the score [40].

Sequences often change their length with increasing evolutionary distance. This is the result of insertions or deletions of amino acids. In an alignment, those mutations are seen as gaps in one of the sequences. To limit the introduction of gaps, a gap penalty is used. In the Needleman-Wunsch algorithm, this is implicitly done, when the maximum value of a field is equal to the value of the field to the left or top of it. The gap penalties used to score gaps are important; if a gap is given a lower score, more gaps are likely to be found, if a higher score is given, less will be found. Usually, different gap scores are given for creating, extending and closing a gap.

A progression of the Needleman-Wunsch algorithm is the Smith-Waterman algorithm that produces optimal local alignments of two proteins. It has a slightly changed backtracking, so it does not only find one optimal global alignment, but many optimal aligned pieces.

These algorithms produce good results; however, they are slow as they have to compute a full alignment of two sequences. The runtime of the (serial) Needleman-Wunsch Algorithm is $\mathbf{O}(n^2)$. Consider a database with millions or sequences that one unknown sequence has to be compared against. This is not a trivial task and requires an algorithm with maximal speed to be done in an acceptable time.

2.4 Blast

BLAST uses a different approach and is usually faster than Needleman-Wunsch. As it uses heuristics, it cannot provide an optimal alignment, statistics can be used to counteract and score the found alignment based on the significance of appearance in the searched database.

Blast searches in its initial state for small identical words in the database. A word in this respect is a k-mer of identical residues of the two sequences that would score above a certain threshold T if it was aligned with the query k-mer. It uses finite-state automata to search these words. The input of the automaton is the sequence splitted in its symbols; for each possible input (each combination of amino acids) there is a defined response from the automaton. The score is computed using a substitution matrix such as BLOSUM62 and explicit gap penalties. The query sequence is divided in all possible k-mers and all words in the complete database are found. Originally, these words were then extended in both directions until the score drops off by some amount. Newer version of the Blast-Algorithm use a so called two-hit method: The idea behind that is that the significant alignments have probably more than one word in their alignment. The algorithm searches for a second word within the realm of a certain distance. If a second word is found, it is ungapped extended. If this extension does not yield a score above a threshold S_x, it is discarded. If it does, a dynamic programming approach is used to determine a gapped alignment.

If a DNA sequence is to be compared to an amino acid sequence, one has to pay attention to the reading frame. There are six possible ways to translated proteins; if there are additional insertions or deletions due to sequencing error, frame shifts can occur. For the purpose of this work, I consider only one reading frame and assume that all errors are eliminated.

As mentioned earlier, the Blast-Score can be used to find a significant alignment in the given database. The total Score S of an alignment is the sum of its pairwise scores. From that, the so called bit-score S can be computed, a normalized score that is a function of the raw score, the scoring matrix, and the amino acid frequency in the database $S = \frac{(\lambda S) ln(K)}{ln(2)}$ With λ being a constant depending on the substitution matrix, K being a constant depending on the amino acid frequency in the database. The expected value of S (so called E-Value) is then $E = Kmne^{\lambda S}$ with m, n being the length of the sequences. This is the expected number of database hits with a score at least S, the observed bit-score. The smaller the E-Value, the better: Alignments with a small E-Value are not likely to be found by chance in the database; this indicates that biological significance might be the crucial factor to explain why an alignment scores so well. Typically, alignments that achieve an E-Value below 1^{-10} are said to be homologous.

2.5 MaFFT

Instead of incorporating information of just two sequences, one could look at multiple sequences to find conserved regions. It seems intuitive that a residue that is conserved in multiple sequences must be valuable to the protein, whereas a residue that is only conserved in two of the many sequences may not be as valuable something might not be detected when looking at only two sequences. There are many programs that compute a multiple sequence alignment. The program used here is called MaFFT [13], Multiple alignment by Fast-Fourier Transformation.

MaFFT represents each amino acid in the sequence as a vector consisting of the polarity and the volume of the amino acid. The vectors are then normalized and the correlation between two sequences based on those vectors is computed. This computed correlation peaks, if the sequences have homologous regions. These peaks are used to find homologous regions, which guide a dynamic programming approach to find an alignment: With the information that the alignment must pass some explicit regions, the dynamic programming table can be reduced and the computation time can be improved. Reducing the dynamic programming table means dividing it into sub-matrices as indicated by the homologous regions and only aligning those regions. After computing this initial alignment, it is iteratively refined [5]

MaFFT uses a scoring matrix based on the previously discussed PAM substitution matrix, but normalized by the frequency of occurrence of the amino acids. To determine the order of the alignments that are to be aligned, a distance is calculated based on the number of 6-tuples shared by two sequences. From this distance matrix, a guide tree is built. This guide tree is computed by using the UPGMA method (Unweighted Pair Group Method with Arithmetic mean)[42]. Building such a tree is fast, but it infers a uniform rate of evolution, an assumption which is not necessarily true. Still, MaFFT performs very well and is faster than most of its competitor programs [12].

2.6 InterProScan

The information known about protein sequences is stored in the databases like the UniProt-Database, especially the manually curated UniProt Knowledgebase (UniProtKB). UniProt is the central resource for protein-related information. Protein sequences can be used to query this database to find information for example about its function, substrate specificity (in case of an enzyme), location, GO-Terms, etc.

A more sensitive approach is not to search every single protein but create protein signatures, mathematical descriptions of the sequence or structure of the protein, and search with the help of that signature for protein families. These signatures can be regular expressions used in Prosite [41], build from multiple sequence alignments [9] or based on Hidden Marko Models [15]. Although there are many databases, they all have their main focus on different things - using only one in a query could lead to bad results because the analyzed protein did not lie in the focus area of the database. This problem was addressed by InterPro, a database combining now more than ten of these signature based databases [10]. The InterPro database holds various information about the information, one of them a list of precomputed mathes to the UniProtKB database. Using the InterProScan tool (IPS) [46], a sequence can be scanned against the Interpro database to find the matching InterPro entry and thus the UniProtKB entries.

2.7 Phyre

Proteins consist of four stages of protein sequences. The primary structure is the linear chain of amino acid, the secondary structure is this chain ordered in secondary structure motifs, the most prominent being alpha-helices and beta-sheets, the tertiary structure is a three-dimensional arrangement of those motifs as one would expect in vivo. The quaternary structure of a protein consists of several tertiary structures together as a complex.

Although Anfinsen's Paradigm [3] states that all information needed to create the tertiary structure lies within the sequence of the protein itself, finding this sequence is not trivial. The process of folding lowers the Gibbs free energy of the protein and the folded protein will have the lowest possible free energy. In other words, finding an energetic favorable structure for a given sequence will yield the structure of the folded protein. Based on this thought, many molecular dynamic (MD) simulations were constructed, to find the structure with the lowest energy by computing the force on the atoms of the protein and thus the change of their position over a given time frame. This yields good results in general but it consumes too much time and computational power. Typical MD-Simulations only simulate a few hundred nanoseconds, while a complete folding of a protein can take several microseconds.

Although a lot of sequences are known, the respective structures remain unsolved. As of July 2012, there were about 75,000 solved protein structures and about 6,000 solved nucleic acid and protein/nucleic acid complexes. The number of unique folds on the other hand is comparably slow and not as fast-growing as the total number structures. A lot of programs exploit this fact. They are based on the idea that although the sequence does not fully determine the structure of the protein, it biases it into the right direction. It should therefore be possible to infer the structure of a query protein by looking at the structure of its known homologues. This is referred to as homology modeling. Prominent example of this method are for example Rosetta [37] or the here used Phyre [14].

A submitted query protein us searched against a database of non-redundant protein sequences using the tool PSI-Blast [1]. This is an development of the original BLAST algorithm, that uses so-called profiles, to iteratively find more homologous sequences. The secondary structure of the found sequences is computed using the tools PsiPred [11], SSPro [35] and JNet [7], also the ordered and disordered parts of the proteins are computed using Disopred [25]. The profiles found by PSI-BLAST and the secondary structure predictions are then scanned against a database of known folds to achieve an E-Value similar to that obtained in a traditional BLAST-search. The highest scoring known folds are then combined to yield a resulting fold for the query protein.

3 Workflow Realization

The jABC workflow now does several things. First, it tries to find homologous proteins via a Blast search. With those homologous proteins, a multiple sequence alignment is created using MaFFT. Simultaneously, the sequence is classified structural and functional using an InterProScan. The third part is finding information about the overall fold and structure. This is done using Phyre.

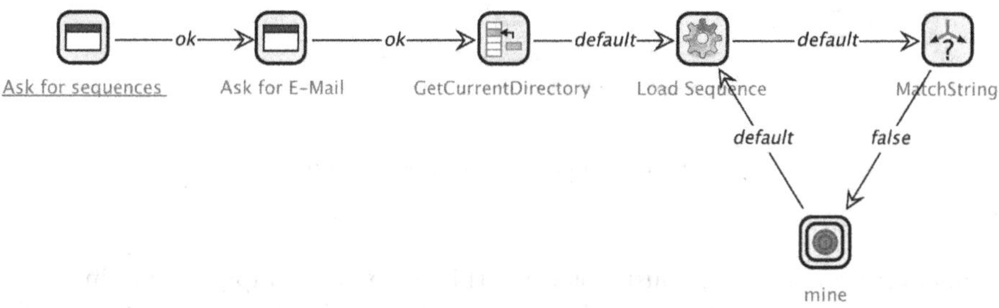

Fig. 1. Main procedure of this jABC workflow. It repeatedly loads a sequence from a file and sends it to the second procedure, here called *mine*, until the file is empty.

The workflow consists of two parts: The main part (see Figure 1) that is only used to set settings and load the sequences from the specified files, and the sub-workflow that realizes the actual gene annotation (see Figure 2).

The main procedure asks for the path of the sequence file. That is, a plain text file consisting of unknown sequences, one line each. It proceeds to ask for a valid e-mail address. This is necessary, since most of the online tools need it

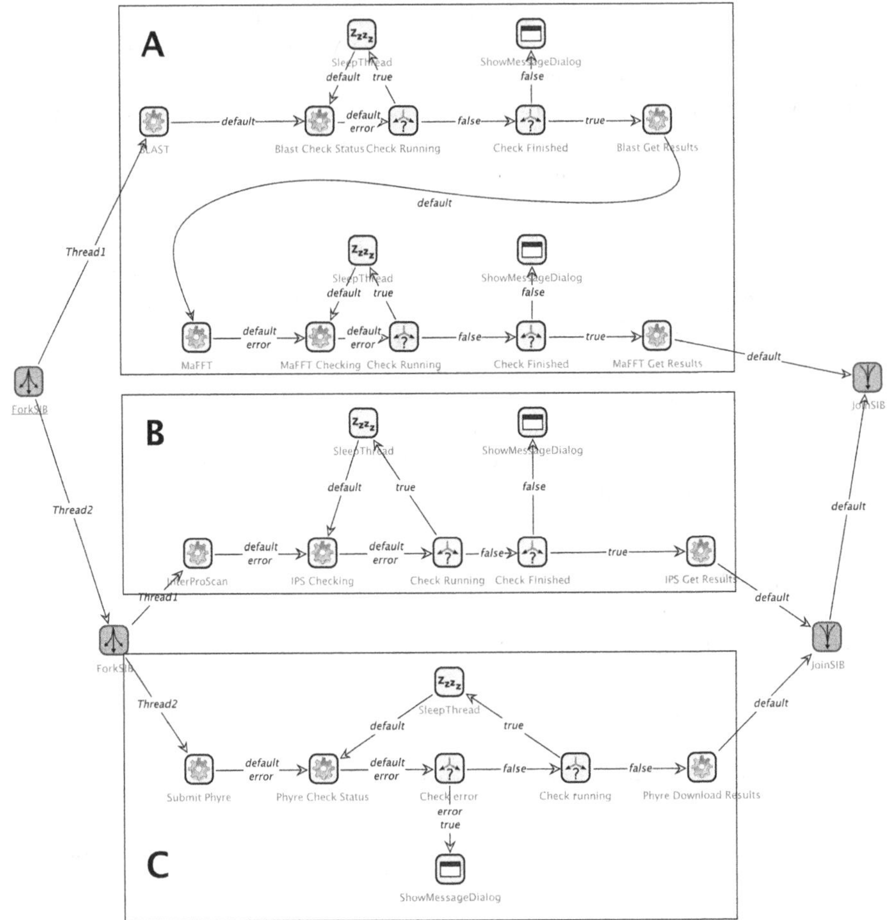

Fig. 2. Actual gene annotation workflow

to function properly. You must not leave this dialog box empty. It continues to determine the current directory. It is assumed that the directory is the jABC main directory, the shell scripts are assumed to be in jABC/Nat2/. A shell script is executed that splits off the first sequence of the sequence file and starts the mine-procedure.

The sub-workflow that realizes the actual gene annotation is then divided into three parts: part A creates the multiple alignment, part B searches the InterPro database using Interproscan, and part C searches for structural homologous using Phyre. These parts run in parallel in different threads created by a *Fork-SIBs*. At the end, they are all joined by *Join-SIBs*. This is necessary to prevent the main procedure from beginning with the next sequence, when the first has not completely finished. This drags down the speed of the procedure due to the different speeds of the Alignment, IPS and Phyre tools. This is mainly due to the small capacity of the Phyre-Server; in peak-times the queue is comparably long so that a job may have to wait for more than an hour. This is a problem and should be addressed in further versions of this workflow.

3.1 Blast and Multiple Alignment

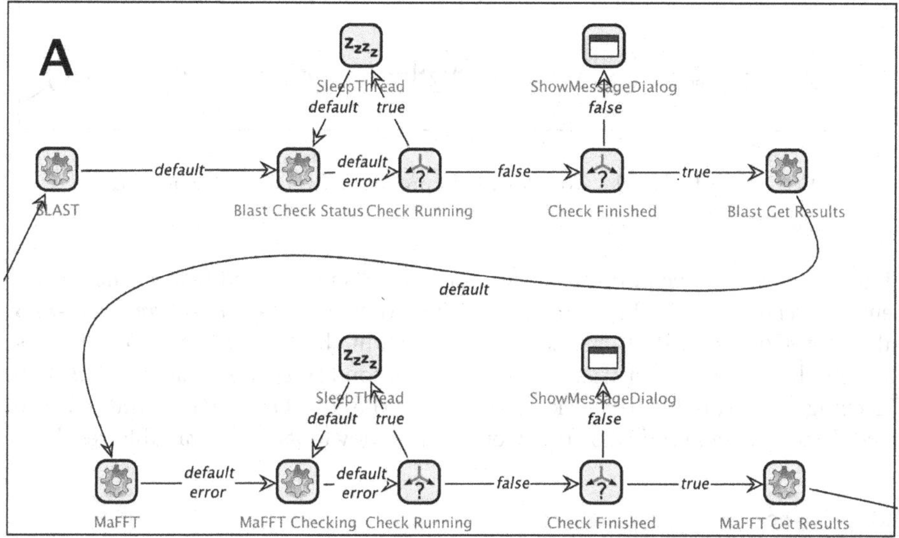

Fig. 3. Part A of the workflow: Blast and multiple alignment

In Figure 3 you see the workflow for the Blast and MSA procedures. The implementation is very straightforward. The first *ExecuteCommand*-SIB (termed BLAST) sends the sequence to the BLAST web service of the EBI. It returns the Job-ID, and identifier that can be used to check the status of the Job and download the results. The former task is done by the second *ExecuteCommand*-SIB (Check Running). It checks, if the job has already finished. If it hasn't, it waits for ten seconds, then checks again. After the job has finished, the third *ExecuteCommand*-SIB (Blast Get Results) downloads the results and stores them in the folder jABC/nat2/blast-results/[Job-ID]/.

The Blast results are then used as an input for the multiple sequence alignment. The first *ExecuteCommand*-SIB, MaFFT, loads the found homologous and sends them to the MaFFT service at the EBI. It returns a Job-ID, that the second *ExecuteCommand*-SIB (MaFFT Checking) uses to access the status of the job. If it is stilled running of queued, the workflow waits for thirty seconds, than queries the status again. After the Alignment is done, the third *ExecuteCommand*-SIB (MaFFT Get Results) downloads the results and stores them at jABC/nat2/mafft-results/[Job-ID]/.

3.2 InterProScan

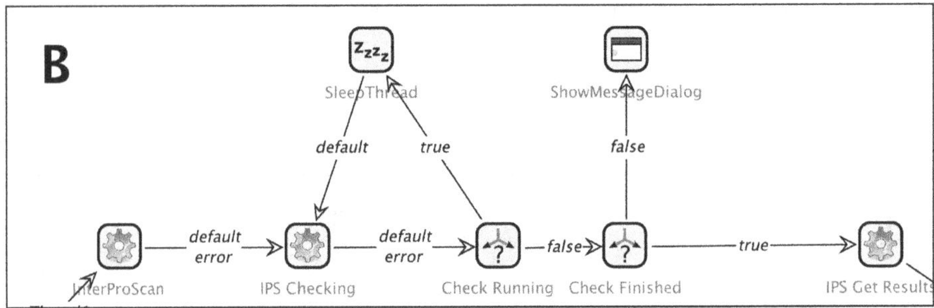

Fig. 4. Part B of the workflow: InterproScan of the query sequences

Figure 4 shows the second part of the workflow. As mentioned before, Interpro is being searched by IPS. The sequence is given to the first *ExecuteCommand*-SIB called InterProScan. It starts the online-search in the InerPro database. It uses the default values and returns a Job-ID. The second *ExecuteCommand*-SIB, IPS Checking, uses this ID to check the status of the job. Once it has finished, the third *ExecuteCommand*-SIB, IPS Get Results, downloads all available results.

3.3 Phyre

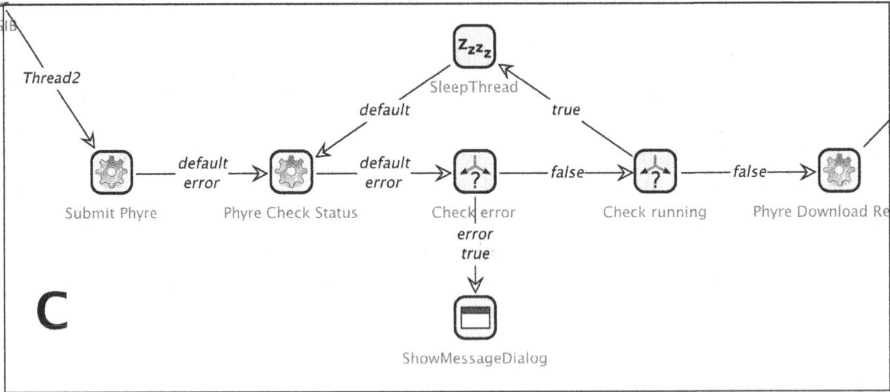

Fig. 5. Part C of the workflow: Structural modeling and homology search with Phyre

The last part of the workflow is depicted in Figure 5. Phyre is used to assess the overall fold of the protein. The implementation is as straightforward as in the case of the IPS or MSA. Phyre is run on a server of the Imperial College London. It does not provide an explicit API and thus does not meet all criteria for a traditional web service. However, as Phyres web-page structure is very simple, it is easy to access it via cURL.

The first *ExecuteCommand*-SIB (Submit Phyre) submits the query sequence to the Phyre sever. The second *ExecuteCommand*-SIB checks the status of the Job. If the job is running, the process halts for thirty seconds and then queries the status again. When the job is finished, it is downloaded by the third *ExecuteCommand*-SIB, Phyre Download Results. The results are saved at jABC/nat2/phyre-results/[Job-ID]/.

4 Conclusion

With the advent of Next Generation Sequencing mechanism, Big Data in Biology is now a highly discussed topic. One of the problems is still the gap between the number of known sequences and the amount of information known about these sequences.

The goal of this jABC project was to - at least partially - automate the steps to annotate an unknown protein sequence and thus put them in a meaningful biological context. This goal was reached - the workflow presented here is an easy way to mine the databases for information about an unknown protein. The use of online services guarantees huge databases that can searched very performant, while keeping the requirements for the user in terms of hardware and cost low. Also, the workflow is easily expandable to incorporate new services or new options for the existing services as they arise.

Still, it should be noted that the jABC workflow was not as extensively tested, as one would do for a program for the productive use. The results should be treated with extreme caution. Also, the use of online-services may offer some disadvantages in terms of privacy, as the results of the queries are openly available.

There are various ways how this project could be extended. First, the operability could be improved by displaying the expected running time of the services, so the user always knows if and which program is running. Secondly, more services could be used to gain more information. An interesting idea would be to create a 3D-model in Rosetta, as this is a tool known to be very performant and accurate. Unfortunately, the Rosetta server that handles automatic model generation requires a log-in and it can not be expected of all users to have an account. Still, a local version of Rosetta could be used to locally compute the model of the protein. A third way to further improve the protein would be an automatic upload of the protein to UniProt along with all known information about the protein. A drawback of this workflow is the running time - especially the phyre-search runs very slowly and can take for longer proteins at peak-times up to some hours. A simple way to address this problem would be to rearrange the submit- and download-scripts. If at first all queries are submitted before the first download of the results is begun, the workflow will probably run a lot faster, as the download scripts of InterProScan and MaFFT would not have to wait for Phyre to finish. This asynchronous work could improve the running time by a many-fold but could not be tested due to time concerns.

Another drawback of the current workflow is its strong platform dependency due to the use of the ExecuteCommand SIBs and shell scripts in a fashion that requires a particular directory structure. Here, platform independency could be achieved by using appropriate REST or jETI SIBs instead.

This article is part of a larger evaluation [18], which aimed at illustrating the power of simplicity-oriented development [30] by validating the claim that process modeling can indeed be handed over to the domain experts by providing them with a graphical modeling framework [43] that covers low-level details in a service-oriented fashion [32], integrates high-level modeling in the overall development process in a way that user-level models become directly executable [31,28], and supports ad-hoc adaptations and evolution [27,29].

The project described in this article can be characterized as follows:

- Scientific domain: bioinformatics
- Number of models: 2
- Number of hierarchy levels: 2
- Total number of SIBs: 38
- SIB libraries used (cf. [23]): common-sibs
- Service technologies used: REST web services

The bioinformatics part of this volume contains five other articles on workflow applications in this domain [36,24,38,39,45]. Further examples of workflow projects with he bioinformatics-specific incarnation of the jABC framework, called Bio-jETI [20], have been described, for example, in [19,21,8]. As shown in [20,22,17], bioinformatics is also a suitable field for the application of semantics-based (semi-) automatic workflow composition techniques (as provided by, e.g., [33]) to support the workflow design process.

References

1. Altschul, S.: Gapped BLAST and PSI-BLAST: a new generation of protein database search programs. Nucleic acid research 25, 3389–3402 (1997)
2. Altschul, S., Gish, W., Miller, W., Myers, E., Lipman, D.: Basic local alignment search tool. J. Mol. Biol. 215(3), 403–410 (1990)
3. Anfinsen, C., Haber, E., Sela, M., White. Jr., F.: The kinetics of formation of native ribonuclease during oxidation of the reduced polypeptide chain. PNAS 47(9), 1309–1314 (1961)
4. Benson, D., Karsch-Mizrachi, I., Lipman, D., Ostell, J., Sayers, E.: Genbank. Nucleic Acids Res. 7, D32–D37 (2011)

5. Berger, M., Muson, M.: A novel randomized iterative strategy for aligning multiple protein sequences. Comput. Appl. Biosci. 7, 479–484 (1994)
6. Berman, H., Westbrook, J., Feng, Z., Gilliland, G., Bhat, T., Weissig, H., Shindyalov, I., Bourne, P.: The Protein Data Bank. Nucleic Acids Research 28, 235–242 (2000)
7. Cole, C., Barber, J., Barton, G.: The Jpred 3 secondary structure prediction server. Nucleic Acids Res. 36(Web server issue), W197–W201 (2008)
8. Ebert, B.E., Lamprecht, A.-L., Steffen, B., Blank, L.M.: Flux-P: Automating Metabolic Flux Analysis. Metabolites 2(4), 872–890 (2012)
9. Gribskov, M., Luthy, R., Eisenberg, D.: Profile Analysis. Methods in Enzymology 183, 146–159 (1990)
10. Hunter, S., Jones, P., Mitchell, A., et al.: InterPro in 2011: new developments in the family and domain prediction database. Nucleic Acids Research 40, D306–D312 (2011)
11. Jones, D.: Protein secondary structure prediction based on position-specific scoring matrices. J. Mol. Biol. 292, 195–202 (1999)
12. Katoh, K., Misawa, K., et al.: MAFFT version 5: Improvement in accuracy of multiple sequence alignment. KNucleic Acids Research 33(2), 411–518 (2005)
13. Katoh, K., Misawa, K., Kuma, K., Miyata, T.: MaFFT: a novel method for rapid multiple sequence alignment based on fast Furier transform. Nucleic Acids Res. 30(14), 3059–3066 (2002)
14. Kelley, L., Sternberg, M.: Protein structure prediction on the web: a case study using the Phyre server. Nature Protocols 4, 363–371 (2009)
15. Krogh, A., Brown, M., Mian, I., Sjolander, K., Haussle, D.: Hidden Markov models in computational biology. Applications to protein modeling. Journal of Molecular Biology 235(5), 1501–1531 (1994)
16. Labarga, A., Valentin, F., Anderson, M., Lopez, R.: Web services at the European bioinformatics institute. Nucleic Acids Research 35(Web Server issue), W6–W11 (2007)
17. Lamprecht, A.-L.: User-Level Workflow Design. LNCS, vol. 8311. Springer, Heidelberg (2013)
18. Lamprecht, A.-L., Margaria, T. (eds.): Process Design for Natural Scientists: An Agile Model-Driven Approach. CCIS, vol. 500. Springer, Heidelberg (2014)
19. Lamprecht, A.-L., Margaria, T., Steffen, B.: Seven variations of an alignment workflow - an illustration of agile process design and management in bio-jETI. In: Măndoiu, I., Wang, S.-L., Zelikovsky, A. (eds.) ISBRA 2008. LNCS (LNBI), vol. 4983, pp. 445–456. Springer, Heidelberg (2008)
20. Lamprecht, A.-L., Margaria, T., Steffen, B.: Bio-jETI: a framework for semantics-based service composition. BMC Bioinformatics 10(Suppl 10), S8 (2009)
21. Lamprecht, A.-L., Margaria, T., Steffen, B., Sczyrba, A., Hartmeier, S., Giegerich, R.: GeneFisher-P: variations of GeneFisher as processes in Bio-jETI. BMC Bioinformatics 9(Suppl 4), S13 (2008)
22. Lamprecht, A.-L., Naujokat, S., Margaria, T., Steffen, B.: Semantics-based composition of EMBOSS services. Journal of Biomedical Semantics 2(Suppl 1), S5 (2011)
23. Lamprecht, A.-L., Wickert, A.: The Course's SIB Libraries. In: Lamprecht, A.-L., Margaria, T. (eds.) Process Design for Natural Scientists. CCIS, vol. 500, pp. 30–44. Springer, Heidelberg (2014)
24. Lis, M.: Constructing a Phylogenetic Tree. In: Lamprecht, A.-L., Margaria, T. (eds.) Process Design for Natural Scientists. CCIS, vol. 500, pp. 101–109. Springer, Heidelberg (2014)

25. Marchler-Bauer, A., et al.: CDD: a conserved domain database for interactive domain family analysis. Nucleic Acids Res. 35(Database issue), D237–D240 (2007)
26. Margaria, T., Nagel, R., Steffen, B.: jETI: A tool for remote tool integration. In: Halbwachs, N., Zuck, L.D. (eds.) TACAS 2005. LNCS, vol. 3440, pp. 557–562. Springer, Heidelberg (2005)
27. Margaria, T., Steffen, B.: Agile IT: Thinking in User-Centric Models. In: Margaria, T., Steffen, B. (eds.) Leveraging Applications of Formal Methods, Verification and Validation. CCIS, vol. 17, pp. 490–502. Springer, Heidelberg (2009)
28. Margaria, T., Steffen, B.: Business Process Modelling in the jABC: The One-Thing-Approach. In: Cardoso, J., van der Aalst, W. (eds.) Handbook of Research on Business Process Modeling. IGI Global (2009)
29. Margaria, T., Steffen, B.: Continuous Model-Driven Engineering. IEEE Computer 42(10), 106–109 (2009)
30. Margaria, T., Steffen, B.: Simplicity as a Driver for Agile Innovation. Computer 43(6), 90–92 (2010)
31. Margaria, T., Steffen, B.: Service-Orientation: Conquering Complexity with XMDD. In: Hinchey, M., Coyle, L. (eds.) Conquering Complexity, pp. 217–236. Springer, London (2012)
32. Margaria, T., Steffen, B., Reitenspieß, M.: Service-oriented design: The roots. In: Benatallah, B., Casati, F., Traverso, P. (eds.) ICSOC 2005. LNCS, vol. 3826, pp. 450–464. Springer, Heidelberg (2005)
33. Naujokat, S., Lamprecht, A.-L., Steffen, B.: Loose programming with PROPHETS. In: de Lara, J., Zisman, A. (eds.) Fundamental Approaches to Software Engineering. LNCS, vol. 7212, pp. 94–98. Springer, Heidelberg (2012)
34. Needleman, S., Wunsch, C.: A general method applicable to the search for similarities in the amino acid sequence of two proteins. Journal of Molecular Biologie 48, 443–453 (1970)
35. Pollastri, G., Przybylski, D., Rost, B., Baldi, P.: Improving the prediction of protein secondary structure in three and eight classes using recurrent neural networks and profiles. Proteins 47, 228–235 (2002)
36. Reso, J.: Protein Classification Workflow. In: Lamprecht, A.-L., Margaria, T. (eds.) Process Design for Natural Scientists. CCIS, vol. 500, pp. 65–72. Springer, Heidelberg (2014)
37. Rohl, C., Strauss, C., Misura, K.: DBaker. Protein structure prediction using rosetta. Methods in Enzymology 383, 66–93 (2004)
38. Schulze, G.: Workflow for Rapid Metagenome Analysis. In: Lamprecht, A.-L., Margaria, T. (eds.) Process Design for Natural Scientists. CCIS, vol. 500, pp. 88–100. Springer, Heidelberg (2014)
39. Schütt, C.: Identification of Differentially Expressed Genes. In: Lamprecht, A.-L., Margaria, T. (eds.) Process Design for Natural Scientists. CCIS, vol. 500, pp. 127–139. Springer, Heidelberg (2014)
40. Zvelebil, M., Baum, J.: Understanding Bioinformatics. Garland Science (2008)
41. Sigrist, C., Cerutti, L., Hulo, N., Gattiker, A., Falquet, L., Pagni, M., Bairoch, A., Bucher, P.: PROSITE: A documented database using patterns and profiles as motif descriptos. Briefigs in Bioinformatics 3, 265–275 (2002)
42. Sokal, R., Michener, C.: A statistical method for evaluation systematic relationships. The University of Kansas science bulletin 28, 1409–1438 (1958)
43. Steffen, B., Margaria, T., Nagel, R., Jörges, S., Kubczak, C.: Model-driven development with the jABC. In: Bin, E., Ziv, A., Ur, S. (eds.) HVC 2006. LNCS, vol. 4383, pp. 92–108. Springer, Heidelberg (2007)

44. Thomas, T., Gilbert, J., Meyer, F.: Metagenomics - a guide from sampling to data analysis. Microbial Informatics and Experimentation 2(3) (2012)
45. Vierheller, J.: Exploratory Data Analysis. In: Lamprecht, A.-L., Margaria, T. (eds.) Process Design for Natural Scientists. CCIS, vol. 500, pp. 110–126. Springer, Heidelberg (2014)
46. Zdobnov, E., Apweiler, R.: InterProScan - an integration platform for the signature-recognition methods in InterPro. Bioinformatics 17(9), 847–848 (2001)

Workflow for Rapid Metagenome Analysis

Gunnar Schulze

Potsdam University, Potsdam, D-14482, Germany
gschulze@uni-potsdam.de

Abstract. Analyses of metagenomes in life sciences present new opportunities as well as challenges to the scientific community and call for advanced computational methods and workflows. The large amount of data collected from samples via next-generation sequencing (NGS) technologies render manual approaches to sequence comparison and annotation unsuitable. Rather, fast and efficient computational pipelines are needed to provide comprehensive statistics and summaries and enable the researcher to choose appropriate tools for more specific analyses. The workflow presented here builds upon previous pipelines designed for automated clustering and annotation of raw sequence reads obtained from next-generation sequencing technologies such as 454 and Illumina. Employing specialized algorithms, the sequence reads are processed at three different levels. First, raw reads are clustered at high similarity cutoff to yield clusters which can be exported as multifasta files for further analyses. Independently, open reading frames (ORFs) are predicted from raw reads and clustered at two strictness levels to yield sets of non-redundant sequences and ORF families. Furthermore, single ORFs are annotated by performing searches against the Pfam database.

Keywords: bioinformatics, metagenome,cd-Hit-algorithm, clustering, protein family, annotation.

1 Introduction: Workflow Scenario

Metagenomics in life sciences provides insights into whole ecosystems and has facilitated the understanding of biological processes, organismal interactions and genetics of various biomes throughout the world. The scientific progress in this field has been significantly enhanced by the advent of next-generation sequencing technologies which provide researchers with ever-increasing amounts of sequencing data. However, to make full use of these opportunities, new approaches of (sequence) data analysis have to be employed. Typical metagenomic datasets consist of large collections of raw sequence reads as outputted by NGS-technologies like 454-sequencing or Illumina, organized in multiple sequence files in FASTA format and come along with associated metadata (e.g. sampling location, environmental conditions, DNA isolation protocols and the type of sequencing technology used). The specific characteristics of this type of sequence data (short sequence lengths and large amounts of sequences) rendered it incompatible to prior approaches which where suitable for datasets obtained by

A.-L. Lamprecht et al. (Eds.): Process Design for Natural Scientists, CCIS 500, pp. 88–100, 2014.
DOI: 10.1007/978-3-662-45006-2_7

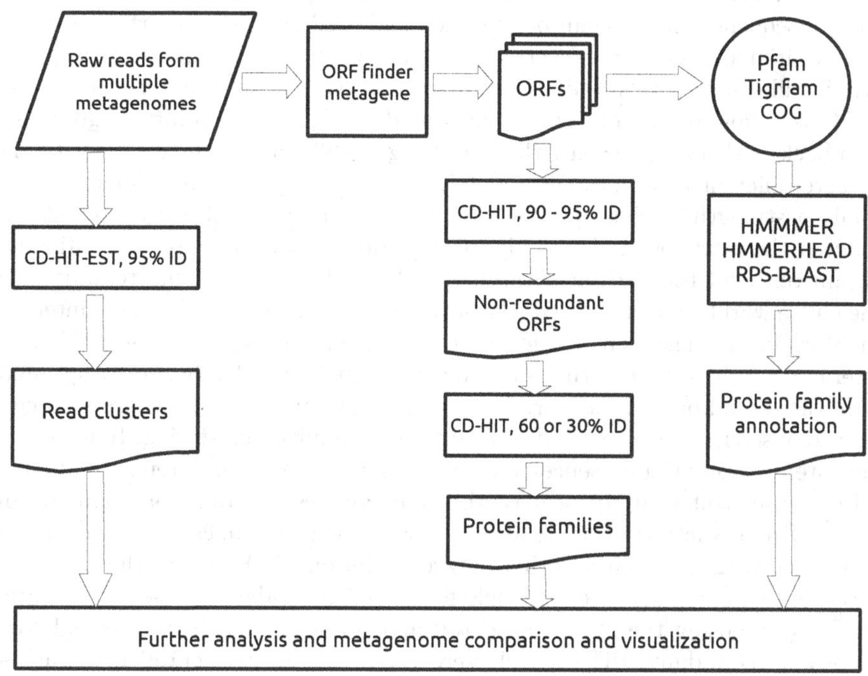

Fig. 1. Overview of the RAMMCAP (rapid analysis of multiple metagenomes with a clustering annotation pipeline) workflow following [12]

Sanger sequencing. Apart from specialized algorithms and data structures for sequence alignment and genome assembly, especially for metagenome data the computational pipelines for functional analyses are of great importance since they allow for structural insights into the genetic composition of biomes and possible implications for ecology of particular habitats.

The workflow presented here offers both a first insight in such functionalities (if present) and a basis for further, more detailed analyses. It takes a single multiple sequence FASTA file as input and provides the user with a structured dataset comprising sequence clusters at different levels of similarity and functional annotation of a subset of sequences by Pfam. The general structure of the workflow is very similar to the one depicted in figure 1.

The actual workflow consists of three major parts which are largely independent and may thus be processed in parallel. Starting from a single FASTA file containing (possibly thousands of) raw reads, the input sequences are first clustered to obtain groups of highly similar sequences. Clustering of the raw reads is a powerful tool and simplifies downstream processing since it can be used to reduce redundancies in the dataset which is of course not possible by manual interpretation of the data if the size of the dataset is large. Furthermore, by selecting an appropriate similarity (ID%) threshold the user gains a first overview of the dataset and the overall similarity of the sequences. A set of representatives of sequence clusters can be obtained and used as input to further analyses and additionally, clusters of certain size can be exported as multiple sequence FASTA files themselves and analyzed separately. An important feature of the jABC workflow framework can be exploited here. The possibility of going one step backwards and repeating the clustering at different levels of similarity and observe different outcomes without having to repeat the entire pipeline is certainly a strength of this approach. The user gains the ability to interactively proceed the workflow and may decide to redo certain analyses after adjusting parameters and then go on with the results rather than having to wait until the entire workflow has finished. By providing a suitable graphical user interface the workflow management framework can turn this somewhat tedious task in an interactive process while other tasks may already be tackled in the background.

In the second part of the workflow, open reading frames (ORFs) are predicted from raw sequencing reads independently of the initial clustering. Since ORFs indicate the potential presence of a gene in the raw reads this step is fundamental to subsequent analyses of potential gene families and functions (annotation steps). The predicted ORFs are already a valuable result an can be stored e.g. to be merged with results from other datasets later on. ORFs are further clustered successively in two more steps to yield first a non-redundant (nr) set of the initial ORFs by choosing the clustering cutoff at high similarity. In the second step, these non-redundant ORFs are clustered at a conservative cutoff to obtain so called families of ORFs. Following this approach the outcome of the clustering implicitly attains a hierarchical structure. Both the non-redundant set and the family set of ORFs can be useful for further analyses. Although the parameters for clustering may depend on the way the sequence data was obtained (see [12]), the idea is again to give the user more flexibility here and allow for iterative clustering to decide on the most appropriate clustering scheme.

Finally, the third part of the workflow carries out the protein family annotation of predicted ORFs. The Pfam [22] database provides comprehensive libraries of protein families and can be used to potentially assign ORFs to proteins/domains which in turn yields insights into the genetic content of samples. This can be considered a first step into the characterization of the biome. Additionally, more specialized databases like Tigrfam and COG can be employed to address e.g. phylogenetic issues, too.

2 Service Analysis

A central task in the workflow is the clustering of sequences both at the DNA level (raw reads) as well as at the level of ORFs (amino acid sequences). Due to the large amount of input sequences, a fast and memory-efficient clustering algorithm should be used. The cd-hit-suite which was published by Li *et al.* [13] in 2006 provides the user with a collection of algorithms to perform such clustering both on the DNA and on the protein sequence level and offers some basic tools to extract clustering statistics and further process the sequence data according to clustering information. The cd-hit algorithms are for example available at the corresponding webserver [1] and also part of the full RAMMCAP workflow which is accessible by scripts from the WebMGA server [27] but can also be downloaded at `http://www.bioinformatics.org/downloads/index.php/cd-hit/`. The suite can be installed locally and executed using the ExecuteCommand-SIB in jABC.

Apart from clustering, two other essential services need to be included into the workflow. Firstly, an algorithm to detect open reading frames from raw input reads is preliminary to any protein-level analysis and functional annotation. There are various programs available to call ORFs from multifasta files and e.g the WebMGA server uses `orf_finder`, `metagene` and `fraggene_scan` as tools for this task. Alternatively, the `getorf` program as part of the european molecular biology open software suite (`EMBOSS`) is already available as a SIB and can be used. Second, the annotation of the detected ORFs regarding potential memberships in gene families can be performed by using different web services. In this case, only Pfam is used to annotate single ORFs, while in theory more specialized databases could be included (see conclusion section) to match the more specific demands of the user. Nevertheless, the annotation of ORFs by Pfam yields important first insights and provides the basis for further analyses. Some of the web services provided by Pfam are already available as SIBs and in this case, the `SequenceSearch-SIB` can be employed to search the Pfam database for domain hits. To create single sequences from a FASTA file containing multiple ORFs yet another tool has to be employed. The EMBOSS provides large collections of file editing tools, e.g. the `seqretsplit` program, which is used here to split the multi FASTA file as outputted by the getorf program into single FASTA files which are in turn used as input to the SequenceSearch SIB. Since the seqretsplit program is not yet included into the collection of EBI SIBs present in jABC, a local `EMBOSS` installation is required additionally to call the program (see Conclusions). The most recent version of the `EMBOSS` can be downloaded at sourceforge.net [2].

Apart from these preliminaries (local installations of `EMBOSS` and the cd-Hit-suite) no further configurations have to be set by the user. For installation details please refer to the documentation which is available in the download versions of cd-hit and `EMBOSS` respectively. Currently the workflow also requires some basic Linux command-line tools which should be easily replaceable by specialized SIBs in the future thus making the workflow independent of the operating system.

3 Workflow Realization

Following the general structure of the RAMMCAP workflow as described in the introduction, the SIBs and external services are employed at three different stages of the workflow. Although these stages can be largely parallelized, the Annotation and clustering of ORFs depend on the previous prediction step. The three stages (raw reads clustering, ORF prediction and clustering, Pfam annotation) are linked by two fork SIBs which indicate tasks that can be run

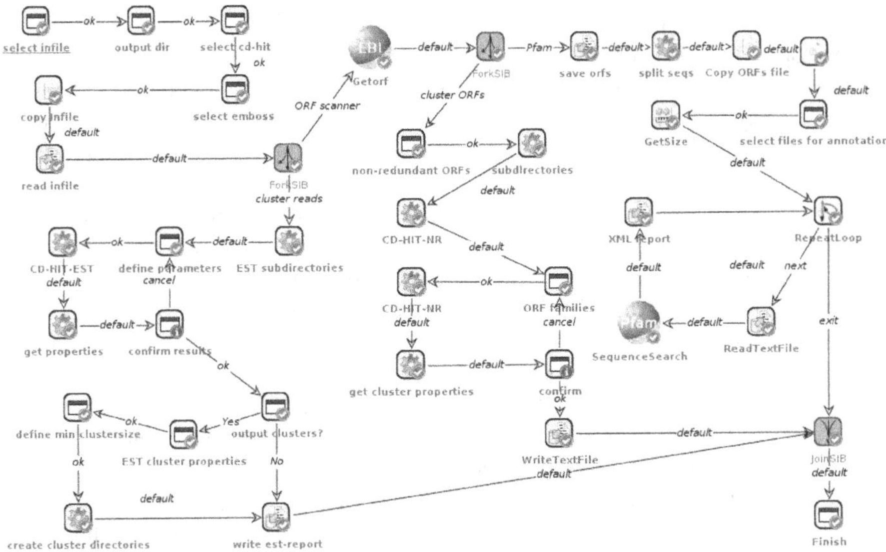

Fig. 2. Overview of the workflow with fork and join SIBs marked by triangles and inverted triangles, respectively.The different stages of the workflow and important intermediary steps are indicated by boxes and descriptions

in parallel 2. To make use of the specialized services and SIBS described in the previous section, additional `Common-SIBs` have to be employed and interactions with the user are required at some critical steps.

3.1 Basic Readin and Setup

At the beginning of the workflow the user is asked to set up some basic parameters, e.g. select an appropriate input file which should be a file in FASTA format containing multiple sequences. The `ShowFileChooser-SIB` allows for browsing the file system and selecting such files in a simple way. Analogously, the user is allowed to select or create an output directory which serves as working directory throughout the entire workflow. Two additional selections are necessary to specify the paths to cd-hit-suite and EMBOSS executables. Note that both suites keep all scripts in a single directory which allows for a single selection to gain access to all programs provided. After this general setup, the `CopyFile` SIB is used to copy the input file to the new working directory and rename it for easier access.

3.2 EST Clustering

After the basic readin the first `fork-SIB` is reached and the input is processed by the `getorf-SIB` to yield ORFs while raw reads are clustered via the `cd-hit-est`

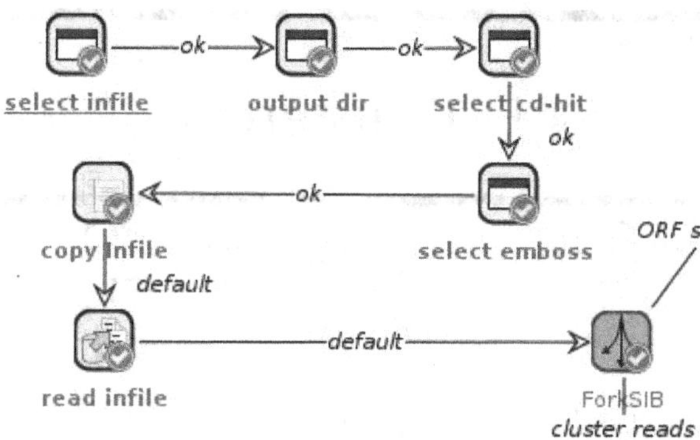

Fig. 3. Basic readin: Selection of the input data and general setups at the beginning of the workflow

algorithm 4. Before the actual clustering takes place, subdirectories for cd-hit-est output are created inside the intitial output directory by calling the Linux command-line tool `mkdir` via the `ExecuteCommand`-SIB. For the actual clustering, two important parameters which have to be specified by the user are a similarity cutoff (%ID) and the corresponding wordsize which is a parameter similar to the one used in `Blast` searches and in this case influences the running time and memory consumption of the `cd-hit-est` algorithm. The user can provide these two parameters by modifying initial values which represent snippets of the command-line parameters via the `ShowInputDialog-SIB`. In the next step the `ExecuteCommand-SIB` is again used to call the cd-hit-est program with the modified parameters and the output is written to the subdirectories created before. The cd-hit-suite provides scripts to extract additional information, e.g. an overview of the size of clusters and contained sequences. The `plot_len1.pl` script is called by another `ExecuteCommand-SIB` and outputs a tabular overview of the clustersizes which can be important for later analyses and is saved into a context variable. The `ShowConfirmDialog-SIB` allows the user to check if clustering was successful. If clustering was not successful or the outcome is not suitable for further analyses, the researcher can decide to refine the (possibly to strict) clustering parameters and repeat the analysis. Otherwise, the user might want to prepare some multifasta files as representatives of the larger clusters which can again be done by employing another tool from the cd-hit-suite. The user is first asked if such additional output is wanted and may then (based on the clustering information collected beforehand) decide on the minimal size of a cluster to be written into a multiple sequence FASTA file in an additional subdirectory. The SIBs required for this task are (in order) `ShowBranchingDialog`, `ShowTextDialog`, `ShowInputDialog` and `ExecuteCommand`. Finally, regardless of these choices, a report summarizing the clustering results is written into a simple text file in the EST-subdirectory.

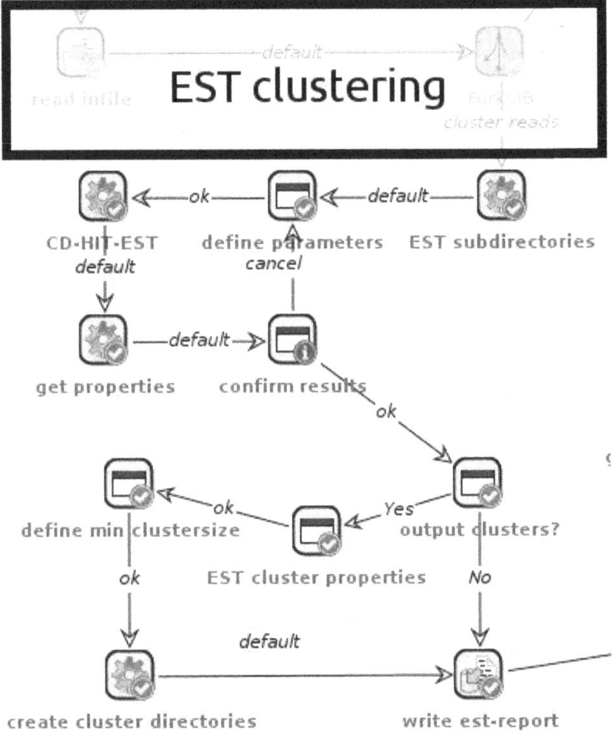

Fig. 4. The raw reads clustering stage of the workflow

3.3 ORF Prediction and Clustering

Following the other branch of the first `fork-SIB`, the raw reads (multiple sequences in a single FASTA file) are used as input to the `getorf` program to predict open reading frames. The output is a again a single FASTA file containing the predicted ORFs. Note that in this step nucleic acid sequences are converted into amino acid (protein) sequences automatically which is the also required for Pfam searches in the third stage of the workflow. Another `fork-SIB` is employed to yield two new threads for ORF clustering and Pfam annotation based on the `getorf` output.

The clustering of ORFs (see Fig. 6) is performed in two steps. First, the set of predicted ORFs is restricted to a set of non-redundant (nr) ORFs which are then further clustered into so called ORF families. To obtain a non-redundant set of ORFs the user is asked to specify a similarity threshold e.g. 95% ID at which ORFs will be considered to be redundant. After creating subdirectories for non-redundant and family sets of ORFs, this parameter is presented to the `cd-hit-algorithm` which is called by the `ExecuteCommand-SIB` analogously to the algorithm used for raw reads clustering. The resulting non-redundant set of ORFs serves as input to another clustering at lower similarity to yield family sets

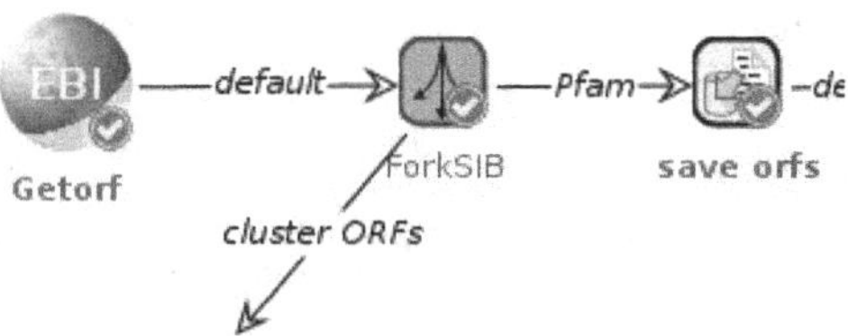

Fig. 5. Intermediate step: ORF prediction using the `getorf`-SIB

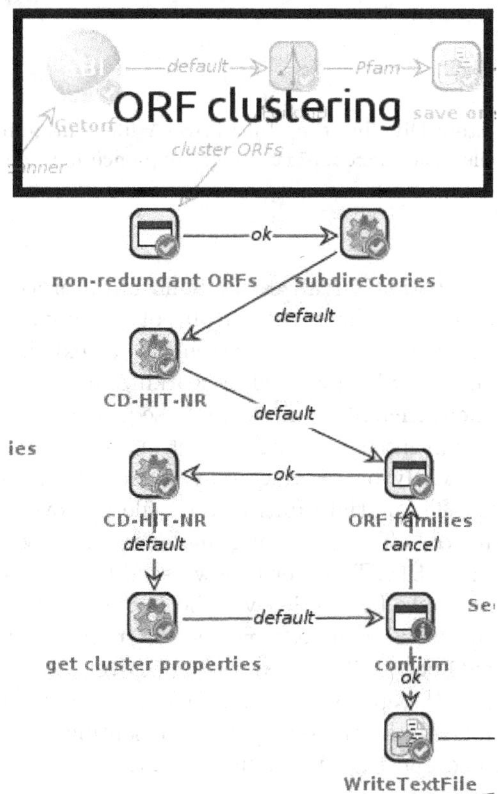

Fig. 6. ORF clustering using the cd-hit algorithm sequentially at two different similarity cutoffs

of ORFs. Here again the user is asked to enter appropriate cutoff and wordsize parameters and has the opportunity to redo the clustering to adjust parameters if necessary. Eventually, the ORF family clustering output is saved into a separate directory for further use.

3.4 Pfam Annotation

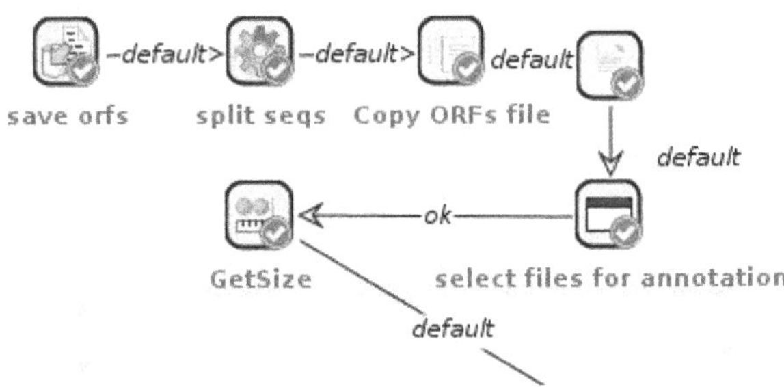

Fig. 7. Intermediary step: Dividing the Multi-FASTA file containing predicted ORFs into single sequence files via `seqretsplit`. Single sequence files can be used as input to `SequenceSearch`

The third stage of the workflow realizes the annotation process of ORFs which where predicted by `getorf`. First, the output of the `getorf` program which was saved in a context variable is now written into a text file in a separate directory called "singleseqs" which is used as working directory in the following. Since the `SequenceSearch-SIB` requires single sequences as input, the Multi-FASTA file has to be split into separate files containing single sequences (ORFs). This can be done efficiently by the `seqretsplit` script which is called by the `ExecuteCommand-SIB`. The initial Multi-FASTA file is moved from the "singleseqs" directory leaving only files containing single sequences which can be read in by the `SequenceSearch-SIB`. The user is now asked to select some of the single sequence files which should be queried via the `ShowFileChooser`-SIB and the size of the overall input to `SequenceSearch` is determined by the `getSize-SIB`. A repeat loop (`RepeatLoop-SIB`) is used to iterate over all query-sequences and to receive and write XML-reports into an annotation subdirectory. After finishing all annotation queries, the three threads representing the different stages of the workflow are joined and the successful completion of all tasks is stated.

4 Conclusion

The workflow presented here can be used to rapidly prepare raw sequence data for further analysis and allows the researcher to possibly gain first insights into

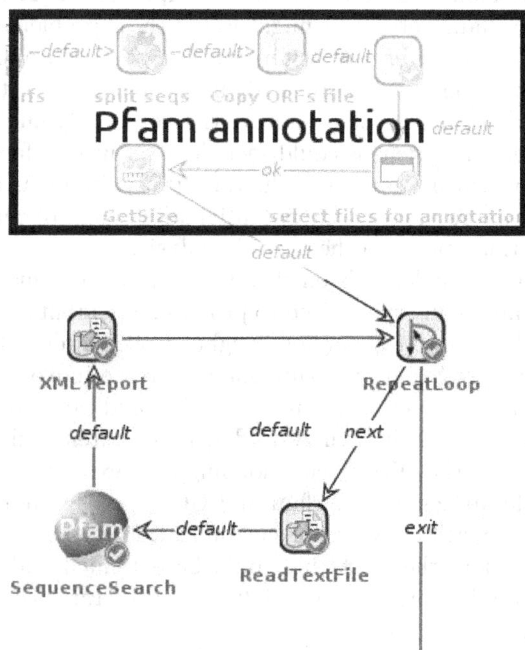

Fig. 8. Pfam annotation using the `SequenceSearch-SIB` and single query sequences as input

the contents of a particular sample. From a single Multi-FASTA file, clusters of sequences at different levels of similarity can be generated by a flexible procedure allowing for input-specific choice of optimal parameters. While the use of single web services and command-line tools may lead to tedious manual interconnection steps and all-in-one scripts lack flexibility, the jABC workflow framework allows for automation and flexibility when needed. Furthermore, independent tasks (threads) can be run in parallel which saves unnecessary waiting time. Although the workflow currently depends on some Linux specific command-line tools and some software has to be installed beforehand, these issues could be resolved in future versions, e.g. the `seqretsplit` script could be added to the existing collection of EBI-SIBS. Alternatively, the `jETI` toolserver could be employed to provide access to a large collection of EBI-SIBs without the need for single SIB implementations. This approach would also allow and simplify additional customization of the workflow if needed. The annotation using `SequenceSearch` currently only works for single sequences and requires the splitting of sequences and separate XML-reports are generated for every single ORF which is certainly overkill, since many ORFs might have no hit in the Pfam database. Additionally, representatives from large ORF family clusters could be extracted and queried against Pfam to restrict the search to sequences which are likely to be matched in the database.

Including the possibility of a Multi-FASTA input to `SequenceSearch` as is also possible at the Pfam web server might lessen these problems and also allow for a more comprehensive overview. Alternatively, a procedure to automatically extract node information from many XML files could provide the user with a single report which summarizes the results of the potentially hundreds of queries performed. Another improvement could include a setup interface at the beginning of the workflow which summarizes the various user inputs in a single request to restrict the user interactions to the potential adjustment of clustering parameters later on and thus speed up the overall analysis.

The workflow critically depends on the clustering algorithms taken from the cd-hit-suite which are highly specialized to process large inputs of short sequence reads. However, other clustering methods might be used alternatively and a generalization of the input-output structure could increase independence from one particular clustering approach which in turn offers additional opportunities for further analyses. One strength of the workflow is the extensibility at almost every stage. For example, the ORF annotation might be extended to include other, more specialized databases like Tigrfam and COG (as is done in the RAMM-CAP workflow) while still allowing for customization to match the researchers preferences. In addition, the clustering could be extended and the user might define his own clustering protocol, e.g. following a hierarchical structure as is outlined in [12].

In its current state the workflow presented here can be considered both a preprocessing tool as well as a template for the rapid analysis of metagenomic data. The workflow might be extended itself or be included in other related workflows and future versions might include additional services which allow for a more specialized and customizable processing of the input data.

This article is part of a larger evaluation [6], which aimed at illustrating the power of simplicity-oriented development [18] by validating the claim that process modeling can indeed be handed over to the domain experts by providing them with a graphical modeling framework [25] that covers low-level details in a service-oriented fashion [20], integrates high-level modeling in the overall development process in a way that user-level models become directly executable [19,16], and supports ad-hoc adaptations and evolution [15,17].

The project described in this article can be characterized as follows:

- Scientific domain: bioinformatics
- Number of models: 1
- Number of hierarchy levels: 1
- Total number of SIBs: 40
- SIB libraries used (cf. [11]): common-sibs (38), ebi-sibs (1), pfam-sibs (1)
- Service technologies used: SOAP web services, REST web services

The bioinformatics part of this volume contains five other articles on workflow applications in this domain [23,3,14,24,26]. Further examples of workflow projects with he bioinformatics-specific incarnation of the jABC framework, called Bio-jETI [8], have been described, for example, in [7,9,4]. As shown in [8,10,5], bioinformatics is also a suitable field for the application of semantics-based (semi-) automatic workflow composition techniques (as provided by, e.g., [21]) to support the workflow design process.

References

1. `http://weizhong-lab.ucsd.edu/cd-hit/`
2. `ftp://emboss.open-bio.org/pub/EMBOSS/`
3. Blaese, L.: Data Mining for Unidentified Protein Sequences. In: Lamprecht, A.-L., Margaria, T. (eds.) Process Design for Natural Scientists. CCIS, vol. 500, pp. 73–87. Springer, Heidelberg (2014)
4. Ebert, B.E., Lamprecht, A.-L., Steffen, B., Blank, L.M.: Flux-P: Automating Metabolic Flux Analysis. Metabolites 2(4), 872–890 (2012)
5. Lamprecht, A.-L.: User-Level Workflow Design. LNCS, vol. 8311. Springer, Heidelberg (2013)
6. Lamprecht, A.-L., Margaria, T.: Scientific Workflows and XMDD. In: Lamprecht, A.-L., Margaria, T. (eds.) Process Design for Natural Scientists. CCIS, vol. 500, pp. 1–13. Springer, Heidelberg (2014)
7. Lamprecht, A.-L., Margaria, T., Steffen, B.: Seven Variations of an Alignment Workflow - An Illustration of Agile Process Design and Management in Bio-jETI. In: Măndoiu, I., Wang, S.-L., Zelikovsky, A. (eds.) ISBRA 2008. LNCS (LNBI), vol. 4983, pp. 445–456. Springer, Heidelberg (2008)
8. Lamprecht, A.-L., Margaria, T., Steffen, B.: Bio-jETI: A framework for semantics-based service composition. BMC Bioinformatics 10(suppl. 10), S8 (2009)
9. Lamprecht, A.-L., Margaria, T., Steffen, B., Sczyrba, A., Hartmeier, S., Giegerich, R.: GeneFisher-P: variations of GeneFisher as processes in Bio-jETI. BMC Bioinformatics 9 (suppl. 4), S13 (2008)
10. Lamprecht, A.-L., Naujokat, S., Margaria, T., Steffen, B.: Semantics-based composition of EMBOSS services. Journal of Biomedical Semantics 2(suppl. 1), S5 (2011)
11. Lamprecht, A.-L., Wickert, A.: The Course's SIB Libraries. In: Lamprecht, A.-L., Margaria, T. (eds.) Process Design for Natural Scientists. CCIS, vol. 500, pp. 30–44. Springer, Heidelberg (2014)
12. Li, W.: Analysis and comparison of very large metagenomes with fast clustering and functional annotation. BMC Bioinformatics (2009)
13. Li, W., Godzik, A.: Cd-hit: A fast program for clustering and comparing large sets of protein or nucleotide sequences. Bioinformatics 22(13), 1658–1659 (2006)
14. Lis, M.: Constructing a Phylogenetic Tree. In: Lamprecht, A.-L., Margaria, T. (eds.) Process Design for Natural Scientists. CCIS, vol. 500, pp. 101–109. Springer, Heidelberg (2014)
15. Margaria, T., Steffen, B.: Agile IT: Thinking in User-Centric Models. In: Margaria, T., Steffen, B. (eds.) ISoLA 2008. CCIS, vol. 17, pp. 490–502. Springer, Heidelberg (2009)
16. Margaria, T., Steffen, B.: Business Process Modelling in the jABC: The One-Thing-Approach. In: Cardoso, J., van der Aalst, W. (eds.) Handbook of Research on Business Process Modeling. IGI Global (2009)

17. Margaria, T., Steffen, B.: Continuous Model-Driven Engineering. IEEE Computer 42(10), 106–109 (2009)
18. Margaria, T., Steffen, B.: Simplicity as a Driver for Agile Innovation. Computer 43(6), 90–92 (2010)
19. Margaria, T., Steffen, B.: Service-Orientation: Conquering Complexity with XMDD. In: Hinchey, M., Coyle, L. (eds.) Conquering Complexity, pp. 217–236. Springer, London (2012)
20. Margaria, T., Steffen, B., Reitenspieß, M.: Service-Oriented Design: The Roots. In: Benatallah, B., Casati, F., Traverso, P. (eds.) ICSOC 2005. LNCS, vol. 3826, pp. 450–464. Springer, Heidelberg (2005)
21. Naujokat, S., Lamprecht, A.-L., Steffen, B.: Loose Programming with PROPHETS. In: de Lara, J., Zisman, A. (eds.) Fundamental Approaches to Software Engineering. LNCS, vol. 7212, pp. 94–98. Springer, Heidelberg (2012)
22. Punta, M., Coggill, P., Eberhardt, R., Mistry, J., Tate, J., Boursnell, C., Pang, N., Forslund, K., Ceric, G., Clements, J., Heger, A., Holm, L., Sonnhammer, E., Eddy, S., Bateman, A., Finn, R.: The pfam protein families database. Nucleic Acids Research (2012)
23. Reso, J.: Protein Classification Workflow. In: Lamprecht, A.-L., Margaria, T. (eds.) Process Design for Natural Scientists. CCIS, vol. 500, pp. 65–72. Springer, Heidelberg (2014)
24. Schütt, C.: Identification of Differentially Expressed Genes. In: Lamprecht, A.-L., Margaria, T. (eds.) Process Design for Natural Scientists. CCIS, vol. 500, pp. 127–139. Springer, Heidelberg (2014)
25. Steffen, B., Margaria, T., Nagel, R., Jörges, S., Kubczak, C.: Model-Driven Development with the jABC. In: Bin, E., Ziv, A., Ur, S. (eds.) HVC 2006. LNCS, vol. 4383, pp. 92–108. Springer, Heidelberg (2007)
26. Vierheller, J.: Exploratory Data Analysis. In: Lamprecht, A.-L., Margaria, T. (eds.) Process Design for Natural Scientists. CCIS, vol. 500, pp. 110–126. Springer, Heidelberg (2014)
27. Wu, S., Zhu, Z., Fu, L., Niu, B., Li, W.: Webmga: A customizable web server for fast metagenomic sequence analysis (2011)

Constructing a Phylogenetic Tree

Monika Lis

Potsdam University, Potsdam, D-14482, Germany
monlis@uni-potsdam.de

Abstract. In this project I constructed a workflow that takes a DNA sequence as input and provides a phylogenetic tree, consisting of the input sequence and other sequences which were found during a database search. In this phylogenetic tree the sequences are arranged depending on similarities. In bioinformatics, constructing phylogenetic trees is often used to explore the evolutionary relationships of genes or organisms and to understand the mechanisms of evolution itself.

Keywords: Bioinformatics, sequence alignment, BLAST, phylogenetic trees.

1 Introduction: Workflow Scenario

The evolutionary development of the recent organisms is one of the most important or at least interesting questions in biology. These days available data enables bioinformatics to search for a tree of life, which could visualize the way from microorganisms to high complex mammals, including humans. But not only the visualization of genetic ancestry, but also other aspects like behavior of organisms can be investigated using phylogenetic trees [22].

In my workflow, the user can input a DNA sequence, which will be translated into a protein sequence and used as a template in a search for similar sequences. The result is a phylogenetic tree, which is constructed from the input sequence and the best hits of the search.

DNA (deoxyribonucleic acid) is a biomolecule and the carrier of the genetic information of all living organisms. It is organized as a double helix, consisting of two polymers which are built up by four different components: the nucleotides. The nucleotides can be distinguished by their organic bases: adenine A, thymine T, guanine G and cytosine C. Certain sections of DNA are called genes. Genes encode genetic information for proteins or molecules. The sequence of bases determines the genetic information. This base sequence can be determined by sequencing via for example the Sanger method.

The DNA sequence can be translated into a protein sequence using the genetic code, a set of rules how DNA sequences are translated into proteins, which is universal for almost all organisms. It defines how the codons (formed from three nucleotides) specify which amino acid in a protein sequence (Figure 1).

There are many databases storing DNA and protein sequences, so that an amount of sequences is freely available for investigations. Examples are GenBank (DNA database) and UniProt (protein database).

A.-L. Lamprecht et al. (Eds.): Process Design for Natural Scientists, CCIS 500, pp. 101–109, 2014.
DOI: 10.1007/978-3-662-45006-2_8

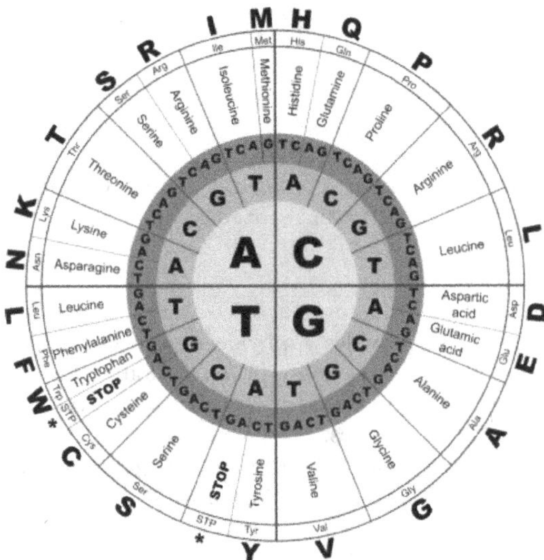

Fig. 1. The genetic code

Both DNA and protein sequences, can be used for a sequence alignment. A sequence alignment is a comparison of different sequences by searching for pairwise matches between their characters (amino acids or nucleotides) [4]. It is of great importance for bioinformatics, since it enables the comparison of organisms not only by morphology, but on genetic information. Also the comparison between genes (and not between organisms) is possible, which can give insights into evolutionary processes at the genetic level. Also it can be used for the identification of conserved motifs or domains, for database searches and for gene prediction. Sequence alignments are performed using dynamic programming, since the construction and scoring of all possible alignments is too complex and therefore time-consuming.

Multiple sequence alignments can be used for the construction of a phylogenetic tree. A phylogenetic tree represents the evolutionary relationships between organisms, genes etc. [5]. The differences and similarities of the alignment are used for the construction of the tree, where there are many possible methods for the construction (for example maximum-likelihood, neighbor-joining, etc.). In the phylogenetic tree the organisms or genes which are more similar are close to each other. The goal of building phylogenetic trees is to reconstruct and understand the evolution of genes and therefore of organisms (Figure 2).

My workflow simplifies the way from a single DNA sequence via a database search for distantly related protein sequences to a phylogenetic tree. So far, this procedure required lot of manual work, the search for suitable services and the adjustment of many parameters. Now you just need to input your sequence and specify the size of the resulting phylogenetic tree, the rest is done automatically.

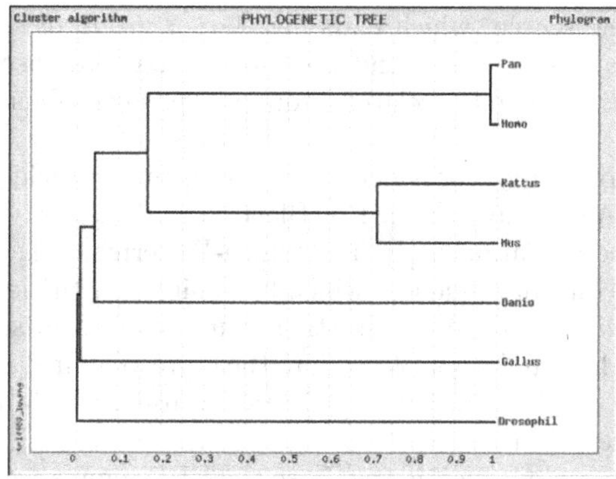

Fig. 2. Phylogenetic tree

2 Service Analysis

For the principal steps of the described phylogenetic analysis, suitable services are publicly available. For instance, the European Bioinformatics Institute (EBI) provides a number of web services for different sequence analysis steps [7], and the forester software libraries for evolutionary biology and comparative genomics research [29] (formerly ATV [30]) can be used for tree visualization. Note here that some of the services that I originally wanted to use did not work as expected , so that I had to find alternative services before I could get the workflow running. For instance, first I wanted to use the NcbiBlast to do a multiple sequence alignment, but the service seemed to be unable to access the database I selected. The following describes the services which I finally used for realizing the workflow.

```
AAB24882      TYHMCQFHCRYVNNHSGEKLYECNERSKAFSCPSHLQCHKRRQIGEKTHEHNQCGKAFPT 60
AAB24881      --------------------YECNQCGKAFAQHSSLKCHYRTHIGEKPYECNQCGKAFSK 40
                                  ****: .***:  * *:** * :****.:* *******..

AAB24882      PSHLQYHERTHTGEKPYECHQCGQAFKKCSLLQRHKRTHTGEKPYE-CNQCGKAFAQ- 116
AAB24881      HSHLQCHKRTHTGEKPYECNQCGKAFSQHGLLQRHKRTHTGEKPYMNVINMVKPLHNS 98
               **** *:***********:***:**.: .**************    :  *.: :
```

Fig. 3. Sequence alignment

BLAST [2] is a tool that searches for sequences in a database by using an input sequence. The idea of a Blast search is that true match alignments are likely to contain short stretches of high similarity. These regions are used as seeds, which get extended step by step to longer alignments (Figure 3). PSI-Blast is a BLAST variant that searches for distant members of a protein family. The first step is to create a list of very similar proteins, which have been found in the chosen database. Those protein sequences are averaged to a "profile". This profile is used to start a new search, which ends in a larger group of sequences. Those sequences again can be averaged and used for a next database search. In this way you can identify distantly related protein sequences. This method is very sensitive.

PSI-Search is now a tool (provided as EBI web service) which combines the Smith-Waterman-Algorithm with a PSI-Blast to find distantly related protein sequences in a selected database [1]. The Smith-Waterman-Algorithm for alignments is advantageous for sequences which have high similarities limited to certain areas (local alignment). When starting from nucleic acid sequences, like in my workflow, they have to be translated into the corresponding protein sequences before PSI-Search can be run. I use EMBOSS transeq, which also provided as an EBI web services, for this step.

For constructing a phylogenetic tree I use the EBI's emma web service, which is a convenient interface to the ClustalW multiple sequence alignment algorithm [27]. In addition to the actual sequence alignment, it also computes the phylogenetic tree that is implied by the alignment process. The forester libraries then provide functionality for creating graphical representations from the specific format in which the trees are described.

3 Workflow Realization

The complete workflow is shown in Figure 4. In addition to the EBI web services (recognizable by the green, "EBI"-labeled globe icon) and the forester SIB (recognizable by the icon resembling a small forest) described above, it comprises a number of SIBs from the CommonSIB library of the jABC.

First, the SIB ShowInputDialog opens a pop-up window (Figure 5), where the input DNA sequence must be entered. After this, in the next input dialog the user must specify the number of branches he wants to have in the resulting phylogenetic tree (excluding the input sequence). That is the number of sequences found in the PSI-Search, which will be used to construct the phylogenetic tree in combination with the input sequence (Figure 6).

After this, transeq translates the Sequence into a protein sequence using the genetic code. This SIB offers the Trim-parameter, which removes the characters "*" and "X" from the protein sequence, which stand for stop and ambiguity. This parameter is optional, the selected setting is "true" because this is required for the construction of the phylogenetic tree later in the workflow.

The next step is the database search using PSI-Search. The searched database is UniProtKB/Swiss-Prot, a high quality resource of protein sequence which is manually annotated and reviewed. PSI-Search results in a set of distant members of the input sequence. There are several result files, of which two are used in the next steps of the workflow by extracting patterns using regular expressions with the ExtractPattern-SIB. The goal of this part of the workflow is to obtain the relevant information about the found sequences in the PSI-Search, which in the present case is especially their ID and the sequence of amino acids.

With the help of a RepeatLoop and the information extracted by the regular expressions, the input sequences for ClustalW are then assembled stepwise by

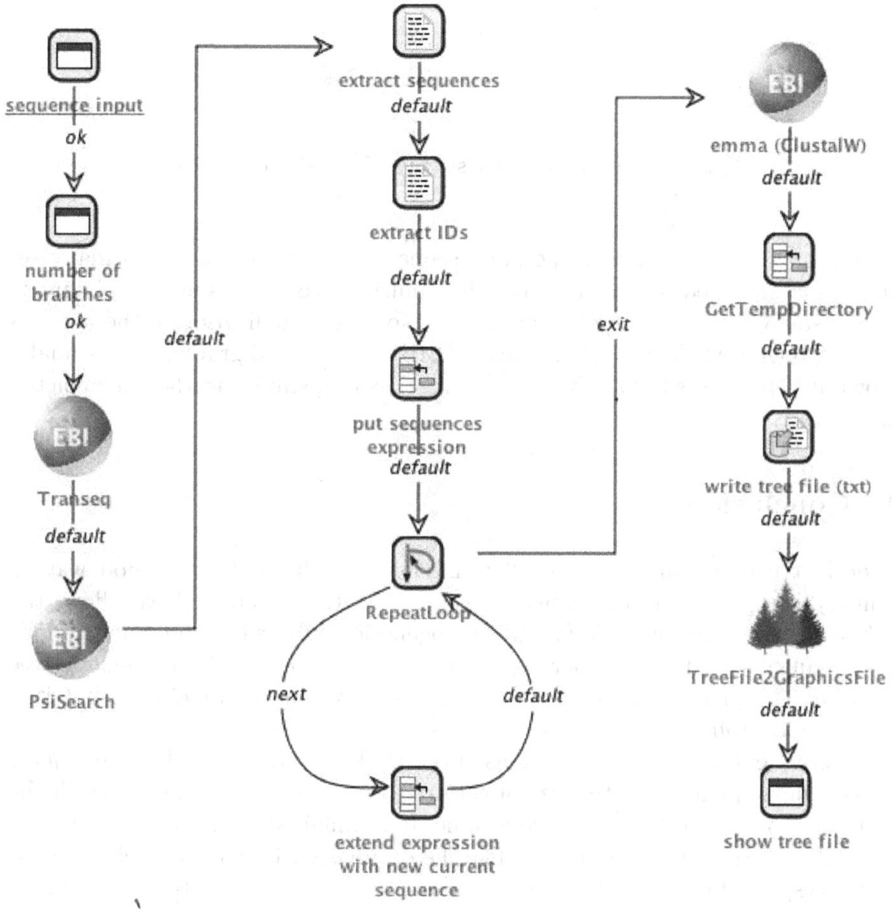

sequence input
ok
number of branches
ok
Transeq
default
PsiSearch
default
extract sequences
default
extract IDs
default
put sequences expression
default
RepeatLoop
next
default
extend expression with new current sequence
exit
emma (ClustalW)
default
GetTempDirectory
default
write tree file (txt)
default
TreeFile2GraphicsFile
default
show tree file

Fig. 4. The workflow

Sequence Input
Please input your sequence!
Abbrechen
OK

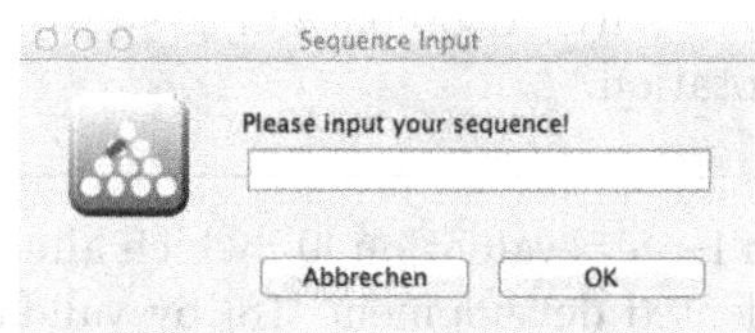

Fig. 5. Pop-up window for entering the input sequence

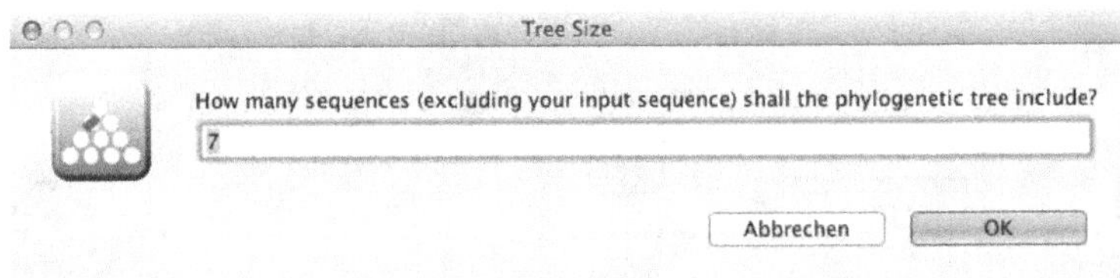

Fig. 6. Pop-up window for specifying the size of the tree

adding one ID and the corresponding sequence per iteration, for as many sequences as specified before. The resulting multiple sequence is used as the input for ClustalW2, whose output again is used for the visualization of the tree via the forester-based TreeFile2GraphicsFile SIB. The created graphics file is finally shown in a pop-up window (SIB ShowImageDialog), similar to the one depicted in Figure 2.

4 Conclusion

Overall it can be said that workflow modeling with jABC is a good way to simplify complex and time-consuming work. With the created workflow, the only things the user must do for the phylogenetic analysis is to provide an input DNA sequence and to consider how complex the constructed phylogenetic tree shall be. The more branches it has, the more information is included, but it is also more complicated to analyze it.

Different extensions and variations of the workflow are thinkable: The request for the put sequence and the size of the tree are not the only things, which the user could or should be able to determine. It is imaginable to give the users the possibility to set other parameters, like the database, where Psi-Search looks for sequences, or which clustering method is used for constructing the phylogenetic tree. Also there could be the possibility for the user to take a protein sequence as query. In this case there must be an additional question whether the input sequence is a DNA or a protein sequence.

Furthermore, this workflow represents only one little step of a possible, big study. Not only short sequences, but also whole chromosomes or genomes could be taken into account for constructing trees, so that they would result in species trees and not in gene trees only. Also continuing steps are possible, such as a gene prediction and annotation.

This article is part of a larger evaluation [9], which aimed at illustrating the power of simplicity-oriented development [18] by validating the claim that process modeling can indeed be handed over to the domain experts by providing them with a graphical modeling framework [26] that covers low-level details in a service-oriented fashion [20], integrates high-level modeling in the overall development process in a way that user-level models become directly executable [19,16], and supports ad-hoc adaptations and evolution [15,17].

The project described in this article can be characterized as follows:

- Scientific domain: bioinformatics
- Number of models: 1
- Number of hierarchy levels: 1
- Total number of SIBs: 14
- SIB libraries used (cf. [14]): common-sibs (10), ebi-sibs (3), forester-sibs (1)
- Service technologies used: SOAP web services

The bioinformatics part of this volume contains five other articles on workflow applications in this domain [23,3,24,25,28]. Further examples of workflow projects with he bioinformatics-specific incarnation of the jABC framework, called Bio-jETI [11], have been described, for example, in [10,12,6]. As shown in [11,13,8], bioinformatics is also a suitable field for the application of semantics-based (semi-) automatic workflow composition techniques (as provided by, e.g., [21]) to support the workflow design process.

References

1. Altschul, S., Madden, T., Schaffer, A., Zhang, J., Zhang, Z., Miller, W., Lipman, D.: Gapped blast and psi-blast: A new generation of protein database search programs. Nucleic Acids Res. 25(17), 3389–3402 (1997)
2. Altschul, S.F., Gish, W., Miller, W., Myers, E.W., Lipman, D.J.: Basic local alignment search tool. Journal of Molecular Biology 215(3), 403–410 (1990)
3. Blaese, L.: Data Mining for Unidentified Protein Sequences. In: Lamprecht, A.-L., Margaria, T. (eds.) Process Design for Natural Scientists. CCIS, vol. 500, pp. 73–87. Springer, Heidelberg (2014)
4. Chenna, R., Sugawara, H., Koike, T., Lopez, R., Gibson, T.J., Higgins, D.G., Thompson, J.D.: Multiple sequence alignment with the clustal series of programs. Nucleic Acids Res. 31(13), 3497–3500 (2003)
5. Delsuc, F., Brinkmann, H., Philippe, H.: Phylogenomics and the reconstruction of the tree of life. Nature Reviews Genetics 6, 361–375 (2005)
6. Ebert, B.E., Lamprecht, A.-L., Steffen, B., Blank, L.M.: Flux-P: Automating Metabolic Flux Analysis. Metabolites 2(4), 872–890 (2012)
7. Labarga, A., Valentin, F., Anderson, M., Lopez, R.: Web services at the European bioinformatics institute. Nucleic Acids Research 35(Web Server issue), W6–W11 (2007)
8. Lamprecht, A.-L.: User-Level Workflow Design. LNCS, vol. 8311. Springer, Heidelberg (2013)
9. Lamprecht, A.-L., Margaria, T.: Scientific Workflows and XMDD. In: Lamprecht, A.-L., Margaria, T. (eds.) Process Design for Natural Scientists. CCIS, vol. 500, pp. 1–13. Springer, Heidelberg (2014)

10. Lamprecht, A.-L., Margaria, T., Steffen, B.: Seven Variations of an Alignment Workflow - An Illustration of Agile Process Design and Management in Bio-jETI. In: Măndoiu, I., Wang, S.-L., Zelikovsky, A. (eds.) ISBRA 2008. LNCS (LNBI), vol. 4983, pp. 445–456. Springer, Heidelberg (2008)
11. Lamprecht, A.-L., Margaria, T., Steffen, B.: Bio-jETI: a framework for semantics-based service composition. BMC Bioinformatics 10(suppl. 10), S8 (2009)
12. Lamprecht, A.-L., Margaria, T., Steffen, B., Sczyrba, A., Hartmeier, S., Giegerich, R.: GeneFisher-P: variations of GeneFisher as processes in Bio-jETI. BMC Bioinformatics 9(suppl. 4), S13 (2008)
13. Lamprecht, A.-L., Naujokat, S., Margaria, T., Steffen, B.: Semantics-based composition of EMBOSS services. Journal of Biomedical Semantics 2(suppl. 1), S5 (2011)
14. Lamprecht, A.-L., Wickert, A.: The Course's SIB Libraries. In: Lamprecht, A.-L., Margaria, T. (eds.) Process Design for Natural Scientists. CCIS, vol. 500, pp. 30–44. Springer, Heidelberg (2014)
15. Margaria, T., Steffen, B.: Agile IT: Thinking in User-Centric Models. In: Margaria, T., Steffen, B. (eds.) ISoLA 2008. CCIS, vol. 17, pp. 490–502. Springer, Heidelberg (2009)
16. Margaria, T., Steffen, B.: Business Process Modelling in the jABC: The One-Thing-Approach. In: Cardoso, J., van der Aalst, W. (eds.) Handbook of Research on Business Process Modeling. IGI Global (2009)
17. Margaria, T., Steffen, B.: Continuous Model-Driven Engineering. IEEE Computer 42(10), 106–109 (2009)
18. Margaria, T., Steffen, B.: Simplicity as a Driver for Agile Innovation. Computer 43(6), 90–92 (2010)
19. Margaria, T., Steffen, B.: Service-Orientation: Conquering Complexity with XMDD. In: Hinchey, M., Coyle, L. (eds.) Conquering Complexity, pp. 217–236. Springer, London (2012)
20. Margaria, T., Steffen, B., Reitenspieß, M.: Service-Oriented Design: The Roots. In: Benatallah, B., Casati, F., Traverso, P. (eds.) ICSOC 2005. LNCS, vol. 3826, pp. 450–464. Springer, Heidelberg (2005)
21. Naujokat, S., Lamprecht, A.-L., Steffen, B.: Loose Programming with PROPHETS. In: de Lara, J., Zisman, A. (eds.) FASE 2012. LNCS, vol. 7212, pp. 94–98. Springer, Heidelberg (2012)
22. Nygaard, S., Zhang, G., Schiott, M.: The genome of the leaf-cutting ant acromyrmex echinatior suggests key adaptations to advanced social life and fungus farming. Genome Res. 21, 1339–1348 (2011)
23. Reso, J.: Protein Classification Workflow. In: Lamprecht, A.-L., Margaria, T. (eds.) Process Design for Natural Scientists. CCIS, vol. 500, pp. 65–72. Springer, Heidelberg (2014)
24. Schulze, G.: Workflow for Rapid Metagenome Analysis. In: Lamprecht, A.-L., Margaria, T. (eds.) Process Design for Natural Scientists. CCIS, vol. 500, pp. 88–100. Springer, Heidelberg (2014)
25. Schtt, C.: Identification of Differentially Expressed Genes. In: Lamprecht, A.-L., Margaria, T. (eds.) Process Design for Natural Scientists. CCIS, vol. 500, pp. 127–139. Springer, Heidelberg (2014)
26. Steffen, B., Margaria, T., Nagel, R., Jörges, S., Kubczak, C.: Model-Driven Development with the jABC. In: Bin, E., Ziv, A., Ur, S. (eds.) HVC 2006. LNCS, vol. 4383, pp. 92–108. Springer, Heidelberg (2007)

27. Thompson, J.D., Higgins, D.G., Gibson, T.J.: CLUSTAL W: improving the sensitivity of progressive multiple sequence alignment through sequence weighting, position-specific gap penalties and weight matrix choice. Nucleic Acids Research 22(22), 4673–4680 (1994)
28. Vierheller, J.: Exploratory Data Analysis. In: Lamprecht, A.-L., Margaria, T. (eds.) Process Design for Natural Scientists. CCIS, vol. 500, pp. 110–126. Springer, Heidelberg (2014)
29. Zmasek, C.M.: forester | software libraries for evolutionary biology and comparative genomics research (November 2012), `http://www.phylosoft.org/forester/` (online; last accessed December 06, 2012)
30. Zmasek, C.M., Eddy, S.R.: ATV: display and manipulation of annotated phylogenetic trees. Bioinformatics 17(4), 383–384 (2001)

Exploratory Data Analysis

Janine Vierheller

Potsdam University, Potsdam, D-14482, Germany
vierhell@uni-potsdam.de

Abstract. In bioinformatics the term exploratory data analysis refers to different methods to get an overview of large biological data sets. Hence, it helps to create a framework for further analysis and hypothesis testing. The workflow facilitates this first important step of the data analysis created by high-throughput technologies. The results are different plots showing the structure of the measurements. The goal of the workflow is the automatization of the exploratory data analysis, but also the flexibility should be guaranteed. The basic tool is the free software R.

Keywords: bioinformatics, data exploration, high-throughput technologies, data sets, heatmap, principal components analysis, hierarchical clustering.

1 Introduction

1.1 Workflow Scenario

Biological systems have a high complexity which can be measured with high-troughput technology targeting the genome, transcriptome and metabolome. These different levels of a living creature are also referred to as 'omics'. The data sets created by omics technologies are usually large and it is difficult to get any information by taking only a look at the measurements. In bioinformatics there are different methods to enable an insight into the structure of the data sets. These methods are known under the name exploratory data analysis and allow a fast visual inspection.

The workflow enables the user to use three well-known methods to investigate either an own data set or a new data set. It is possible to perform all three methods serially or only single methods in an arbitrary order. The results from the analysis will be saved in your working directory and can be useful for the development of the further analysis.

1.2 Purpose

The exploratory data analysis of a data set can become a tedious manual task, because there are many different methods with a lot of parameters leading to a lot of combinations and possibilities. If there is more than one data set, all steps have to be repeated. But already one data set can lead to several reruns, because

A.-L. Lamprecht et al. (Eds.): Process Design for Natural Scientists, CCIS 500, pp. 110–126, 2014.
DOI: 10.1007/978-3-662-45006-2_9

the right combination of methods and parameters to get the best possible insight of the underlying structure of the data has to be found. The workflow allows to do the analysis in an automated manner, but also enables the user to use only some of the methods. This makes the analysis flexible and allows the user to decide how to go on after each step. The results are different plots of the data set which can be inspected directly in the workflow and are also saved for later usage.

2 Service Analysis

2.1 Services

The workflow uses R which is a free software environment for statistical computing and graphics [4]. This has to be downloaded and installed. There are already many functions available in R and further functions can often be included by installing packages and loading libraries. Furthermore, it is possible to write ones own functions. The software can be started from the command line by typing 'R'. Afterwards the R prompt appears and commands can be used to start calculations. It is possible to load data, to write text to files and to create plots and save them. These functions are necessary for the workflow.

In addition the GEOquery package is used, which is an interface to Gene Expression Omnibus (GEO) at the NCBI (National Center of Biotechnology Information) [2]. This is a public functional genomics data repository where you can get transcriptomics data.

2.2 Implementation

The workflow was created and tested on a Linux operating system (Fedora 12), hence the workflow will probably not work on other operating systems. It would be possible to use it on other systems, if the shell-scripts were changed.

It was not necessary to implement new SIBs. The Common-SIBs which are already given enable one to have access to the input data, use R and to show the results. If you use your own data set, you can access it via the ShowFileChooser-SIB. The user's chosen variables can be inserted with the ShowInputDialog-SIB and the created plots are shown with the ShowImageDialog-SIB. R-scripts were written to create the plots in an automated way. Unfortunately, the R-scripts can not directly be started with the ExecuteCommand-SIB. Hence, there were shell-scripts written which were executed by the ExecuteCommand-SIB and start the R-scripts. Thus for each R-script exists a corresponding shell-script with the same name, but with the file extension .sh. All necessary files have to be in the same directory as the workflow.

The R-scripts need some libraries which have to be installed beforehand. The *lattice* package can be installed within R by typing: install.packages("lattice"). Moreover, BioConductor, the package *bioLite* and the GEO libraries have to be downloaded by typing the following in R:

```
source("http://bioconductor.org/biocLite.R")
biocLite()
biocLite("GEOquery")
```

This can take a while, but it has to be done only once. Administrator privileges and Internet are necessary to install the packages. If you want to use a new data set for the workflow it will be downloaded from a FTP server. The download time depends on the size of the files. It might be important to have the R-package *Rcurl* installed to provide a connection to the FTP server. Perhaps the download will not be provided, if the host resolutions does not work.

R saves all created files and plots automatically within the directory, where it was started, hence it is by default the jABC folder. If you wish to save them somewhere else, you have to specify the path and the output names appropriately.

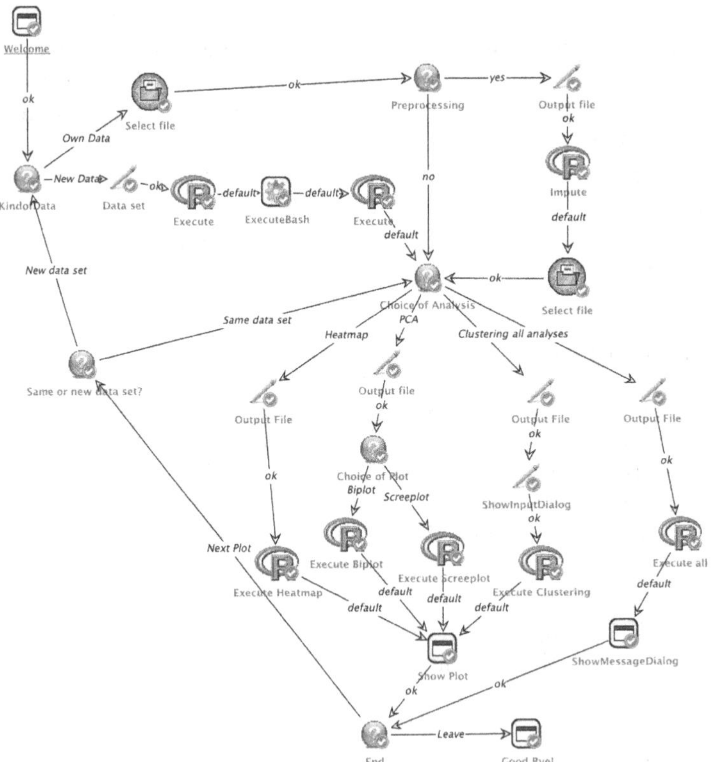

Fig. 1. The workflow

3 Workflow Realization

The workflow guides you from the selection of the input data to the choice of the analysis until one or more plots are created. Then you can rerun the process or quit. The user has only to click several times and to type the desired names of the files.

3.1 Input

The workflow starts with the question which data you want to use for your analysis. You can choose between your own data set and a new microarray data set. Your own data has to fulfill some criteria. It has to be already in the same directory as your workflow, has to be a txt-file and should be in the structure of a table or matrix. The new microarray data set will be downloaded to your directory, where the workflow is located.

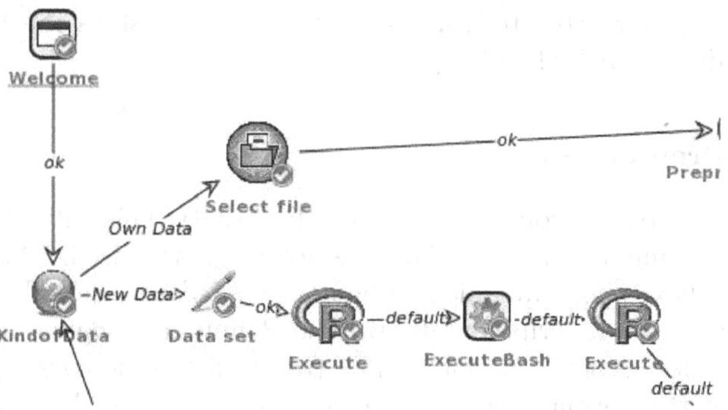

Fig. 2. Workflow: data set

3.2 Own Data

If you choose to use your own data, you can select it via the ShowFileChooser-SIB. You have to click through the directory levels to get to the working directory. The name of the selected file will be saved in the variable *selectedFile* and is used as input for later R-scripts. The idea is to use files deriving from high-throughput technologies, which are often large data sets. But technically every matrix or dataframe saved in a txt-file would yield results. There is already an example data set which can be used to demonstrate the function of the workflow. The file is called Blood.txt and contains measurements of blood samples of 16 volunteers from the Slovenian healthy study (as part of the SYSTHER project [6,10]). The importance of the blood was already highlighted by Huzarewich, Siemens and Booth [11]: The blood circulates throughout the whole body and contains a lot of metabolites which can be used as biomarkers. The complexity of the composition of the blood and the fact that it contains information about the whole body and not one tissue in particular, makes it one of the most difficult tissues to analyze using omic technologies. The data set is the complete blood count which is a screening test to observe diseases like anemia [1].

3.3 New Data

If you choose to use a new data set, you have to specify a GEO-number of a microarray-experiment. An example is already given as initial value in the ShowInputDialog-SIB: GSE20986. Microarray measurements increase in reliability, reproducibility and accuracy [8] and are used increasingly. In this experiment iris, retina and choroidal microvascular endothelial cells were isolated from donor eyes. The GEO Platform is GPL570 – the GEO short code for the Affymetrix Human Genome U133 Plus 2.0 Array, a commonly used microarray chip for human transcriptome studies [31]. First of all the raw data are acquired directly from GEO and are saved in a new directory. The .tar-file is a compressed archive of the CEL files (the Affymetrix native file format) which are decompressed in R. Afterwards, the data are deposited using the GC-RMA algorithm, loaded in R, normalized and written to a new txt-file. For these steps the R-scripts are MA.R, writedata.R and MA2.R.

3.4 Data Preprocessing

It is possible to prepare your own data set (Figure 3). This will be necessary, if some values are missing and the data are not yet normalized. This step is not necessary and hence not available for the downloaded data set. The preprocessing is done with the R-script Impute.R. The R function *impute* does not exist anymore, therefore a new function was written to fill in the missing values with the mean. For the normalization the function *scale* is used. You have to select the name of the file which will be created, the default name is Datanorm.txt. After the preparation you have to select the new file, though the file name will be

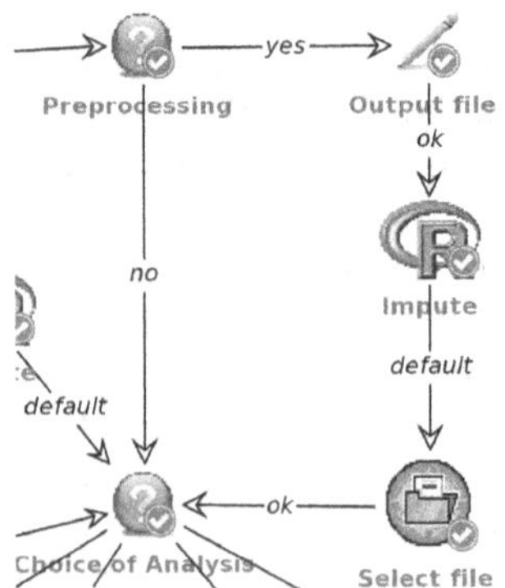

Fig. 3. Workflow: Preprocessing

saved in the variable *selectedFile*. The preparation will lead to different results, hence maybe it will be necessary to take a look at the plots with raw data and compare them with the imputed and normalized data.

3.5 Methods

After the loading and the preparation of the data file, you can decide which analysis you would like to perform. The exploratory data analysis is used to get an overview of the underlying structure of the data. You can select in the ShowBranchingDialog between "Heatmap","PCA","Clustering" and "all analyses". The heatmaps can reveal extreme variables and the variance of the measurements. The hierarchical clustering groups samples or variables together, because of their similarities and uncovers connections among them. The principal component analysis demonstrate the main directions of the measurements.

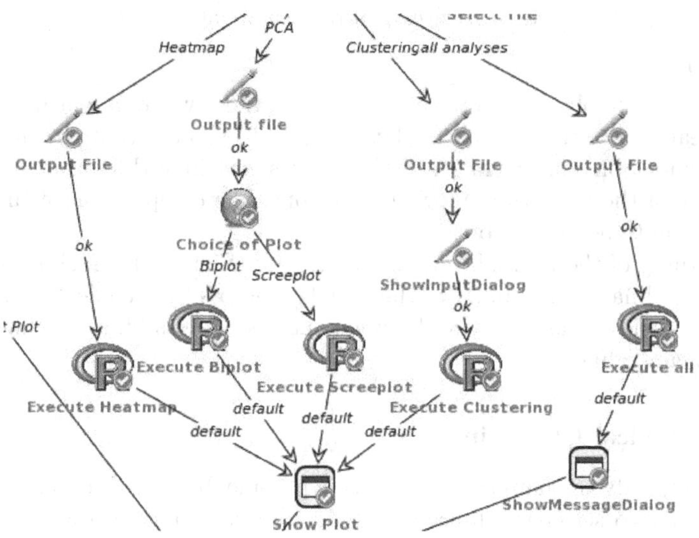

Fig. 4. Workflow: choice of analysis

3.6 Heatmap

You have to specify the name of the png-file which will be created afterwards via the ShowInputDialog-SIB by default it is heatmap. The heatmap is created using the R function *levelplot* of the package **lattice**, the corresponding script is called heatmap.R. The plot will be automatically saved under the specified name. A heatmap is a graphical method assigning each value within a table to a color. The colors represent the level of the measurements [3]. Thereby it is possible to visually show unusual high or low values or even patterns.

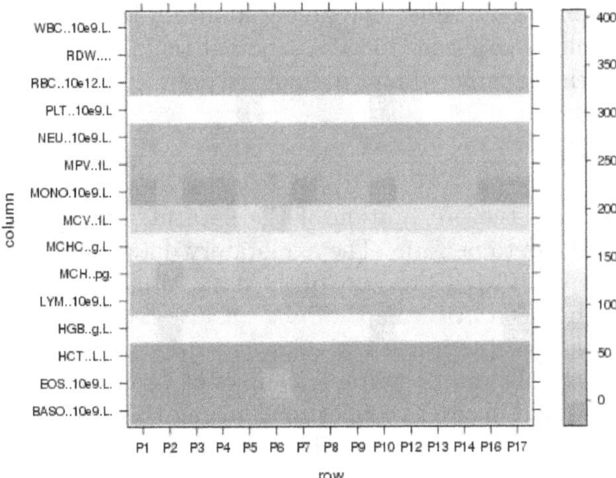

Fig. 5. Heatmap of raw blood data

Heatmaps of the blood data were created with the rows representing the people. The heatmap of the raw blood data (Figure 5) showed that the mean corpuscular hemoglobin concentration (MCHC) was very high (blue color) whereas the majority of the values were low (pink color). The composition of the blood seems to be quite heterogeneous.

The heatmap of the normalized blood variables (Figure 6) can show whether there is a coordinated variability of the variables across the people. It can reveal low or high values. The deviation between the people was high and fluctuated around a mean value.

3.7 Hierarchical Clustering

You have to specify the name of the resulting png-file, by default it is hclust.png. Then you have to select the linkage method, the default is average. The most common used methods are "average", "single" and "complete", but also "ward", "mcquitty", "median" or "centroid" would be possible. Both selections are done by the ShowInputDialog-SIB. If the method is not specified or because of a typo not recognizable, the default method "complete" will be used. The cluster is created with the R functions *dist* and *hclust*, the corresponding script is hclust.R.

The procedure of the hierarchical clustering was already described in [32]: It starts with the calculation of a proximity matrix D, therefore the pairwise dissimilarities ($D_{ii'}$) between the two observations (i, i') were calculated using for example the Euclidean distance.

$$d_j(x_{ij}, x_{i'j}) = (x_{ij} - x_{i'j})^2 \tag{1}$$

The index j represent the number of the pairwise dissimilarities which are then combined to one dissimilarity matrix. The objects were grouped together

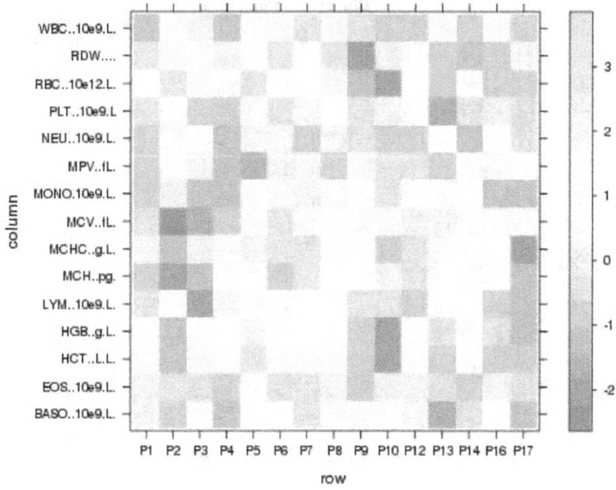

Fig. 6. Heatmap of normalized blood data

according to their distances, where a small distance between two objects represents their similarity. The three most common methods to group the objects are Single linkage (SL), Complete linkage (CL) and Average linkage (AL). The distance of every pair is computed and the methods join the objects together according to their lowest (SL), highest (CL) or average distance (AL). For the hierarchical clustering it is not necessary to define the number of clusters beforehand.

The plot (Figure 7) shows the hierarchical clustering of the persons. Members of one group have similar blood values.

The other both common linkage methods (Figures 8, 9) represent almost the same result, only the vizualization is slightly different.

3.8 Principal Component Analysis (PCA)

Via the ShowInputDialog-SIB you have to specify the output name, by default it is pca.png. Afterwards, you have to decide whether you want the result represented in a biplot or a screeplot via the ShowBranchingDialog-SIB. For the PCA the R function *princomp* was used as well as the functions *biplot* or *screeplot*. The corresponding R-scripts are biplot.R and screeplot.R.

Principal component analysis is a mathematical method for dimension reduction and was described in [32]: A data set is represented by a matrix X in which the n rows are the samples and the p columns are the variables. Each variable of a data set represents one dimension (axis) of the space. The interpretation of high dimensional data sets is difficult or even impossible. Using an orthogonal transformation a new coordinate system can be created with uncorrelated variables which are the principal components (PC) and the first one has the highest variance among all linear combinations. The first few principal components carry

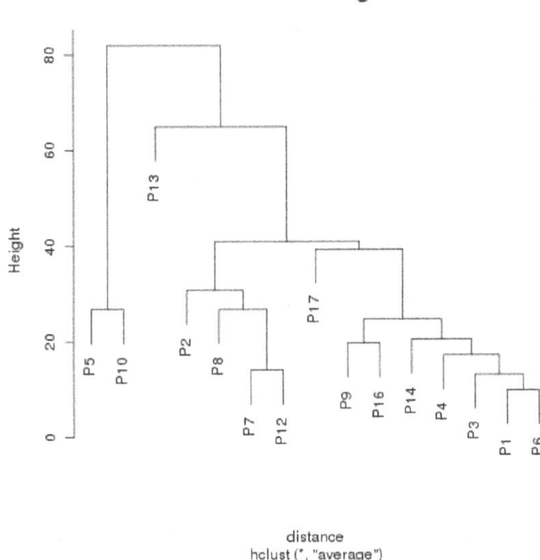

Fig. 7. Hierarchical clustering (Average Linkage)

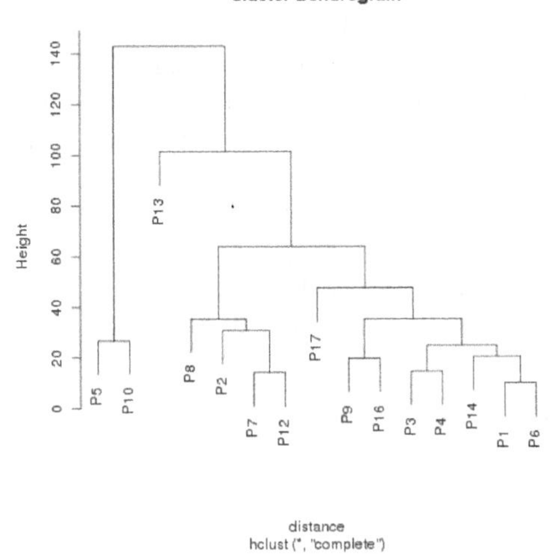

Fig. 8. Hierarchical clustering (Complete Linkage)

the most of the information and thus sometimes some principal components can be left out without great information loss if the variance is small. This leads to a coordinate system of smaller dimension and the interpretation is easier. PCA reveals relationships between the variables or objects.

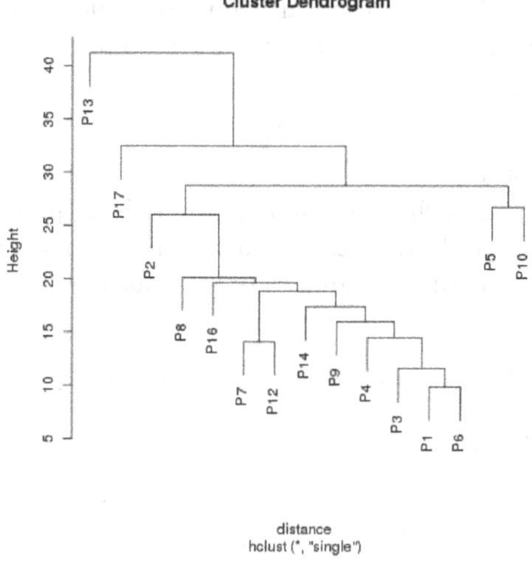

Fig. 9. Hierarchical clustering (Single Linkage)

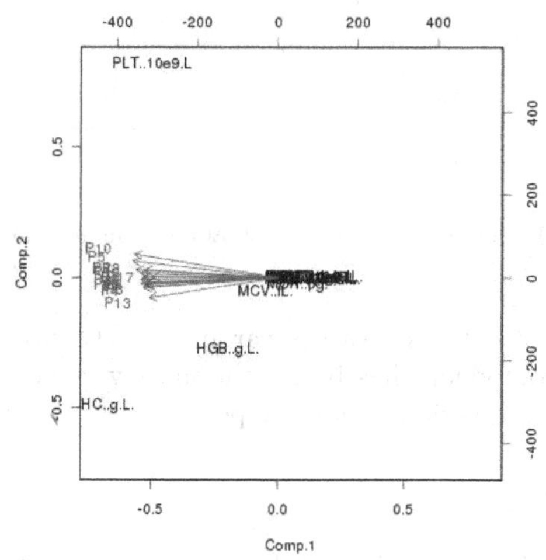

Fig. 10. Biplot of the principal component analysis

Biplot. The results of the method PCA can be represented in a biplot (R function *biplot*). Two scatterplots of the axis loadings of the first two principal components are combined in one plot. A scatterplot plots objects given by their Cartesian coordinates to reveal relationships between objects [5]. The samples are represented as points and the variables as vectors which represent their contribution to the principal axis [32].

In the biplot (Figure 10) the blood variables are represented by the labels and the persons are indicated by arrows. Almost all blood variables where arranged in one small area, except for four variables. The biplot demonstrates the wide range of the variables, because they are separated along the direction of the first principal component. Whereas the variance among the people was low in comparison to the variables.

Screeplot. The other representation is a screeplot which plots the variances against the number of the principal component. This helps to decide how many principal components should be considered in further analysis and which components can be left out without high loss of information.

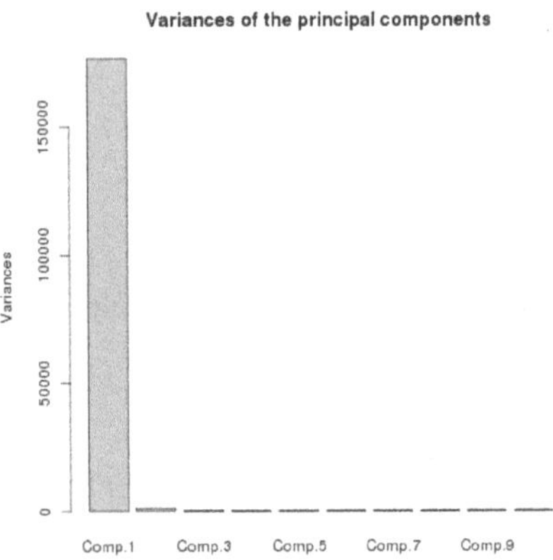

Fig. 11. Screeplot of the principal component analysis

The screeplot (Figure 11) shows the variance of the principal components. The first principal component has by far the most variance. Hence, the blood variables are much more variable than the persons.

3.9 Image

The described methods yield a plot which is saved as a png-file. In the workflow the resulting plot is shown via the ShowImageDialog-SIB. The window has to be closed, otherwise you will have many open windows.

3.10 All Analyses

Furthermore it is possible to do all three analyses in row. In this case you only have to select the linkage method for the hierarchical clustering, by default it is again average. The R-script allanalyses.R will perform hierarchical clustering with the specified linkage method, create a heatmap, perform the principal component analysis and create a biplot and a screeplot.

The plots are automatically saved with the names 1hclust.png, 2heatmap.png, 3biplot.png and 4screeplot.png. The naming facilitates to recover the files, but

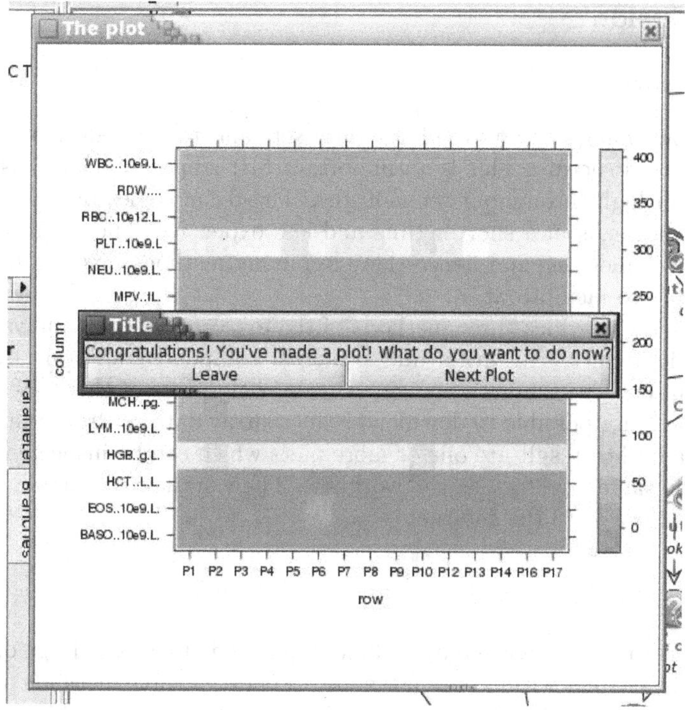

Fig. 12. Workflow: ShowImageDialog-SIB

it is necessary to rename them afterwards, otherwise they will be overwritten during the next run of "all analyses". The plots will not be shown within the workflow, hence you have to take a look at them outside of the workflow.

3.11 Rerun

After the analysis you can decide to leave the workflow ("Leave") or rerun it ("Next plot") (Figure 12). You can select a whole new data set to create a plot or you use the same file again to do another analysis, but then it will not be asked for preprocessing again (Figure 13).

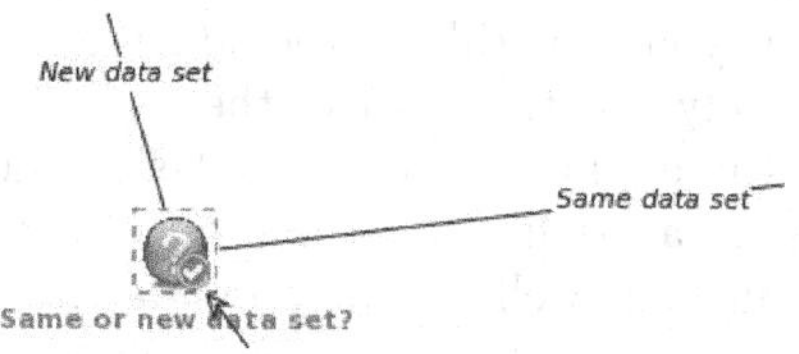

Fig. 13. Workflow: New or old data set?

4 Conclusion

4.1 Summary

The workflow enables to analyze large data sets and to get a deeper insight of the underlying structure. This is an important first step in the analysis of data deriving from high-throughput technologies. The technologies produce increasingly large data sets in a shorter time and less expensive. The management of such data is challenging and hence there are many methods investigated in the bioinformatics to facilitate it.

The workflow provides three methods of the exploratory data analysis: heatmap, hierarchical clustering and principal component analysis. All these methods can be done on one data set, but also only parts of them. Beside own data sets, it is also possible to download a microarray data set from the Internet and analyze it. The result are one or more plots which can be inspected and are stored in the same directory as the workflow. The workflow requires R, some R packages and access to the Internet.

4.2 Discussion

The goal was to facilitate the tedious first step of the analysis of large data sets. The workflow enables within only few steps to perform three methods on a data set and save the results in four png-files. Furthermore, it is possible to do only single methods. The created plot is shown directly in the workflow, hence you can decide whether the result is satisfying or any other analysis would be of interest. Even if the workflow is highly automated, it is still flexible. You can select the linkage method for the hierarchical clustering and the output names can be chosen, too.

If you do these analyses manually it takes a while and a lot of steps have to be repeated. This can become an annoying but still necessary procedure. The workflow accelerates the analysis, because you only have to click a few times and type the names of the output files or you use just the given default names. You can search in your directories for the input file, decide what analysis you prefer and you will see the result immediately. Any further analysis on the same data set will take even less time. If you would do this in R by yourself, you would have to know the exact name and the location of your own input file, type all necessary commands and save the plot. Using the workflow you do not have to know much about R, but you can still use the advantages of R.

The workflow shows only one tiny part of the possibilities of R and provide only three methods of the explorative data analysis. The own input data has to be already in format of a txt-file and the form of a table or a matrix. You can load other formats in R as well and manipulate them. This would have to be done before the start of the workflow. If you want for example some rows or columns of your data to be excluded or the whole matrix transformed, which is easily possible in R, you have to do it again apart from the workflow. You are restricted to use files in the way they are prepared. If you notice within the workflow that some changes in the data would be of interest, you have to leave the workflow and manipulate the data before you restart the workflow.

The limited three methods for the analysis are done in a standardized way. You are not able to change any parameter for the methods except the linkages for hierarchical clustering. Moreover, the labels or the colors in the plots can not be changed dynamically. Only changes in the R- and shell-scripts will provide further flexibility, but also more complexity.

The implementation of the workflow with jABC was not always intuitive, because you start with the functions you already know, which are some CommonSIBs. If you search for a specific SIB of which you think it might exists, you have to have a clear idea how this could be named. This problem will be solved in the future automatically, because the documentation and number of problem reports will increase when jABC becomes more known. The ShowFileChooser loads only the name of the file and not the data themselves. This happens not until the R scripts are started. The file has to be in the same directory as the workflow, because only the name of the file is assigned to the parameter and not the whole path. It will be necessary to change the subsequent read of the parameters which would improve the workflow.

Having all the input files, R- and shell-scripts and the created output files in the same directory will lead to complexity which should be avoided, for example by moving the plots to a new directory. The management of the output files is easily possible by assigning not only the names of the output files, but also the absolute or relative path. The workflow could be improved if more possibilities were included for creating new directories and assigning paths.

The main SIB of this workflow is the ExecuteCommand-SIB, because it starts all R-scripts. Usually, you can start a R-script on the command line, hence it was expected to do it in a similar way in the ExecuteCommand-SIB, but it did not work. It is necessary to write a shell-script and to pass the parameters so that then the actual R-script will be started on the command line. Thus, you have to write for each R-script a corresponding shell-script. Although the shell-scripts are small, the required files are doubled. Each further extension will consists of at least two files more. Thus the main usage of the ExecuteCommand-SIB is not recommended and it would be better to integrate the scripts on a jETI server and to create platform-independent SIBs.

The ShowInputDialog-SIB enables to assign one parameter, but for the "all analyses" part it would be practical to assign four parameters: the four names of the output files. Then it would not be necessary to give default names and rename the files afterwards. Furthermore, the created four plots are not shown in the workflow, because using the ShowImage-SIB four time in a row does not seem acceptable. An idea is to create only one pdf with all four plots, but it is not always desired to have only one file. It would be possible to integrate it as a further choice.

4.3 Outlook

Although the workflow enables to analyze data in an easier way, it is still possible to extend methods and to improve the choice of parameters and to achieve a better structure of the files. You could add more methods to the workflow by writing more R-scripts. These could be not only methods from the explorative data analysis, but also methods from machine learning, regression analysis and so on. The software R and its packages provide a huge amount of possibilities. It would be an idea to write one universal shell-script and to pass the name of the R-script as a parameter. This would reduce the number of required files. As described the workflow facilitates only the first major part of the analysis of large data sets, of course the workflow could be extended by any subsequent method.

This article is part of a larger evaluation [13], which aimed at illustrating the power of simplicity-oriented development [23] by validating the claim that process modeling can indeed be handed over to the domain experts by providing them with a graphical modeling framework [30] that covers low-level details in a service-oriented fashion [25], integrates high-level modeling in the overall development process in a way that user-level models become directly executable [24,21], and supports ad-hoc adaptations and evolution [20,22].

The project described in this article can be characterized as follows:

- Scientific domain: bioinformatics
- Number of models: 1
- Number of hierarchy levels: 1
- Total number of SIBs: 28
- SIB libraries used (cf. [18]): common-sibs
- Service technologies used: R scripts

The bioinformatics part of this volume contains five other articles on workflow applications in this domain [27,7,19,28,29]. Further examples of workflow projects with he bioinformatics-specific incarnation of the jABC framework, called Bio-jETI [15], have been described, for example, in [14,16,9]. As shown in [15,17,12], bioinformatics is also a suitable field for the application of semantics-based (semi-) automatic workflow composition techniques (as provided by, e.g., [26]) to support the workflow design process.

References

1. Complete Blood Count, `http://www.labtestsonline.org/understanding/analytes/cbc/test.html` (last accessed October 2, 2012)
2. Gene Expression Omnibus, `http://www.ncbi.nlm.nih.gov/geo` (last accessed October 2, 2012)

3. R Documentation: Levelplot, http://stat.ethz.ch/R-manual/R-devel/library/lattice/html/levelplot.html (last accessed October 2, 2012)
4. R-project, http://www.r-project.org (last accessed October 2, 2012)
5. Scatterplot, http://www.stat.yale.edu/Courses/1997-98/101/scatter.htm (last accessed October 2, 2012)
6. SYSTHER project, http://systher.biologie.hu-berlin.de (last accessed October 2, 2012)
7. Blaese, L.: Data Mining for Unidentified Protein Sequences. In: Lamprecht, A.-L., Margaria, T. (eds.) Process Design for Natural Scientists. CCIS, vol. 500, pp. 73–87. Springer, Heidelberg (2014)
8. Cahan, P., Rovegno, F., Mooney, D., Newman, J.C., Laurent III, S., McCaffrey, T.A., McCaffrey, T.A.: Meta-Analysis of Microarray Results: Challenges, Opportunities, and Recommendations for Standardization, NIH-PA Author Manuscript (2007)
9. Ebert, B.E., Lamprecht, A.-L., Steffen, B., Blank, L.M.: Flux-P: Automating Metabolic Flux Analysis. Metabolites 2(4), 872–890 (2012)
10. Gruden, K., Hren, M., Herman, A., Blejec, A., Albrecht, T., Selbig, J., Bauer, C., Schuchardt, J., Or-Guil, M., Zupani, K., Svajger, U., Tabuc, B., Ihan, A., Kopitar, A., Ravnikar, M., Knezevic, M., Rozman, P., Jeras, M.: Large scale omics assessment of physiological variation in constituents of human blood periodically taken from a group of healthy volunteers (in preparation)
11. Huzarewich, R.L.C.H., Siemens, C.G., Both, S.A.: Application of omics to Prion Biomarker Discovery. Journal of Biomedicine and Biotechnology (2010)
12. Lamprecht, A.-L.: User-Level Workflow Design. LNCS, vol. 8311, pp. 1–202. Springer, Heidelberg (2013)
13. Lamprecht, A.-L., Margaria, T.: Scientific Workflows and XMDD. In: Lamprecht, A.-L., Margaria, T. (eds.) Process Design for Natural Scientists. CCIS, vol. 500, pp. 1–13. Springer, Heidelberg (2014)
14. Lamprecht, A.-L., Margaria, T., Steffen, B.: Seven variations of an alignment workflow - an illustration of agile process design and management in bio-jETI. In: Măndoiu, I., Wang, S.-L., Zelikovsky, A. (eds.) ISBRA 2008. LNCS (LNBI), vol. 4983, pp. 445–456. Springer, Heidelberg (2008)
15. Lamprecht, A.-L., Margaria, T., Steffen, B.: Bio-jETI: a framework for semantics-based service composition. BMC Bioinformatics 10(Suppl 10), S8 (2009)
16. Lamprecht, A.-L., Margaria, T., Steffen, B., Sczyrba, A., Hartmeier, S., Giegerich, R.: GeneFisher-P: variations of GeneFisher as processes in Bio-jETI. BMC Bioinformatics 9(Suppl 4), S13 (2008)
17. Lamprecht, A.-L., Naujokat, S., Margaria, T., Steffen, B.: Semantics-based composition of EMBOSS services. Journal of Biomedical Semantics 2(Suppl 1), S5 (2011)
18. Lamprecht, A.-L., Wickert, A.: The Course's SIB Libraries. In: Lamprecht, A.-L., Margaria, T. (eds.) Process Design for Natural Scientists. CCIS, vol. 500, pp. 30–44. Springer, Heidelberg (2014)
19. Lis, M.: Constructing a Phylogenetic Tree. In: Lamprecht, A.-L., Margaria, T. (eds.) Process Design for Natural Scientists. CCIS, vol. 500, pp. 101–109. Springer, Heidelberg (2014)
20. Margaria, T., Steffen, B.: Agile IT: Thinking in User-Centric Models. In: Margaria, T., Steffen, B. (eds.) Leveraging Applications of Formal Methods, Verification and Validation. CCIS, vol. 17, pp. 490–502. Springer, Heidelberg (2009)
21. Margaria, T., Steffen, B.: Business Process Modelling in the jABC: The One-Thing-Approach. In: Cardoso, J., van der Aalst, W. (eds.) Handbook of Research on Business Process Modeling, IGI Global (2009)

22. Margaria, T., Steffen, B.: Continuous Model-Driven Engineering. IEEE Computer 42(10), 106–109 (2009)
23. Margaria, T., Steffen, B.: Simplicity as a Driver for Agile Innovation. Computer 43(6), 90–92 (2010)
24. Margaria, T., Steffen, B.: Service-Orientation: Conquering Complexity with XMDD. In: Hinchey, M., Coyle, L. (eds.) Conquering Complexity, pp. 217–236. Springer, Heidelberg (2012)
25. Margaria, T., Steffen, B., Reitenspiess, M.: Service-oriented design: The roots. In: Benatallah, B., Casati, F., Traverso, P. (eds.) ICSOC 2005. LNCS, vol. 3826, pp. 450–464. Springer, Heidelberg (2005)
26. Naujokat, S., Lamprecht, A.-L., Steffen, B.: Loose Programming with PROPHETS. In: de Lara, J., Zisman, A. (eds.) Fundamental Approaches to Software Engineering. LNCS, vol. 7212, pp. 94–98. Springer, Heidelberg (2012)
27. Reso, J.: Protein Classification Workflow. In: Lamprecht, A.-L., Margaria, T. (eds.) Process Design for Natural Scientists. CCIS, vol. 500, pp. 65–72. Springer, Heidelberg (2014)
28. Schulze, G.: Workflow for Rapid Metagenome Analysis. In: Lamprecht, A.-L., Margaria, T. (eds.) Process Design for Natural Scientists. CCIS, vol. 500, pp. 88–100. Springer, Heidelberg (2014)
29. Schütt, C.: Identification of Differentially Expressed Genes. In: Lamprecht, A.-L., Margaria, T. (eds.) Process Design for Natural Scientists. CCIS, vol. 500, pp. 127–139. Springer, Heidelberg (2014)
30. Steffen, B., Margaria, T., Nagel, R., Jörges, S., Kubczak, C.: Model-driven development with the jABC. In: Bin, E., Ziv, A., Ur, S. (eds.) HVC 2006. LNCS, vol. 4383, pp. 92–108. Springer, Heidelberg (2007)
31. Swan, D.: Analysing micorarray data in Bioconductor, `http://bioinformatics.knowledgeblog.org/2011/06/20/analysing-microarray-data-in-bioconductor` (last accessed October 2, 2012)
32. Trevor Hastie, R.T., Friedman, J.: The elements of Statistical Learning: Data Mining, Inference, and Prediction, 2nd edn. Springer (2009)

Identification of Differentially Expressed Genes

Christine Schütt

Potsdam University, Potsdam, D-14482, Germany
cschuett@uni-potsdam.de

Abstract. With the jABC it is possible to realize workflows for numerous questions in different fields. The goal of this project was to create a workflow for the identification of differentially expressed genes. This is of special interest in biology, for it gives the opportunity to get a better insight in cellular changes due to exogenous stress, diseases and so on. With the knowledge that can be derived from the differentially expressed genes in diseased tissues, it becomes possible to find new targets for treatment.

Keywords: bioinformatics, gene expression, differentially expressed genes, disease, stress response.

1 Introduction: Workflow Scenario

The basis of every living being are genes. These are parts of the DNA which encodes proteins or other functional units and are needed to maintain every cell of an organism and to transmit its hereditary information. All organisms have many genes corresponding to various biological characteristics such as eye color or number of petals, which are immediately visible, but also others which are not, such as blood type, increased risk for specific diseases, or the thousands of basic biochemical processes that comprise life. Moreover damages / changes in genes or in the expression of genes can lead to defects or diseases, which can but do not need to be lethal. Changes in the expression of genes mean that these sections of the DNA are not transcribed to RNA in the normal amount. Either it is transcribed more often or less. This could lead to a different number of proteins or the like.

Generally spoken the goal of this project is to identify those genes which are differentially expressed under a certain condition. Through high throughput sequencing and screening techniques it is possible to simultaneously examine a tissue for the expression of all known genes from the organism. Therefore certain sequences are labeled on two-dimensional arrays, the so called microarrays or chips. The sequences are 25 bases long oligonucleotides and each is called a probe set. They are specific for one gene but for each gene multiple probe sets exist. So that one gene can bind up to eleven different probe sets on different positions of the chip. This ensures that a gene can be detected even if a probe set is defective or if a whole region of the chip is damaged. Various types of arrays are available on the market, which are specific for different species. One example is the whole human genome expression array provided by Affymetrix which

A.-L. Lamprecht et al. (Eds.): Process Design for Natural Scientists, CCIS 500, pp. 127–139, 2014.
DOI: 10.1007/978-3-662-45006-2_10

contains 54675 probe sets [23]. The results from several of such experiments are stored in the public database ArrayExpress at the European Bioinformatics Institute (EBI) server (http://www.ebi.ac.uk/arrayexpress/) in form of CEL files. These files contain the raw expression data from experiments. Files of interest can be downloaded in this format for further studies.

In order to find differentially expressed genes one has to search ArrayExpress for experiments with tissues of interest under a control condition and for the same tissue under a different condition which should be examined (diseased or stressed). The expression data from the different experiments are afterwards analyzed for genes that are stronger or weaker represented on the chips for the test condition. These genes are the differentially expressed genes. Those which are stronger represented under the test condition are up-regulated in comparison to the control condition and those which are weaker represented are down-regulated.

With the chosen expression data one has to do several steps until one can identify the differentially expressed genes. A first major step is to do a log 2 transformation and to normalize the data from the different arrays to compensate differences between the conditions that just result from different experimental conditions and to see the systematic biological differences more clearly.[26] For the normalization different approaches are possible, such as mean, median or quantile normalization. Here in this project the quantile normalization will be used. The next step is to find the probe sets that are expressed on the chips at all. Therefore all probe sets are filtered out whose expression values lay below a certain threshold, which can be determined by the first quantile. Then, to identify the differentially expressed genes, two more conditions had to be fulfilled by the genes. One will be covered with the help of Students t-test. This test examines whether the different expression values between the two groups (test and control condition) are random or significant[18]. Due to the large amount of probe sets on a chip and with that due to the larger number of hypothesis that have to be tested simultaneously, a multiple testing procedure must be used. But the problem of this test method is that the chance of getting false positive results increases. That is why it is necessary to adjust for this with special correction methods, e. g. Bonferroni, Benjamini and Hochberg, Holm, etc. [22]. In this implementation of the project the Benjamini and Hochberg procedure will be the default setting. So the first of the two condition which has to be fulfilled is that the probe set has a p-value less or equal to a critical value (typically 0.05 or 0.01). The second condition takes the log fold-change into deliberation. Which means that the difference of the log 2 transformed expression values should be greater than or equal to one (a log fold-change of one means that the expression of the gene in one condition is twice or half the size than the expression under the other condition). The log fold-change is calculated by the following equations.

$$\mathbf{T}est - \mathbf{C}ontrol \geq 1 \Longrightarrow \textsf{up-regulated in test}$$

$$\mathbf{C}ontrol - \mathbf{T}est \geq 1 \Longrightarrow \textsf{down-regulated in test}$$

All probe sets which fulfill these conditions can be identified as differentially expressed probe sets. Afterwards it is possible to search for these probe sets and to figure out which gene is expressed differentially.

The realization of this workflow in jABC should make it possible to automate the tedious manual task of identifying differentially expressed genes so that anyone can find those genes without the need of advanced knowledge of computer sciences. And furthermore to have the possibility to change single parameters without changing the scripts and through that to get more or less stringent results. The following parts contain more information about the concrete work with jABC.

2 Service Analysis

The workflow of this project is mainly based on scripts with Gnu R-specific commands. R is an open source software which is provided by CRAN. With the help of R it is possible to do statistical computing and to generate graphics [24]. The functionality of R can be extended through downloading specific packages from Bioconductor (`http://www.bioconductor.org/`), for example packages for analyzing high-throughput genomic data.

The scripts can be accessed from the workflow via the ExecuteCommand-SIB. These are in this project responsible for the execution of shell scripts. For each R script a shell script exists which is necessary to execute the R script. The shell scripts are structured as shown in the following figure (Figure 1). Because of the use of shell scripts with Linux-specific commands the whole workflow is currently restricted to the operating system Linux.

```
#!/bin/sh
R < R_Skripte/diffexpr.r --vanilla --args ${1}
```

Fig. 1. Shell script that is used in the ExecuteCommand-SIB to execute the R script for the identification of differentially expressed genes

Furthermore it is necessary to (down-) load all Gnu R packages in R that are used for the identification of the differentially expressed genes. Which are the following packages: "affy", "preprocessCore", "vsn", "multtest". All together three more or less different R scripts are written for this project. Two of these are responsible for the loading of the control and test data (Figures 2 and 3) and the other is used for the actual identification (Figure 4).

The user of the workflow needs to download the raw data (CEL files) of the experiments that should be analyzed, before the workflow is executed. Additionally a list with the chosen CEL files for the control condition and a list with the files of the test condition needs to be constructed and stored under the names "control.csv" and "test.csv". The CEL files and the files with the list of the CEL

```
##Loading of the data or the single control experiments

#(down-)loading of the libraries
source("http://bioconductor.org/biocLite.R")
biocLite("affy")
source("http://bioconductor.org/biocLite.R")
biocLite("vsn")
source("http://bioconductor.org/biocLite.R")
biocLite("multtest")
library(affy)
library(vsn)

#loading of the expression data
setwd("Kontrolle")
pd_k =read.AnnotatedDataFrame("kontrolle.csv",header=FALSE, row.names=1)
a_k =ReadAffy(filenames=rownames(pData(pd_k)), phenoData=pd_k, verbose=TRUE)

x_k =expresso(a_k ,bg.correct=FALSE, normalize=FALSE, pmcorrect.method="pmonly", summary.method="medianpolish")

exprs_k = exprs(x_k)
colnames(exprs_k)=pData(pd_k)
all(colnames(exprs_k)==rownames(pData(pd_k)))

#saving of the expression data in the working directory
setwd("../")
save.image("K.RData")
```

Fig. 2. R script for loading of control files

```
##Loading of the data or the single test experiments

#(down-)loading of the libraries
source("http://bioconductor.org/biocLite.R")
biocLite("affy")
source("http://bioconductor.org/biocLite.R")
biocLite("vsn")
source("http://bioconductor.org/biocLite.R")
biocLite("multtest")
library(affy)
library(vsn)

#loading of the expression data
setwd("Test")
pd_t =read.AnnotatedDataFrame("test.csv",header=FALSE, row.names=1)
a_t =ReadAffy(filenames=rownames(pData(pd_t)), phenoData=pd_t, verbose=TRUE)

x_t =expresso(a_t ,bg.correct=FALSE, normalize=FALSE, pmcorrect.method="pmonly", summary.method="medianpolish")

exprs_t = exprs(x_t)
colnames(exprs_t)=pData(pd_t)
all(colnames(exprs_t)==rownames(pData(pd_t)))

#saving of the expression data in the working directory
setwd("../")
save.image("T.RData")
```

Fig. 3. R script for loading of test files

files need to be stored together in special directories, which should be named "Control" and "Test". These directories should lie in the same working directory, which should contain all the results of the analysis that arises during the execution of the workflow as well. These are important steps for the analysis that cannot be easily included in the workflow and requires a little work from the user.

Note that it is also possible to store all the scripts and libraries on a jETI server and generate platform-independent SIBs for accessing them, so that the workflow can be used independent from the platform on which the user works. Therefore some further work and changes in the workflow are needed, which might be done in future work.

```
##Identification of differentially expressed genes

args=commandArgs(TRUE)

#read in and normalization of the expression data

load("K.RData")
load("T.RData")
integratedset=as.matrix(cbind(exprs_k,exprs_t))
nr_k=ncol(exprs_k)
nr_t=ncol(exprs_t)

library(preprocessCore)

integratedsetnorm=normalize.quantiles(integratedset)
rownames(integratedsetnorm)=rownames(integratedset)

#1. filter (expression treshold)

K_Median = apply(integratedsetnorm[,1:nr_k],1,median)
T_Median = apply(integratedsetnorm[,nr_k+1:nr_t],1,median)

quant = quantile(integratedsetnorm)[2]

finalset=integratedsetnorm[-intersect(which(K_Median<=quant),which(T_Median<=quant)),]

#2. filter

library(multtest)
cl=c(rep(0,nr_k),rep(1,nr_t))
t=mt.teststat(finalset, classlabel=cl,test="t.equalvar")
pt=2*pt(-abs(t),df=ncol(finalset)-2)
pAdj=mt.rawp2adjp(pt, proc=c("BH"))
pBH=pAdj$adjp[order(pAdj$index),"BH"]

K=apply(finalset[,1:nr_k],1,median)
T=apply(finalset[,nr_k+1:nr_t],1,median)


downFilter=rownames(finalset)[which(K-T>=1)]
upFilter=rownames(finalset)[which(T-K>=1)]

pwert=args[1]

downexpr=intersect(downFilter,rownames(finalset)[which(pBH <= pwert)])
upexpr=intersect(upFilter,rownames(finalset)[which(pBH <= pwert)])

#saving of the identified up/down expressed probe sets

sink("up.txt")
print(upexpr)
sink()
sink("down.txt")
print(downexpr)
sink()
```

Fig. 4. R script for the identification of differentially expressed probe sets

3 Workflow Realization

All together the following SIBs were used beside the ExecuteCommand-SIB: ShowFileChooser, ShowConfirmDialog, ShowInputDialog and ShowTextDialog from the GUI SIBS and furthermore the ReadTextFile-SIB (IO SIB) and the Fork- and Join-SIB (Control SIBs). How these SIBs are combined in the workflow can be seen in the following figure (figure 5). The most important parts are the loading and the identification part, both are emphasized through rectangles.

The most interesting and determining parts of the workflow are generally speaking those where the path of the workflow splits up to more than one branch. The first SIB in this project which is followed by a split up is the ShowConfirmDialog (here called Shortcut). This SIB is somehow a shortcut as the name already suggests. It provides a possibility to avoid an unnecessary long execution time by skipping the loading part. The next split ups are caused by the Fork-SIB. A Fork-SIB offers the possibility of executing two threads simultaneously and thus to save time in the execution process. The Fork-SIB can be found twice in the workflow, one in the loading part and another in the identification part. The first Fork-SIB ensures through a downstream Join-SIB that the workflow just continues if both threads coming from the Fork-SIB are completed. This is necessary for the following steps because those need the results from both threads.

Now if the user has loaded all necessary data, the execution of the workflow can be started. The first SIB in this workflow is the ShowFileChosser-SIB, which requests the user to choose the working directory in which the directories for the raw data, a directory with the R scripts (named R_Scripts) and the shell scripts should be contained. In the next step, the decision for the shortcut, the user is needed again. Here he has to say whether he has already loaded the data in R, which means that the workflow was already, at least once, executed. If the workflow was not executed once up to then one would reach the loading part of the workflow. The next SIB is then the Fork-SIB. From here on two threads are executed simultaneously. One is responsible for loading the CEL files from the control data into R and the other thread is responsible for loading the data that should be tested. Thereafter is a Join-SIB, waiting for both of the threads to be completed. This part of the workflow is therefore responsible for loading the data into R.

It is followed by the identification part. As the first step in this part the user is demanded to choose the critical p-value. This value gets then transmitted to the last ExecuteCommand-SIB, which calls the R script for the identification of differentially expressed genes. Here the expression data get normalized and the differentially expressed probe sets identified. The up-/ down-regulated probe sets are stored in separate text files by R (up.txt and down.txt). These files will be loaded after another Fork-SIB into the workflow context via the ReadTextFile-SIB. Finally the results will be shown with the ShowTextDialog-SIB in two windows, one for the up- and another for the down-regulated probe sets. These parts are again emphasized through rectangles in the workflow.

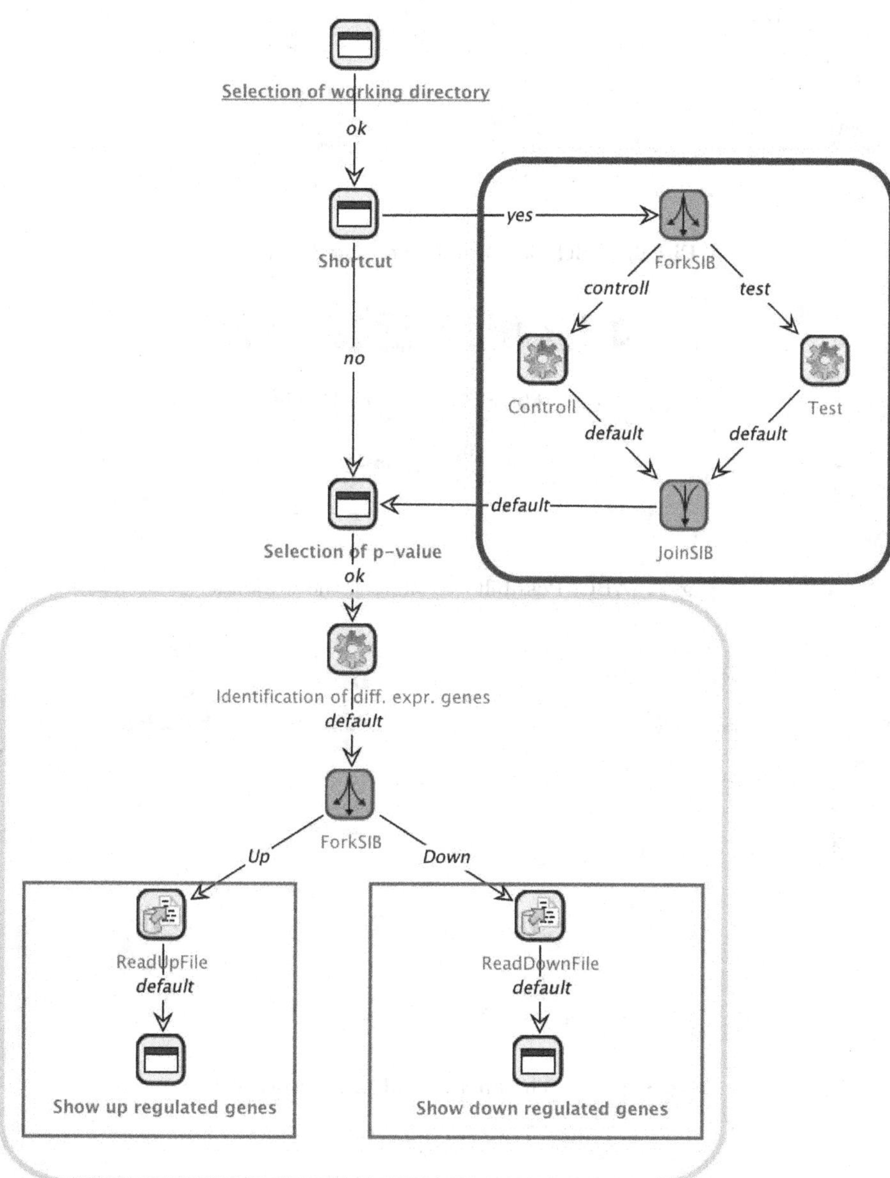

Fig. 5. Project realization with jABC

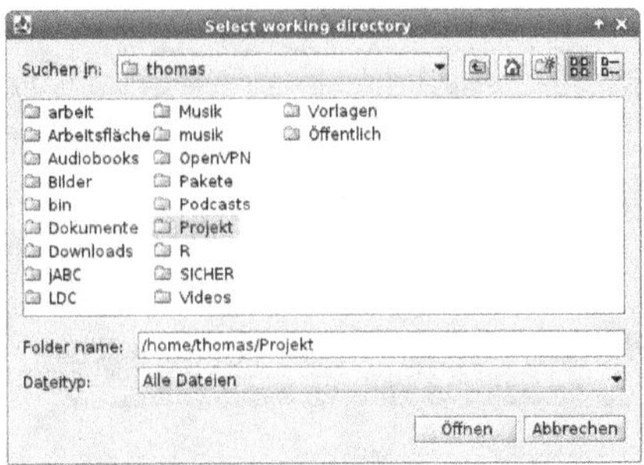

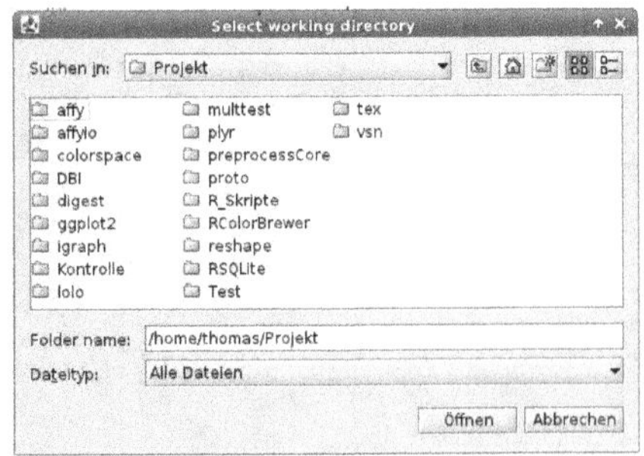

Fig. 6. jABC: Selection of working directory

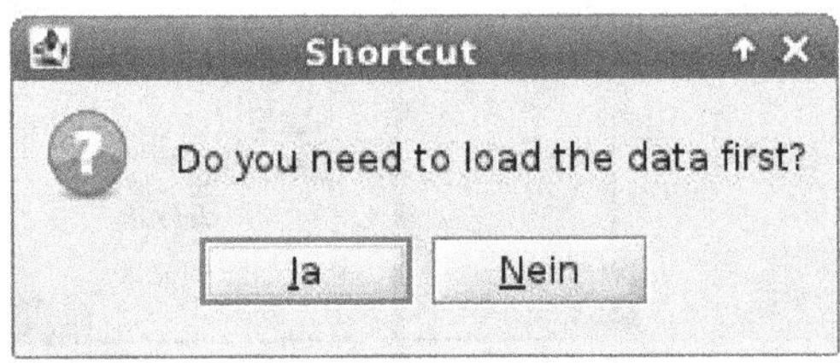

Fig. 7. jABC: Possibilty to shorten the workflow

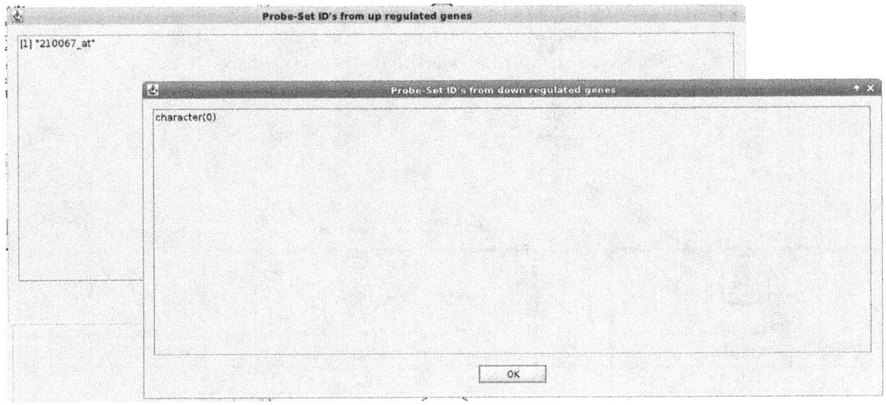

Fig. 8. jABC: The final output of the workflow

And now at the end of this section, the major points of what is requested by the user before and during the execution of this workflow will be shortly summarized. The first steps of the user should be to select and download the data of interest from ArrayExpress and store these in directories accordingly. Furthermore the user needs to compile a list for the CEL files which will be used from the single experiments. These should be stored in the corresponding

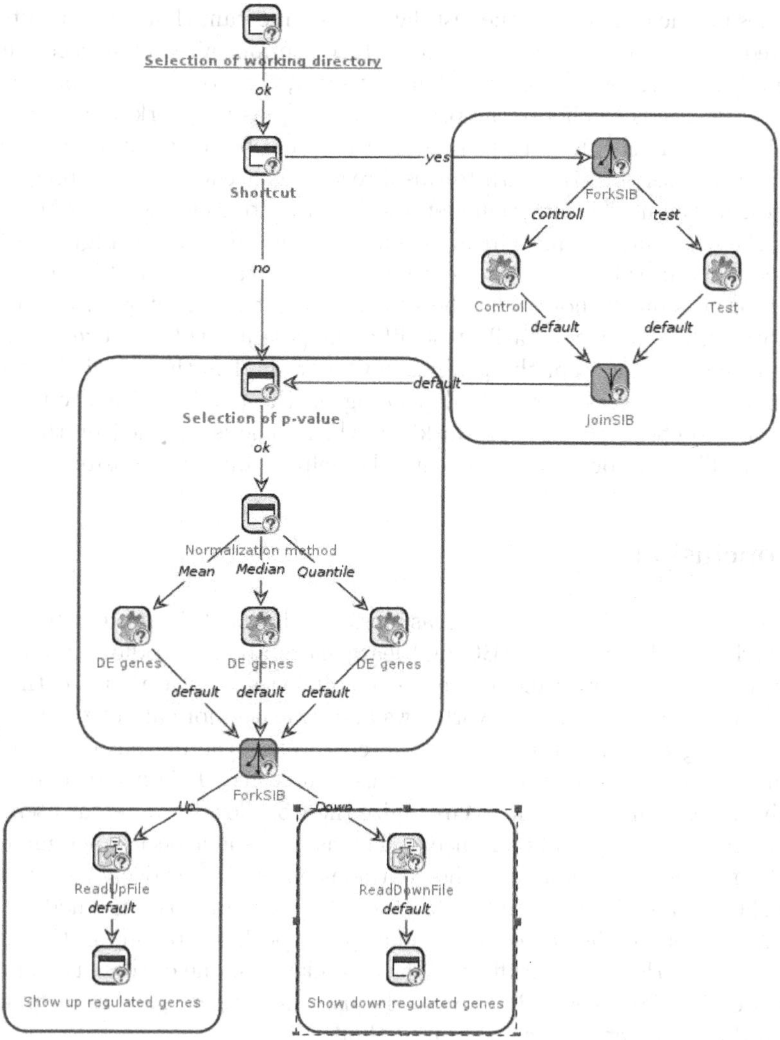

Fig. 9. Alternative workflow

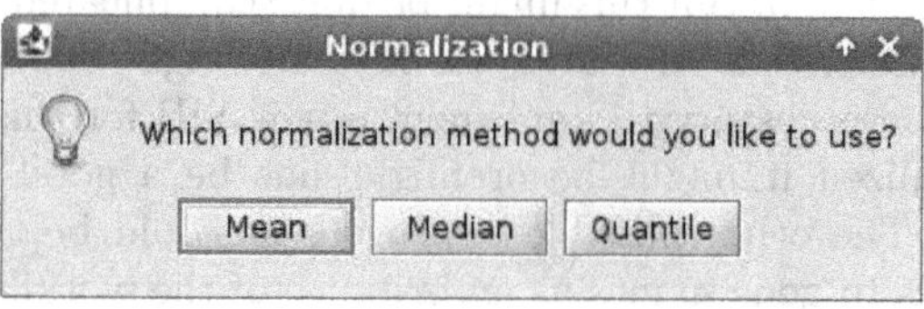

Fig. 10. jABC: Selection between different normalization methods

directories for the control and the test data. It is important that these directories are stored in the directory of the project, which contains already project-specific files and directories. After this was done correctly, the workflow can be started. Here the user needs to choose the project directory as the working directory at first (Figure 6). This is important because this could be stored at different locations by every user, but the path to this directory is needed in the subsequently processes. At the next interaction step the user has to decide whether he or she can use the shortcut, and has already loaded the data, or not (see Figure 7). The last task of the user is to choose the wanted p-value as shown in Figure 8. This interaction possibility shows why the shortcut might be of interest. Because of this shortcut, the user can easily test different p-values without executing the most time-consuming step, the loading. So he or she has the possibility to get more or less probe sets as results depending on the p-values. Finally the user might want to check beyond the workflow which gene is encoded by the single probe sets. This can be easily done with the help of different websites.

4 Conclusion

To finally conclude, in general it was possible during this project to realize the intended workflow with jABC and learn more about workflows thereby as well. It was quite interesting to see the possibilities that are offered through the realization of projects with workflows and to learn more about the usage of workflows. A great advantage is here offered through the option of interacting with the user with the help of a graphic user interface. This makes it possible to easily change parameters or to customize the workflow for different users and to meet their different wants and needs. This is also one aspect which might be interesting to develop further in the continuation of this project. For example one might include the possibilities for the user to change the method for the normalization or for the correction of multiple hypotheses testing in the course of the workflow. How the workflow might look like with one of these two options can be seen in Figures 9 and 10. Here the user would get the chance to select between three different normalization methods.

Two more things are imaginable for the improvement of the workflow: One is to integrate the loading of the raw data into the workflow and the generation of the list of CEL files as well. But this might be quite complicated and maybe even pointless, for the user needs to search the files and right experiments anyway. However it would be necessary to implement a new SIB for this and depending on how this is realized it might be or might not be a good addition to the existing workflow. The other possible improvement could be the "translation" from probe sets IDs to gene names as an instance of the workflow, which might be done via a specific website or with the help of a package in R. This somehow could lead to some limitation of the workflow that has not been mentioned yet. Because of certain packages that have to be used in this project realization, the user would be restricted to a certain microarray, for example the hgu133plus2.0, a microarray that is frequently used in experiments with genetic material of human. If other chips should be used the packages has to be loaded for those as well. But if the user just wants to work with the aforementioned array this workflow would work just fine.

That some of the aforementioned additional options could not be included in the workflow yet is principally due to some minor difficulties with R, which could be certainly solved with further work on the scripts. But still the result of the project is totally satisfying and builds a good foundation for future work. As a final result a workflow is thinkable which offers the possibility to identify differentially expressed genes independent of the examined species.

This article is part of a larger evaluation [4], which aimed at illustrating the power of simplicity-oriented development [14] by validating the claim that process modeling can indeed be handed over to the domain experts by providing them with a graphical modeling framework [21] that covers low-level details in a service-oriented fashion [16], integrates high-level modeling in the overall development process in a way that user-level models become directly executable [15,12], and supports ad-hoc adaptations and evolution [11,13].

The project described in this article can be characterized as follows:

- Scientific domain: bioinformatics
- Number of models: 1
- Number of hierarchy levels: 1
- Total number of SIBs: 13 /16
- SIB libraries used (cf. [9]): common-sibs
- Service technologies used: R scripts

The bioinformatics part of this volume contains five other articles on workflow applications in this domain [19,1,10,20,25]. Further examples of workflow projects with he bioinformatics-specific incarnation of the jABC framework, called Bio-jETI [6], have been described, for example, in [5,7,2]. As shown in [6,8,3], bioinformatics is also a suitable field for the application of semantics-based (semi-) automatic workflow composition techniques (as provided by, e.g., [17]) to support the workflow design process.

References

1. Blaese, L.: Data Mining for Unidentified Protein Sequences. In: Lamprecht, A.-L., Margaria, T. (eds.) Process Design for Natural Scientists. CCIS, vol. 500, pp. 73–87. Springer, Heidelberg (2014)
2. Ebert, B.E., Lamprecht, A.-L., Steffen, B., Blank, L.M.: Flux-P: Automating Metabolic Flux Analysis. Metabolites 2(4), 872–890 (2012)
3. Lamprecht, A.-L. (ed.): User-Level Workflow Design - A Bioinformatics Perspective. LNCS, vol. 8311. Springer, Heidelberg (2013)

4. Lamprecht, A.-L., Margaria, T.: Scientific Workflows and XMDD. In: Lamprecht, A.-L., Margaria, T. (eds.) Process Design for Natural Scientists. CCIS, vol. 500, pp. 1–13. Springer, Heidelberg (2014)
5. Lamprecht, A.-L., Margaria, T., Steffen, B.: Seven Variations of an Alignment Workflow - An Illustration of Agile Process Design and Management in Bio-jETI. In: Măndoiu, I., Wang, S.-L., Zelikovsky, A. (eds.) ISBRA 2008. LNCS (LNBI), vol. 4983, pp. 445–456. Springer, Heidelberg (2008)
6. Lamprecht, A.-L., Margaria, T., Steffen, B.: Bio-jETI: a framework for semantics-based service composition. BMC Bioinformatics 10(suppl. 10), S8 (2009)
7. Lamprecht, A.-L., Margaria, T., Steffen, B., Sczyrba, A., Hartmeier, S., Giegerich, R.: GeneFisher-P: variations of GeneFisher as processes in Bio-jETI. BMC Bioinformatics 9(suppl. 4), S13 (2008)
8. Lamprecht, A.-L., Naujokat, S., Margaria, T., Steffen, B.: Semantics-based composition of EMBOSS services. Journal of Biomedical Semantics 2(suppl. 1), S5 (2011)
9. Lamprecht, A.-L., Wickert, A.: The Course's SIB Libraries. In: Lamprecht, A.-L., Margaria, T. (eds.) Process Design for Natural Scientists. CCIS, vol. 500, pp. 30–44. Springer, Heidelberg (2014)
10. Lis, M.: Constructing a Phylogenetic Tree. In: Lamprecht, A.-L., Margaria, T. (eds.) Process Design for Natural Scientists. CCIS, vol. 500, pp. 101–109. Springer, Heidelberg (2014)
11. Margaria, T., Steffen, B.: Agile IT: Thinking in User-Centric Models. In: Margaria, T., Steffen, B. (eds.) ISoLA 2008. CCIS, vol. 17, pp. 490–502. Springer, Heidelberg (2009)
12. Margaria, T., Steffen, B.: Business Process Modelling in the jABC: The One-Thing-Approach. In: Cardoso, J., van der Aalst, W. (eds.) Handbook of Research on Business Process Modeling. IGI Global (2009)
13. Margaria, T., Steffen, B.: Continuous Model-Driven Engineering. IEEE Computer 42(10), 106–109 (2009)
14. Margaria, T., Steffen, B.: Simplicity as a Driver for Agile Innovation. Computer 43(6), 90–92 (2010)
15. Margaria, T., Steffen, B.: Service-Orientation: Conquering Complexity with XMDD. In: Hinchey, M., Coyle, L. (eds.) Conquering Complexity, pp. 217–236. Springer, London (2012)
16. Margaria, T., Steffen, B., Reitenspieß, M.: Service-Oriented Design: The Roots. In: Benatallah, B., Casati, F., Traverso, P. (eds.) ICSOC 2005. LNCS, vol. 3826, pp. 450–464. Springer, Heidelberg (2005)
17. Naujokat, S., Lamprecht, A.-L., Steffen, B.: Loose programming with PROPHETS. In: de Lara, J., Zisman, A. (eds.) FASE 2012. LNCS, vol. 7212, pp. 94–98. Springer, Heidelberg (2012)
18. Rasch, B., Friese, M., Hofmann, W., Naumann, E.: Quantitative Methoden. Einführung in die Statistik für Psychologen und Sozialwissenschaftler, vol. 1. Springer (2009)
19. Reso, J.: Protein Classification Workflow. In: Lamprecht, A.-L., Margaria, T. (eds.) Process Design for Natural Scientists. CCIS, vol. 500, pp. 65–72. Springer, Heidelberg (2014)
20. Schulze, G.: Workflow for Rapid Metagenome Analysis. In: Lamprecht, A.-L., Margaria, T. (eds.) Process Design for Natural Scientists. CCIS, vol. 500, pp. 88–100. Springer, Heidelberg (2014)

21. Steffen, B., Margaria, T., Nagel, R., Jörges, S., Kubczak, C.: Model-Driven Development with the jABC. In: Bin, E., Ziv, A., Ur, S. (eds.) HVC 2006. LNCS, vol. 4383, pp. 92–108. Springer, Heidelberg (2007)
22. Stranger, B.E., Forrest, M.S., Clark, A.G.: Genome-wide associations of gene expression variation in humans. PLoS Genetics 1, 695–704 (2005)
23. Strothmann, K.: Gen-Chips–eine Einführung in die Technologie der moderenen Genexpressionsanalyse. Pharm Unserer Zeit 29(5), 303–308 (2000)
24. Venables, W.N., Smith, D.M.: An Introduction to R. R Core Team (2012)
25. Vierheller, J.: Exploratory Data Analysis. In: Lamprecht, A.-L., Margaria, T. (eds.) Process Design for Natural Scientists. CCIS, vol. 500, pp. 110–126. Springer, Heidelberg (2014)
26. Zhijin, W., Irizarry, R.A.: Preprocessing of oligonucleotide array data. Nature Biotechnology 22, 656–658 (2004)

Visualization of Data Transfer Paths

Christian Kuntzsch

Potsdam University, Potsdam, D-14482, Germany
ckuntzsc@uni-potsdam.de

Abstract. A workflow for visualizing server connections using the Google Maps API was built in the jABC. It makes use of three basic services: An XML-based IP address geolocation web service, a command line tool and the Static Maps API. The result of the workflow is an URL leading to an image file of a map, showing server connections between a client and a target host.

Keywords: geoinformatics, IP geo locating, Google Maps API.

1 Introduction: Workflow Scenario

The Internet connects billions of people everyday. It has become a common place for sharing news, pictures, movies and other data and there is certainly no way it could be replaced by any other electronic system. In 2010 there was more data transmitted over the Internet than the entire history of the Internet through 2009 [20]. This data travels through millions of miles of cable all around the globe, often several times back and forth between the user and the server. But which way does it actually take? The jABC workflow described in this paper answers this question by visualizing server connections on a map.

First some background information on how the Internet works: Simply put, it is a global local area network, working just like any other network i.e. in an office or university. If the user for example wants to view a certain website, an URL is typed into the browser and the response is a website that corresponds to that exact URL. This concept is called the client-server model. The user acts as a client who sends a request to a server, and the server sends a response, which can be anything from simple text to a complex website. But this request of data does not directly go to the server. Instead, it follows a path of several servers, called gateways, that are divided into a number of tiers, that connect cities, countries and finally continents (see Fig. 1).

The actual workflow goes like this: First, the user's IP address is determined. Next, the user is asked the IP address or the URL of a specific server that he wants the connection to be visualized. Every gateway between the user and the server is then determined by IP addresses, which are then converted into geographic coordinates that can be mapped out. Usually the number of gateways between a client and a server varies around five to fifteen, this means the process of converting an IP address into geographic coordinates has to be repeated that many times. By automating these steps, a simple workflow is put together.

A.-L. Lamprecht et al. (Eds.): Process Design for Natural Scientists, CCIS 500, pp. 140–148, 2014.
DOI: 10.1007/978-3-662-45006-2_11

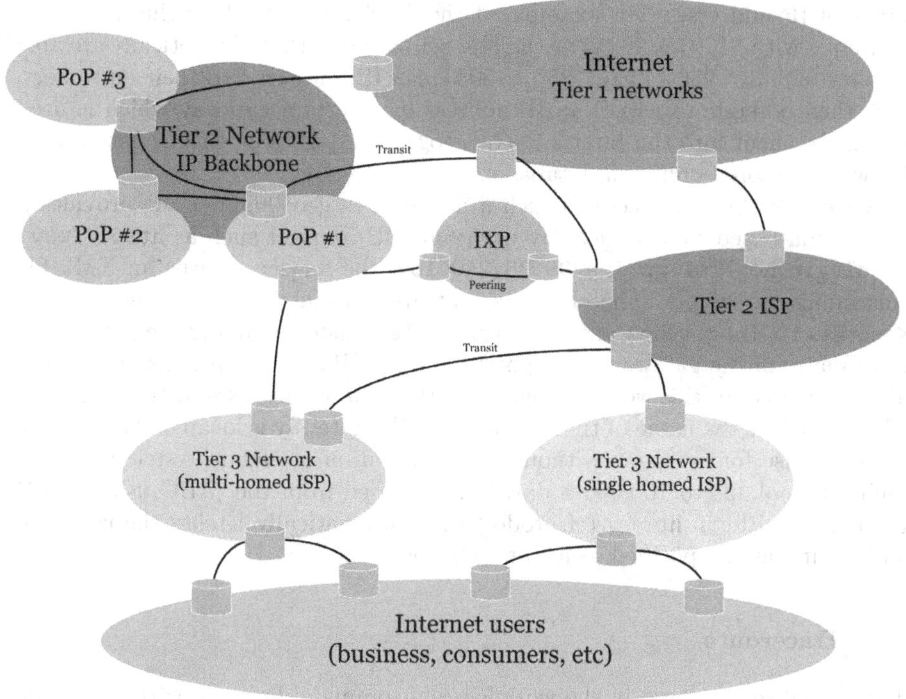

Fig. 1. General structure of the Internet. ISP = Internet Service Provider. PoP = Point of presence. IXP = Internet exchange point. Following [11].

Finally, an URL is generated, containing each coordinate. This URL leads to a picture of a map, showing each gateway connection from client to server.

2 Service Analysis

There are only three major services needed to realize the workflow: a web service which converts an IP address into geographic coordinates, a simple command line tool to resolve the connection between client and server and the Google Maps API.

2.1 IP-Geolocating

Several different websites offer a service for IP-geolocating, but all work in the same manner: An IP address is a unique numerical label containing four 8-bit digits, separated by a dot (i.e. 82.128.101.24). Every time an electronic device connects to the Internet, an IP address is assigned to it. What the IP address reads is not random, but determined through the user's Internet Service Provider (ISP), like AT&T and Telekom. An ISP buys and holds the rights to a certain range of IP addresses. For example, if the Telekom holds the rights for all IP addresses with 81, 91 and 212 as the first set of digits, they theoretically are able to distribute 3 * 256 * 256 * 256 = 50331648 IP addresses to their customers. It is then possible to assign an IP address to a certain gateway which is used to log the client into the Internet. The geographic position of these gateways is known and stored online in databases.

A web service that accesses such a database is geoPlugin [1]. It provides a simple xml-based web service. By using an URL request such as `http://www.geoplugin.net/xml.gp?ip=209.85.249.182`, the service returns an XML-file containing the results. The elements that are relevant for this application are `<geoplugin_longitude>` and `<geoplugin_latitude>`,defining the geographic coordinates of the gateway corresponding to the IP address. An element that is also being used for this workflow but is not that important is `<geoplugin_city>`, which provides the name of the city in which the gateway is located. This service is free to use for everyone without any registration or signup restrictions, but limits its lookups to 100,000 a day. It is accessed from the jABC using a SIB from the geoPlugin library (cf. [todo]) that automatically fetches the user's IP address if none is specified as a ContextExpression.

2.2 Traceroute

The second service used in the workflow is a command line tool with one single command in it:

```
tracert -d %URL
```

This sends several packets of data from the client to the target host, listing every gateway server on its way. It is usually used as a network diagnostic tool for measuring transit delays. This specific command line is written to be working in Microsoft Windows operating systems. It is also available on most other operating systems, for instance as "traceroute" on Apple Mac OS or as "tracepath" on Linux installations. Of course, the platform-specific version of this command line tool has to be installed in order to successfully execute the workflow.

The parameter `-d` has the effect that IP addresses are not resolved to host names, so the output of the command line tool is smaller. The expression `%1` acts as a placeholder variable and is replaced upon usage of the executable via jABC by the client's IP address. An example of the output of this small tool is shown in Figure 2.

2.3 Google Maps API

Finally, one last service is needed to complete the workflow. In order to get an impression which path the user's data takes, a cartographic view on every connection between the gateways is required. This is accomplished by using the Google Maps API, specifically the Static Maps API V2 [2]. It provides a wide range of functionalities, ranging from a simple extract map of a certain geographic region to highly complex maps with point, line or polygon information.

```

C:\Users\Christian Kuntzsch\Documents\jABC>tracert -d www.google.de

Routenverfolgung zu www-cctld.l.google.com [173.194.69.94] ?ber maximal 30 Abschnitte:

  1     9 ms    13 ms    10 ms  10.215.31.254
  2    11 ms     8 ms    12 ms  10.72.192.254
  3    12 ms    10 ms    11 ms  62.117.3.113
  4     9 ms     9 ms     9 ms  89.16.128.161
  5    12 ms    11 ms    10 ms  89.16.128.163
  6    15 ms     8 ms    10 ms  89.16.128.164
  7    14 ms    13 ms    11 ms  193.178.185.100
  8    10 ms    11 ms    11 ms  209.85.249.184
  9    11 ms    11 ms    13 ms  66.249.95.219
 10    11 ms    12 ms    10 ms  64.233.174.55
 11    10 ms    11 ms    13 ms  173.194.69.82
 12    10 ms    20 ms    14 ms  173.194.69.94

Ablaufverfolgung beendet.

```

Fig. 2. Example output of the command line tool `tracreroute`

The Google Static Map service creates a map based on URL parameters without requiring JavaScript or any other dynamic script language. For this workflow, some parameters are predefined. These are the size of output map, which is set to 1280 x 720 px, the basemap that is used, which is a topographic representation and the color and width of the lines connecting the gateway servers, which are red and 5 px. An example of such an URL reads as follows:

`http://maps.googleapis.com/maps/api/staticmap?size=1280x720&sensor=false&path=color:red|weight:5|longPoint1,latPoint1|longPoint2,latPoint2`

When executing the workflow, the parameters `longPoint1`, `latPoint1` and so forth are replaced by actual geographic coordinates, determined by the location of the sever gateways. These points are then inserted into the map and connected via straight red lines. The result is a PNG-file that can be accessed via the final URL.

There was no SIB for acquiring an image or any other file through an URL before, so one had to be created.

3 Workflow Realization

Figure 3 shows the complete workflow built in the jABC. Yellow areas represent SIBs where user interaction is required, the green area shows the iteration process.

At first, the user is welcomed by a small message, using the CommonSIB "Show Message Dialog". As a next step, the Static Maps URL is being prepared and the predefined parameters are set. This is accomplished using the CommonSIB "Put String". Next, the geoPlugin SIB is being used for the first time, to resolve the user's geographic position by geolocating his IP address. The city in

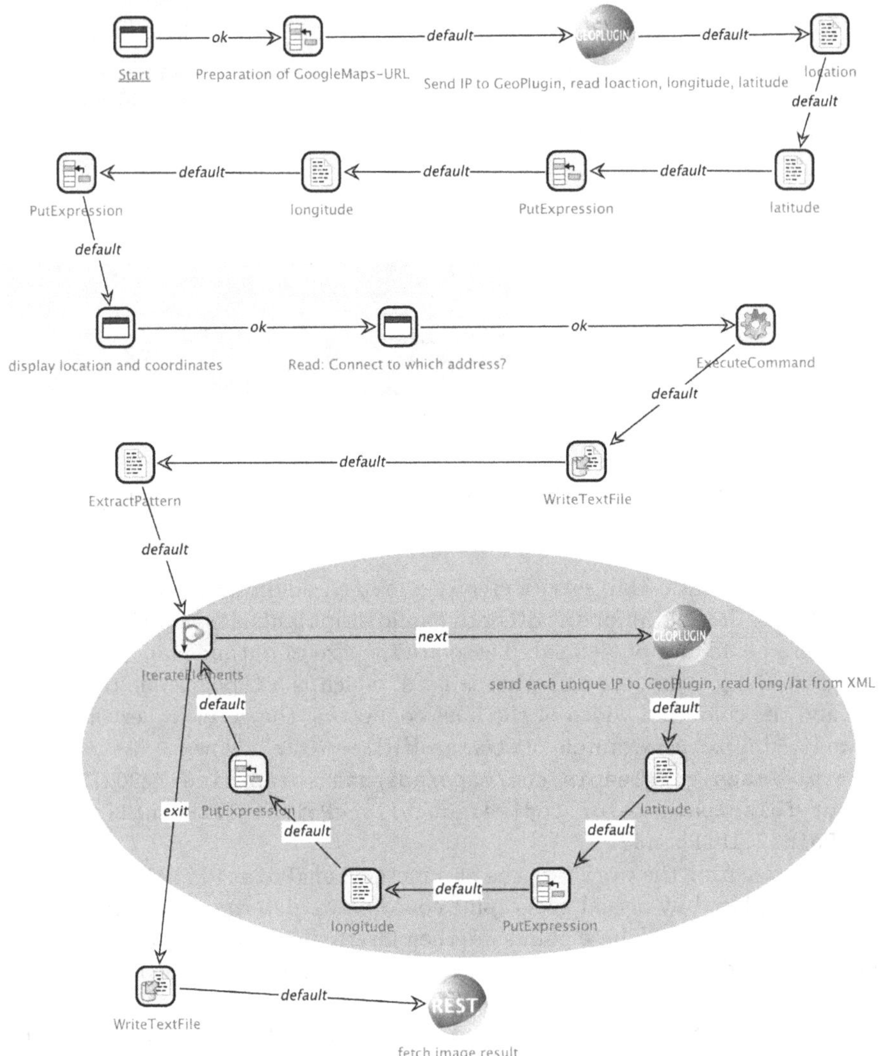

Fig. 3. Workflow built in the jABC

which the user is currently located is extracted from the resulting XML-hash and stored as a variable. Also, the user's geographic longitude and latitude are extracted as well and directly appended to the URL. This means, the first point is already established. These steps are accomplished by using the CommonSIBs "Extract Pattern" and, again, "Put String".

Continuing on, the user is presented the city he currently resides in and his corresponding geographic coordinates. He is then asked the IP address or URL of a website, to which the connection should be established. Next, the command line

Fig. 4. An example result map

tool "traceroute" receives this string. The former placeholder %1 is replaced by it and then, the tool is executed using the CommonSIB "Execute Command". The traceroute command takes several seconds to complete and the result is written into a text file via the CommonSIB "WriteTextFile", so that the user can comprehend and see every IP address of all the gateways that the data passes. The IP addresses are then extracted and temporarily stored.

The next thing to do is to loop the request made by the geoPlugin-SIB. This step that was already done before for the user's current IP address and is now repeated over and over again for every IP address from the command line tool result. This is accomplished by using the CommonSIB "Iterate Elements". Every time the loop passes a round, a new pair of coordinates is appended to the URL. If the last IP address has been processed, the resulting URL is written to a text file for later usage.

The last step is to fetch the resulting image file of the map using the aforementioned RestSIB "FetchImageURL2File". It is then stored to the same directory as all the other files that were created before. Figure 4 shows a sample result map visualizing a server connection from the University of Potsdam to `www.guardian.co.uk`.

4 Conclusion

Realizing the workflow with the jABC was relatively simple. Most of the services needed for a complete working process were provided through the CommonSIBs that are integrated into jABC. The interaction with the user is reduced to a minimum, but could easily be expanded i.e. by letting the user decide which basemap the visualization should use or what color the lines connecting the servers should be. Also, some of the steps included in the workflow are not required, such as the output of the command line tool result being written into a text file.

There is one problem that is still not resolved: The geoPlugin web service sometimes seems to be unreachable, resulting in a plugin status 404 error. In this case, the workflow will not be completed, or the map will show no connections. A solution to this problem could be the usage of a different geolocation web service, requiring to program a new SIB. Likewise, the workflow will not be completed if the server that traceroute is trying to contact is currently offline. Then the output will be empty and jABC will not find any IP addresses to process.

Since every service but one is web-based, and the command line "traceroute" is present on most operating systems, this workflow can be used on any machine, independent from the OS.

This article is part of a larger evaluation [7], which aimed at illustrating the power of simplicity-oriented development [15] by validating the claim that process modeling can indeed be handed over to the domain experts by providing them with a graphical modeling framework [24] that covers low-level details in a service-oriented fashion [17], integrates high-level modeling in the overall development process in a way that user-level models become directly executable [16,13], and supports ad-hoc adaptations and evolution [12,14].

The project described in this article can be characterized as follows:

- Scientific domain: geoinformatics
- Number of models: 1
- Number of hierarchy levels: 1
- Total number of SIBs: 21
- SIB libraries used (cf. [10]): common-sibs (18), geoplugin-sibs (2), rest-sibs (1)
- Service technologies used: REST web services

The geoinformatics part of this volume contains eight other articles on workflow applications in this domain [19,5,25,4,22,21,3,23]. Further geoinformatics workflow projects with the jABC have recently been started. Ongoing work is also exploring how to apply semantics-based (semi-) automatic workflow composition techniques (as provided by, e.g., [18]) to support the workflow design process, as described in [8,9,6] for the bioinformatics domain.

References

1. geoPlugin. Plugin to geo-targeting and unleash your site's potential (2012), http://www.geoplugin.net/
2. Google. Static Maps API V2 Developer Guide (2012), https://developers.google.com/maps/documentation/staticmaps/index
3. Hibbe, M.: Spotlocator Project Documentation. In: Lamprecht, A.-L., Margaria, T. (eds.) Process Design for Natural Scientists. CCIS, vol. 500, pp. 149–158. Springer, Heidelberg (2014)
4. Holler, R.: GraffDok: A Graffiti Documentation Application. In: Lamprecht, A.-L., Margaria, T. (eds.) Process Design for Natural Scientists. CCIS, vol. 500, pp. 235–247. Springer, Heidelberg (2014)
5. Kind, J.: Creation of Topographic Maps. In: Lamprecht, A.-L., Margaria, T. (eds.) Process Design for Natural Scientists. CCIS, vol. 500, pp. 225–234. Springer, Heidelberg (2014)
6. Lamprecht, A.-L.: User-Level Workflow Design. LNCS, vol. 8311. Springer, Heidelberg (2013)
7. Lamprecht, A.-L., Margaria, T.: Scientific Workflows and XMDD. In: Lamprecht, A.-L., Margaria, T. (eds.) Process Design for Natural Scientists. CCIS, vol. 500, pp. 1–13. Springer, Heidelberg (2014)
8. Lamprecht, A.-L., Margaria, T., Steffen, B.: Bio-jETI: a framework for semantics-based service composition. BMC Bioinformatics 10(suppl. 10), S8 (2009)
9. Lamprecht, A.-L., Naujokat, S., Margaria, T., Steffen, B.: Semantics-based composition of EMBOSS services. Journal of Biomedical Semantics 2(suppl. 1), S5 (2011)
10. Lamprecht, A.-L., Wickert, A.: The Course's SIB Libraries. In: Lamprecht, A.-L., Margaria, T. (eds.) Process Design for Natural Scientists. CCIS, vol. 500, pp. 30–44. Springer, Heidelberg (2014)
11. Ludovic, F.: Internet Connectivity Distribution & Core (2010), http://en.wikipedia.org/wiki/Internet
12. Margaria, T., Steffen, B.: Agile IT: Thinking in User-Centric Models. In: Margaria, T., Steffen, B. (eds.) ISoLA 2008. CCIS, vol. 17, pp. 490–502. Springer, Heidelberg (2009)
13. Margaria, T., Steffen, B.: Business Process Modelling in the jABC: The One-Thing-Approach. In: Cardoso, J., van der Aalst, W. (eds.) Handbook of Research on Business Process Modeling. IGI Global (2009)
14. Margaria, T., Steffen, B.: Continuous Model-Driven Engineering. IEEE Computer 42(10), 106–109 (2009)
15. Margaria, T., Steffen, B.: Simplicity as a Driver for Agile Innovation. Computer 43(6), 90–92 (2010)

16. Margaria, T., Steffen, B.: Service-Orientation: Conquering Complexity with XMDD. In: Hinchey, M., Coyle, L. (eds.) Conquering Complexity, pp. 217–236. Springer, London (2012)
17. Margaria, T., Steffen, B., Reitenspieß, M.: Service-Oriented Design: The Roots. In: Benatallah, B., Casati, F., Traverso, P. (eds.) ICSOC 2005. LNCS, vol. 3826, pp. 450–464. Springer, Heidelberg (2005)
18. Naujokat, S., Lamprecht, A.-L., Steffen, B.: Loose programming with PROPHETS. In: de Lara, J., Zisman, A. (eds.) Fundamental Approaches to Software Engineering. LNCS, vol. 7212, pp. 94–98. Springer, Heidelberg (2012)
19. Noack, F.: CREADED: Coloured-Relief Application for Digital Elevation Data. In: Lamprecht, A.-L., Margaria, T. (eds.) Process Design for Natural Scientists. CCIS, vol. 500, pp. 182–195. Springer, Heidelberg (2014)
20. Parr, B.: More Data Was Transmitted Over the Internet in 2010 Than All Previous Years Combined [VIDEO]. Mashable Tech. (2011), `http://mashable.com/2011/10/20/kirk-skaugen-web-2/`
21. Respondeck, T.: A Workflow for Computing Potential Areas for Wind Turbines. In: Lamprecht, A.-L., Margaria, T. (eds.) Process Design for Natural Scientists. CCIS, vol. 500, pp. 196–211. Springer, Heidelberg (2014)
22. Scheele, L.: Location Analysis for Placing Artificial Reefs. In: Lamprecht, A.-L., Margaria, T. (eds.) Process Design for Natural Scientists. CCIS, vol. 500, pp. 212–224. Springer, Heidelberg (2014)
23. Sens, H.: Web-Based Map Generalization Tools Put to the Test. In: Lamprecht, A.-L., Margaria, T. (eds.) Process Design for Natural Scientists. CCIS, vol. 500, pp. 171–181. Springer, Heidelberg (2014)
24. Steffen, B., Margaria, T., Nagel, R., Jörges, S., Kubczak, C.: Model-driven development with the jABC. In: Bin, E., Ziv, A., Ur, S. (eds.) HVC 2006. LNCS, vol. 4383, pp. 92–108. Springer, Heidelberg (2007)
25. Teske, D.: Geocoder Accuracy Ranking. In: Lamprecht, A.-L., Margaria, T. (eds.) Process Design for Natural Scientists. CCIS, vol. 500, pp. 159–170. Springer, Heidelberg (2014)

Spotlocator – Guess Where the Photo Was Taken!

Marcel Hibbe

Potsdam University, Potsdam, D-14482, Germany
mhibbe@gmail.com

Abstract. Spotlocator is a game wherein people have to guess the spots of where photos were taken. The photos of a defined area for each game are from panoramio.com. They are published at `http://spotlocator.drupalgardens.com` with an ID. Everyone can guess the photo spots by sending a special tweet via Twitter that contains the hashtag #spotlocator, the guessed coordinates and the ID of the photo. An evaluation is published for all tweets. The players are informed about the distance to the real photo spots and the positions are shown on a map.

Keywords: Geoinformation, Spotlocator, panoramio, twitter, game, google static maps, REST.

1 Introduction: Workflow Scenario

The basic idea of this project is a game wherein people have to guess the spots of where photos were taken. It should improve people's geographical knowledge about their neighborhood. The administrator can define the search area of the current game. Thereafter information about geo-referenced photos are downloaded from Panoramio (`www.panoramio.com`) for the specified area. For every photo a unique ID is generated which gets stored in a file containing additional data such as the coordinates and the author. The photos are published on the website `http://spotlocator.drupalgardens.com` together with their IDs. The challenge for the players is to search the photo locations on site. For that they need a Twitter account (`www.twitter.com`), and a smartphone with GPS support. When a player has found a photo location, he sends a tweet in the following format:

#spotlocator 52.123456,13.123456 id:123

The hashtag #spotlocator is the name of the game and is used to identify tweets containing information about the assumed photo locations. The numbers in the middle are geographical coordinates which have to be modified by the player for the current photo. The ID refers to the Photo-ID published on the website. This way, every person having a Twitter account and owning a smartphone can join the game.

For evaluation all the tweets containing the Hashtag #spotlocator are downloaded. The distance to the original photo locations is calculated by comparing

A.-L. Lamprecht et al. (Eds.): Process Design for Natural Scientists, CCIS 500, pp. 149–160, 2014.
DOI: 10.1007/978-3-662-45006-2_12

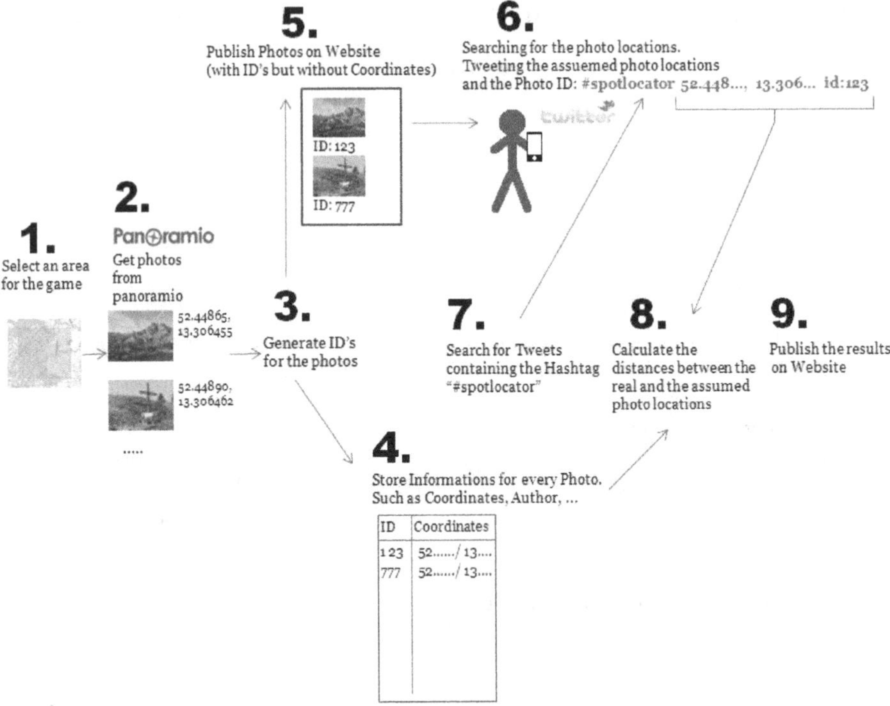

Fig. 1. Workflow of the game

the assumed coordinates with the coordinates stored in the file containing the original photo information. The results are published on the website, so everyone can check how accurate his assumption was. Figure 1 shows the workflow of the game.

The reason for using Panoramio was that there is already a pool of data that can be used and there is no need to create an own data basis. The reason for using Twitter was the wide distribution of the service so that people don't have to register any additional account for playing the game.

2 Service Analysis

The services needed for realizing the workflow is the Panoramio REST API [21] to get the photo Information and the Twitter REST API to download the tweets. Additional tools are Dropbox, which is used to publish the generated HTML sites. The content management system Drupal has been used to design a website where the generated HTML sites are embedded via an iFrame.

A site that uses the Panoramio API can show photos that appear on Panoramio free of charge. The site must credit the photographer and link to the original photo page. You must also display the text "Photos provided by Panoramio are under the copyright of their owners" under Panoramio-photos. To use, copy, print, or download a photo from Panoramio, you must get explicit permission from the photographer [22]. For this reason the spotlocator program will not have a print-function. To use the REST API in jABC, you have to do a GET on an URL like this:

```
http://www.panoramio.com/map/get_panoramas.php?set=public&from=
0&to=20&minx=-180&miny=-90&maxx=180&maxy=90&size=medium&mapfilter=
true
```

Minx, miny, maxx and maxy define the area to show photos from. "set=public" means that only popular photos are used and "size=medium" specifies the image size. You can define the number of photos to be displayed using "from=X" and "to=Y", where Y-X is the number of photos included. The value 0 represents the latest photo uploaded to Panoramio. For example, "from=0 to=20" will extract a set of the last 20 photos uploaded to Panoramio, "from=20 to=40" the previous set of 20 photos and so on. The result data is formatted using JavaScript Object Notation (JSON) [3]. To do a GET command in jABC, the REST SIB "FetchTextualDataFromURL" is used. It fetches textual content behind the given URL and puts the result into the execution context. To use the Twitter REST API [28] a GET command is used as well and the result data is formatted using JavaScript Object Notation (JSON), too. The URL to search for Tweets with the hashtag #spotlocator is:

```
http://search.twitter.com/search.json?q=40spotlocator
```

As the Twitter search is mainly a real-time search, it's only possible to find Tweets of the last few days (between 4 and 10 days). This is enough to fit the needs of the spotlocator game.

As a result of the jABC workflow there are generated HTML files containing the current game, the results of the guesses and an archive for old games. These files get stored in the public folder of Dropbox, which has to be installed at the local machine. For each HTML file there is a public URL (rightclick - copy public URL). These URLs are used to display these sites via an iframe in a website created using the content management system Drupal Gardens. As creating a website is not a topic of this seminar paper, this documentation will limit to the generation of the HTML files via jABC. The website can be visited at `http://spotlocator.drupalgardens.com`.

All in all, the only requirement to run the program is the desktop version of Dropbox. As the guesses published by the Twitter users refer to the photos on the Website `http://spotlocator.drupalgardens.com` (currently updated by the author), it is not recommended to send tweets referring to photos which have been generated by another machine. This would lead to redundant photo IDs so that the evaluation would show up wrong results. Because of this it is allowed to run this program on another machine, but tweets should always refer to the photos on the website which is administrated by the author.

3 Workflow Realization

At the beginning of the program there is the possibility to make some configurations. If the program is running on another machine, you can set the paths where the program data will be saved. If you are using Dropbox to publish the generated HTML files, you have to choose the Dropbox public folder. The table depicted in Figure 2 shows all the files used by the program.

File	action	description
Spotlocator_NewGame.htm	write (Dropbox)	HTML file containing the current game
Spotlocator_Archive.htm	read / write (Dropbox)	HTML file containing the old games
Spotlocator_Report.htm	write (Dropbox)	HTML file containing the evaluation for the tweets
Spotlocator_photoinfo.htm	read / write	File containing all photo informations (ID's, coordinates, author, ...)
Spotlocator_current_number.txt	read / write	File containing the current photo-counter

Fig. 2. Files used by the program

After configuration there is an option (ShowBranchingDialog) between creating a new game or evaluating the tweets from Twitter. The following 2 Chapters will describe each option.

3.1 Create a New Game

To create a new game, the user first has to enter four geographical coordinates (ShowInputDialog) to define a bounding box in which the photo spots must be guessed. The site http://www.openstreetmap.org/export is suitable to get the coordinates. In another Input Dialog the user can enter the number of photos that have to be guessed in the specified area. These inputs are stored in variables that are used to build the GET URL for Panoramio:

```
http://www.panoramio.com/map/get_panoramas.
php?set=public&from=0&to=${number_of_photos}&minx=${area_west}&
miny=${area_south}&maxx=${area_east}&maxy=${area_north}&
size=medium&mapfilter=true
```

The GET request is performed using the REST-SIB "FetchTextualDataFromURL". The result containing the JSON-Code is stored in the variable "panoramio_get". For one photo the code looks like the following:

```
{
  "count": 773840,"photos": [
    {
      "photo_id": 532693,
      "photo_title": "Wheatfield in afternoon light",
      "photo_url": "http://www.panoramio.com/photo/532693",
      "photo_file_url":
"http://static2.bareka.com/photos/medium/532693.jpg",
      "longitude": 11.280727,
      "latitude": 59.643198,
      "width": 500,
      "height": 333,
      "upload_date": "22 January 2007",
      "owner_id": 39160,
      "owner_name": "Snemann",
      "owner_url": "http://www.panoramio.com/user/39160",
    }
}
```


The next task is to extract the strings that are needed in the program. This is done for every string with the SIB "ExtractPattern" by using regular expressions [20].
The expression to extract the pattern for the photo file URL is:

```
"photo_file_url":"([\p{Graph}[\p{Space}]&&[^"]]+)
```

This command is searching for the text "photo_file_url":". After this string there is the URL that has to be extracted. "Graph" and "Space" define the characters that are allowed to be extracted. The symbols

```
[^"]
```

mean that the next quote defines the end of the extraction and "+" means that this search is done until there are no more matching patterns. As a result, the ExtractPattern SIB stores all photo file URL in an array. This procedure is also done for latitude, longitude, photo_id and owner_name. At this point the JSON-Code is no longer needed because all information has been extracted into arrays.
The next four SIBs are for creating an archive for old games. If the program is executed for the first time a new file called "Spolocator_Archive.htm" is created without content. The next time the program runs, the previous game ("Spotlocator_NewGame.htm") will always be added to the archive. This is done by the SIBs "ReadTextFile" and "WriteTextFile". The SIB "PutExpression" merges the previous game and the old archive into one variable that becomes the content of the new archive. After that, the photo information "Spotlocator_photoinfo.htm" of earlier games is loaded from hard drive with the "ReadTextFile" SIB. If there is no such file it will be created by the "WriteTextFile" SIB.

The following "PutExpression" SIB is for creating the beginning of the HTML file "Spotlocator_NewGame.htm". To give the players an overview where they have to search for the photo spots, there are 2 Google Maps (Google Static Maps [1]) that show the bounding box in 2 different zoom levels. The links for the maps are created by using the variables that the user defined at the beginning. Additionally, there is the option to open the bounding box in OpenStreetMap.

```
<head>
    <style>
    body{ font-size:13px; font-family:Helvetica; }
    </style>
</head>

<center>
<b>the photos are form the following area:</b>
<br><br>
<img src="http://maps.google.com/maps/api/staticmap?
path=color:0x0000FF80|weight:4|
${area_north},${area_west}|${area_nord},${area_east}|
${area_south},${area_east}|${area_south},${area_west}|
${area_north},${area_west}&size=300x300&zoom=7&sensor=true">
  

<img src="http://maps.google.com/maps/api/staticmap?
path=color:0x0000FF80|weight:5|
${area_north},${area_west}|${area_nord},${area_east}|
${area_south},${area_east}|${area_south},${area_west}|
${area_north},${area_west}&size=500x300&sensor=true">

<br><br>
To view this area in OpenStreetMap
<a href="http://www.openstreetmap.org/?minlon=${area_west}
&minlat=${area_south}&maxlon=${area_east}
&maxlat=${area_north}&box=yes" target="_blank">click here</a>.
<br><hr><br><br>
</center>
```

The next SIB "ReadTextFile" reads the current counter of the photo IDs from the file "Spotlocator_current_number.txt". Storing the ID on the hard drive is necessary, because otherwise the counter would start at 0 again at every program start. If the file with the counter does not exist, it will be created. The following loop show in Figure 3 is a main part of creating a new game. The loop summarizes the information for every photo and adds it to the Information about the other Photos. Then the HTML-part for the current photo is generated which is added to the whole HTML Code. After that the photo ID and the loop number is increased.

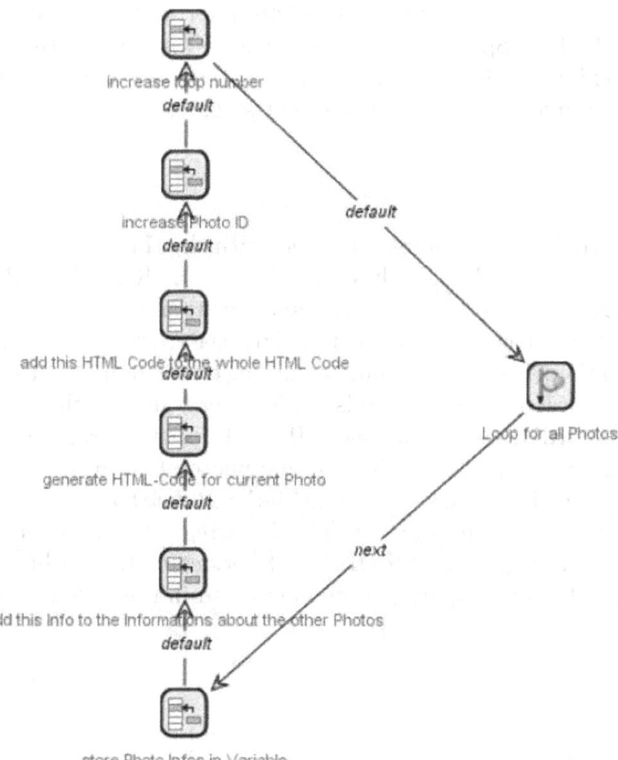

Fig. 3. Loop for summarizing photo information

```
<center>
<h2>photo number: ${photonumber}</h2>
<a href="http://www.panoramio.com/photo/
${panoramio_int_photoid[loopnumber]}"
target="_blank">
<img src="${panoramio_photoadresses[loopnumber]}"></a>

<br><small>Copyright of this photo:
<i>${panoramio_ownername[loopnumber]}</i></small>
<br><br>

You know where this photo was taken?
Send a tweet with the following text:
 #spotlocator <i>latitude</i><b>,</b><i>longitude</i>
 id:<b>${photonumber}</b>
</center>
```

After the loop, the current photo ID and all the photo informations are saved to hard drive. The HTML file "Spotlocator_NewGame.htm" is saved into the Dropbox public folder. The user gets a confirmation that the game was created successfully and additional information about the next steps.

3.2 Game Evaluation

The Game evaluation starts by downloading all tweets with the Hashtag #spotlocator. This is done by the REST SIB "FetchTextualDataFromURL". The URL is: `http://search.twitter.com/search.json?q=spotlocator`.

The answer in JSON-Format is the basis for the ExtractPattern SIBs to extract the desired information. Like at the game creation, this is done by using regular expressions. The extracted information is the Twitter Names of the owners, their nicknames, the coordinates and the photo ID of the photo they refer to. In the next step, the photo information ("Spotlocator_photoinfo.htm") that is stored on the hard drive is read with the "ReadTextFile" SIB. "ExtractPattern" is used again to store the information as arrays. The following "PutExpression" SIB is for creating the beginning of the HTML file "Spotlocator_Report.htm". The loop shown in Figure 4 is to compare photos mentioned in the tweets with the original photo information.

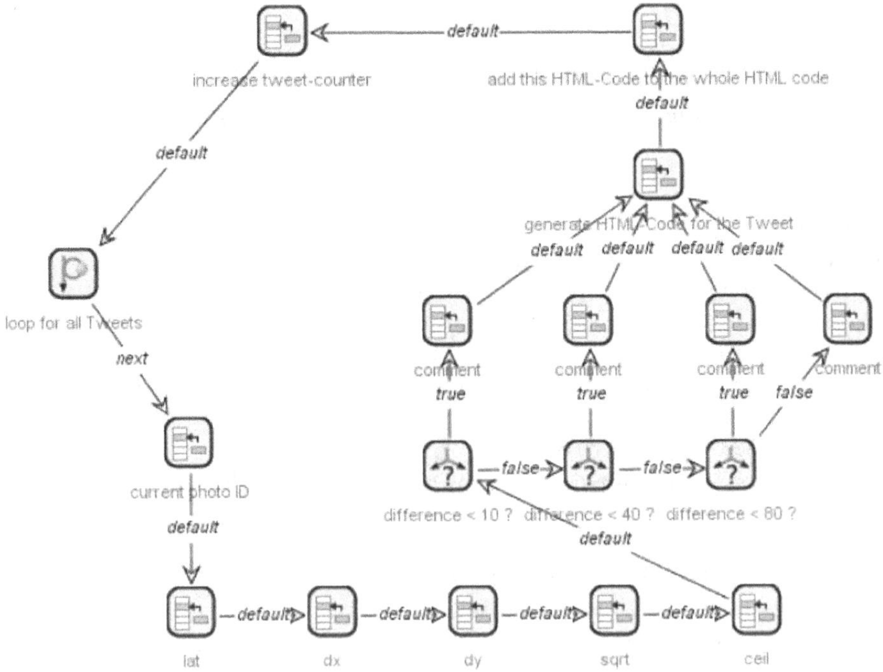

Fig. 4. Loop for photo comparison

At the beginning of the loop, the current photo ID that is mentioned in the tweet is written into a variable with the value $tweets_photoid[tweetnumber]. The next 5 SIBs calculate the distance between the assumed photo locations and the real photo locations. This is realized by using the theorem of Pythagoras while considering that the distance between lines of longitude varies with the latitude. The algorithm for this is [5]:

```
lat = (lat_real + lat_twitter) / 2 * 0.01745
dx = 111.3 * cos(lat) * (lon_real - lon_twitter)
dy = 111.3 * (lat_real - lat_twitter)
distance = sqrt(dx * dx + dy * dy)*1000
```

Lat and lon are the geographical coordinates in degree. Distance has the unit meter. The distance is rounded up with the command "ceil". The next "EvaluateCondition" and "PutExpression" SIBs generate a comment like "very good" or "not so good! good luck for the next time" for the different ranges of difference. Afterwards the HTML part for the current tweet is generated. This is added to the whole HTML Code. After that the loop number is increased. After the loop the HTML file "Spotlocator_Report.htm" is saved into the Dropbox public folder. The user gets a confirmation that the game was evaluated successfully and additional information about the next steps.

4 Conclusion

The workflow could be realized as planned and the game is running without problems. A current inconvenience is that the game creation and evaluation have to be executed manually, so that the website `http://spotlocator.drupalgardens.com` is not always up to date. Ideally, the program would be running continuously on a server so that the information will update in real time. Another constraint is that there can be problems if a Twitter user did not obey to the required tweet format. In future versions this will be improved by changing the regular expressions. At this time, a new game can only be created by the jABC administrator. A better solution for this would have to be realized in future versions, too. An idea is that everyone can create his own game via a special tweet. Furthermore the evaluation could be improved by ranking the best tips for a photo. To build more complex websites a SIB would be useful which is able to post blog entries. Another possibility to interact with the players would be to directly reply to the tweets by tweeting the results. This would require a special SIB as well. All in all, this project could be realized as a jABC workflow without problems. As the results are nearly solely HTML files which have to be published via a web server, PHP would be a good alternative. On the other hand the advantage of jABC is the flexibility to quickly make modifications and to have an overall view of the game.

This article is part of a larger evaluation [8], which aimed at illustrating the power of simplicity-oriented development [15] by validating the claim that process modeling can indeed be handed over to the domain experts by providing them with a graphical modeling framework [26] that covers low-level details in a service-oriented fashion [17], integrates high-level modeling in the overall development process in a way that user-level models become directly executable [16,13], and supports ad-hoc adaptations and evolution [12,14].

The project described in this article can be characterized as follows:

- Scientific domain: geoinformatics
- Number of models: 1
- Number of hierarchy levels: 1
- Total number of SIBs: 79
- SIB libraries used (cf. [11]): common-sibs (18), rest-sibs (2)
- Service technologies used: REST web services

The geoinformatics part of this volume contains eight other articles on workflow applications in this domain [6,19,4,27,2,24,23,25]. Further geoinformatics workflow projects with the jABC have recently been started. Ongoing work is also exploring how to apply semantics-based (semi-) automatic workflow composition techniques (as provided by, e.g., [18]) to support the workflow design process, as described in [9,10,7] for the bioinformatics domain.

References

1. GOOGLE. Google Static Maps API V2 Developer Guide (last accessed July 24, 2012), `https://developers.google.com/maps/documentation/staticmaps/`
2. Holler, R.: GraffDok — A Graffiti Documentation Application. In: Lamprecht, A.-L., Margaria, T. (eds.) Process Design for Natural Scientists. CCIS, vol. 500, pp. 239–251. Springer, Heidelberg (2014)
3. Json.Org. JavaScript Object Notation (last accessed July 24, 2012), `http://www.json.org/`
4. Kind, J.: Creation of topographic maps. In: Lamprecht, A.-L., Margaria, T. (eds.) Process Design for Natural Scientists. CCIS, vol. 500, pp. 229–238. Springer, Heidelberg (2014)
5. Kompf, M.: Entfernungsberechnung (last accessed July 24, 2012), `http://www.kompf.de/gps/distcalc.html`
6. Kuntzsch, C.: Visualization of data transfer paths. In: Lamprecht, A.-L., Margaria, T. (eds.) Process Design for Natural Scientists. CCIS, vol. 500, pp. 140–148. Springer, Heidelberg (2014)
7. Lamprecht, A.-L.: User-Level Workflow Design. LNCS, vol. 8311. Springer, Heidelberg (2013)
8. Lamprecht, A.-L., Margaria, T.: Scientific workflows and XMDD. In: Lamprecht, A.-L., Margaria, T. (eds.) Process Design for Natural Scientists. CCIS, vol. 500, pp. 1–13. Springer, Heidelberg (2014)

9. Lamprecht, A.-L., Margaria, T., Steffen, B.: Bio-jETI: a framework for semantics-based service composition. BMC Bioinformatics 10(suppl. 10), S8 (2009)
10. Lamprecht, A.-L., Naujokat, S., Margaria, T., Steffen, B.: Semantics-based composition of EMBOSS services. Journal of Biomedical Semantics 2(suppl. 1), S5 (2011)
11. Lamprecht, A.-L., Wickert, A.: The course's SIB libraries. In: Lamprecht, A.-L., Margaria, T. (eds.) Process Design for Natural Scientists. CCIS, vol. 500, pp. 30–44. Springer, Heidelberg (2014)
12. Margaria, T., Steffen, B.: Agile IT: Thinking in User-Centric Models. In: Margaria, T., Steffen, B. (eds.) Leveraging Applications of Formal Methods, Verification and Validation. CCIS, vol. 17, pp. 490–502. Springer, Heidelberg (2009)
13. Margaria, T., Steffen, B.: Business Process Modelling in the jABC: The One-Thing-Approach. In: Cardoso, J., van der Aalst, W. (eds.) Handbook of Research on Business Process Modeling. IGI Global (2009)
14. Margaria, T., Steffen, B.: Continuous Model-Driven Engineering. IEEE Computer 42(10), 106–109 (2009)
15. Margaria, T., Steffen, B.: Simplicity as a Driver for Agile Innovation. Computer 43(6), 90–92 (2010)
16. Margaria, T., Steffen, B.: Service-Orientation: Conquering Complexity with XMDD. In: Hinchey, M., Coyle, L. (eds.) Conquering Complexity, pp. 217–236. Springer, London (2012)
17. Margaria, T., Steffen, B., Reitenspiess, M.: Service-Oriented Design: The Roots. In: Benatallah, B., Casati, F., Traverso, P. (eds.) ICSOC 2005. LNCS, vol. 3826, pp. 450–464. Springer, Heidelberg (2005)
18. Naujokat, S., Lamprecht, A.-L., Steffen, B.: Loose Programming with PROPHETS. In: de Lara, J., Zisman, A. (eds.) FASE 2012. LNCS, vol. 7212, pp. 94–98. Springer, Heidelberg (2012)
19. Noack, F.: CREADED: Colored-Relief Application for Digital Elevation Data. In: Lamprecht, A.-L., Margaria, T. (eds.) Process Design for Natural Scientists. CCIS, vol. 500, pp. 182–195. Springer, Heidelberg (2014)
20. ORACLE. Pattern, `http://docs.oracle.com/javase/6/docs/api/java/util/regex/Pattern.html` (last accessed August 1, 2012)
21. PANORAMIO. Panoramio API Zeigen Sie Fotos von Panoramio auf Ihrer Webseite an, `http://www.panoramio.com/api/data/api.html` (last accessed July 2, 2012)
22. PANORAMIO. Panoramio Copyright, `http://www.panoramio.com/help/copyright` (last accessed July 23, 2012)
23. Respondek, T.: A Workflow for Computing Potential Areas for Wind Turbines. In: Lamprecht, A.-L., Margaria, T. (eds.) Process Design for Natural Scientists. CCIS, vol. 500, pp. 200–215. Springer, Heidelberg (2014)
24. Scheele, L.: Location analysis for placing artificial reefs. In: Lamprecht, A.-L., Margaria, T. (eds.) Process Design for Natural Scientists. CCIS, vol. 500, pp. 216–228. Springer, Heidelberg (2014)
25. Sens, H.: Web-based map generalization tools put to the test: A jABC workflow. In: Lamprecht, A.-L., Margaria, T. (eds.) Process Design for Natural Scientists. CCIS, vol. 500, pp. 175–185. Springer, Heidelberg (2014)
26. Steffen, B., Margaria, T., Nagel, R., Jörges, S., Kubczak, C.: Model-Driven Development with the jABC. In: Bin, E., Ziv, A., Ur, S. (eds.) HVC 2006. LNCS, vol. 4383, pp. 92–108. Springer, Heidelberg (2007)

27. Teske, D.: Geocoder accuracy ranking. In: Lamprecht, A.-L., Margaria, T. (eds.) Process Design for Natural Scientists. CCIS, vol. 500, pp. 161–174. Springer, Heidelberg (2014)
28. TWITTER. Twitter Developers, `https://dev.twitter.com/docs` (last accessed August 1, 2012)

Geocoder Accuracy Ranking

Daniel Teske

Potsdam University, Potsdam, D-14482, Germany
daniel.teske@uni-potsdam.de

Abstract. Finding an address on a map is sometimes tricky: the chosen map application may be unfamiliar with the enclosed region. There are several geocoders on the market, they have different databases and algorithms to compute the query. Consequently, the geocoding results differ in their quality. Fortunately the geocoders provide a rich set of metadata. The workflow described in this paper compares this metadata with the aim to find out which geocoder is offering the best-fitting coordinate for a given address.

Keywords: address, querying, geocoder, geocoding, yahoo maps, bing maps, google maps, open street maps, coordinate, accuracy, metadata, analysis, visualization, custom sib.

1 Introduction: Workflow Scenario

Geocoding describes the process of locating an address. Locating means to find the best-fitting coordinate for a given address. This is an important and basic function in many applications and can be used for example to search for an address on a map such as "August-Bebel-Strasse 89, 14482 Potsdam". Obviously, all navigation tools must geocode the target-address of a trip. But also the geomarketing industry needs to geocode entire datasets of customer addresses, for instance to calculate catchment area of supermarkets, banks or diners.

Geocoding-providers, here named *geocoders*, are the service-providers which receive the query-address, process the geocoding task and put out the result. The geocoder is the adapter between address and coordinate. All three objects are correlated in a simple functional manner:

$$coordinate_i = geocoder_i(address)$$

All geocoders offer the same function: geocoding. Except for the documentation of the service connection, each service provider itself is a black box. The service-provider hides there information about the volume and structure of the database and of course of the algorithm behind. The quality of the resulting coordinate is mainly influenced by the quality and quantity database of the geocoder and the query algorithm that uses these database. The geocoding-quality of each geocoder can vary from area to area, from country to country and of course from street to street, too.

A.-L. Lamprecht et al. (Eds.): Process Design for Natural Scientists, CCIS 500, pp. 161–174, 2014.
DOI: 10.1007/978-3-662-45006-2_13

Fig. 1. Example address in Yahoo Maps

Fig. 2. Example address in Bing Maps

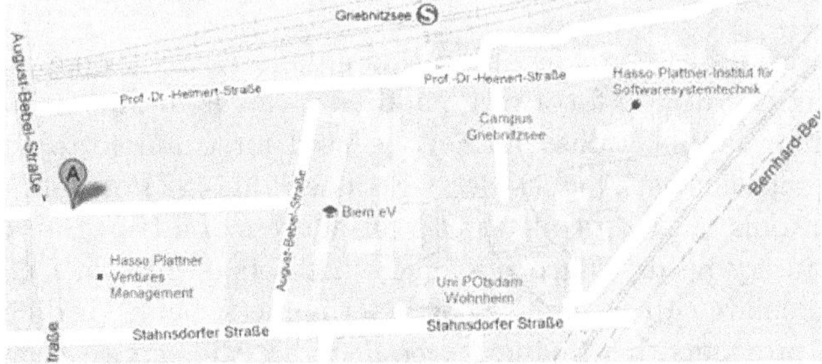

Fig. 3. Example address in Google Maps

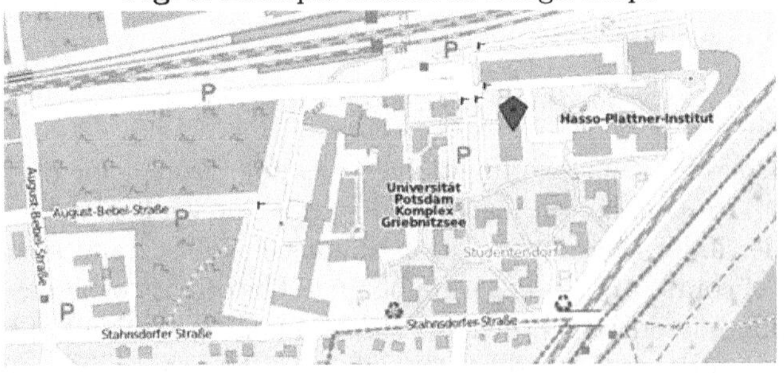

Fig. 4. Example address in Open Street Maps

An example: To find the address of the Institute of Computer Science of the Potsdam University on a map the user has to search the address "August-Bebel-Strasse 89, 14482 Potsdam" in the adopted map service application which uses an internal geocoder. Possible map applications are Yahoo Maps (Fig. 1), Bing Maps (Fig. 2), Google Maps (Fig. 3) and also Open Street Maps (Fig. 4). If the address is obviously wrongly located like in Fig. 1, where the address is placed at the forest, the user will turn to the next map application and start the next try until he finds a "better" location. The best fitting to the real world location is calculated by OSM in Fig. 4

To handle huge address datasets like customer information of shops or addresses of fellow students the processing must be automated. In this case the user applies the adopted API to process the list of addresses. There is no time to verify each single coordinate if it looks "right". So which geocoder is the best one? And first of all: What is actually meant by "best"?

Well, in geo-information the accuracy of coordinates is very important. Accuracy describes how exact the coordinate fits to the real world object. However the geocoder has got two meanings of accuracy, firstly the accuracy of query fitting and secondly the accuracy of the coordinate. All those information come with the resulting coordinate as metadata. So comparing the geocoders means to compare the metadata.

Aim of this project is to show the user the confidence and reliability of a set of geocoders to a given address. Furthermore the automated processing of address datasets will use all geocoders instead of one. It will pick up the coordinate with the best given accuracy. The delimitation will be that only the accuracy of the coordinate will be included, not the accuracy of the query.

2 Service Analysis

The four geocoders which will be part of the challenge are:

- "Yahoo! PlaceFinder",
- "Bing Maps Locations API",
- "Google Maps Geocoding API" in second edition, which has been marked as deprecated and
- "Google Maps Geocoding API" in third edition, which is the currently supported API.

All considered geocoders are free and web-based, which means they are available by plain HTML GET-requests. Unfortunately the Open Street Maps geocoder named Nominatim is not part of the challenge because its metadata does not possess any sensible accuracy-attributes [6].

2.1 Yahoo! PlaceFinder

The "Yahoo! PlaceFinder", in this article simply called "Yahoo", has a well documented metadata set. To use the WebServices of Yahoo a registration is needed. The received AppId must be part of the request. Yahoos response is clear and offers the following coordinate and accuracy-details.

The quality tag stands for one of 28 codes. Eight accuracy-levels (99-80) are reserved for point based qualities. Five accuracy-levels (75-70) are reserved for coordinate qualities on street level. The other 15 accuracy-levels (64-9) will be used for coordinates with an area based quality. The used quality-levels represent a quite even distribution from the best fitting (99 is a concrete coordinate) over a "airport"-sized area (level 64) to the worst fitting (9 is a country). It is very eye-catching and astonishing that more than the half accuracy-levels are used for the poorer area-based quality levels [2].

```
http://where.yahooapis.com/geocode?q=August-Bebel-Strasse%2089,
%2014482%20Potsdam&appid=yahooappid
```

<latitude>52.391460</latitude>
<longitude>13.123140</longitude>
<quality>86</quality>

2.2 Bing Maps Locations API

The "Bing Maps Locations API", in this article easily named "Bing", is not as well documented like the one of Yahoo. The services of Bing need also a registration to receive a BingKey.

The metadata of Bings response include many cascaded information, so the correct accuracy-details are not easy to find. The information for the coordinate accuracy is divided in four levels: "Rooftop", "Parcel", "InterpolationOffset" and "Interpolation". All four accuracy-levels stand for a quite well fitting, for example the difference of the two worst accuracy-levels is that the InterpolationOffset has included the correct street side of an address [5].

```
http://dev.virtualearth.net/REST/v1/Locations/14482%20Potsdam,%
20August-Bebel-Strasse%2089/?o=xml&maxResults=1&key=bingkey
```

<Latitude>52.392732</Latitude>
<Longitude>13.127103</Longitude>
<CalculationMethod>Rooftop</CalculationMethod>

2.3 Google Maps Geocoding API (version 3)

The third edition of the "Google Maps Geocoding API", in this article titled "GMv3", is the current version of the popular Maps API from Google. Google shows a very good documentation of its services with many samples. The connection to the WebService does not need any registration. As an unique feature Google offers information about the map-coverage of its database [4]. The use is free, but also limited to 2.500 requests daily per IP.

The result is much easier to interpret than in Bing. The coordinate accuracy has four different characteristics which are quite similar to those of Bing:

"ROOFTOP", "RANGE_INTERPOLATED", "GEOMETRIC_CENTER", "APPROXIMATE". [3]

```
http://maps.googleapis.com/maps/api/geocode/xml?address=
August-Bebel-Strasse%2089,%2014482%20Potsdam&sensor=false
```

<lat>52.3934502</lat>
<lng>13.1302285</lng>
<location_type>ROOFTOP</location_type>

2.4 Google Maps Geocoding API (version 2)

The second edition of the "Google Maps Geocoding API", in this article shortly named "GMv2", is marked as deprecated. So the service could be switched off every moment without any premonition. But it has nine accuracy-levels, so the comparison of GMv2 and GMv3 is quite interesting. The service requires an API-Key from Google, but it seems that the service provider has disabled the validation of the API-Key. So every API-Key is working now.

The accuracy-levels are numerical attributes, ranged from nine to one where nine stands for the highest accuracy and one for the lowest. It is very exciting that the number of accuracy-levels was reduced in the current version three of the Google Maps Geocoding API. Furthermore the used accuracy-levels are evenly spread like those from Yahoo. [1]

```
http://maps.googleapis.com/maps/geo?q=August-Bebel-Strasse+89,
+14482+Potsdam&output=xml&sensor=false&key=googleapikey
```

<AddressDetails Accuracy="8">
<coordinates>13.1302285,52.3934502,0</coordinates>

2.5 Metadata Comparison

The metadata of each geocoder have their own documentation. They are not normalized and not appropriate to comparison. So each single accuracy-level of a geocoder must be contrasted with all accuracy-levels of the other geocoders. That is a difficult undertaking because each documentation of the geocoders accuracy-levels uses just chunky keywords with fluffy descriptions.

In a first step the accuracy-levels of the geocoder with the most accuracy-levels (Yahoo) will be sorted by its correctness and will further state as reference for the next steps. In the next step the accuracy-levels of the geocoder with the second most accuracy-levels (GMv2) are tried to fit to the first. In the last step the providers with four accuracy-levels (GMv3 and Bing) must be adapted to the previous. The resulting arrangement is shown in the table 1.

2.6 Test Data

To get a representative overview about the coordinate accuracies from all selected geocoders a test run was performed. As test data 232 Potsdam points of interest addresses (POI) were used. The data comes from the `www.potsdam.de/poi` portal which contains addresses of shopping malls, libraries, casinos, hostels and many more. They are available in diverse formats. The processing of this address dataset was automated with a custom Java program which reads addresses and geocodes them with the selected geocoder. Finally a CSV file is exported which adds all accuracy-information. Fig. 5 shows the POIs in the Google Earth. In Table 1 the geocode-analysis is summarized. The table contains also the results of the test data precessing.

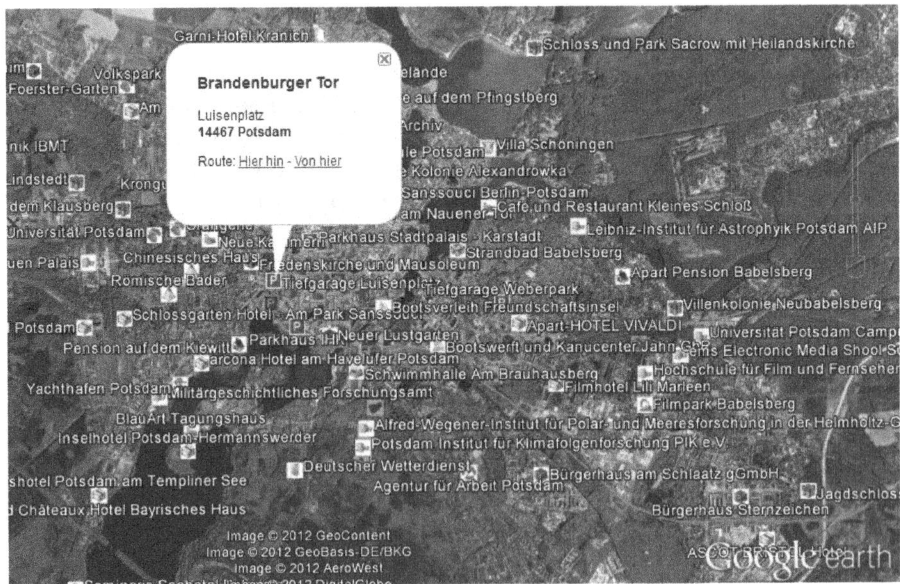

Fig. 5. Potsdam POIs visualized in Google Earth

The data was also analyzed by the sum of winnings and their average rank. A geocoder wins a challenge when the mapped accuracy-rank of the given accuracy-level is better or equal then the others. The average rank is a simple calculation of the average of achieved and mapped accuracy-levels.

3 Workflow Realization

The workflow is partitioned into one very tiny and three large parts, as illustrated in Fig. 6. At first the address must be entered by the user. Second the geocoders are requested. Third the responses will be investigated and finally the results are visualized.

Table 1. Alignment of all accuracy-levels, leading to a normalized accuracy-ranking

accuracy-ranking	Yahoo	GMv2	GMv3	Bing
1	**99**			
2	**90**	**9** (4/2%)		
3	**87** (88/38%)	**8** (176/76%)	**ROOFTOP** (167/71%)	**Rooftop** (146/63%)
4	**86** (14/6%)			**Parcel**
5	**85**			**Interpolation Offset**
6	**84**			**Interpolation** (53/23%)
7	**82**		**RANGE_ INTERPO LATED** (9/4%)	
8	**80**	**7**		
9	**75**		**GEOMETRIC_ CENTER** (41/18%)	
10	**74**			
11	**72**	**6** (41/18%)		
12	**71** (10/4%)			
13	**70**			
14	**64**			
15	**63**		**APPROX IMATE** (10/4%)	
16	**62**			
17	**60** (106/46%)	**5** (3/1%)		
18	**59** (3/1%)			
19	**50**			
20	**49** (6/3%)			
21	**40** (4/2%)	**4**		
22	**39** (1/<1%)			
23	**30**	**3**		
24	**29**			
25	**20**	**2**		
26	**19**			
27	**10**	**1**		
28	**9**			
unknown	0	7/3%	5/2%	33/14%
winnings	88/38%	97/42%	45/19%	179/77%
average ranking	10.9	5.4	4.8	3.8

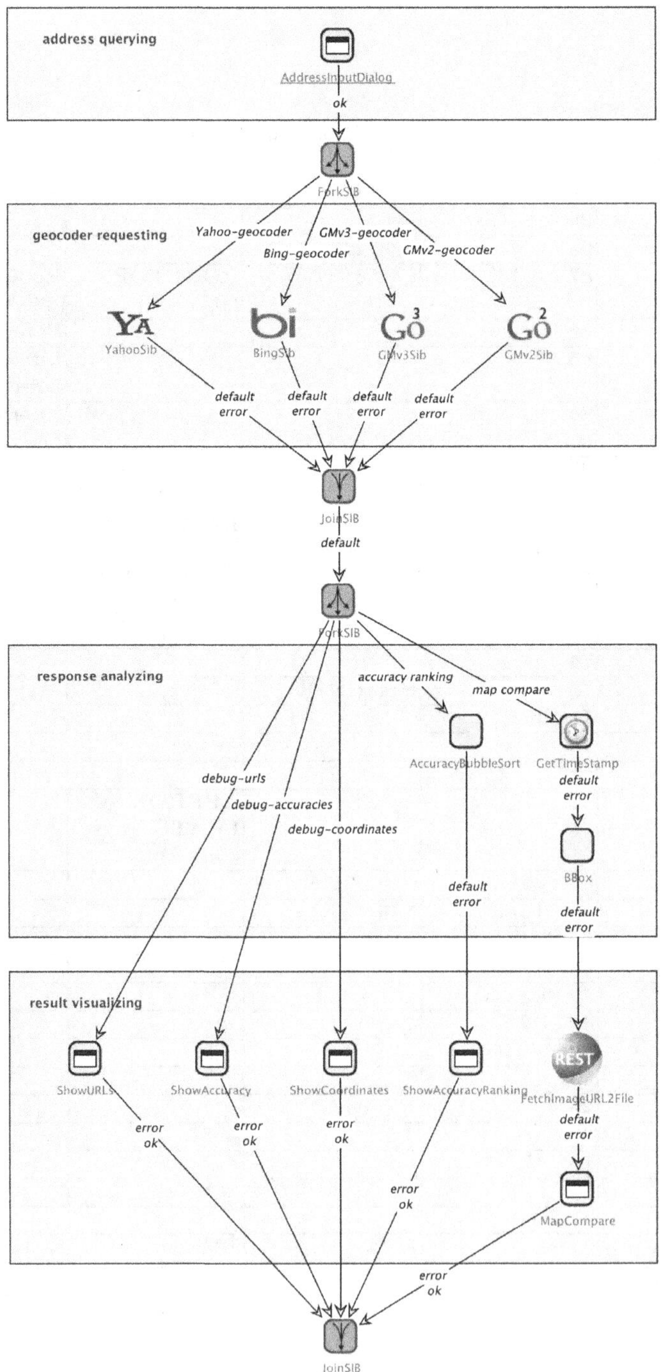

Fig. 6. The complete jABC workflow

3.1 Address Querying

This is just a common ShowInputDialog where the address can be inserted, see Fig. 7. The address will be saved in the ContextKey *address_query*.

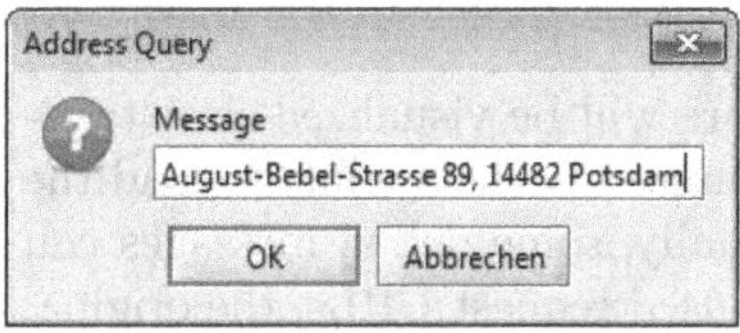

a) A precise address

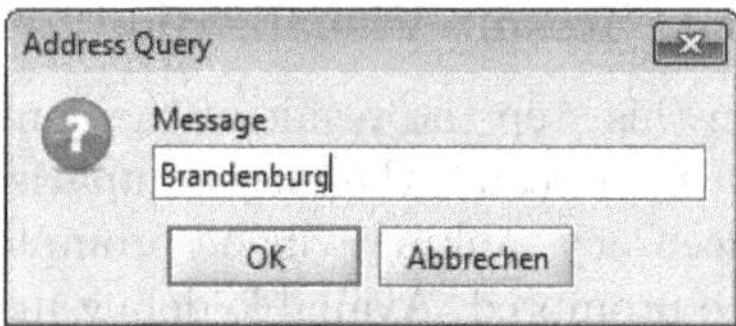

b) An imprecise address

Fig. 7. Address queries

3.2 Geocoder Requesting

In this step all selected geocoders as described in the previous section are requested simultaneously. All these SIBs are custom SIBs. The input of these custom SIBs is just the *address_query* ContextKey as ContextExpression. Internally they are building the URL to request the geocoder and parsing the XML-response to filter the coordinate and accuracy-information. If a geocoder needs a registration key, this it is configured in the SIB internally.

The resulting ContextKeys are separated parts of the coordinate named *coodinate_lon* and *coordinate_lat* and the original value of the accuracy field named *accuracy*.

The used geocoders can easily be extended. The type of the geocoder is not limited to web-based geocoders, for example a new custom geocoder could be a local geodatabase or a simple CSV text-file parser.

3.3 Response Analysis

The response analyzing can be understood as a necessary preprocessing of the received coordinates and accuracies from the step before. Currently two analyzing tasks are implemented: the ranking-calculation of the geocoders and the bounding-box-calculation.

The ranking calculation is realized by the mapping from the accuracy-levels to the accuracy-ranking as seen in table 1. This is of course a custom SIB. The input-ContextExpression is a concatenation of the names of the geocoder with their accuracy-levels. The output-ContextKey *formatted_ranking* is a formatted string where the names of the geocoders are ordered by their rank.

The bounding-box-calculation finds out the minimal bounding rectangle of a list of points. It is needed for the map-visualization in the next step. The input-ContextExpressions are a concatenation of all received *coordinates* by the pattern [gc1_lon],[gc1_lat];[gcn_lon],[gcn_lat] and a *buffer*. The buffer describes the free space between the minimal bounding rectangle and the map-corners. It is a percentage value. With a buffer of 0.2 the resulting maps will get a very pleasant layout.

3.4 Result Visualization

In this step the result of the complex steps before will be visualized simultaneously. Because the map-comparison of the coordinates needs a while to load the accuracy-ranking will be prompted first. Optionally, some debug messages can be prompted. Available debug messages are the used request URLs, the original accuracy-levels and the resulting coordinates of all geocoders.

The accuracy-ranking is a common ShowMessageDialog which prompts the generated String from the step before, see Fig. 8.

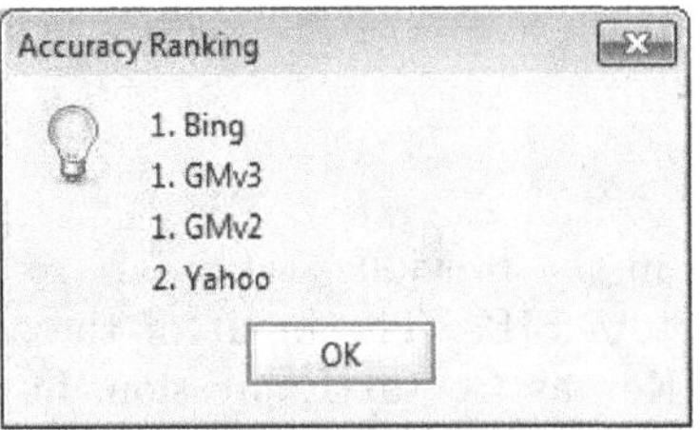

a) precise address

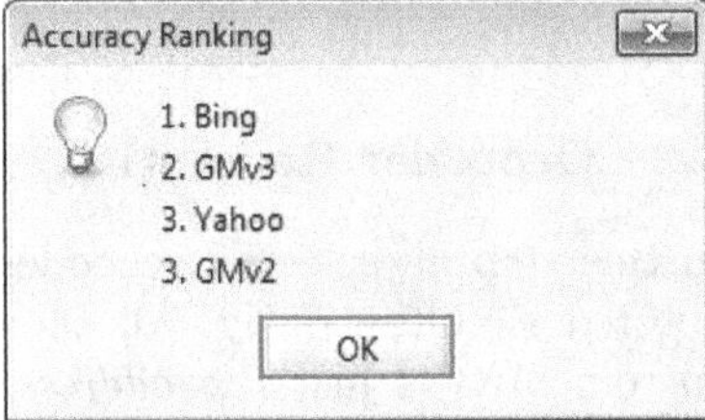

b) imprecise address

Fig. 8. Visualisation of the accuracy-ranking

The map-comparison needs a little workaround: Because there is no SIB that shows an image from an online resource it must be downloaded first via the FetchImageURL2File-SIB which was developed ad-hoc by an advisor of this jABC-course. In the next step this image can be prompted by the common ShowImageDialog, see Fig. 9. The map is received by a static map service which uses Open Street Map data. Furthermore it is possible to add markers onto the static map [24].

Like the geocoders, the visualization methods can be extended very easily. First a diagram-visualization was scheduled, but the interpretation of a bar- or box-plot with it was very imprecise. The problem is that an accuracy-placement on a diagram with a scale-range from 0 to 100 (or 1 to 28 of course) suggests an equal data-range. That is why accuracies of Yahoo and Bing cannot be plotted on the same diagram.

4 Conclusion

The geocoders can now be compared. Gone are the times of evaluating all known map application to make sure that the address is correctly geocoded. But the comparison by a simple mapping is disappointing.

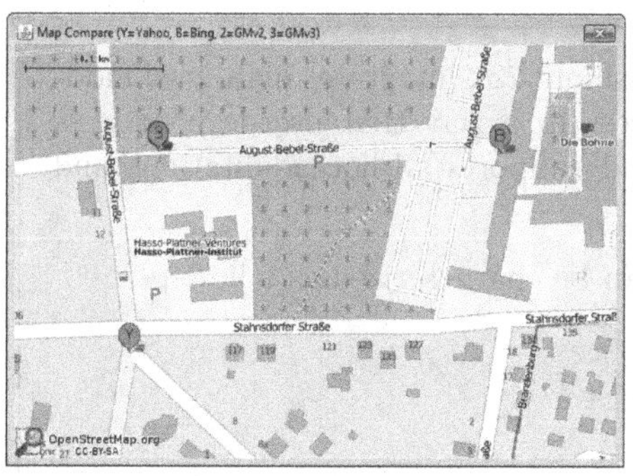

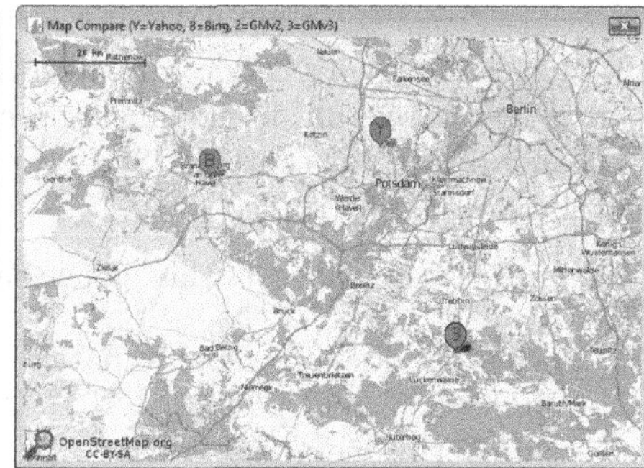

a) precise address b) imprecise address

Fig. 9. Visualization of coordinates on a map

Bing has found an easy way pretending to have good-fitting data: Their accuracy-levels are only good fitting-levels. A further expertise is that GMv2 and GMv3 delivering the same coordinates, but the accuracy-levels in GMv2 have a finer resolution than in GMv3.

The metadata of the geocoders offer more interesting information than accuracy. For example Yahoo has more information like radius which provides information about the radius of the matching area. Bing got a MatchCode which provides information about the matching inside the internal administration-level hierarchy. Furthermore it is a pity that the Open Street Map geocoder Nominatim does not provide accuracy-metadata. But facts could be gained by interpreting multiple information of the place metadata like the attributes *class* with values like "place", "highway" or "boundary" and the attribute *type* with values like "residential", "city" or "administrative".

During the work on this jABC project, in the end of May, Gisgraphy published a so called "result comparator" on `http://www.gisgraphy.com/compare/` which does exactly what the Geocoding Accuracy Ranking does: It compares several geocoders. But the result comparator tells nothing about which one possesses the better coordinates.

Also during the work on this project, in the middle of July, James Fees was blogging on http://spatiallyadjusted.com about "Google Maps Is More Accurate Because They Say It Is". He galls about Brian McClendon, the head of Google Earth and Maps, who says that "There is no way to mix the best of one company's product with the best of another" [7]. Apparently, the comparison of the available geocoders is currently a field of high activity.

This article is part of a larger evaluation [13], which aimed at illustrating the power of simplicity-oriented development [20] by validating the claim that process modeling can indeed be handed over to the domain experts by providing them with a graphical modeling framework [29] that covers low-level details in a service-oriented fashion [22], integrates high-level modeling in the overall development process in a way that user-level models become directly executable [21,18], and supports ad-hoc adaptations and evolution [17,19].

The project described in this article can be characterized as follows:

- Scientific domain: geoinformatics
- Number of models: 1
- Number of hierarchy levels: 1
- Total number of SIBs: 18
- SIB libraries used (cf. [16]): common-sibs (11), rest-sibs (1), own sibs (6)
- Service technologies used: REST web services

The geoinformatics part of this volume contains eight other articles on workflow applications in this domain [11,25,10,9,27,26,8,28]. Further geoinformatics workflow projects with the jABC have recently been started. Ongoing work is also exploring how to apply semantics-based (semi-) automatic workflow composition techniques (as provided by, e.g., [23]) to support the workflow design process, as described in [14,15,12] for the bioinformatics domain.

References

1. Caruana, R., Lawrence, S., Giles, C.L.: Overfitting in neural networks: backpropagation. In: Proceedings of 13th Conference on Advances Neural Information Processing Systems, USA, pp. 402–408 (2001)
2. Documentation of the Yahoo PlaceFinder metadata (Online last accessed July 31, 2012) `http://developer.yahoo.com/geo/placefinder/guide/responses.html#address-quality`
3. Google Maps Javascript API V3 Reference (Online; last accessed October 2, 2013)
4. Google Spreadsheets Autofilter (information about the Google Maps data-coverage) (Online; last accessed October 2, 2013), `http://gmaps-samples.googlecode.com/svn/trunk/mapcoverage_filtered.html`
5. Location Data (documentation of the Bing Locations metadata) (Online; last accessed October 2, 2013), `http://msdn.microsoft.com/en-us/library/ff701725.aspx`
6. Nominatim - OpenStreetMap Wiki (Online; last accessed October 2, 2013), `http://wiki.openstreetmap.org/wiki/Nominatim`
7. Fee, J.: Google maps is more accurate because they say it is - spatially adjusted (Online; last accessed October 2, 2013), `http://spatiallyadjusted.com/2012/07/20/google-maps-is-more-accurate-because-they-say-it-is/`
8. Hibbe, M.: Spotlocator – Guess Where the Photo Was Taken! In: Lamprecht, A.-L., Margaria, T. (eds.) Process Design for Natural Scientists. CCIS, vol. 500, pp. 149–160. Springer, Heidelberg (2014)

9. Holler, R.: GraffDok — A graffiti documentation application. In: Lamprecht, A.-L., Margaria, T. (eds.) Process Design for Natural Scientists. CCIS, vol. 500, pp. 239–251. Springer, Heidelberg (2014)
10. Kind, J.: Creation of topographic maps. In: Lamprecht, A.-L., Margaria, T. (eds.) Process Design for Natural Scientists. CCIS, vol. 500, pp. 229–238. Springer, Heidelberg (2014)
11. Kuntzsch, C.: Visualization of data transfer paths. In: Lamprecht, A.-L., Margaria, T. (eds.) Process Design for Natural Scientists. CCIS, vol. 500, pp. 140–148. Springer, Heidelberg (2014)
12. Lamprecht, A.-L.: User-Level Workflow Design. LNCS, vol. 8311, pp. 1–202. Springer, Heidelberg (2013)
13. Lamprecht, A.-L., Margaria, T.: Scientific workflows and XMDD. In: Lamprecht, A.-L., Margaria, T. (eds.) Process Design for Natural Scientists. CCIS, vol. 500, pp. 1–13. Springer, Heidelberg (2014)
14. Lamprecht, A.-L., Margaria, T., Steffen, B.: Bio-jETI: a framework for semantics-based service composition. BMC Bioinformatics 10(Suppl.10), S8 (2009)
15. Lamprecht, A.-L., Naujokat, S., Margaria, T., Steffen, B.: Semantics-based composition of EMBOSS services. Journal of Biomedical Semantics 2(Suppl. 1), S5 (2011)
16. Lamprecht, A.-L., Wickert, A.: The course's SIB libraries. In: Lamprecht, A.-L., Margaria, T. (eds.) Process Design for Natural Scientists. CCIS, vol. 500, pp. 30–44. Springer, Heidelberg (2014)
17. Margaria, T., Steffen, B.: Agile IT: Thinking in User-Centric Models. In: Margaria, T., Steffen, B. (eds.) Leveraging Applications of Formal Methods, Verification and Validation. CCIS, vol. 17, pp. 490–502. Springer, Heidelberg (2009)
18. Margaria, T., Steffen, B.: Business Process Modelling in the jABC: The One-Thing-Approach. In: Cardoso, J., van der Aalst, W. (eds.) Handbook of Research on Business Process Modeling. IGI Global (2009)
19. Margaria, T., Steffen, B.: Continuous Model-Driven Engineering. IEEE Computer 42(10), 106–109 (2009)
20. Margaria, T., Steffen, B.: Simplicity as a Driver for Agile Innovation. Computer 43(6), 90–92 (2010)
21. Margaria, T., Steffen, B.: Service-Orientation: Conquering Complexity with XMDD. In: Hinchey, M., Coyle, L. (eds.) Conquering Complexity, pp. 217–236. Springer, Heidelberg (2012)
22. Margaria, T., Steffen, B., Reitenspiess, M.: Service-oriented design: The roots. In: Benatallah, B., Casati, F., Traverso, P. (eds.) ICSOC 2005. LNCS, vol. 3826, pp. 450–464. Springer, Heidelberg (2005)
23. Naujokat, S., Lamprecht, A.-L., Steffen, B.: Loose programming with PROPHETS. In: de Lara, J., Zisman, A. (eds.) Fundamental Approaches to Software Engineering. LNCS, vol. 7212, pp. 94–98. Springer, Heidelberg (2012)
24. Niechoda, P.: Documentation of Pawel's OSM Static maps API (Online; last accessed July 31, 2012), `http://pafciu17.dev.openstreetmap.org/`
25. Noack, F.: CREADED: Colored-relief application for digital elevation data. In: Lamprecht, A.-L., Margaria, T. (eds.) Process Design for Natural Scientists. CCIS, vol. 500, pp. 186–199. Springer, Heidelberg (2014)
26. Respondek, T.: A workflow for computing potential areas for wind turbines. In: Lamprecht, A.-L., Margaria, T. (eds.) Process Design for Natural Scientists. CCIS, vol. 500, pp. 200–215. Springer, Heidelberg (2014)

27. Scheele, L.: Location analysis for placing artificial reefs. In: Lamprecht, A.-L., Margaria, T. (eds.) Process Design for Natural Scientists. CCIS, vol. 500, pp. 216–228. Springer, Heidelberg (2014)
28. Sens, H.: Web-based map generalization tools put to the test: A jABC workflow. In: Lamprecht, A.-L., Margaria, T. (eds.) Process Design for Natural Scientists. CCIS, vol. 500, pp. 175–185. Springer, Heidelberg (2014)
29. Steffen, B., Margaria, T., Nagel, R., Jörges, S., Kubczak, C.: Model-driven development with the jABC. In: Bin, E., Ziv, A., Ur, S. (eds.) HVC 2006. LNCS, vol. 4383, pp. 92–108. Springer, Heidelberg (2007)

Web-Based Map Generalization Tools Put to the Test: A jABC Workflow

Henriette Sens

Potsdam University, Potsdam, D-14482, Germany
hsens@uni-potsdam.de

Abstract. Geometric generalization is a fundamental concept in the digital mapping process. An increasing amount of spatial data is provided on the web as well as a range of tools to process it. This jABC workflow is used for the automatic testing of web-based generalization services like mapshaper.org by executing its functionality, overlaying both datasets before and after the transformation and displaying them visually in a .tif file. Mostly Web Services and command line tools are used to build an environment where ESRI shapefiles can be uploaded, processed through a chosen generalization service and finally visualized in Irfanview.

Keywords: map generalization, geo-visualization, cartography, CSISS, GDAL, geo-processing.

1 Introduction: Workflow Scenario

A cartographic map - unlike other forms of cartographic or map-like products such as sketch maps, infographics or chorèmes - requires by definition some kind of generalization of the visual representation applied to the geographic data being used [25]. The basic concept is that elements on a map always represent real world phenomena at a scale smaller than their actual size. Therefore, they must be graphically transformed and fitted to the map scale while keeping and even emphasizing their typical and significant appearance. Not semantic but geometric generalization is the key aspect of the present workflow. Geometric generalization means that the size and degree of detail of map objects should de- or increase linear to scale change.

Having been considered "difficult for a computer to execute well" and a rather "human characteristic of judgement" [1] in the early 1990s, with the rise of digital data processing and online on-demand mapping services such as Google Maps, map generalization is now an integral part of the digital cartographic modeling pipeline. But can automated processing achieve what the human eye and aesthetic perception have done for centuries in the map making process?

Generalization tools are widely implemented in desktop GIS or spatial databases like PostGIS, but online free and ready-to-use services are rare. One example of those services is mapshaper.org, a flash-based web tool that uses line simplification algorithms to reduce the complexity of a given polygon by eliminating a calculated subset of outline vertices. Manual alteration and vertex

A.-L. Lamprecht et al. (Eds.): Process Design for Natural Scientists, CCIS 500, pp. 175–185, 2014.
DOI: 10.1007/978-3-662-45006-2_14

editing is also offered. So the aim of this project is to create a testing environment for different generalization tools.

It consists of the following principal steps:

1. Choose a generalization tool
2. Execute it and store the new data as SHP (ESRI shapefile)
3. Convert it to GML (Geography Markup Language) format
4. Overlay and intersect the two data layers
5. Convert the intersection layer into TIFF (Tagged Image File Format) format
6. Display the TIFF in a new Irfan View instance

The idea is to provide a process that includes the data processing as well as the visualization and gets the user to choose between several tools. Input data required is a polygon or polyline dataset in ESRIs shapefile format. It is then being altered by the chosen web service which again has a shapefile output. To be processed in the CSISS overlay web service [3], it needs be converted to GML data format. Finally, the result of the overlay is rasterized to a TIF file which is displayed in Irfan View, a small free-ware program that lets one open and to a small extent, alter pictures.

2 Service Analysis

The fundamental concept of the workflow is to execute several services programmatically - mostly via the Execute Command SIB that addresses command line tools.

- **Mapshaper - URL (Execute Command)**
  Up to the present date, only one generalization service could be found on the web which is the mapshaper.org. It is therefore the only selectable service and the workflow will be based upon it. The flash-based web-application mapshaper.org comes with a client interface, shown in Figure 1, that can be addressed through a web browser via the URL `http://mapshaper.com/test/MapShaper.swf`. The SIB Mapshaper - URL addresses the command prompt "mapshaper.cmd" which opens a firefox browser instance and loads the given URL.
  Naturally, this SIB needs a web browser and a flash plug-in as a requirement. The service is platform independent and its parameters (e.g. generalization algorithms or detail level) can only be altered manually through the browser GUI and not via jABC.
  The application uses ESRI-Shapefiles which is a proprietary vector file system that consists of the 3 basic files .SHP (stores geometric feature information), .SHX (linkage between .SHP and .DBF) and .DBF (stores feature attributes).
  The service contains three different line-simplification algorithms to choose from (Douglas-Peucker, Weight-Visvalingham and Visvalingham-Wyatts) and

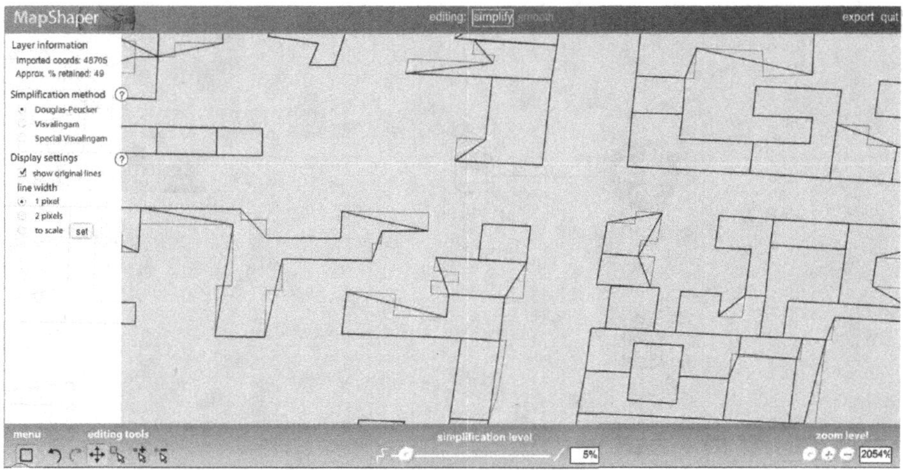

Fig. 1. Web Service Mapshaper.org

apparently eliminates topological errors such as overlap and gaps between adjacent polygons. The level of generalization can also be altered. Additional vertex editing tools can be used as well. The outcome can be viewed on-the-fly.

- **GDAL - Geospatial Data Abstraction Library (Execute Command)**
  GDAL is a C++ open source translator library for raster and vector geospatial data formats and uses command line utilities for data translation and processing. It contains different subcomponents such as "OGR" or the utility program "GDAL_RASTERIZE". The first is a simple feature library that provides read and write access to a variety of vector file formats facilitating conversion between them [4]. The latter is used to burn vector data into existing raster files. The library needs to be downloaded and installed and can be addressed via command line. A batch file called "SDKShell.bat" comes with the installation and needs to be run first before executing the commands. It sets up the environment for using the command line tools. It runs on all modern Unix-based operation systems and most Windows versions.
- **Geobrain - Geospatial Web Services (CSISS) (Webservice)**
  The Geobrain Geospatial Web Services are a collection of services to process and manipulate many geodata formats, e.g. satellite images, raster data, vector maps etc. Developed by the Center for Spatial Information Science and Systems of the George Mason University in Fairfax, Virginia, the services are SOAP based. In this workflow, the Service Raster Overlay is used to intersect both the raw and the generalized vector datasets.
- **IrfanView (Execute Command)**
  The generated TIF file is opened in an instance of the small programm Irfanview. Irfanview needs to be installed, the programm is adressed under C:\Program Files (x86)\IrfanView\i_view32.exe.

3 Workflow Realization

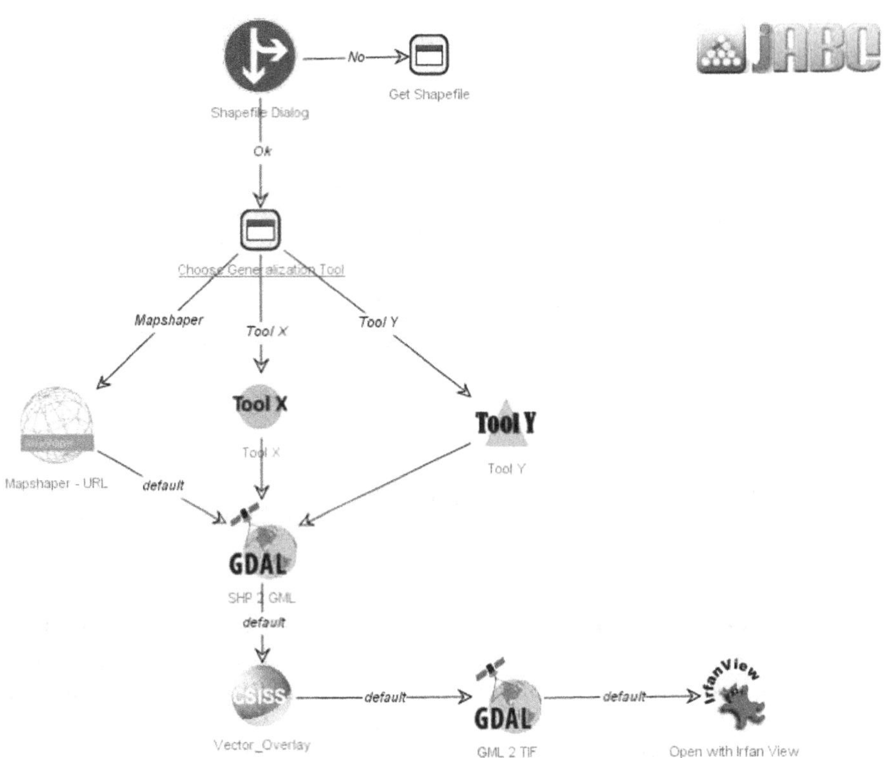

Fig. 2. jABC Workflow

Having the services characterized in the previous section, the realization of the actual workflow in jABC will now be described. It is a linear process with no sub-models or loops. The only interaction with the user is necessary in the welcome dialog where the user has to choose the generalization tool (see Fig.2).

The workflow begins with a reminder to have a shapefile ready for the generalization (see Fig. 3) and if not, to provide one (ShowMessageDialog, see Fig. 4). What follows is a dialog window (Show.Branching.Dialog) in which the user is asked to choose a generalization tool to perform the workflow with.

Tools X and Y are represented by prototype SIBs which can later be replaced by other actual tools. The only executable tool is Mapshaper.

The generalization web service is then being executed through the Execute Command SIB "Mapshaper - URL". It simply addresses the command file "mapshaper.cmd" in a local folder which opens a Firefox instance with the mapshaper.org - URL (see Fig. 6).

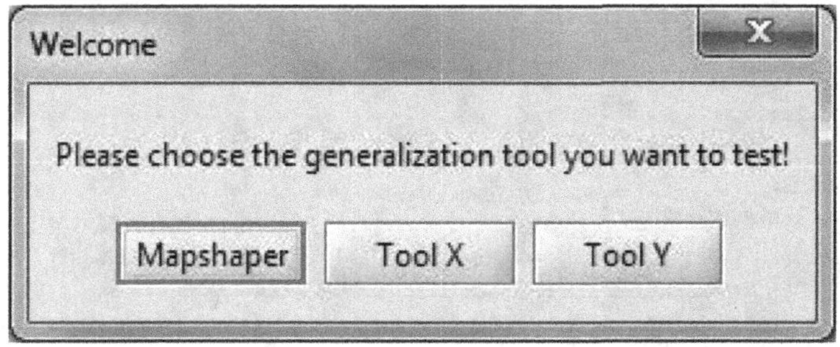

Fig. 3. Branching dialog: choose a generalization tool

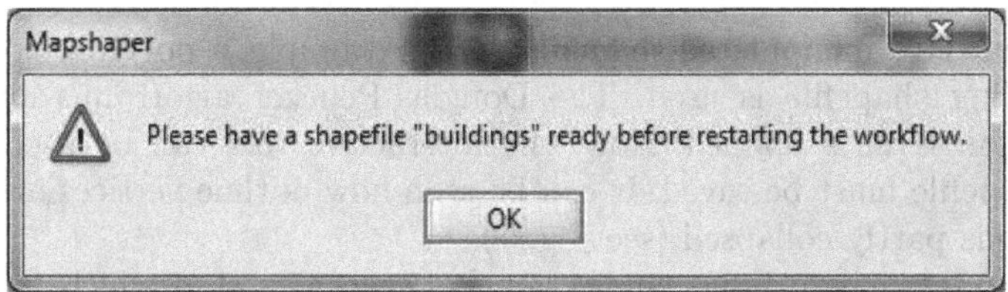

Fig. 4. Message dialog: please provide a shapefile

Fig. 5. Message dialog: tool not yet available

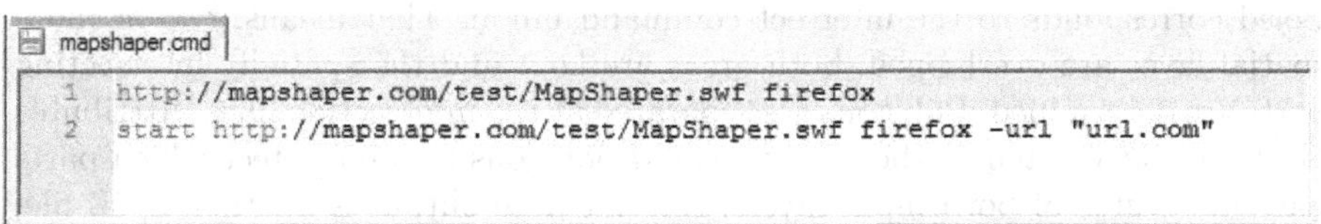

Fig. 6. Commandline: opens firefox browser with specific URL

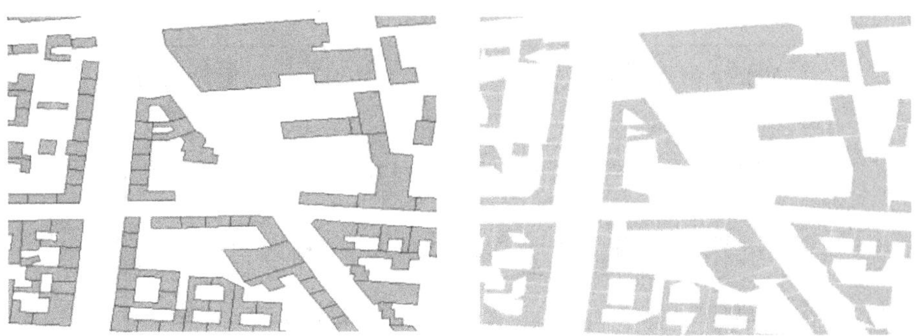

Fig. 7. Buildings before (left) and after generalization (right)

The result is a manipulated shapefile. In the example, a polygon Open Street Map building shapefile is used. The Douglas-Peucker algorithms and a 5%-simplification level is applied. Now, the interactive tool can be used and the output shapefile must be saved. It can be seen how outline vertices are reduced and polygons partly collapsed (see Fig. 7).

Unfortunately, there is no connection between this step which is still performed in the mapshaper.org web environment and the rest of the workflow, so it needs to be restarted manually at that point in the process.

shp_2_gml.cmd

```
ogr2ogr -f "GML" buildings_gen.gml buildings_gen.shp
ogr2ogr -f "GML" buildings.gml buildings.shp

```

Fig. 8. Commandline: converts shapfiles to GML

In the next step, the shapefiles are converted to GML format. This is done by the command line translator OGR 2 OGR (see Fig. 8). The new files are saved in the same folder.

At this point comes the CSISS Vector Overlay SIB into play. Its service performs the overlay between two GML files by the operator OR which in the GIS world corresponds to the intersect command union. That means, two or more spatial layer are overlapped, both areas are kept and the spatially intersecting parts are determined. Polygons are separated at the intersection lines. Attributes are kept and written to the newly created polygons to later detect which parts have attributes of both input layers. Intermediate output is another GML file, in this case named buildings_union.gml.

Another conversion task is executed in the next step. Using the GDAL_ RASTERIZE command, the source GML file is rasterized into a target TIF file which gml_2_tif.cmd

```
gdal_rasterize -burn 255 -l buildings_union buildings_union.gml buildings.tif
```

Fig. 9. Commandline: rasterizes GML to TIF

comes with a world file .TFW for spatial reference. The command line contains the following parameters [4] (see Fig. 9):

- burn: puts a fixed value into a band for all objects, in this case it is the value for red, 255.
- l: indicates the layers from the datasource that will be used for input features, both the GML and TIF file.

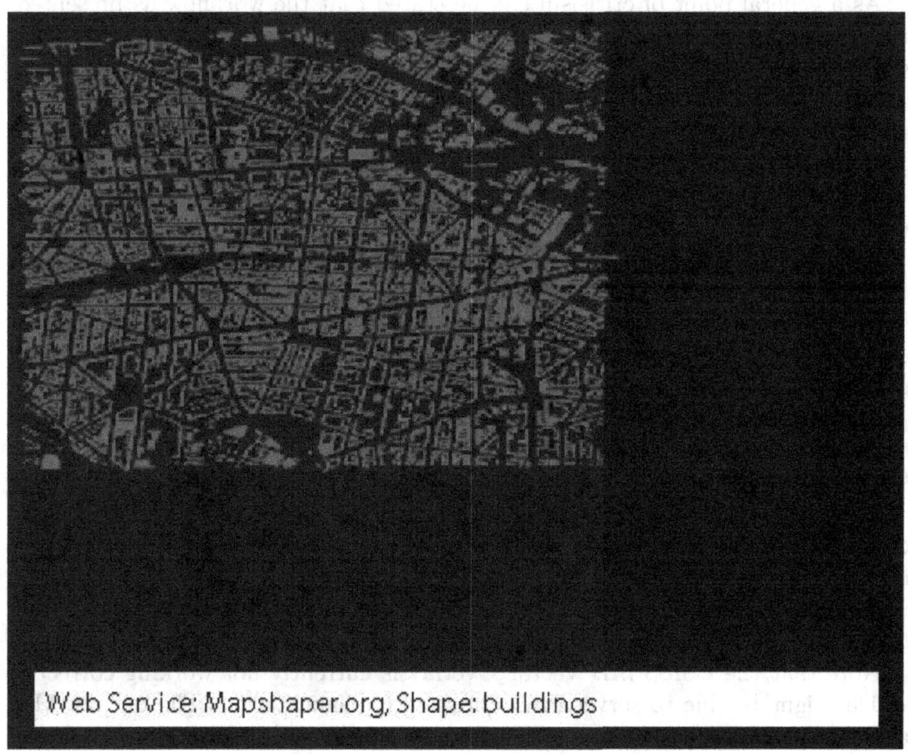

Fig. 10. Final output TIF as seen in Irfanview

Finally, the image is opened and displayed in the program Irfan View (see Fig. 10).

4 Conclusion

Webtools for visualization are numerous and the results already achieve high design standards. Examples like "prettymaps" (http://prettymaps.stamen.com/), "Open Street Map" (http://www.openstreetmap.org/) or "Polymaps" (http:// www.polymaps.org/) give good results. Geodata is also increasingly available on the web, free and ready-to-use as one can easily connect to a geographic database and retrieve information upon request [2]. This is what most web services can offer and interchange standards are also set.

The only missing link from data acquisition to visualization in the pipeline of web based on-demand map production is the actual data processing. Transformation should alter the data geometry and/or semantics. That goes beyond the adaptive zoom function many visualization services offer. At present, free tools and services for geoprocessing and even generalization are rare, but might increasingly be developed as demand is rising. The development should benefit from progression in the other two fields.

As a general point of critisism can be stated that the workflow as presented was realized with just one generalization service, mapshaper.org. If more services were available, a real comparison could be performed at the end of the workflow. Different output datasets of the same input data could be contrasted with one another. The discrepancy of altered and/or collapsed polygon areas could be calculated and displayed. Since the principal concept of the designed workflow has been the comparison between different generalization tools on the web, implementing just one web service does not comply with the initial goal.

As for the concrete form of the current workflow implementation, the workflow could certainly embody more user interaction. Not only choosing a tool to be tested, but also setting its generalization parameters or selecting an algorithm and the input data would enhance the workflows usability. Unfortunately, the nature of the tool mapshaper.org does not allow programmatic access to its parameters in jABC, as it is a highly interactive flash environment. Maybe other tools will be easier to address and maybe some form of interface standards will be developed in the future.

Likewise, it would also be nice to include more interaction dialogues when converting the files. Input files and output file names and directories should be chosen by using the ShowFileChooser SIB. As another idea, a loop could be embedded between the viewing of the outcome in Irfanview and the generalization tool so that in case outputs are not satisfying, the process could be iterated.

Note that the CSISS SIB Vector Overlay is currently not working correctly which might be due to server errors or false implementation. The output TIF also needs alteration in terms of color management and displayed data. There should be an preceding selection command that filters the GML and assigns certain colors according to a SQL-statement.

To conclude the evaluation, we take a closer look at the Mapshaper-Tool. One important question is if the service delivered results that could be used in the further process. The outcome is a shapefile, a proprietary vector format set by the GIS program company ESRI. That format alone can be handled through conversion by other services which is seen as an advantage. But it also comes with great disadvantages: The outcome data of mapshaper.org misses spatial projection. That means no coordinate system is assigned even though the input data (shapefile buildings from Open Street Map) has one. That will cause problems a few steps later with the Vector Overlay, when two data layers should be spatially intersected. The SIB cannot handle unprojected data. Open Street Map data sometimes comes geometrically and/or topologically incorrect. For example, outline rings are not closed and polygons have zero area values. Fixing those data errors is not originally planned to be part of the workflow but should be included since it is crucial to have manageable data to continue the process. To work with the data in the present workflow, those errors were corrected separately in a desktop GIS. Maybe the data should be checked beforehand.

This article is part of a larger evaluation [10], which aimed at illustrating the power of simplicity-oriented development [17] by validating the claim that process modeling can indeed be handed over to the domain experts by providing them with a graphical modeling framework [24] that covers low-level details in a service-oriented fashion [19], integrates high-level modeling in the overall development process in a way that user-level models become directly executable [18,15], and supports ad-hoc adaptations and evolution [14,16].

The project described in this article can be characterized as follows:

- Scientific domain: geoinformatics
- Number of models: 1
- Number of hierarchy levels: 1
- Total number of SIBs: 9
- SIB libraries used (cf. [13]): common-sibs (8), csiss-sibs (1)
- Service technologies used: SOAP web services, web applications, command line tools

The geoinformatics part of this volume contains eight other articles on workflow applications in this domain [8,21,7,26,6,23,22,5]. Further geoinformatics workflow projects with the jABC have recently been started. Ongoing work is also exploring how to apply semantics-based (semi-) automatic workflow composition techniques (as provided by, e.g., [20]) to support the workflow design process, as described in [11,12,9] for the bioinformatics domain.

References

1. Arlinghaus, S.: Practical handbook of digital mapping: terms and concepts. CRC Press, Florida (1994)
2. Burghardt, D., Neun, M., Weibel, R.: Generalization Services on the Web Classification and an Initial Prototype Implementation. Cartography and Geographic Information Science 32(4), 257–268 (2005)

3. Center for Spatial Information Science and Systems (CSISS). CSISS Geospatial Web Services. George Mason University, Fairfax (2011)
4. GDAL Development Team. GDAL - Geospatial Data Abstraction Library, Version 1.9.1. Open Source Geospatial Foundation (2012)
5. Hibbe, M.: Spotlocator Project Documentation. In: Lamprecht, A.-L., Margaria, T. (eds.) Process Design for Natural Scientists. CCIS, vol. 500, pp. 154–163. Springer, Heidelberg (2014)
6. Holler, R.: GraffDok: A Graffiti Documentation Application. In: Lamprecht, A.-L., Margaria, T. (eds.) Process Design for Natural Scientists. CCIS, vol. 500, pp. 235–247. Springer, Heidelberg (2014)
7. Kind, J.: Creation of Topographic Maps. In: Lamprecht, A.-L., Margaria, T. (eds.) Process Design for Natural Scientists. CCIS, vol. 500, pp. 225–234. Springer, Heidelberg (2014)
8. Kuntzsch, C.: Visualization of Data Transfer Paths. In: Lamprecht, A.-L., Margaria, T. (eds.) Process Design for Natural Scientists. CCIS, vol. 500, pp. 140–148. Springer, Heidelberg (2014)
9. Lamprecht, A.-L.: User-Level Workflow Design. LNCS, vol. 8311. Springer, Heidelberg (2013)
10. Lamprecht, A.-L., Margaria, T.: Scientific Workflows and XMDD. In: Lamprecht, A.-L., Margaria, T. (eds.) Process Design for Natural Scientists. CCIS, vol. 500, pp. 1–13. Springer, Heidelberg (2014)
11. Lamprecht, A.-L., Margaria, T., Steffen, B.: Bio-jETI: a framework for semantics-based service composition. BMC Bioinformatics 10(suppl. 10), S8 (2009)
12. Lamprecht, A.-L., Naujokat, S., Margaria, T., Steffen, B.: Semantics-based composition of EMBOSS services. Journal of Biomedical Semantics 2(suppl. 1), S5 (2011)
13. Lamprecht, A.-L., Wickert, A.: The Course's SIB Libraries. In: Lamprecht, A.-L., Margaria, T. (eds.) Process Design for Natural Scientists. CCIS, vol. 500, pp. 30–44. Springer, Heidelberg (2014)
14. Margaria, T., Steffen, B.: Agile IT: Thinking in User-Centric Models. In: Margaria, T., Steffen, B. (eds.) Leveraging Applications of Formal Methods, Verification and Validation. CCIS, vol. 17, pp. 490–502. Springer, Heidelberg (2009)
15. Margaria, T., Steffen, B.: Business Process Modelling in the jABC: The One-Thing-Approach. In: Cardoso, J., van der Aalst, W. (eds.) Handbook of Research on Business Process Modeling. IGI Global (2009)
16. Margaria, T., Steffen, B.: Continuous Model-Driven Engineering. IEEE Computer 42(10), 106–109 (2009)
17. Margaria, T., Steffen, B.: Simplicity as a Driver for Agile Innovation. Computer 43(6), 90–92 (2010)
18. Margaria, T., Steffen, B.: Service-Orientation: Conquering Complexity with XMDD. In: Hinchey, M., Coyle, L. (eds.) Conquering Complexity, pp. 217–236. Springer, London (2012)
19. Margaria, T., Steffen, B., Reitenspieß, M.: Service-Oriented Design: The Roots. In: Benatallah, B., Casati, F., Traverso, P. (eds.) ICSOC 2005. LNCS, vol. 3826, pp. 450–464. Springer, Heidelberg (2005)
20. Naujokat, S., Lamprecht, A.-L., Steffen, B.: Loose programming with PROPHETS. In: de Lara, J., Zisman, A. (eds.) Fundamental Approaches to Software Engineering. LNCS, vol. 7212, pp. 94–98. Springer, Heidelberg (2012)
21. Noack, F.: CREADED: Coloured-Relief Application for Digital Elevation Data. In: Lamprecht, A.-L., Margaria, T. (eds.) Process Design for Natural Scientists. CCIS, vol. 500, pp. 182–195. Springer, Heidelberg (2014)

22. Respondeck, T.: A Workflow for Computing Potential Areas for Wind Turbines. In: Lamprecht, A.-L., Margaria, T. (eds.) Process Design for Natural Scientists. CCIS, vol. 500, pp. 196–211. Springer, Heidelberg (2014)
23. Scheele, L.: Location Analysis for Placing Artificial Reefs. In: Lamprecht, A.-L., Margaria, T. (eds.) Process Design for Natural Scientists. CCIS, vol. 500, pp. 212–224. Springer, Heidelberg (2014)
24. Steffen, B., Margaria, T., Nagel, R., Jörges, S., Kubczak, C.: Model-driven development with the jABC. In: Bin, E., Ziv, A., Ur, S. (eds.) HVC 2006. LNCS, vol. 4383, pp. 92–108. Springer, Heidelberg (2007)
25. Stern, B., Hurni, L., Werner, M., Wiesmann, S.: Generalisation of Map Data (2011), `http://www.gitta.info/Generalisati/en/text/Generalisati.pdf`
26. Teske, D.: Geocoder Accuracy Ranking. In: Lamprecht, A.-L., Margaria, T. (eds.) Process Design for Natural Scientists. CCIS, vol. 500, pp. 159–170. Springer, Heidelberg (2014)

CREADED: Colored-Relief Application for Digital Elevation Data

Franziska Noack

Potsdam University, Potsdam, D-14482, Germany
fnoack@uni-potsdam.de

Abstract. In the geoinformatics field, remote sensing data is often used for analyzing the characteristics of the current investigation area. This includes DEMs, which are simple raster grids containing grey scales representing the respective elevation values. The project CREADED that is presented in this paper aims at making these monochrome raster images more significant and more intuitively interpretable. For this purpose, an executable interactive model for creating a colored and relief-shaded Digital Elevation Model (DEM) has been designed using the jABC framework. The process is based on standard jABC-SIBs and SIBs that provide specific GIS functions, which are available as Web services, command line tools and scripts.

Keywords: geoinformatics, remote sensing, digital elevation model, geovisualization, geoprocessing, shaded relief, raster image.

1 Introduction: Workflow Scenario

The idea for this project is based on the workflow presented by the GIS specialist Tim Sutton [30]: To get elevation data visualized is a standard demand in geoinformatics and remote sensing. The resulting colored relief models are generally used to gain an overview of the respective investigation area. The required functions for visualizing digital elevation data are provided by common GIS software products. The approach of the CREADED project was to integrate these consecutive work steps into a stand-alone application. To achieve this, several Web services, command line tools and scripts were integrated into the jABC framework. Thus, no complex GIS program is needed on the local computer. Instead, the designated DEM file can be processed in a user-friendly way and during all process units different options and settings can be selected to obtain the desired result.

At the beginning of the workflow, the user selects the DEM raster dataset that should be processed from his local file system. After uploading the raster file, it has to be transformed in the geographic coordinate system WGS 84. This is a requirement of Web services used later in the process. For this projection, the user needs to insert the EPSG code (an international conventional code system for identifying coordinate systems) of the current system. A list of the supported coordinate systems with both name and EPSG code can be displayed as needed.

A.-L. Lamprecht et al. (Eds.): Process Design for Natural Scientists, CCIS 500, pp. 186–199, 2014.
DOI: 10.1007/978-3-662-45006-2_15

If desired, the DEM can then be clipped to an area of interest. This area can be defined either by the edge coordinates of a rectangle or by a polygon, that needed to be available in the common shapefile format. Afterwards a shaded relief image can be created from the elevation data contained in the DEM file. A shaded relief is intended to imitate illumination, shading and shadows on the topography. The influencing variables, like azimuth and altitude angle, are arbitrary. The next step is to colorize the DEM with a specific color ramp. The user can use his own color definitions stored in a txt-file, or simply choose from a collection of common color tables. In a final step, the shaded relief and the colored image are merged into one combined image as shown in Figure 1. This illustration contrasts an original grey scale DEM with a clipped area, which has passed through the whole workflow. In comparison to the original raster image, the topography within the manipulated area can be more easily interpreted.

Fig. 1. Comparison of the original DEM and the processed area

2 Service Analysis

To make the workflow components executable some preparations and adaptions are required. For the intermediate storage of files during the process, a FTP folder is used (`jabc.bplaced.net`). This requires a permanent internet connection and implies a limitation in file sizes, especially concerning the DEM file. The login information for the FTP folder is contained in the respective SIBs. For both the FTP upload and the fetching of data to the local file system, specific SIBs have been developed and provided by the staff of the Potsdam university. For the local installation of required programs and the storage of resulting data, the local workspace *D:\jABC* has to be created.

The first part of the process is the projection of the current coordinate system. For that a command line tool from the Geospatial Data Abstraction Library [3] has been used. GDAL offers a variety of command line utilities for the processing of raster data. For executing the SIB, download and installation of the GDAL software [24] are required. In the jABC workflow, the projection tool has been integrated by using the jABC ExecuteCommand-SIB.

Also for clipping the DEM raster by using a polygon shapefile, GDAL [3] offers a command line tool. Hence this function was implemented in the Execute-Command-SIB as well. For clipping the DEM based on edge coordinates, the Center for Spatial Information Science and Systems (CSISS) [1] provides a WSDL service named *Raster_LatLonBBoxClip*. A SIB accessing this Web service has been developed and provided by the institute staff. The coordinates which are handed over as parameters need to be in the EPSG 4326 coordinate system, because of which the transformation has been executed at the beginning of this workflow.

The next step is the creation of a shaded relief map based on elevation data. For this a SIB based on the CSISS service *Raster_TopographicShading* [1] has been used. The CSISS services accept only an URL to the source file as an input parameter, therefore the FTP upload function has been integrated.

For coloring the DEM image based on percentage-classified RGB color values (self-defined or selected from existing color tables) the Geospatial Data Abstraction Library provides an adequate command line tool [2]. This has been integrated into another ExecuteCommand-SIB.

The last step is the merging of the colored and the relief-shaded DEM. To realize this process the Open Source Geospatial Foundation OSGeo provides a useful script beyond their Python samples [23]. Hence it is possible to execute this script by using a command line, it has been implemented in an ExecuteCommand-SIB as well. But to successfully execute this SIB, a couple of preparations are necessary: If not already existing, the Python software [25] and the release specific GDAL program needs to be installed [4]. Furthermore the additional package *NumPy* is required [4].

3 Workflow Realization

The main part of the model is displayed in Figure 2. In the jABC framework, thematically self-contained parts of the model can be exported into separate subgraphs by using macros. This causes no modification of the functionality, but is recommended for more visual clarity. The submodels used in the project CREADED are illustrated in Figures 3 to 9.

In the whole application an extensive error reporting has been integrated. If the FTP upload or download fails, the program returns a specific error message. For all integrated services and command line tools the error messages contain the specific error text retrieved either by the Web service or by the console. Moreover all user inputs that have to be in a specific range (like the coordinates for clipping the DEM) are evaluated by using the EvaluateCondition-SIB. Invalid inputs result in an error and in a reopening of the input dialog.

For the user interaction (information and conditional branching) the Common-SIBs ShowMessageDialog and ShowBranchingDialog are used. The workflow starts with the request to select the DEM file that should be processed. For this selection the ShowFileChooser-SIB has been used. This Common-SIB allows the specification of a default file type, here the file extension tif has been preset. The selected file is then stored in the execution context as a variable by using a ContextKey. A branching dialog gives the user the option to start the projection submodel, if the DEM file is not in the WGS84 coordinate system. Otherwise the file will be directly uploaded to the FTP folder. The projection subgraph (see Fig. 3) starts with the demand if the EPSG code of the current coordinate system is known. If the user confirms this question, he will be directly forwarded to the input formula. Otherwise the list of supported EPSG codes will be displayed. For this the csv-file containing this list is retrieved from the FTP folder (where it has been stored beforehand to be accessible from other computers) by using the FetchDataURL2File-SIB. The thus locally stored file is put in the execution context by using the ReadTextFile-SIB. Now it can be displayed by simply integrating the chosen ContextKey in the ShowTextDialog-SIB. After inspecting this list the user will be redirected to the input dialog. The inserted code will be validated by using the EvaluateCondition-SIB and only codes between 3819 and 5546 will be accepted. If the chosen value is outside this range, the user gets an error message and the code list displayed again. Here it is necessary to load the list from the FTP folder again. Otherwise, if the user has selected the direct opening of the input formula in the first branching dialog, the list would not be available. After evaluating the code, the ExecuteCommand-SIB executes the projection. If successfully created, the thus locally stored projected file is put in the execution context as a variable by defining a ContextKey. To complete this part, the projected file will be stored in the FTP folder.

In the next branching dialog the user has to decide if and how the DEM image should be clipped (see second part in Fig. 2). If clipping is not desired by the user, the image will be fetched from the FTP URL, stored in the execution context by using a new variable name and uploaded again on the FTP server.

Main Model

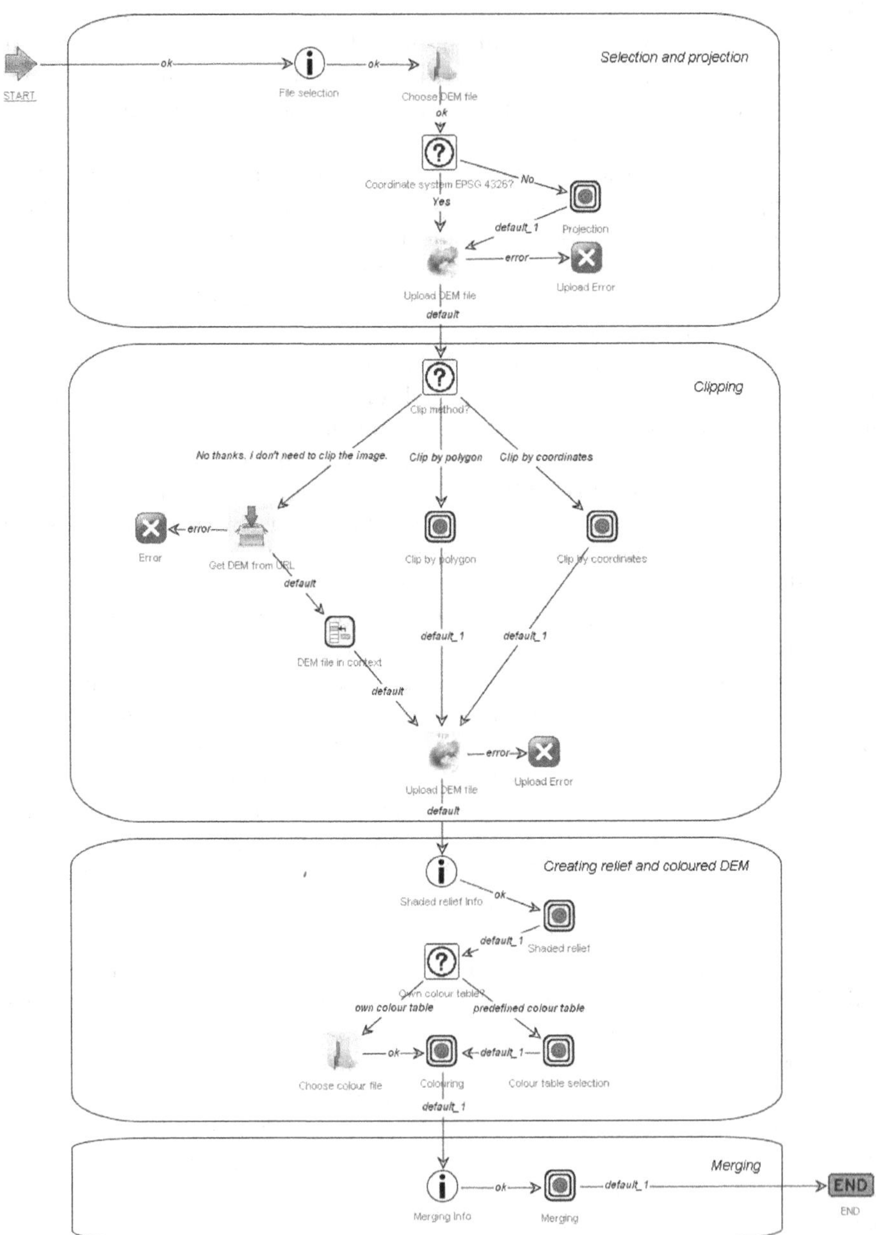

Fig. 2. Main workflow without extracted submodels

Submodel I: Projection

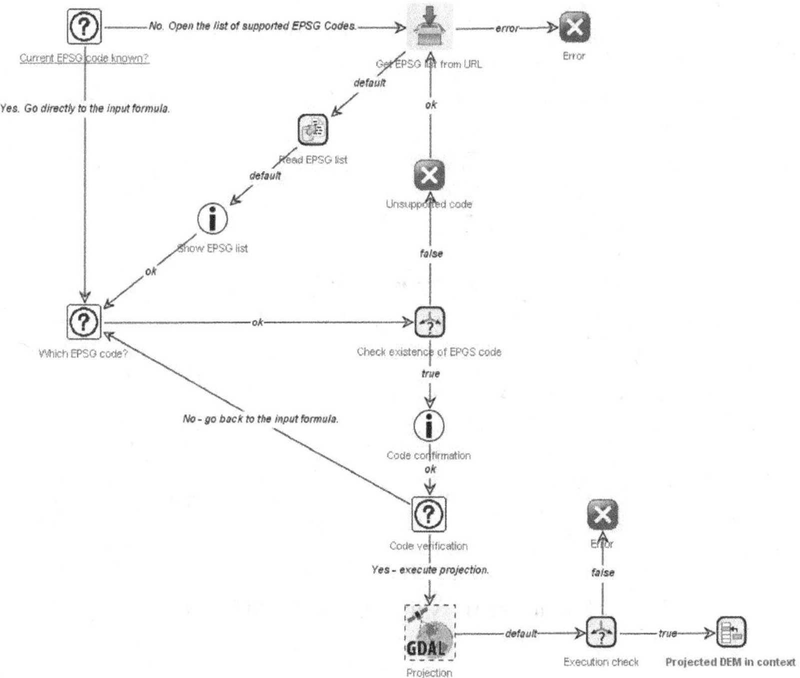

Fig. 3. Submodel I - Projection of the DEM file

This procedure is used to ensure one unique filename when the parallel branches join at the end. This is required for further processing stages.

If the user wants to clip the DEM by using a polygon shapefile, the second submodel will be invoked (see Fig. 4). The ESRI® shapefile is a vector data format consisting of several files. Required files for this process are: shape format (*.shp), shape index format (*.shx), attribute format (*.dbf) and projection format (*.prj). The user has to select these files consecutively. For this the ShowFileChooser-SIB (with respective default settings for file extensions) has been integrated. All files are uploaded on the FTP server and then stored in the local workspace, but only the shp-file has to be stored in the execution context. The clipping command line tool requires only the shp-file as an input parameter, but the corresponding files need to be accessible and stored in the same folder. Otherwise the ExecutionCommand-SIB would return an error. Instead of uploading and fetching the files, the user could have been asked to copy them manually into the workspace folder. However, due to the automatic character of the whole project, the other option has been chosen. Finally, the clipped image will be stored in the execution context and uploaded to the FTP server.

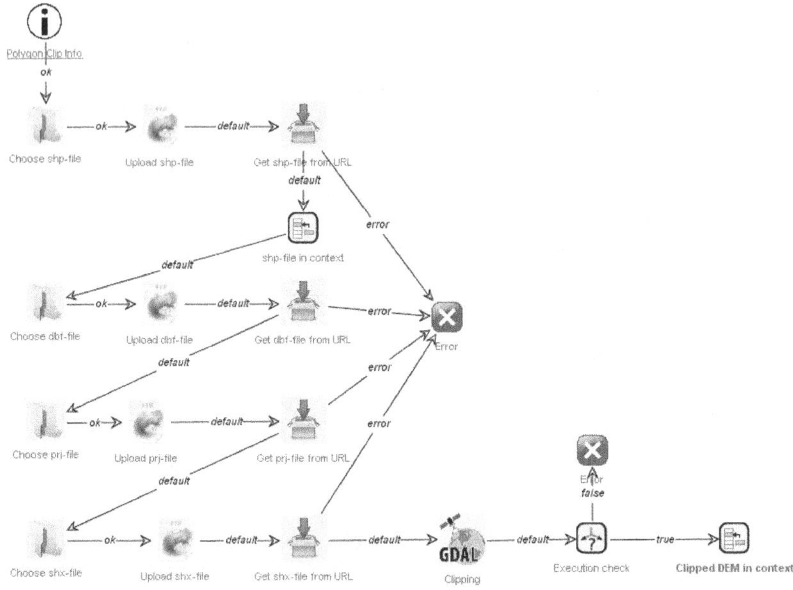

Fig. 4. Submodel II - Clipping the DEM by polygon

The third branch (see second part of Fig. 2) stands for the option to clip the DEM by coordinates, representing the edges of a rectangle. This process has been exported into a submodel (see Fig. 5). After validating the inserted coordinate values, the CSISS-SIB executes the clipping of the DEM file. The resulting dataset is stored in a variable and can be fetched to the local workspace using the FetchDataURL2File-SIB. Finally, the file is put in the execution context and uploaded into the FTP folder for further processing.

Contrary to the proposed sequence by Tim Sutton [30], the clipping part has not been integrated as the last process part of the workflow. The reason lies in the file size of digital elevation models: the workflow becomes more efficient if the image is clipped first and only the required part is further processed.

In the next process step, the shaded relief will be created (see Fig. 6). Different factors are influencing the resulting topographic shaded image, like altitude and azimuth angle for defining the sun's position. These values can be set by the user (default values are given). The entries will be checked and validated before they are processed by the CSISS-SIB. The resulting shaded relief is fetched from the variable, stored into the execution context and uploaded to the FTP server.

The process part for coloring the DEM contains two branches (see third part in Fig. 2): the user can load own color rules or select between given color ramps. The own color table has to be a simple text file and must have the following

Submodel III: Clip by Coordinates

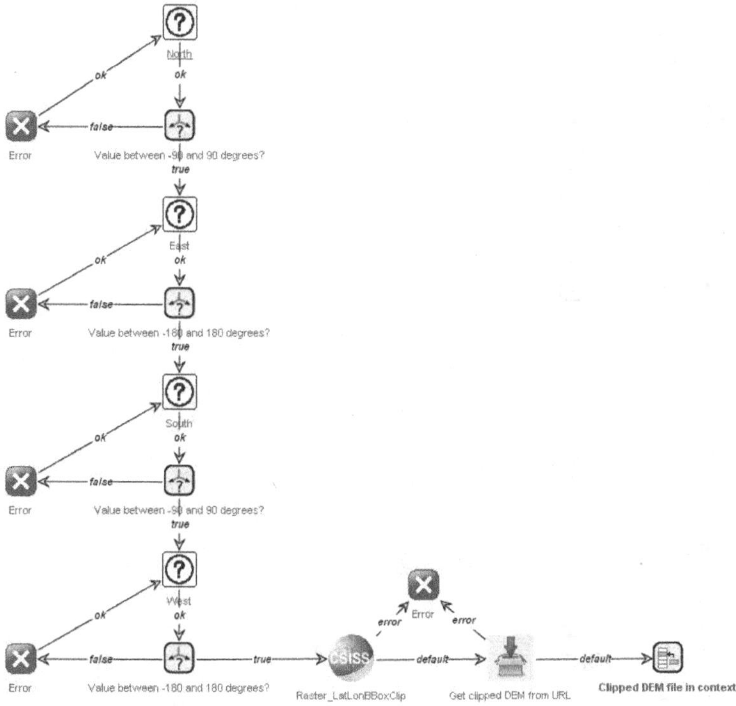

Fig. 5. Submodel III - Clipping the DEM by coordinates

structure (percentaged thresholds and RGB color values):

```
0% 0:230:0
20% 0:160:0
35% 50:130:0
55% 120:100:30
75% 120:130:40
90% 170:160:50
100% 255:255:100
```

The color rules file can be selected by using the ShowFileChooser-SIB and is passed as a variable to the coloring function.

The other branch leads to the color selection submodel (see Fig. 7). The user can go directly to the input formula if the name of the color table is known. The employed color tables are standard GRASS color ramps [22]. The list of supported colors has been stored beforehand in the FTP folder and is here fetched to a local file and then put into the execution context by using the ReadTextFile-SIB. The ShowTextDialog-SIB allows the display of the color information. In advance, the list of supported color tables has been restricted to

Submodel IV: Shaded Relief

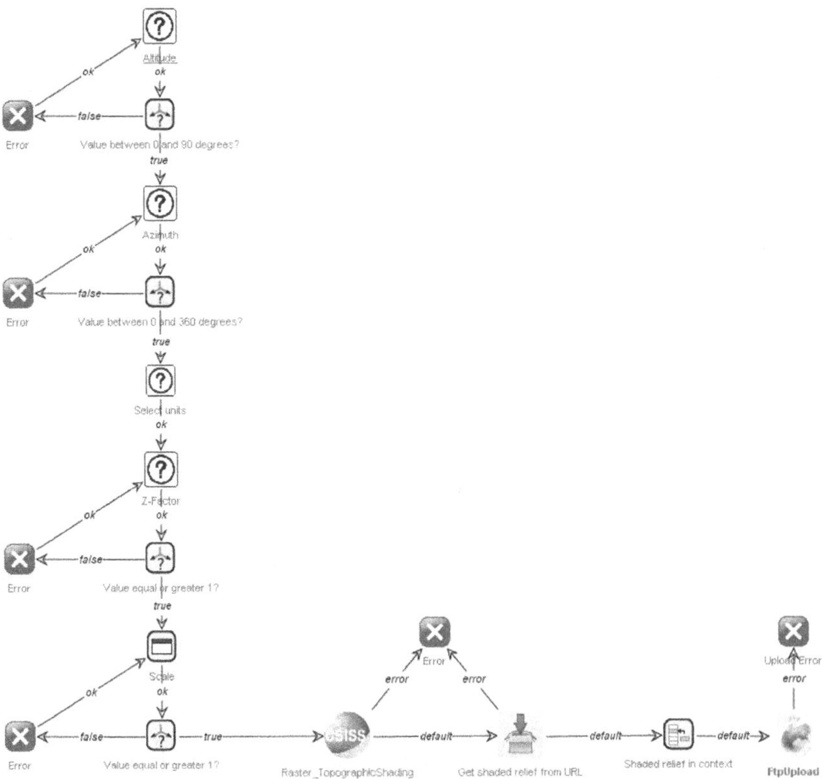

Fig. 6. Submodel IV - Creation of a shaded relief image

those that are defined by percentage values, because that is a limitation of the command line tool that executes the coloring. After inspecting the list of supported color ramps the user will be redirected to the input dialog. The inserted name is stored as a variable and a subsequent test checks if this name is on the list and can be processed. If this is the case, then the specific color rules for the selected color ramp can be fetched from the respective website - for this the URL to the GRASS color tables [22] will be expanded with the specific color name that has been stored in the variable. The resulting URL leads to the color rules of the desired color table and they will be stored in a local text file. Then this file is put in the execution context and uploaded into the FTP folder.

Wether self-defined or loaded from the GRASS website, a color table is now stored on the FTP server and can be processed by the coloring command line tool (see Fig. 8). The colored DEM is stored in the execution context and uploaded into the FTP folder for further processing.

Submodel V: Colour Table Selection

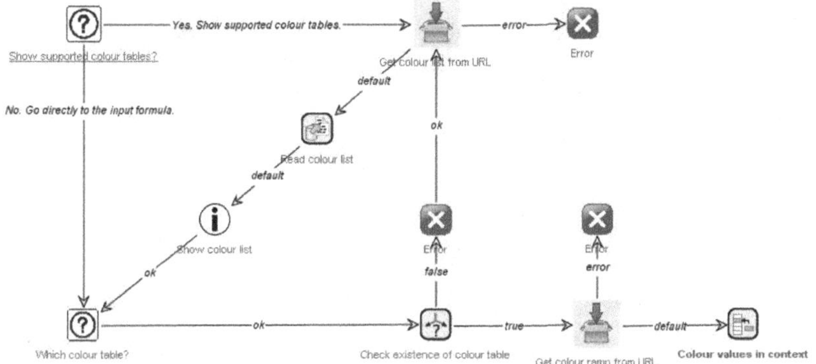

Fig. 7. Submodel V - Color table selection

Submodel VI: Colouring

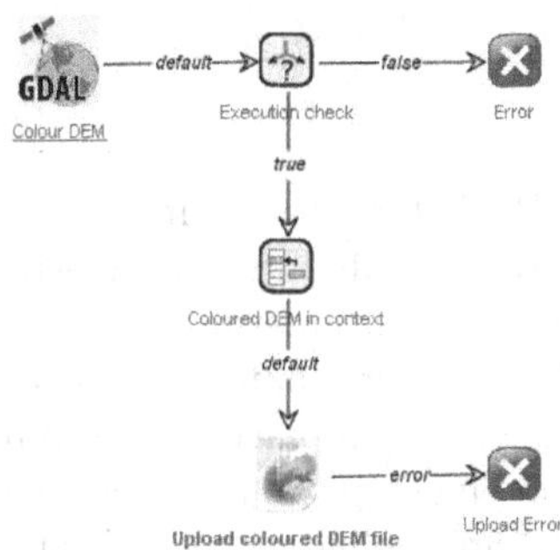

Fig. 8. Submodel VI - Colouring of the DEM

The initial plan was to parallelize the creation of the shaded relief and the colored image, because they are both based on the DEM file and not interdependent. This could have been realized by using the Fork- and the Join-SIB. But due to the fact that both processes contain user interactions, they are executed sequentially.

The last process of the workflow is the creation of the final dataset by merging the colored image with the shaded relief (see Fig. 9). As previously discussed, this will be achieved by using a python script [23]. This is stored locally by using the FetchDataURL2File-SIB. The ExecutionCommand-SIB gets the input files (colored DEM and shaded relief) from variables and runs the script in the local workspace. After the successful execution the created dataset is put in the execution context, uploaded into the FTP folder and then stored as *result.tif* in the local workspace.

Submodel VII: Merging

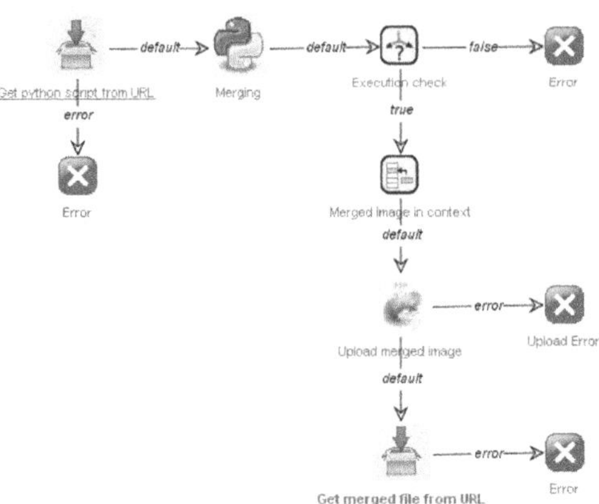

Fig. 9. Submodel VII - Merging of colored DEM and shaded relief image

4 Conclusion

The idea of the project CREADED was to integrate common GIS functions for creating colored relief-shaded DEMs into a stand-alone application. This could be successfully realized. A few adaptions and local extensions arose during the realization. Two CSISS-SIBs (Raster_ChangeColortable and Raster_PolygonClip) did not work as planned and were replaced by command line tools covering the same functionality. None of the employed changes effected the process itself, the workflow works as planned and delivers the desired results. The user can create a colored shaded relief based on a simple raster file containing elevation data for each pixel. Prior to this the DEM can be clipped if only a part of the area is needed for further analyses. The resulting image makes the topography of a monitored area more observable and interpretable. Normally this is done in many separate processing steps and requires a GIS software with the respective functions. By using the CREADED application, the user only has to provide the DEM file and, only if desired, a polygon shapefile or an own color rules file.

One limitation of the application is the usage of small datasets. The FTP server principle results in limitations concerning the file size of the used DEM. Also the CSISS-SIBs quickly reach their limits when it comes to large DEM files. A large file size leads to a decrease in speed and performance. Another problem is related to the projection of the DEM. The used command line tool accepts only a part of the existing EPSG codes as input parameter. For instance five-digit EPSG codes are not supported. This means that if the DEM has an unsupported coordinate system, it cannot be projected. Here an extension to all EPSG codes or the implementation of another service would be desirable.

Another expandability would be to give the user the possibility to choose a local workspace at the beginning of the workflow instead of prescribing it. Furthermore the possibility to load a DEM file of a specific area could be given by integrating an adequate Web service. And finally, the execution on other platforms should be supported, for example by integrating the used tools as jETI services.

This article is part of a larger evaluation [10], which aimed at illustrating the power of simplicity-oriented development [18] by validating the claim that process modeling can indeed be handed over to the domain experts by providing them with a graphical modeling framework [29] that covers low-level details in a service-oriented fashion [20], integrates high-level modeling in the overall development process in a way that user-level models become directly executable [16, 19], and supports ad-hoc adaptations and evolution [15,17].

The project described in this article can be characterized as follows:

- Scientific domain: geoinformatics
- Number of models: 8
- Number of hierarchy levels: 2
- Total number of SIBs: 119
- SIB libraries used (cf. [13]): common-sibs (97), ftp-sibs (8), csiss-sibs (2), rest-sibs (12)
- Service technologies used: REST web services, SOAP web services

The geoinformatics part of this volume contains eight other articles on workflow applications in this domain [5–8,26–28,31]. Further geoinformatics workflow projects with the jABC have recently been started. Ongoing work is also exploring how to apply semantics-based (semi-) automatic workflow composition techniques (as provided by, e.g., [21]) to support the workflow design process, as described in [9, 11, 12] for the bioinformatics domain.

References

1. CSISS Center for Spatial Information Science and Systems. Geospatial web services, `http://geobrain.laits.gmu.edu/grassweb/manuals/index.html` (accessed July 20, 2012)
2. GDAL Geospatial Data Abstraction Library, Gdalem - tools to analyze and visualize dems, `http://www.gdal.org/gdalem.html` (accessed June 28, 2012)
3. GDAL Geospatial Data Abstraction Library. Gdalwarp - image reprojection and warping utility, `http://www.gdal.org/gdalwarp.html` (accessed May 17, 2012)
4. Gohlke, C.: Laboratory for Fluorescence Dynamics, University of California. Unofficial windows binaries for python extension packages, `http://www.lfd.uci.edu/~gohlke/pythonlibs/` (accessed June 05, 2012)

5. Hibbe, M.: Spotlocator Project Documentation. In: Lamprecht, A.-L., Margaria, T. (eds.) Process Design for Natural Scientists. CCIS, vol. 500, pp. 149–158. Springer, Heidelberg (2014)
6. Holler, R.: GraffDok: A Graffiti Documentation Application. In: Lamprecht, A.-L., Margaria, T. (eds.) Process Design for Natural Scientists. CCIS, vol. 500, pp. 235–247. Springer, Heidelberg (2014)
7. Kind, J.: Creation of Topographic Maps. In: Lamprecht, A.-L., Margaria, T. (eds.) Process Design for Natural Scientists. CCIS, vol. 500, pp. 225–234. Springer, Heidelberg (2014)
8. Kuntzsch, C.: Visualization of Data Transfer Paths. In: Lamprecht, A.-L., Margaria, T. (eds.) Process Design for Natural Scientists. CCIS, vol. 500, pp. 140–148. Springer, Heidelberg (2014)
9. Lamprecht, A.-L.: User-Level Workflow Design - A Bioinformatics Perspective. LNCS, vol. 8311. Springer, Heidelberg (2013)
10. Lamprecht, A.-L., Margaria, T.: Scientific Workflows and XMDD. In: Lamprecht, A.-L., Margaria, T. (eds.) Process Design for Natural Scientists. CCIS, vol. 500, pp. 1–13. Springer, Heidelberg (2014)
11. Lamprecht, A.-L., Margaria, T., Steffen, B.: Bio-jETI: a framework for semantics-based service composition. BMC Bioinformatics 10(Suppl 10), S8 (2009)
12. Lamprecht, A.-L., Naujokat, S., Margaria, T., Steffen, B.: Semantics-based composition of EMBOSS services. Journal of Biomedical Semantics 2(Suppl 1), S5 (2011)
13. Lamprecht, A.-L., Wickert, A.: The Course's SIB Libraries. In: Lamprecht, A.-L., Margaria, T. (eds.) Process Design for Natural Scientists. CCIS, vol. 500, pp. 30–44. Springer, Heidelberg (2014)
14. Margaria, T., Nagel, R., Steffen, B.: jETI: A tool for remote tool integration. In: Halbwachs, N., Zuck, L.D. (eds.) TACAS 2005. LNCS, vol. 3440, pp. 557–562. Springer, Heidelberg (2005)
15. Margaria, T., Steffen, B.: Agile IT: Thinking in User-Centric Models. In: Margaria, T., Steffen, B. (eds.) ISoLA 2008. CCIS, vol. 17, pp. 490–502. Springer, Heidelberg (2009)
16. Margaria, T., Steffen, B.: Business Process Modelling in the jABC: The One-Thing-Approach. In: Cardoso, J., van der Aalst, W. (eds.) Handbook of Research on Business Process Modeling. IGI Global (2009)
17. Margaria, T., Steffen, B.: Continuous Model-Driven Engineering. IEEE Computer 42(10), 106–109 (2009)
18. Margaria, T., Steffen, B.: Simplicity as a Driver for Agile Innovation. Computer 43(6), 90–92 (2010)
19. Margaria, T., Steffen, B.: Service-Orientation: Conquering Complexity with XMDD. In: Hinchey, M., Coyle, L. (eds.) Conquering Complexity, pp. 217–236. Springer, London (2012)
20. Margaria, T., Steffen, B., Reitenspieß, M.: Service-Oriented Design: The Roots. In: Benatallah, B., Casati, F., Traverso, P. (eds.) ICSOC 2005. LNCS, vol. 3826, pp. 450–464. Springer, Heidelberg (2005)
21. Naujokat, S., Lamprecht, A.-L., Steffen, B.: Loose Programming with PROPHETS. In: de Lara, J., Zisman, A. (eds.) FASE 2012. LNCS, vol. 7212, pp. 94–98. Springer, Heidelberg (2012)
22. OSGeo SVN Repositories. Colors, `https://svn.osgeo.org/grass/grass/branches/releasebranch_6_4/lib/gis/colors/` (accessed July 21, 2012)
23. OSGeo SVN Repositories, Python samples, `http://svn.osgeo.org/gdal/trunk/gdal/swig/python/samples/hsv_merge.py` (accessed June 05, 2012)

24. OSGeo SVN Repositories. Trac, http://trac.osgeo.org/ (accessed May 16, 2012)
25. Python Software Foundation. Download, http://www.python.org/download/ (accessed June 05, 2012)
26. Respondeck, T.: A Workflow for Computing Potential Areas for Wind Turbines. In: Lamprecht, A.-L., Margaria, T. (eds.) Process Design for Natural Scientists. CCIS, vol. 500, pp. 196–211. Springer, Heidelberg (2014)
27. Scheele, L.: Location Analysis for Placing Artificial Reefs. In: Lamprecht, A.-L., Margaria, T. (eds.) Process Design for Natural Scientists. CCIS, vol. 500, pp. 212–224. Springer, Heidelberg (2014)
28. Sens, H.: Web-Based Map Generalization Tools Put to the Test. In: Lamprecht, A.-L., Margaria, T. (eds.) Process Design for Natural Scientists. CCIS, vol. 500, pp. 171–181. Springer, Heidelberg (2014)
29. Steffen, B., Margaria, T., Nagel, R., Jörges, S., Kubczak, C.: Model-driven development with the jABC. In: Bin, E., Ziv, A., Ur, S. (eds.) HVC 2006. LNCS, vol. 4383, pp. 92–108. Springer, Heidelberg (2007)
30. Sutton, T.: Linfiniti Geo Blog. A workflow for creating beautiful relief shaded dems using gdal, http://linfiniti.com/2010/12/a-workflow-for-creating-beautiful-relief-shaded-dems-using-gdal (accessed August 02, 2012)
31. Teske, D.: Geocoder Accuracy Ranking. In: Lamprecht, A.-L., Margaria, T. (eds.) Process Design for Natural Scientists. CCIS, vol. 500, pp. 159–170. Springer, Heidelberg (2014)

A Workflow for Computing Potential Areas for Wind Turbines

Tobias Respondek

Potsdam University, Potsdam, D-14482, Germany
t.respondek@gmail.com

Abstract. This paper describes the implementation of a workflow model for service-oriented computing of potential areas for wind turbines in jABC. By implementing a re-executable model the manual effort of a multi-criteria site analysis can be reduced. The aim is to determine the shift of typical geoprocessing tools of geographic information systems (GIS) from the desktop to the web. The analysis is based on a vector data set and mainly uses web services of the "Center for Spatial Information Science and Systems" (CSISS). This paper discusses effort, benefits and problems associated with the use of the web services.

Keywords: geoprocessing, CSISS, site analysis, data conversion, vector format.

1 Introduction: Workflow Scenario

With the introduction of the Renewable Energy Sources Act (EEG) in Germany in 2000 the foundation for an accelerated expansion of renewable energies was laid. In this context, the great importance of wind energy to achieve the goals is undeniable by experts and politicians. However, the combination of high space requirements and an acute lack of space, considerably limits the possibilities of decentralized energy supply. Against this background it is therefore necessary to establish the use of information systems whose core competency is to analyze and visualize the potential of energy, to coordinate competing land claims between energy and alternative uses, to illustrate the visual impact of decentralized power stations in the landscape, and to communicate the opportunities of an endogenous development of the municipal to the regional and to the national level clearly.

To meet these demands geographic information systems (GIS) are used, reflecting the enormous importance of the resource "space". For example, these provide a large number of analytical methods and tools for processing spatial data. The recurring analyses while identifying sites can thus greatly be simplified with the help of GIS. The key concept here is geoprocessing. Its primary goal is to automate GIS tasks and perform spatial analysis and modeling. In almost all GIS applications recurring routine tasks have to be performed. Therefore, multi-step processes are summarized to workflows. Thus, a diverse selection of tools can be combined in a particular order within a model. The type of tasks

A.-L. Lamprecht et al. (Eds.): Process Design for Natural Scientists, CCIS 500, pp. 200–215, 2014.
DOI: 10.1007/978-3-662-45006-2_16

to be automated can be quite simple. For example, it may be the automatic conversion of data into other formats. But it can also be quite complex tasks, which are a sequence of operations of complex spatial relationships which are modeled and analyzed. Calculate the optimal paths through a transport network or a comprehensive site analysis are examples. The geoprocessing is based on different data transformation processes. A typical geoprocessing tool performs an operation on a dataset and returns the result of the execution as a new dataset (Figure 1). By each intermediary geoprocessing a small but significant operation is performed for the final result of the geographic data.

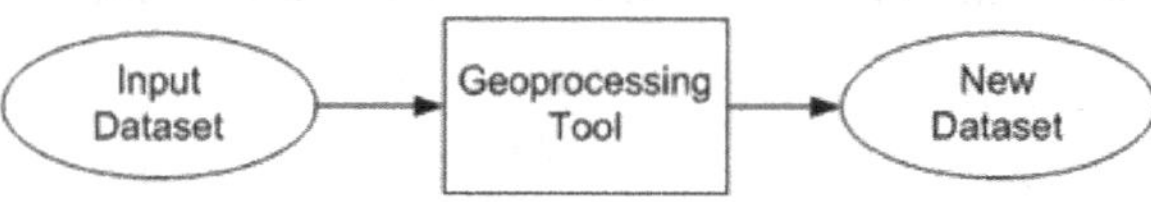

Fig. 1. Geoprocessing [4]

In summary, geoprocessing tools can be concatenated, so that the output of a tool is passed to the subsequent tool. In existing desktop GIS modeling systems support of such processes is already integrated. Most prominent example here is the ArcGIS ModelBuilder by market leader ESRI, which provides an extensive collection of tools and an advanced and user-friendly modeling environment. Following similar principles but using different technologies, the work described in this paper deals with the implementation of a jABC workflow model for the calculation of potential areas for wind turbines based on open web services.

Thematically, the workflow addresses a site analysis in the context of renewable energies, which has to meet certain requirements. The site-requirements of a wind turbine vary, but can be named relatively clearly. The two substantially relevant aspects are the exclusion areas on the one hand and the suitability areas on the other. While exclusion areas are those areas where a power plant construction is not permitted or not possible, the suitable sites are those areas which are particularly well suited for this type of energy. For example exclusion areas can be built-up areas, water areas or protection zones. By contrast, suitable sites are distinguished in addition to the space availability in particular by their potential of wind. The wind speed is the determining factor in whether a wind farm can be operated profitably or not. The actual site analysis is to overly these suitable and exclusion areas. The result then shows the potential locations for wind turbines.

Due to the complexity and clarity there are three rules defined for the preparation of the model, which will be implemented in the project: The mean wind speed in the potential areas must prevail at least 4.3 m / s at 50 m above ground. This guideline reflects a presumed economically viable in official planning processes. The second criterion is to exclude traffic areas. In this process a special feature should be considered: It should be assumed that wind turbines at a distance of less than 40 meters for motorways and trunk roads at 20 meters are not allowed. Finally, the third criterion is to exclude protected areas.

As data base of the implementation vector data of an area from northern Bavaria are used. The available test data consists of three data sets that are in shapefile format. The line data "Verkehr" (traffic) includes various roads and railway lines based on Topographic Map 25 (TK25). Figure 2 visualizes this. Highways are displayed in yellow, trunk roads in red. The polygon data "Schutz" (reserve) deals with the classification of an area in various protected areas and can be used for the restrictions in the model. Accordingly, the two red dashed areas in Figure 3 visualize the nature reserves. Additionally the data set "Wind" (wind) as another polygon data set includes comprehensive wind data from the German Weather Service (DWD) at 50 m above the ground in front. In figure 4 areas with high wind speeds are shown in green, areas with low wind speeds are shown in red.

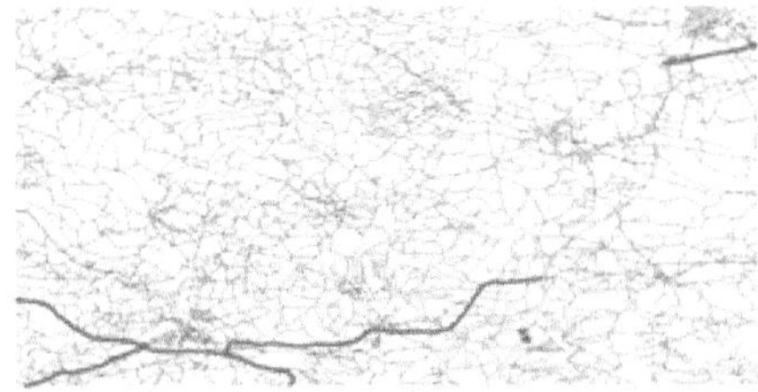

Fig. 2. Initial Dataset "Verkehr"

Fig. 3. Initial Dataset "Schutz"

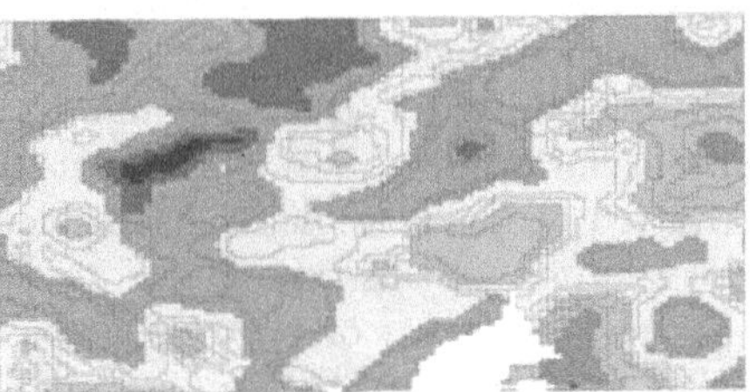

Fig. 4. Initial Dataset "Wind"

The overall objective of this paper is to present and document the implementation of a workflow model for the calculation of potential areas for wind turbines based on vector data. The main focus is on the use of open geoservices provided by the "Center for Spatial Information Science and Systems". With the help of this model the recurring process of siting such plants in the context of the current theme "Renewable Energies" is to be automated and thus simplified. Thereby there should only be a need to enter data and to slightly modify some parameters and not to set up an entire new model. The documentary looks at effort, benefits and problems of the model and finally gives a brief outlook on the possible extension of this.

2 Service Analysis

Considering the rules of the model described in the introduction, it can be quickly determined which tasks the deployed web services for site analysis basically need to provide. For comparative purposes and for clarity, the model was initially implemented in the ArcGIS Model Builder and tested successfully. At this point, the modeled workflow is preceded by the introduction in Figure 5.

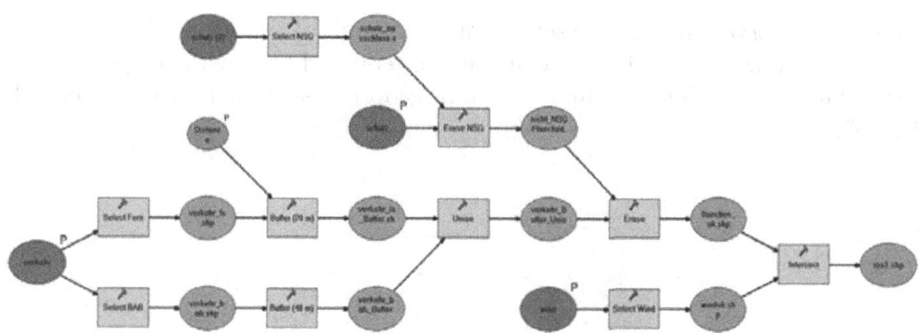

Fig. 5. Implementation of the model in ArcGIS

While the blue ellipses represent the input data, the green ellipses provide the output data. The yellow rectangles in between visualize typical geoprocessing tools. The following tasks can be identified: Since the dataset "Verkehr" includes both motorways and trunk roads, a selection with subsequent extraction of the two different types of conduct is necessary. Thereby the restriction can be maintained, that wind turbines may be placed at different distances, dependent on the particular type of traffic. This is accomplished by buffering of different widths.

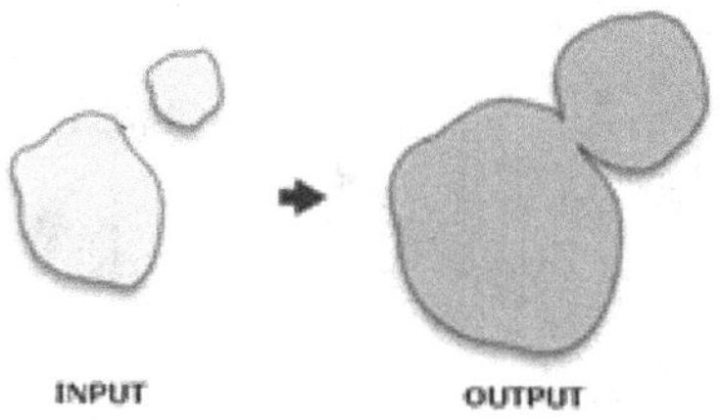

Fig. 6. Operation "Buffer" [3]

Subsequently, the two datasets have to be recombined. This process is called "Union".

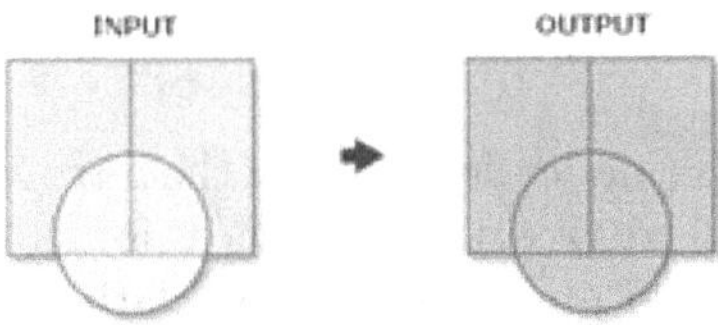

Fig. 7. Operation "Union" [3]

For the reserves in the dataset "Schutz" an initial selection of the nature reserves is necessary as well. These are then intersected back with the protection initial dataset and deleted out of it. The geoprocessing tool to use is called "Erase".

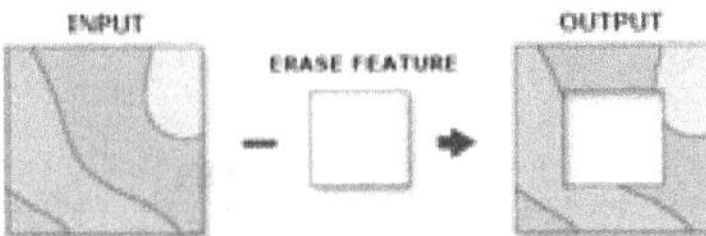

Fig. 8. Operation "Erase" [3]

This creates an area dataset that contains the allowable areas to build power plants without the forbidden nature reserves. From this, the reunited buffered traffic areas have to be erased. This task is performed once again with the "Erase" tool.

Finally, the areas with suitable wind are added. To do this, from the record "Wind" all surfaces with a wind speed of at least 4.3 m / s are selected and extracted. Afterwards, with the help of the tool "Intersection", the suitable areas can be overlayed with the previous data set created.

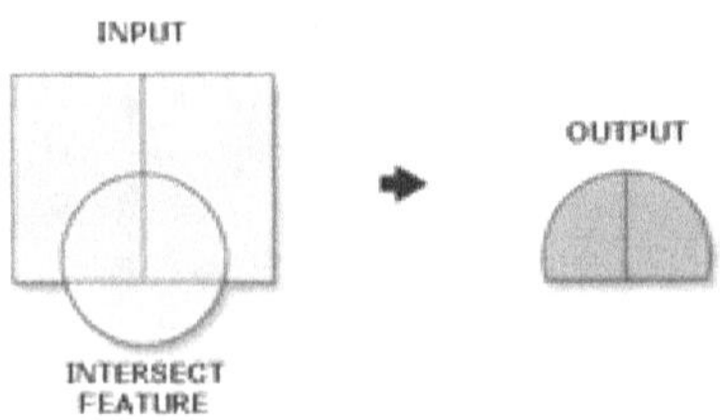

Fig. 9. Operation "Intersection" [3]

This leads to a record that complies with all rules established in the model. Furthermore, five geoprocessing tools are identified, which functionalities must be assumed by web services. "Union", "Intersect" and "Erase" are typically summarized as "Overlay" operations. A "Selection" is similar to a simple SQL query to a database from which a new record has to be created. In addition, the "Buffering" has to be implemented.

As already indicated in the introduction, the "Center for Spatial Information Science and Systems" (CSISS) is developing such geoprocessing tools as web services. Overall, it represents almost 80 available geoservices to enable geoprocessing and analysis based on existing software modules or geoscience. Most services provide functionality to manipulate raster and vector data, or process satellite images. It is based on the Geographic Resources Analysis Support System (GRASS), which represents an open source (GNU GPL'ed), image processing and GIS program. Some of the services are also based on existing web services or developed on other geoscientific modules. On the official website, the services are described as follows:

"These Web services are SOAP based, each service has WSDL description and the service input and output are accessible network points, i.e. URLs (Uniform Resource Locator). As a result, these geospatial Web services could be used easily and invoked independently by any client in any part of the world. All these Web services have been categorized according to OGC standard service type taxonomy and registered into the catalogue services, so that they can be easily searched for use. They have been used in an Online Analysis System (GeOnAS) within the framework of GeoBrain, an open, interoperable, distributed, standard-compliant, multi-tier Web-based geospatial information services and knowledge building system." [2]

From the 15 "GRASS_based geospatial web services for processing vector map" of the 80 services offered, the following services are needed to implement the presented geoprocessing tools:

By using the service "Vector_FeatureExtraction" one can extract vector objects of an existing vector dataset and create a new record with only the selected objects. The tables of a database can thereby be obtained via SQL queries. The service "Vector_Buffer" provides the ability to create a buffer around objects of any type. The service "Vector_Overlay" encapsulates several of the features presented above. Thus, it provides several operators to overlay two vector data sets: Intersection (and), Union (or) and Erase (not).

Since the services require different types of data and produce different outputs, two other services are necessary in addition. The services "Vector_SHP2GML" and "Vector_GML2SHP "allow to convert vector data sets between the data format ESRI shapefile and GML format in both directions.

The acronym GML stands for Geography Markup Language and is a markup language for the exchange of spatial objects ("Features"). GML is an application of XML and defined by schema descriptions. Thus GML allows the transmission of objects with attributes, relations and geometries in the range of spatial. GML is developed by the Open Geospatial Consortium (OGC) in partnership with the ISO TC 211. Like all the results of the OGC process, the documentation is freely available to everyone.

On the other hand, the Shapefile format is a proprietary data from the Environmental Systems Research Institute (ESRI), which has become an industry standard. This is composed of at least three files: a .shp file for the geometry, a .shx file as an index of the geometry and the link to the attribute data and a .dbf file for the actual attribute data. In addition, there are optional files like the .prj file that includes the projection of the data. For some of the CSISS- services this file is required, so the output data must be present in a geo-referenced coordinate reference system.

These last two services thus ensure interoperability between the heterogeneous data formats. The implementation of the workflow in the next section shows that the transformation of data formats is not always straightforward.

In addition to the mandatory data formats, some services have some other conditions: For example, some services do not deal with locally stored data as input. They require a Uniform Resource Locator (URL) as input parameter. It is therefore necessary to manage a web server on which the data used is stored. In the project the provider "bplaced" [1] is used, which provides 1 - 2 GB webspace with no forced advertising. The capacity was sufficient for testing purposes. However, because of this external web space some other services are needed, which automatically upload and download the data onto the ftp server without manual intervention. In this context it is necessary to implement a service, which is able to retrieve an URL and can write the data contained in a file. This was implemented through the REpresentational State Transfer architecture (REST).

All the services described here were implemented as Service Independent Building Block (SIB) in order to be able to use them in jABC. Furthermore, they are supplemented by some common-SIBs, which serve the program flow and control of the execution context.

3 Workflow Realization

Figure 5 already gave an idea how the workflow was modeled. It can be seen that the entire model can be divided into three submodels, each representing one of the model rules. Those the three submodels are executed in parallel through the controlsib "ForkSIB".

3.1 Submodel 1: Extraction of the Wind

The aim of the first submodel is to extract those areas, which meet the requirements of the wind speed form the "Wind" dataset. The implemented jABC-workflow is shown in Figure 10.

Therefore, the SIB "Vector_FeatureExtraction" is particularly used. As input parameters it requires an URL to a GML file. Since the initial file exists as a shapefile, it must first be converted to a GML. This task is performed by the SIB "Vector_SHP2GML" at the beginning of the submodel. This requires an URL

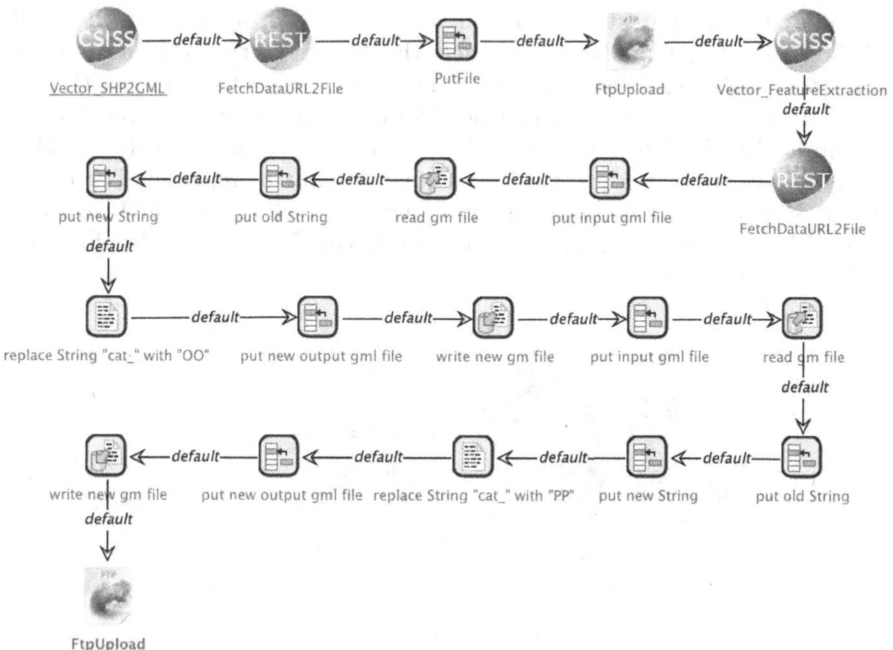

Fig. 10. Extraction of the wind

to a directory on a server as input parameter, where there are the four equally named components of a shapefile. It is the mandatory .shp-, .shx- and .dbf-file, plus the .prj file. Of course, the directory must be accessible to the public here. The input parameter "shapefileDataStoreURL" is therefore the URL to the file including file name without extension. As the return parameter an URL is obtained, that can be accessed using the REST-SIB "FetchDataURL2File" and be written in a file by specifying a desired local directory. This is necessary to re-upload the file with the help of the SIB "FtpUpload" back to the server. Previously, the file must be placed in the execution context by using "Putfile". As input parameters, the ftp-SIB requires the host address of the server, the access, including user name and password, and the output path to the server. Once a GML file is on the server now, the desired areas can be extracted by an SQL query using the SIB "Vector_FeatureExtraction". Correspondingly, a query that refers to an attribute of the input data has to be specified in the WHERE part of the SIB. As well as the input the output is an URL as well. At this point in the following, a critical step is necessary, which is repeated in the other submodels. By processing the SIB "Vector_FeatureExtraction" and other CSISS-SIBs the table schema of the files are changed. If you want to process the output file into another CSISS-SIB, there is a name conflict in the table schema, because the attributes are no longer unique. Therefore, the attribute names have to be renamed before the output file can be edited. After the GML was placed into the execution context with "Putfile", you can read in the GML file itself (SIB "read GML file"). Thereby one gets the content of the GML as a string down into the context. Now you have to create two variables. For one, the old string and secondly, the new string (the old and the new attribute name). With the help of the SIB "ReplaceString" then the old string can be replaced. This process is performed twice, as two column names must be replaced. The newly created GML file is stored with the SIB "write new GML file", and finally is uploaded back to the server with the SIB "FtpUpload". Figure 11 visualizes the Result of the extraction.

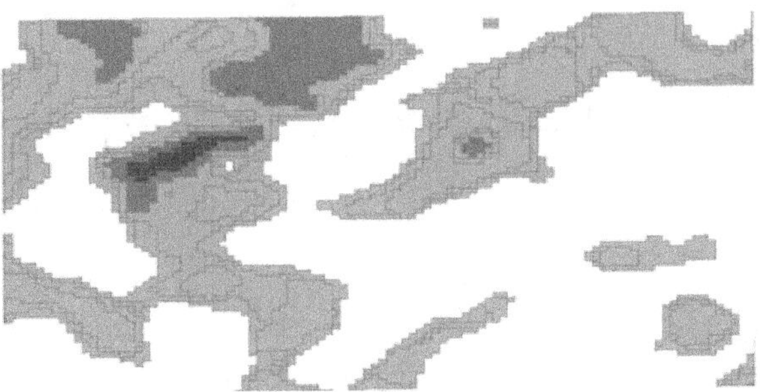

Fig. 11. Result of the extraction

3.2 Submodel 2: Extraction of Natural Reserves

The goal of the second submodel is to extract the natural reserves in the data set "Schutz". Based on these objectives it is clear that the second sub-model has obvious parallels to the first submodel. Thus, the initial data set is first converted to a GML, the nature reserves are extracted, the resulting table schema are renamed and the output file is uploaded to the server. In this case the already known SIBs are used.

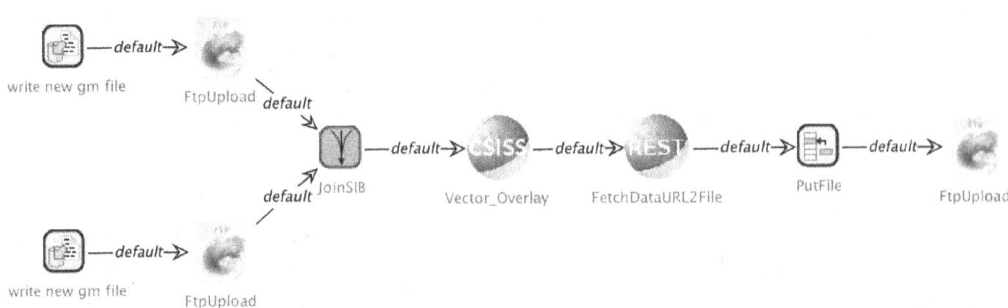

Fig. 12. Deleting the natural reserves from the initial dataset

Subsequently, however, the schema of the initial dataset is renamed as well and the extracted natural reserves are overlayed with the initial data set (Figure 12). Here the SIB "Vector_Overlay" is used. This requires two URLs as input parameters, each representing a link to a GML file. As "ainputURL" the renamed initial dataset and as "binputURL" the extracted natural reserves are used. One also needs to specify an operator. Since the last mentioned data set is to be cut out of the first, the operator "not" must be chosen. This corresponds to the typical geoprocessing tool "Erase". The output is then uploaded to the server and is visualized in Figure 13.

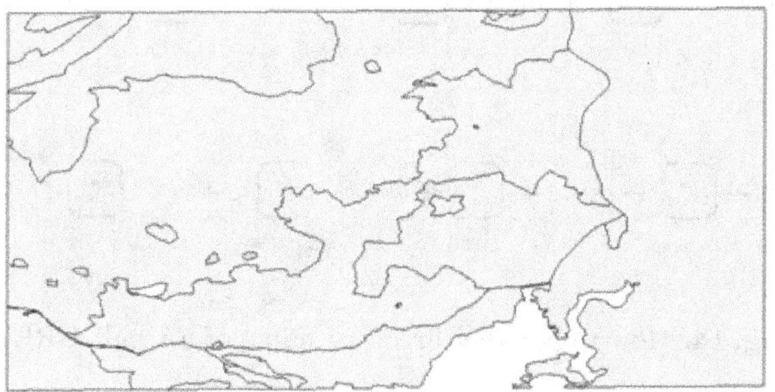

Fig. 13. Result of the extraction and intersection

3.3 Submodel 3: Type-Dependent Buffering of Traffic

In the third submodel, the motorways and trunk roads will be extracted out of the dataset "Verkehr" and then be buffered with different widths. First, according to known procedures the motorways and trunk roads are extracted and uploaded as separate GML files to the server. Since the service "Vector_Buffer" expects a zipped shapefile as input parameters, but the extraction produces a GML, the file must then be converted again. This is the first time the SIB "Vector_GML2SHP" is used. As input and output parameters, it uses URLs. The problem however is the fact that the output parameter points to a ZIP file that is named exactly to the minute by their creation date. If you want to process this file in other SIBs, you have to unpack it. This can be done in an automated workflow, but only if the exact path to the zip file can be specified. Since it is variable in this case, therefore, a workaround must be built to extract the ZIP file and to gain access to the shapefile. Thus, by using "put pattern" a pattern, that makes it possible to extract the dynamically generated folder name, is put. Then it is just done, using "extract directory name". As result you get back a list of hits, but in here is just one element. While iterating through the list, the folder name will be written in the context. This folder name can then be used for following steps. The path standing in the context can thus be used as input parameter for the SIB "UnzipFiles". Thereupon, the unzipped shapefile can be zipped again using "ZipFiles" and this time be stored in a path known. The input parameter "input directory" is now known due to prior extraction. Then again, the zip file can be uploaded to the server and then be served as input parameter for the SIB "Vector_Buffer" (Figure 14).

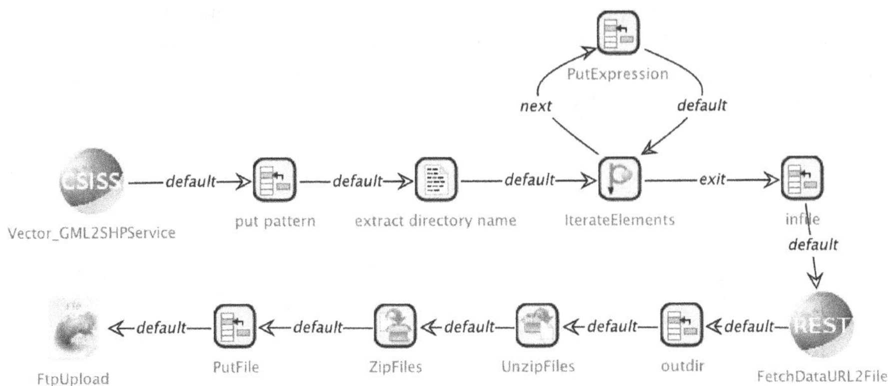

Fig. 14. How to get the directory name of a result URL

Indicating a buffer distance the SIB "Vector_Buffer" will generate a zone around the street, which will later be used as an exclusion area. As output you get a URL that points to a ZIP file. Therefore, the sequence described above has to be integrated at this point again in order to unzip the file. Since the .prj-file of the shapefile is missing in the output folder of the SIB "Vector_Buffer", a workaround has to be implemented at this point. Thus, the three files .shp, .shx and .dbf are first separately uploaded to the server. Then the .prj file must be added separately onto the server so that the shapefile is back into the same folder completely (Figure 15). Only then there exists the possibility of using the SIB "Vector_SHP2GML" to generate a GML file, which is required as a URL in the SIB "Vector_Overlay" in the following.

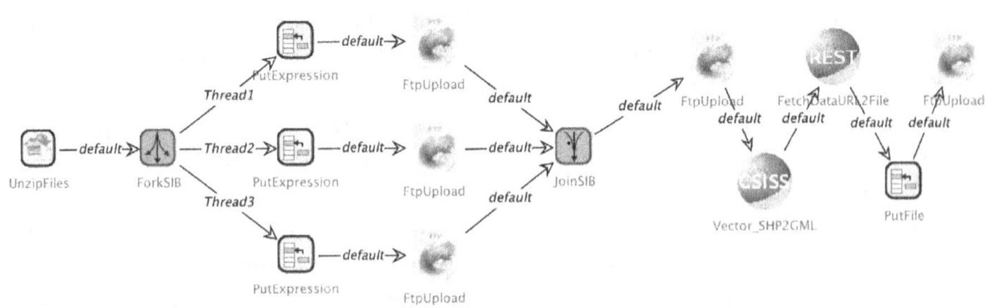

Fig. 15. How to upload the .prj-file seperately

The SIB "Vector_Overlay" in submodel 3 is finally used to union the two concurrent workflows for different buffer widths again (Figure 16). The corresponding operation of this union is achieved due the operator "or".

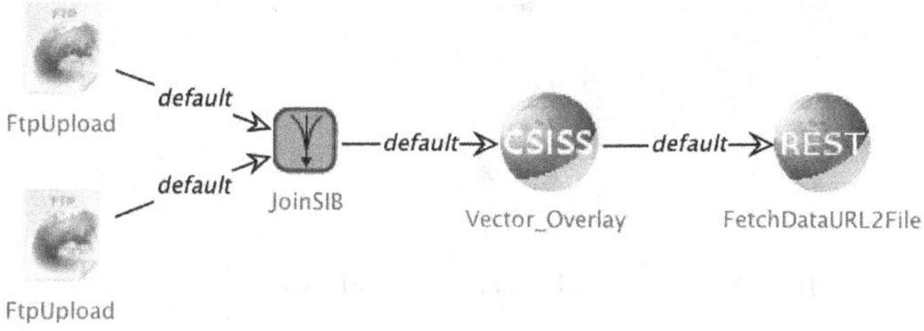

Fig. 16. Union of the roads

Figure 17 shows the extracted and different widths of the buffered roads.

Fig. 17. Buffered Roads

After the three sub-models are constructed, in conclusion, the three resulting datasets have to be overlayed. Here, however, a problem in dealing with the web services occurred, for which no workaround could be found. The intersection between the records of the wind and protected areas worked with the help of the SIB "Vector_Overlay" and specifying the parameter "and". However, a prior intersection of the buffered traffic areas with the protected areas was not possible. This is, because the output data after the buffering is still a line feature. This may not be overlayed with an area in the SIB "Vector_Overlay", so that the operation Erase ("not") cannot be executed. It is possible, however, that the result is displayed in any GIS together with the buffered lines. Thus, for at least visually determine the potential energy surfaces. In the following figure the green areas show the potential areas and the red lines display the exclusion areas of the traffic.

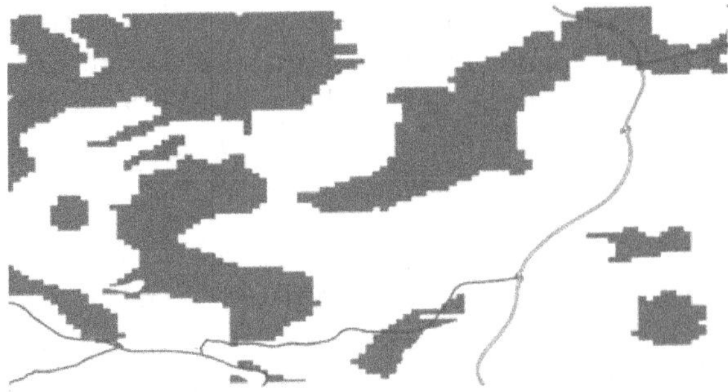

Fig. 18. Potential areas for wind power plants

4 Conclusion

The aim of this study was to conduct a site analysis based on vector data and on web services provided by the CSISS. This should allow simplifying the repetitive tasks of a manual multi-criteria site selection. It was also about to test the usability of available open web services, and ultimately determine how practicable in this case the shift of the functionality of geographic information systems from the desktop to the web is.

It turned out that in the result the initially intended goal could not be reached: Since the web service "Vector_Overlay" does not permit an intersection of line and area data types, one of the last steps of the workflow could not be realized. This was surprising as such an operation is basically possible in all popular desktop GIS. It shows that web services do currently not have the same functionality as common GIS. Towards the end of the project the further loss of the web services prevented testing, so that no practicable workaround could be developed. These facts show that a web based geoprocessing has yet not the same reliability as local processing.

Another notable difference is, that the jABC workflow model that orchestrates the CSISS web services is a lot more complicated than for example a comparable workflow in ArcGIS ModelBuilder. As an indication of this, the sheer number of processing steps can be seen. This effort is mainly necessary because different services require different input parameters. Also, it is often tedious to convert between different data formats and data has to be uploaded or downloaded. Because some web service parameters are not sufficiently specified and documented by the service providers, using them is very often is on a "trial and error" basis. Consequently, it took a while to find out, for example, that a shapefile must not consist of three mandatory files as usual, but additionally requires the .prj file. Amazingly, this file is then lost again while processing some services, which is why they have to be brought in again separately. The semantic conflicts of the table schema name were added as a further difficulty. Also zip and unzip the folders presented a challenge, due to the variable folder names. But is important to note that due to its open interfaces one may find workarounds and that the web services will surely improve. For example, it is planned that in the future it will be possible to use zipped shapefiles as inputs.

Since the web services are based on GRASS GIS, one would certainly have faster and more intuitive success, provided one is familiar with the desktop version. Clear parallels between the GRASS command line commands and the input parameters of the services have been identified.

In terms of the workflow model, there are certainly still possibilities for some expansion. There may be other requirements to be implemented, which should substantially be feasible with the geoprocessing tools used. Also visualization services could be included instead of the pure data output.

This article is part of a larger evaluation [10], which aimed at illustrating the power of simplicity-oriented development [17] by validating the claim that process modeling can indeed be handed over to the domain experts by providing them with a graphical modeling framework [24] that covers low-level details in a service-oriented fashion [19], integrates high-level modeling in the overall development process in a way that user-level models become directly executable [18,15], and supports ad-hoc adaptations and evolution [14,16].

The project described in this article can be characterized as follows:

– Scientific domain: geoinformatics
– Number of models: 1
– Number of hierarchy levels: 1
– Total number of SIBs: 156
– SIB libraries used (cf. [13]): common-sibs (104), ftp-sibs (21), csiss-sibs (16), rest-sibs (15)
– Service technologies used: SOAP web services

The geoinformatics part of this volume contains eight other articles on workflow applications in this domain [8,21,7,25,6,22,5,23]. Further geoinformatics workflow projects with the jABC have recently been started. Ongoing work is also exploring how to apply semantics-based (semi-) automatic workflow composition techniques (as provided by, e.g., [20]) to support the workflow design process, as described in [11,12,9] for the bioinformatics domain.

References

1. Bplaced, `http://www.bplaced.net/` (Online; last accessed January 17, 2012)
2. CSISS. Geospatial Web Services, `http://geobrain.laits.gmu.edu/grassweb/manuals/index.html` (Online; last accessed January 17, 2012)
3. ESRI. Geoprocessing tools, `http://webhelp.esri.com/arcgisdesktop/9.2/index.cfm?TopicName=Geoprocessing_tools` (Online; last accessed January 17, 2012)

4. ESRI. What is geoprocessing?, `http://webhelp.esri.com/arcgisdesktop/9.2/index.cfm?TopicName=What_is_geoprocessing?` (Online; last accessed January 17, 2012)
5. Hibbe, M.: Spotlocator Project Documentation. In: Lamprecht, A.-L., Margaria, T. (eds.) Scientific Workflows. CCIS, vol. 500, pp. 149–158. Springer, Heidelberg (2014)
6. Holler, R.: GraffDok: A Graffiti Documentation Application. In: Lamprecht, A.-L., Margaria, T. (eds.) Scientific Workflows. CCIS, vol. 500, pp. 235–247. Springer, Heidelberg (2014)
7. Kind, J.: Creation of Topographic Maps. In: Lamprecht, A.-L., Margaria, T. (eds.) Scientific Workflows. CCIS, vol. 500, pp. 225–234. Springer, Heidelberg (2014)
8. Kuntzsch, C.: Visualization of Data Transfer Paths. In: Lamprecht, A.-L., Margaria, T. (eds.) Scientific Workflows. CCIS, vol. 500, pp. 140–148. Springer, Heidelberg (2014)
9. Lamprecht, A.-L. (ed.): User-Level Workflow Design. LNCS, vol. 8311. Springer, Heidelberg (2013)
10. Lamprecht, A.-L., Margaria, T.: Scientific Workflows and XMDD. In: Lamprecht, A.-L., Margaria, T. (eds.) Scientific Workflows. CCIS, vol. 500, pp. 1–13. Springer, Heidelberg (2014)
11. Lamprecht, A.-L., Margaria, T., Steffen, B.: Bio-jETI: A framework for semantics-based service composition. BMC Bioinformatics 10(suppl. 10), S8 (2009)
12. Lamprecht, A.-L., Naujokat, S., Margaria, T., Steffen, B.: Semantics-based composition of EMBOSS services. Journal of Biomedical Semantics 2(suppl. 1), S5 (2011)
13. Lamprecht, A.-L., Wickert, A.: The Course's SIB Libraries. In: Lamprecht, A.-L., Margaria, T. (eds.) Scientific Workflows. CCIS, vol. 500, pp. 30–44. Springer, Heidelberg (2014)
14. Margaria, T., Steffen, B.: Agile IT: Thinking in User-Centric Models. In: Margaria, T., Steffen, B. (eds.) ISoLA 2008. CCIS, vol. 17, pp. 490–502. Springer, Heidelberg (2009)
15. Margaria, T., Steffen, B.: Business Process Modelling in the jABC: The One-Thing-Approach. In: Cardoso, J., van der Aalst, W. (eds.) Handbook of Research on Business Process Modeling. IGI Global (2009)
16. Margaria, T., Steffen, B.: Continuous Model-Driven Engineering. IEEE Computer 42(10), 106–109 (2009)
17. Margaria, T., Steffen, B.: Simplicity as a Driver for Agile Innovation. Computer 43(6), 90–92 (2010)
18. Margaria, T., Steffen, B.: Service-Orientation: Conquering Complexity with XMDD. In: Hinchey, M., Coyle, L. (eds.) Conquering Complexity, pp. 217–236. Springer, London (2012)
19. Margaria, T., Steffen, B., Reitenspiess, M.: Service-Oriented Design: The Roots. In: Benatallah, B., Casati, F., Traverso, P. (eds.) ICSOC 2005. LNCS, vol. 3826, pp. 450–464. Springer, Heidelberg (2005)
20. Naujokat, S., Lamprecht, A.-L., Steffen, B.: Loose Programming with PROPHETS. In: de Lara, J., Zisman, A. (eds.) Fundamental Approaches to Software Engineering. LNCS, vol. 7212, pp. 94–98. Springer, Heidelberg (2012)
21. Noack, F.: CREADED: Coloured-Relief Application for Digital Elevation Data. In: Lamprecht, A.-L., Margaria, T. (eds.) Scientific Workflows. CCIS, vol. 500, pp. 182–195. Springer, Heidelberg (2014)

22. Scheele, L.: Location Analysis for Placing Artificial Reefs. In: Lamprecht, A.-L., Margaria, T. (eds.) Scientific Workflows. CCIS, vol. 500, pp. 212–224. Springer, Heidelberg (2014)
23. Sens, H.: Web-Based Map Generalization Tools Put to the Test. In: Lamprecht, A.-L., Margaria, T. (eds.) Scientific Workflows. CCIS, vol. 500, pp. 171–181. Springer, Heidelberg (2014)
24. Steffen, B., Margaria, T., Nagel, R., Jörges, S., Kubczak, C.: Model-Driven Development with the jABC. In: Bin, E., Ziv, A., Ur, S. (eds.) HVC 2006. LNCS, vol. 4383, pp. 92–108. Springer, Heidelberg (2007)
25. Teske, D.: Geocoder Accuracy Ranking. In: Lamprecht, A.-L., Margaria, T. (eds.) Scientific Workflows. CCIS, vol. 500, pp. 159–170. Springer, Heidelberg (2014)

Location Analysis for Placing Artificial Reefs

Lasse Scheele

Potsdam University, Potsdam, D-14482, Germany
lasse.scheele@uni-potsdam.de

Abstract. Location analyses are among the most common tasks while working with spatial data and geographic information systems. Automating the most frequently used procedures is therefore an important aspect of improving their usability. In this context, this project aims to design and implement a workflow, providing some basic tools for a location analysis. For the implementation with jABC, the workflow was applied to the problem of finding a suitable location for placing an artificial reef. For this analysis three parameters (bathymetry, slope and grain size of the ground material) were taken into account, processed, and visualized with the *The Generic Mapping Tools* (GMT), which were integrated into the workflow as jETI-SIBs. The implemented workflow thereby showed that the approach to combine jABC with GMT resulted in an user-centric yet user-friendly tool with high-quality cartographic outputs.

Keywords: Geoinformatics, Location analysis, Exclusion mapping, The Generic Mapping Tools, Geo-visualization, Artificial reef, Balearics.

1 Introduction: Workflow Scenario

The aim of the presented workflow is to find suitable areas for placing an artificial reef in the waters of the Balearic Islands (Spain) in the Mediterranean Sea. An artificial reef is a man-made structure placed in the sea to attract and support marine wildlife [25]. These structures can be discarded and cleaned vessels [29], rail wagons or special objects made for instance out of concrete. Their objective is to become – similar to natural reefs – a hot-spot for plants and fishes. Whether these spots only attract the surrounding flora and fauna or also increase the biomass is a matter of scientific discussion [21]. Regardless, increasingly signs can be found that suggest a positive impact and the reefs certainly do provide shelter and protection to destructive forms of fishing. Furthermore or as a consequence, these reefs often become dive sites and attract a kind of tourism known to be environmentally thoughtful [27]. The installation of artificial reefs is therefore a method for helping the marine wildlife at least locally in a sustainable way.

To make sure that an artificial reef fulfills its purpose, it is necessary to keep the characteristics of the natural habitats of those species in mind, which are meant to benefit from its installation [21]. And to characterize the needs of a species, different parameters (e. g. water depth and temperature) are important. Some plants, for example, need more daylight than others, thereby suggesting

A.-L. Lamprecht et al. (Eds.): Process Design for Natural Scientists, CCIS 500, pp. 216–228, 2014.
DOI: 10.1007/978-3-662-45006-2_17

locating the reef in shallower waters. Moreover, it is essential to ensure the structures safety and to prevent any kind of movement caused by unstable or steep ground material or strong currents. Since the purpose of this project is to show a possible design and implementation of the workflow, only a selection of the wide range of important parameters is taken into account:

Bathymetry is the underwater depth of the ocean floor, which is the height of the water column between ocean floor and water surface.

Slope is the angle of the ocean floor and specifies the slanting compared to a completely horizontal plane.

Grain size of the ground material is given in millimeter and refers to the diameter of particles of the ocean floor.

This simplified approach is reasonable because the consideration of more aspects would be easily implemented by transferring the developed procedure to the new parameters. In any case, this parameter-based approach is typical for location analyses (especially with geographic information systems (GIS)) where every relevant parameter is included via one thematic layer [2]. These layers are intersected to exclude unsuitable locations – a procedure referred to as *Exclusion Mapping*, which is often used and not as error-prone as the analysis of conventional maps. The placing of an artificial reef is therefore an appropriate example for a location analysis and suitable for showing the benefits of this workflow.

The wide range of different species with their specific ecological requirements and the aim of developing a tool that is capable of finding suitable reef-spots for all these various settings, make it necessary to keep the data processing as adjustable and user-based as possible. At the same time, the project also aimed to produce high-quality visualizations in an automated procedure, which focuses the interaction with the user to the content but not the layout. To implement this concept using the *Java Application Building Center* (jABC) [24], some basic datasets containing graphical elements, such as labels for map elements and color scales for the data representation, which are not meant to be changed by the user, are provided and complemented by one spatial grid for each of the three parameters.

In the first step the workflow, the user will process any of the given parameter by itself and one at a time (see Fig. 1). To do so, the user will first get the chance to examine the spatial distribution for the parameter. With the support of this overview a range for the values is declared, beyond which the data will be classified as unsuitable. This classification is subsequently visualized and confirmed or redone. In a second and final step the results for all parameters are summarized in one map, showing suitable locations for placing an artificial reef. This map also depicts for each unsuitable spot which parameter is out of the range entered by the user.

2 Service Analysis

The services chosen to implement the described workflow were *The Generic Mapping Tools* (GMT) developed by the *University of Hawaii* and the *National*

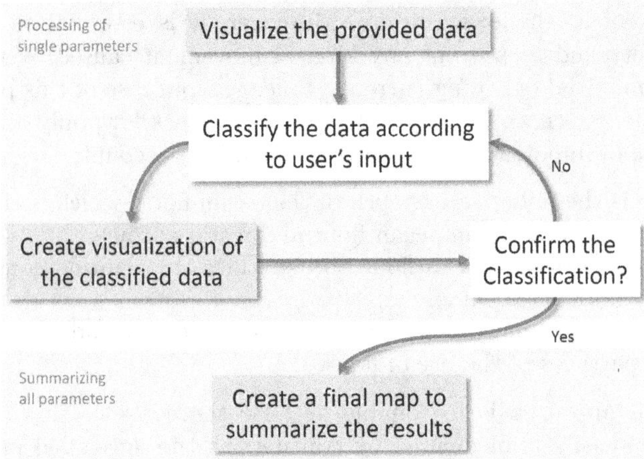

Fig. 1. Schematic diagram for the workflow with stages asking for user's input (white) and automated procedures (grey)

Oceanic and Atmospheric Administration [31] [30]. GMT is an open source command line tool available for the operating systems UNIX/Linux, OSX and Windows and bundling approximately 65 features for spatial data processing and visualization writing, such as in *PostScript*-files. The specific commands used for this workflow are listed and described below:

`pscoast` is used to plot the coastline of the Balearic Islands and to fill the land and water areas with a specified color. In addition it is used to add a frame, title and scale bar to a map.
`grdimage` imports and displays a two-dimensional gridded data.
`pstext` places text strings on a map.
`psscale` adds a legend with a color scale bar to the map.
`grdclip` clips gridded data by limiting the z-values to an upper and/or lower boundary.
`grd2xyz` converts a two-dimensional gridded dataset to a XYZ-table with columns for x- and y-coordinates and the z-value.
`psxyz` plots vector data stored in a XYZ-table.
`ps2raster` converts a PostScript-file to a raster image using the interpreter *Ghostscript* [1].

With GMT it is possible to create new files and also to add content to an already existing file and the added layer is than put on top of the content of the updated file. A creation of a map with GMT is therefore a sequence of commands, building the content from the back- to the foreground (see Chap. 3).

To use GMT (and Ghostscript) as a single tool it may to be installed locally on a platform. But for implementation within a jABC-workflow, an other approach has to be used, since the structure of the commands does not match the requirements of the ExecuteCommand-*Service Independent Building Block*

(SIB). To avoid this problem, the needed tools were integrated via the *Java Electronic Tool Integration Platform* (jETI) [12]. The commands were implemented as single jETI-SIBs with two versions per tool, one for writing in a new file and one for writing in an already existing file. Since some of the GMT commands need input data to be read from a directory and included in the workflow (e. g. the gridded data for `grdimage`) or data to be written to a directory (e. g. the finalized map written as an raster image with `ps2raster`) the jETI-SIBs *ReadFile* and *WriteFile* were necessary to realize the workflow.

3 Workflow Realization

To realize the workflow with jABC the jETI-SIBs were combined with the common jABC-SIBs *ShowConfirmDialog* and *ShowMessageDialog* (showing explanations), *ShowInputDialog* (asking for user's input), *ShowBranchingImageDialog* (showing the maps and asking for confirmation for the classification) and *PutString* (creating a string to pass in the workflow) to create a self-explaining and smooth workflow.

Before explaining the single steps of the workflow, a closer look at the provided data is necessary. The three parameters are included via two-dimensional gridded datasets (GRD-files), which will be processed during the workflow. For the bathymetry an *Earth Topography Digital Dataset* (ETOPO) was used with a spatial resolution of 2 minutes in each direction and the depth values measured in meters [28]. The grid containing the slope values was created from the bathymetry dataset and thus has the same spatial resolution with the angles given in degree. Since data regarding the grain size was not available for the area of interest, a fictitious dataset was created with the same spatial resolution as the first two grids. The datasets additionally provided are not manipulated in the workflow and contain labels and legends (TXT-files) and color scales (CPT-files).

The structure of the workflow – as mentioned in Chapter 1 and illustrated in Figure 2 – shows three parts for the processing of the single parameters bathymetry, slope and grain size, and one part for the generation of the final map summarizing the results. The processing of the different parameters is thereby very similar (simply the topic of the gridded data is exchanged) and below only described exemplary for the bathymetry.

The part of processing a parameter consists of two main steps, which are implemented in jABC with submodels. The first is to create a map showing the spatial distribution of the parameter (see Fig. 3) and the second to get the user's input and create a classification for the parameter based on the input (see Fig. 5). Since the creation of figures with GMT is done in sequences of commands, the visualization of the data basis concerning one parameter (shown in Fig. 3) is created by the following sequence (shown as a workflow in Fig. 4):

1. `pscoast`: specifies the extent of the map and colors the land and water areas
2. `pscoast`: creates a mask following the coastline and the following commands will therefore only alter the water area

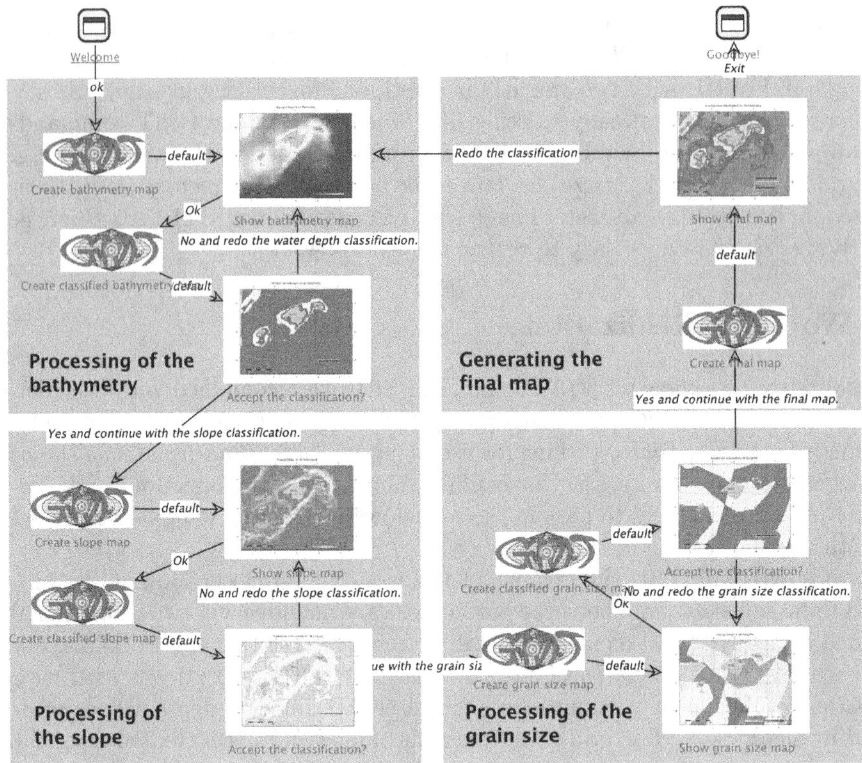

Fig. 2. Realization of the workflow with jABC. The SIBs symbolized with the GMT-logo represent submodels either for creating a map with the original dataset (see Fig. 4) or for classifying and mapping the data according to the user's input (see Fig. 6).

3. `grdimage`: the spatial grid containing the values for the parameter is added on top of the water area
4. `pscoast`: the mask for the coastline is deleted
5. `pscoast`: a mapframe with a scale bar and a title is added
6. `pstext`: labels for the Balearic Islands are added
7. `psscale`: a legend is added corresponding to the colors of the previously added grid
8. `ps2raster`: the final map is converted from PostScript to the *Portable Network Graphics* (PNG) file format

After the map is created and exported to a PNG image, it is shown to the user in order to get an overview of the data. On this basis and with the knowledge of the natural habitats of the species to be supported with the artificial reef, the user should be capable of depicting a range of suitable values, which will lead to a data classification of the processed parameter (see Fig. 5). The sequence of GMT-commands using the user's input is shown in Figure 6. The most important steps are:

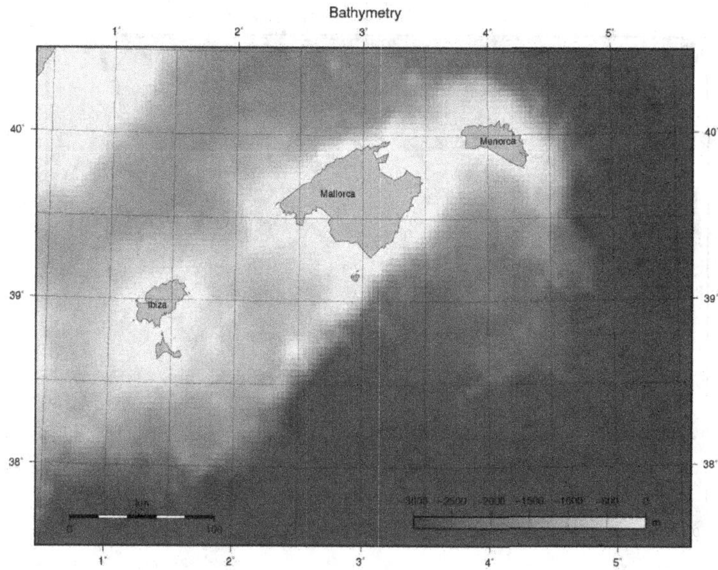

Fig. 3. Map showing the data basis regarding the bathymetry. This map is created with the submodel illustrated in Figure 4 and shown to the user while going through the workflow to help choosing the range for classifiying the water depth.

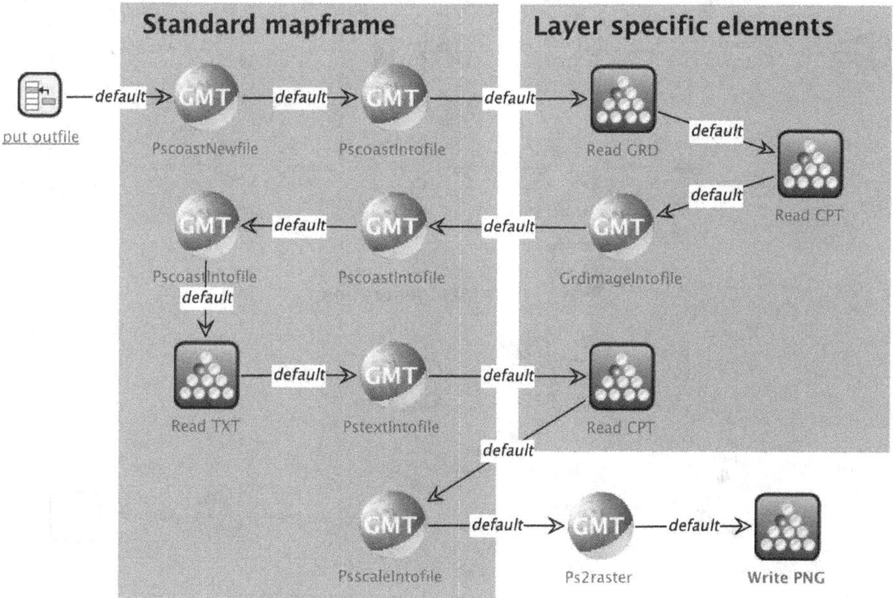

Fig. 4. jABC-Submodel for creating a map showing the data basis for one of the parameters (see Fig. 3). It is emphasized which SIBs create the standard mapframe used for all maps and which SIBs include the thematic layer presented in the map.

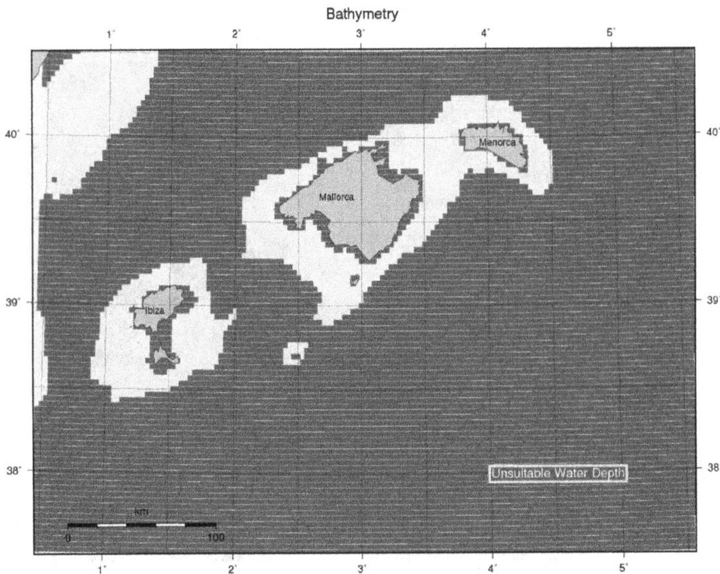

Fig. 5. Map showing a classification regarding the bathymetry. The range used here was −500 to −35 m. This map is created with the submodel illustrated in Figure 6 and shown to the user after choosing the range to review the classification.

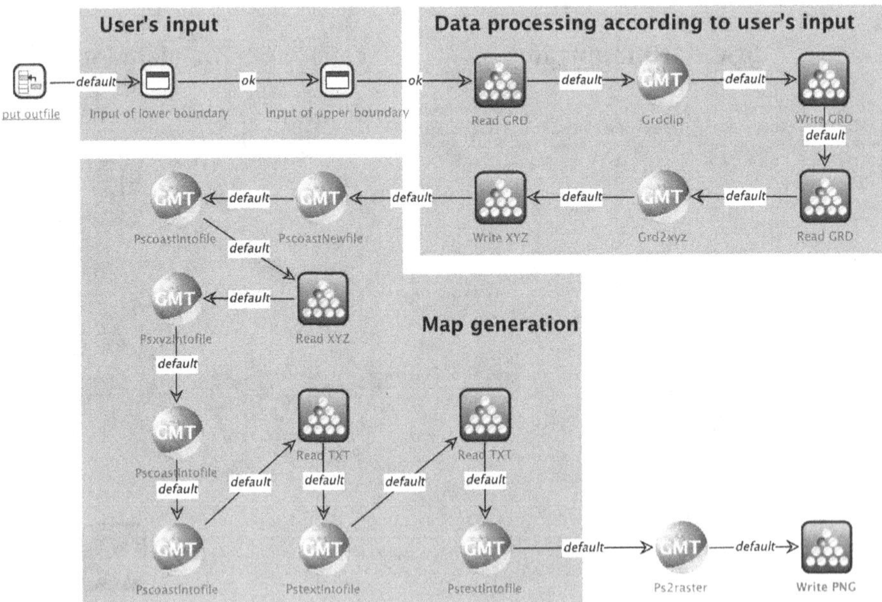

Fig. 6. jABC-Submodel for classifying the data for one parameter and creating a map showing the results of the classification (see Fig. 5). It is emphasized which SIBs take the user's input, which do the data processing according to this input and which create the map with the results.

1. `grdclip`: creating a new version of the original GRD-file with z-values limited to the range specified by the user – the values lower than the lower boundary and higher than the upper boundary are classified as *Not a Number* (NaN)
2. `grd2xyz`: converts the clipped grid to a table (XYZ-file) with one column for the x-, one for the y-coordinate and one for the z-value (containing the value for the parameter)

The following process of the map generation is similar to the submodel previously described; the only difference being that it uses the xyz-table instead of the gridded data. The content is therefore not included as a raster but as single points, each one representing an unsuitable location with an area of the cell size of the original raster. After the classification is done, the results maybe reviewed and redone, if necessary or desired. Otherwise the workflow will continue with the processing of the next parameter.

When the processing of the single parameters is completed, the final step of the workflow will summarize the results in a single map (see Fig. 7). The corresponding submodel is shown in Figure 8 and uses the XYZ-tables created in the previous steps of the workflow. Using these files, the map generation of the final map is similar to the one described above, albeit with a small alteration: since the results for all three parameters have to be included and displayed at the same time without covering one another, a symbolization with different point sizes was chosen, drawing the points on top with the smallest symbol. Thereby it is not only possible to make out suitable spots regarding all parameters, but also to see why (because of which parameter) a spot is marked as unsuitable.

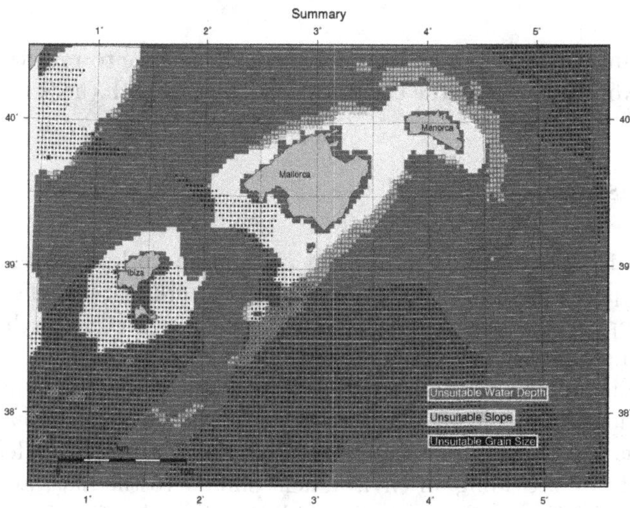

Fig. 7. Final map created with the submodel illustrated in Figure 8 and showing a possible classification for all parameters in one frame. The used ranges were -500 to -35 m for bathymetry, 0 to $4°$ for slope and 0.01 to 20 mm for grain size.

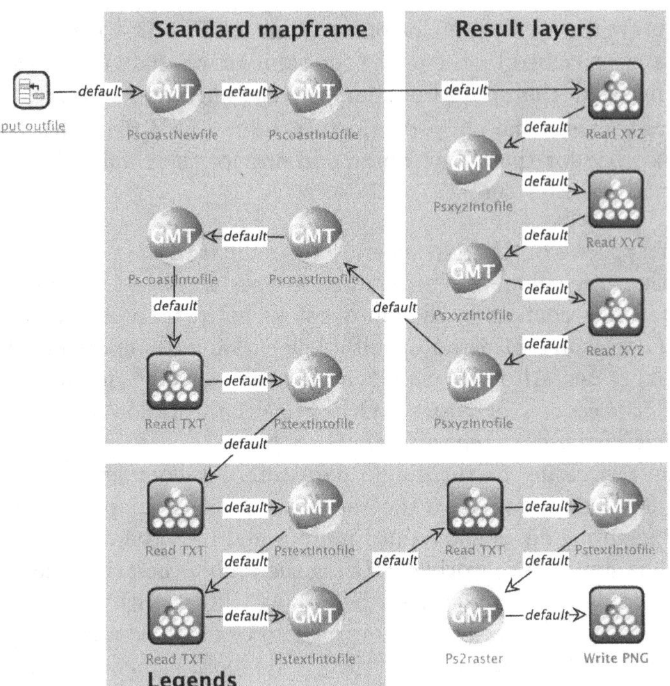

Fig. 8. jABC-Submodel for the final map summarizing the results for all parameters (see Fig. 5). It is emphasized which SIBs create the standard mapframe, which include the classified layers and which add the corresponding legends.

With the final map generated, the user gets the chance to review the results and exit the workflow or redo the classification, starting with the first parameter.

4 Conclusion

The goal of this project was to implement a scientific workflow with jABC that is capable of performing a location analysis and working with the method of exclusion mapping. It aimed to develop a user-centric procedure with adjustable content and high-quality cartographic output.

The scientific problem used as setting for the workflow was the identification of suitable locations for placing artificial reefs in the waters of the Balearic Islands. Artificial reefs are of interest because they can have a positive effect on local marine wildlife by providing an environment similar to the natural habitats of specific species of flora and fauna. The individual needs of various species for different conditions and the importance of many other parameters (e.g. ground stability) made it necessary to realize a workflow that allows the user to specify the limits of acceptable values for the considered parameters. At the same time it was important to achieve a visualization easy to interpret and not prone to errors.

To implement the workflow with jABC, eight GMT-commands were integrated as jETI-SIBs and combined with some common jABC-SIBs. In providing some basic datasets for the three selected parameters bathymetry, slope and grain size and for some graphical elements (like labels and scale bars) the user is able to process the single aspects and to summarize these results. The thematic data is thereby included as gridded data coming with a given spatial resolution. This data has to be acquired and prepared in advance to match the requirements of GMT and jABC. While going through the workflow the unsuitable locations are excluded and visualized for every single parameter, resulting in a final map showing the results in one frame.

The outputs of the workflow can be used in multiple approaches. The easiest and most straightforward is to use the final map and examine suitable locations for placing an artificial reef, retrieved by classifying all parameters. In addition, the symbolization of the parameters in the final map allows a deeper analysis in that spots marked as unsuitable can also be subjects to a qualitative analysis. This might be useful if some parameters are more important than others. In some cases for example, the water depth might be much more relevant than the ground material, which could lead to an overall suitable reef location, even though the values for the grain size are out of the preferred range. If the knowledge of these special circumstances is available, the results of the realized workflow allow the user to establish a ranking of suitability for the different areas, ranging from suitable (e. g. shallow water, flat slope and medium grain size) over suitable with reservations (e. g. shallow water, flat slope and coarse grain size) to unsuitable (e. g. deep water, steep slope and coarse grain size). Thus, even though this step of post-processing is not included in the workflow itself – which might be a useful addition and done in future work – the stage of the workflow already implemented is capable of providing a basis for a profound analysis.

To be suitable as a decision support system, however, many additional parameters would have to be included. Besides some basic parameters describing the natural conditions – like water temperature and current velocities – human interaction would also have to be considered. For instance the trawling and shipping lines are a crucial aspect for a suitable location [2]. Similarly, already existing reefs and highly productive areas might be taken into account. Since the procedures used in the workflow process the parameters one-by-one, this completion is feasible and the most time-consuming part would probably be the acquisition of the data basis for the added parameters.

At the same time the parameter-based location analysis and the design of the workflow is transferable for solving of a lot of other problems related with GIS. This workflow could therefore be used as a kind of template and be adjusted and extended to solve location analyses in other contexts, but with similar databases.

For further development, the integration of vector data might also be useful approach, as it was chosen and described by Tobias Respondek (see corresponding paper in this composure). The support of a combination of raster and vector data would increase the usability of the workflow and further expand the field of application.

In any case, the efforts made to develop an automated and user-friendly workflow for performing a location analysis – especially the design of the process and way the parameters are included and visualized – turned out to be of value and warrant further exploration.

This article is part of a larger evaluation [8], which aimed at illustrating the power of simplicity-oriented development [16] by validating the claim that process modeling can indeed be handed over to the domain experts by providing them with a graphical modeling framework [24] that covers low-level details in a service-oriented fashion [18], integrates high-level modeling in the overall development process in a way that user-level models become directly executable [17,14], and supports ad-hoc adaptations and evolution [13,15].

The project described in this article can be characterized as follows:

- Scientific domain: geoinformatics
- Number of models: 8
- Number of hierarchy levels: 1
- Total number of SIBs: 142
- SIB libraries used (cf. [11]): common-sibs (29), jeti-sibs (113)
- Service technologies used: jETI services

The geoinformatics part of this volume contains eight other articles on workflow applications in this domain [6,20,5,26,4,22,3,23]. Further geoinformatics workflow projects with the jABC have recently been started. Ongoing work is also exploring how to apply semantics-based (semi-) automatic workflow composition techniques (as provided by, e.g., [19]) to support the workflow design process, as described in [9,10,7] for the bioinformatics domain.

References

1. Artifex Software. Overview of Ghostscript (February 2012), http://www.ghostscript.com/doc/9.05/Readme.htm
2. Green, D.R., Ray, S.T.: Using GIS for siting artificial reefs – Data issues, problems and solutions: Real World to Real World. Journal of Coastal Conservation 8, 7–16 (2002)
3. Hibbe, M.: Spotlocator Project Documentation. In: Lamprecht, A.-L., Margaria, T. (eds.) Process Design for Natural Scientists. CCIS, vol. 500, pp. 149–158. Springer, Heidelberg (2014)
4. Holler, R.: GraffDok: A Graffiti Documentation Application. In: Lamprecht, A.-L., Margaria, T. (eds.) Process Design for Natural Scientists. CCIS, vol. 500, pp. 235–247. Springer, Heidelberg (2014)
5. Kind, J.: Creation of Topographic Maps. In: Lamprecht, A.-L., Margaria, T. (eds.) Process Design for Natural Scientists. CCIS, vol. 500, pp. 225–234. Springer, Heidelberg (2014)

6. Kuntzsch, C.: Visualization of Data Transfer Paths. In: Lamprecht, A.-L., Margaria, T. (eds.) Process Design for Natural Scientists. CCIS, vol. 500, pp. 140–148. Springer, Heidelberg (2014)
7. Lamprecht, A.-L.: User-Level Workflow Design. LNCS, vol. 8311. Springer, Heidelberg (2013)
8. Lamprecht, A.-L., Margaria, T.: Scientific Workflows and XMDD. In: Lamprecht, A.-L., Margaria, T. (eds.) Process Design for Natural Scientists. CCIS, vol. 500, pp. 1–13. Springer, Heidelberg (2014)
9. Lamprecht, A.-L., Margaria, T., Steffen, B.: Bio-jETI: A framework for semantics-based service composition. BMC Bioinformatics 10(suppl. 10), S8 (2009)
10. Lamprecht, A.-L., Naujokat, S., Margaria, T., Steffen, B.: Semantics-based composition of EMBOSS services. Journal of Biomedical Semantics 2(suppl. 1), S5 (2011)
11. Lamprecht, A.-L., Wickert, A.: The Course's SIB Libraries. In: Lamprecht, A.-L., Margaria, T. (eds.) Process Design for Natural Scientists. CCIS, vol. 500, pp. 30–44. Springer, Heidelberg (2014)
12. Margaria, T., Nagel, R., Steffen, B.: jETI: A Tool for Remote Tool Integration. In: Halbwachs, N., Zuck, L.D. (eds.) TACAS 2005. LNCS, vol. 3440, pp. 557–562. Springer, Heidelberg (2005)
13. Margaria, T., Steffen, B.: Agile IT: Thinking in User-Centric Models. In: Margaria, T., Steffen, B. (eds.) ISoLA 2008. CCIS, vol. 17, pp. 490–502. Springer, Heidelberg (2009)
14. Margaria, T., Steffen, B.: Business Process Modelling in the jABC: The One-Thing-Approach. In: Cardoso, J., van der Aalst, W. (eds.) Handbook of Research on Business Process Modeling. IGI Global (2009)
15. Margaria, T., Steffen, B.: Continuous Model-Driven Engineering. IEEE Computer 42(10), 106–109 (2009)
16. Margaria, T., Steffen, B.: Simplicity as a Driver for Agile Innovation. Computer 43(6), 90–92 (2010)
17. Margaria, T., Steffen, B.: Service-Orientation: Conquering Complexity with XMDD. In: Hinchey, M., Coyle, L. (eds.) Conquering Complexity, pp. 217–236. Springer, London (2012)
18. Margaria, T., Steffen, B., Reitenspiess, M.: Service-Oriented Design: The Roots. In: Benatallah, B., Casati, F., Traverso, P. (eds.) ICSOC 2005. LNCS, vol. 3826, pp. 450–464. Springer, Heidelberg (2005)
19. Naujokat, S., Lamprecht, A.-L., Steffen, B.: Loose Programming with PROPHETS. In: de Lara, J., Zisman, A. (eds.) Fundamental Approaches to Software Engineering. LNCS, vol. 7212, pp. 94–98. Springer, Heidelberg (2012)
20. Noack, F.: CREADED: Coloured-Relief Application for Digital Elevation Data. In: Lamprecht, A.-L., Margaria, T. (eds.) Process Design for Natural Scientists. CCIS, vol. 500, pp. 182–195. Springer, Heidelberg (2014)
21. Pickering, H., Whitmarsh, D.: Artificial reefs and fisheries exploitation: A review of the attraction versus production debate, the influence of design and its significance for policy. Fisheries Research 31, 39–59 (1997)
22. Respondeck, T.: A Workflow for Computing Potential Areas for Wind Turbines. In: Lamprecht, A.-L., Margaria, T. (eds.) Process Design for Natural Scientists. CCIS, vol. 500, pp. 196–211. Springer, Heidelberg (2014)
23. Sens, H.: Web-Based Map Generalization Tools Put to the Test. In: Lamprecht, A.-L., Margaria, T. (eds.) Process Design for Natural Scientists. CCIS, vol. 500, pp. 171–181. Springer, Heidelberg (2014)

24. Steffen, B., Margaria, T., Nagel, R., Jörges, S., Kubczak, C.: Model-Driven Development with the jABC. In: Bin, E., Ziv, A., Ur, S. (eds.) HVC 2006. LNCS, vol. 4383, pp. 92–108. Springer, Heidelberg (2007)
25. Stephan, C.D., Dansby, B.G., Osburn, H.R., Matlock, G.C., Riechers, R.K., Rayburn, R.: Texas Artificial Reef Fishery Management Plan. Texas Parks and Wildlife Department, Fishery Management Plan Series Number 3 Edition (1990)
26. Teske, D.: Geocoder Accuracy Ranking. In: Lamprecht, A.-L., Margaria, T. (eds.) Process Design for Natural Scientists. CCIS, vol. 500, pp. 159–170. Springer, Heidelberg (2014)
27. U.S. Department of Commerce and National Oceanic and Atmospheric Administration. National Artificial Reef Plan (as Amended): Guidelines for Siting, Construction, Development, and Assessment of Artificial Reefs (February 2007)
28. U.S. Department of Commerce and National Oceanic and Atmospheric Administration and National Environmental Satellite, Data, and Information Service and National Geophysical Data Center. nETOPO2v2 2006 (2006), http://www.ngdc.noaa.gov/mgg/fliers/06mgg01.html
29. U.S. Environmental Protection Agency and United States Maritime Administration. National Guidance: Best Management Practices for Preparing Vessels Intended to Create Artificial Reefs (May 2006)
30. Wessel, P., Smith, W.H.F.: The Generic Mapping Tools – A Map-making Tutorial Version 4.5.8. University of Hawaii at Manoa and National Oceanic and Atmospheric Administration (2012)
31. Wessel, P., Smith, W.H.F.: The generic mapping tools – technical reference and cookbook version 4.5.8. Technical report, University of Hawaii at Manoa and National Oceanic and Atmospheric Administration (2012)

Creation of Topographic Maps

Josephine Kind

Potsdam University, Potsdam, D-14482, Germany
reso@uni-potsdam.de

Abstract. The goal of this project was to create a topographic map of Germany without requiring any knowledge of a GIS program from the user. The resulting workflow autonomously generates a map of a colored digital terrain model with the main rivers, political boundaries, some cities, mountains and a legend key under the map. For the individual steps it mainly uses the Generic Mapping Tools (GMT). GMT is a collection of command line programs, which are run on an external server, so they don't have to be installed at the user's computer. Creating a map of other areas only requires minor changes of the workflow configuration.

Keywords: geovisualization, topographic maps, GMT.

1 Introduction: Workflow Scenario

Topographic maps are detailed and accurate graphic representations of both the natural and man-made features on the ground of a particular terrain [24]. Historically, there exist a variety of methods for the creation of topographic maps, for different purposes. The example described in this paper is concerned with the creation a topographic map of Germany, including big cities, mountains and mountain ranges and some important rivers, as shown in Figure 1.

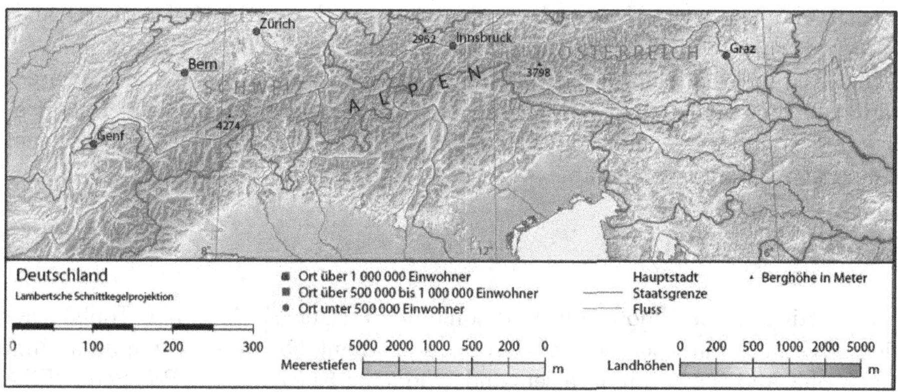

Fig. 1. Part of the created topographic map

A.-L. Lamprecht et al. (Eds.): Process Design for Natural Scientists, CCIS 500, pp. 229–238, 2014.
DOI: 10.1007/978-3-662-45006-2_18

Technically, five principal steps are required for creating a topographic map, as also the workflow diagram in Figure 2 indicates: The first part of the workflow edits all the input data. The second part creates the base map. Third, all the information like cities, mountains or rivers are inserted to the map. Here, all the symbols for instance the cities are plotted and subsequently all the symbols are labeled. Fourth, the workflow creates a legend key under the map. The fifth and last part renders the final map.

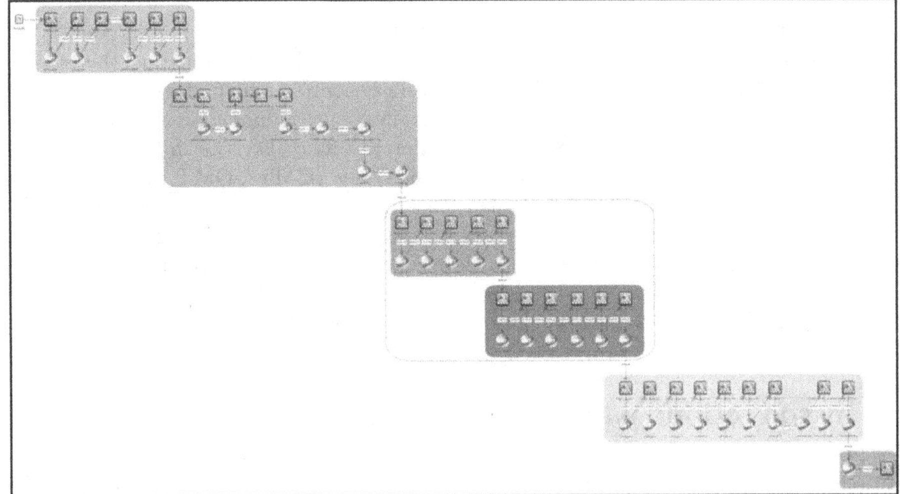

Fig. 2. Workflow overview

With this jABC workflow you can easily create a topographic map, not only of Germany, but of every part in the world. There is no GIS-Program or other programs required to convert the data and there is no special technical knowledge needed. You just have to know where your area is at the graticule of the earth and to provide some text files with all the facts, for example cities or mountains, to be inserted into the map. From this information, the workflow creates a colored digital terrain model with red-colored political boundaries, main rivers and a legend key under the map. It is also possible to add own information which should be inserted to the map.

2 Service Analysis

For realizing the workflow you need some GMT (Generic Mapping Tools) services. "GMT is an open source collection of about 65 tools for manipulating geographic and Cartesian data sets and producing Encapsulated PostScript File (EPS). GMT supports over 30 map projections and transformations and comes with support data such as GSHHS coastlines, rivers, and political boundaries.

GMT is developed and maintained by Paul Wessel and Walter H. F. Smith with help from a global set of volunteers, and is supported by the National Science Foundation. It is released under the GNU General Public License." [23].

Concretely, the following GMT commands are required in this scenario (cf. the GMT Online Man Pages at [23]):

- **xyz2grd**: Converts an ASCII or binary table to grid file format.
- **grdpaste**: Puts two grids together along common edges.
- **grdgradient**: Computes a directional gradient from a 2D grid file.
- **grdimage**: Produces images from 2-D gridded data.
- **pscoast**: Plots coastlines, filled continents, rivers, and political borders.
- **psxy**: Plots the symbols of the cities and the heights.
- **pstext**: Plots the text strings.
- **pslegend**: Plots the legend on the map.
- **ps2raster**: Crops and converts PostScript to raster image, EPS and PDF.

All the Generic Mapping Tools are command line tools. The tools which are needed for the workflow are available as jETI services at a remote server and the corresponding SIBs can simply be used. All the other functionality that is needed is available from the jETI and CommonSIB libraries that are enclosed in the jABC download package.

3 Workflow Realization

As explained in the introduction, the workflow is consists of five principal parts, which are detailed in the following.

3.1 Data Input

The first part edits all the input data. Before starting the workflow you have to create a folder named jABC on the local disk where the data, for example the final map, can be saved. Furthermore all the input data have to be inserted into this folder. The input data consists of three relief datasets:

1. The GLOBE (The Global Land One-km Base Elevation Project)
   It is a 30-arc-second (1-km) gridded, quality-controlled global Digital Elevation Model (DEM). For a map of Germany you need part C (c10g) and G (g10g). These parts and all other parts can be downloaded from `http://www.ngdc.noaa.gov/mgg/topo/gltiles.html` (cf. Figure 4).
2. ETOPO2v2 Global Relief Model
   ETOPO2 is a 2 arc-minute global relief model of Earth's surface that integrates land topography and ocean bathymetry.

At the first part the workflow reads the input data and merges the two parts of the GLOBE data to one land grid using the GMT services xyz2grd and grdpaste as described in Section 2. Then, it calls grdgradient to compute a directional derivative or gradient from the 2D grid file and extracts (with grdcut) the subarea from the ETOPO1 to an ocean grid.

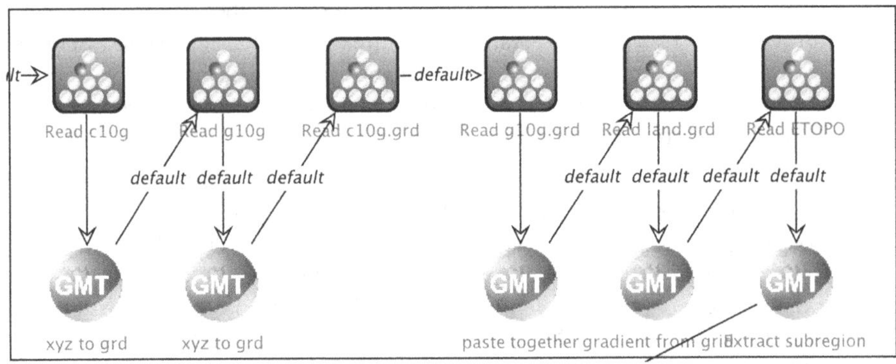

Fig. 3. Data input (Part 1)

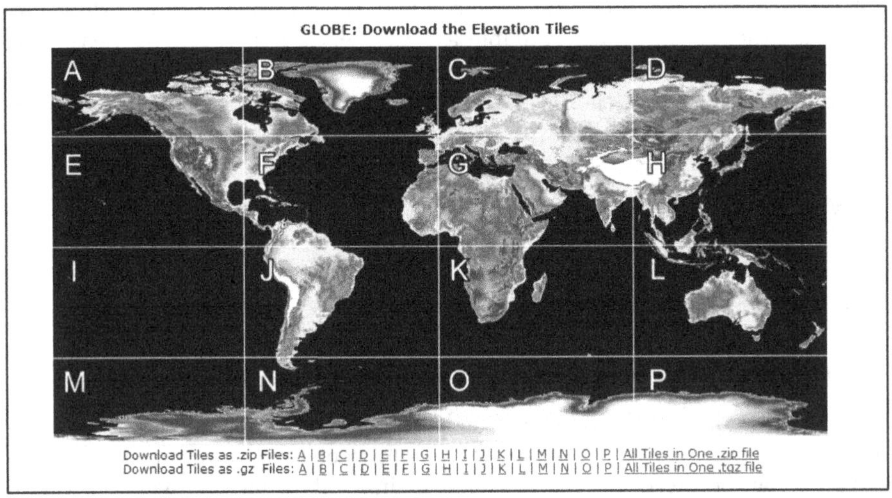

Fig. 4. The GLOBE

3.2 Basemap

At the next part the workflow creates a colored image from the ocean and from the land with the commands grdimage and pscoast. For this part you have to paste the files land.cpt and the ocean.cpt into the jABC folder. Now you have a colored basemap with rivers, coastlines and red political boundaries as shown in Figure 6. The output is a colored PostScript file.

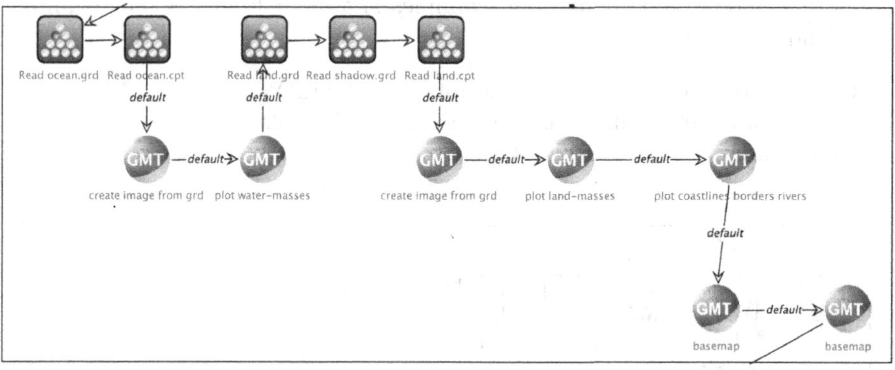

Fig. 5. Basemap (part 2)

3.3 Cities, Rivers, Mountains

In this part the workflow integrates all the information which should be in the final map. There have to be text files for every kind of city and text files with the information about the heights (height_1.txt), the rivers (river.txt) and the

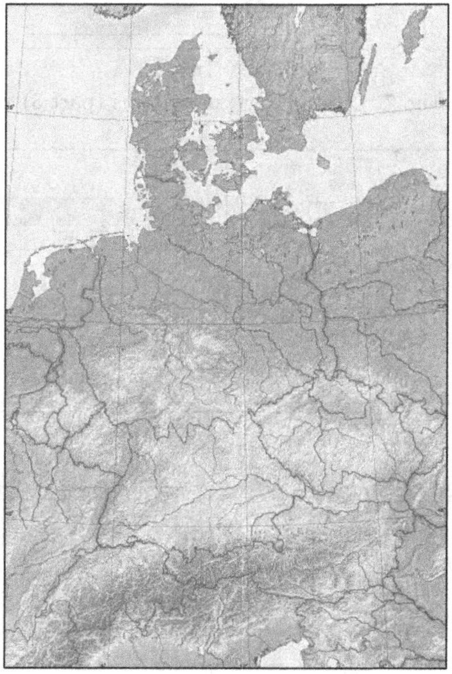

Fig. 6. Basemap

mountains (mountain.txt) like the examples shown in Figure 8. For example three kinds of cities:

1. Cities more than 1 million inhabitants (cities_1.txt)
2. Cities from 500000 till 1million inhabitants (cities_2.txt)
3. Cities under 500000 inhabitants (cities_3.txt)

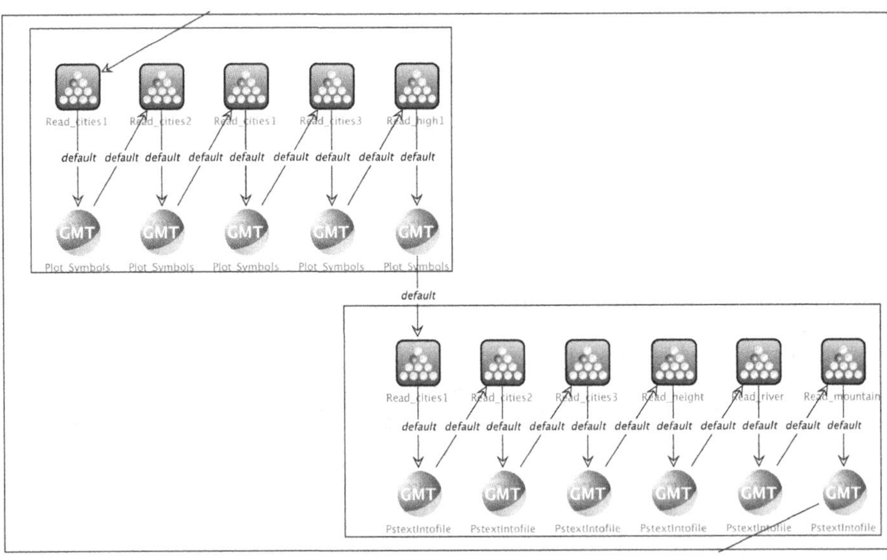

Fig. 7. Cities, rivers, mountains (part 3)

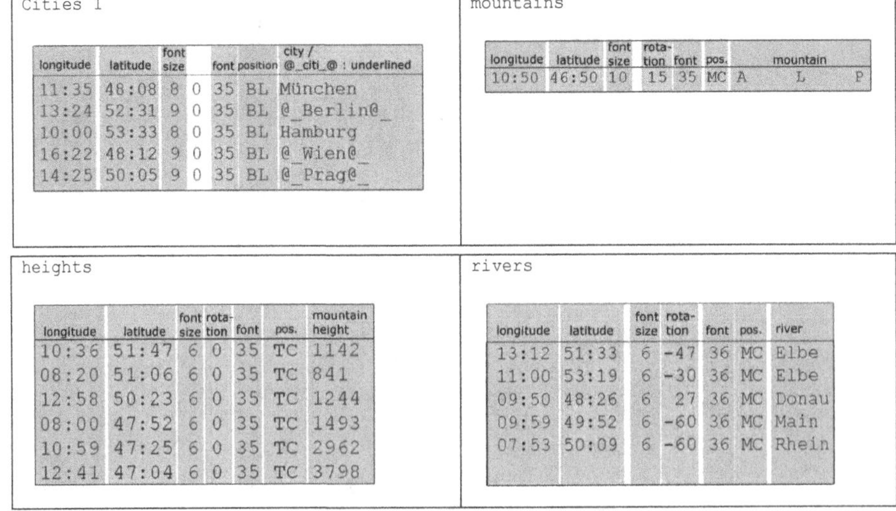

Cities 1

longitude	latitude	font size		font	position	city / @_citi_@ : underlined
11:35	48:08	8	0	35	BL	München
13:24	52:31	9	0	35	BL	@_Berlin@_
10:00	53:33	8	0	35	BL	Hamburg
16:22	48:12	9	0	35	BL	@_Wien@_
14:25	50:05	9	0	35	BL	@_Prag@_

mountains

longitude	latitude	font size	rotation	font	pos.	mountain
10:50	46:50	10	15	35	MC	A L P

heights

longitude	latitude	font size	rotation	font	pos.	mountain height
10:36	51:47	6	0	35	TC	1142
08:20	51:06	6	0	35	TC	841
12:58	50:23	6	0	35	TC	1244
08:00	47:52	6	0	35	TC	1493
10:59	47:25	6	0	35	TC	2962
12:41	47:04	6	0	35	TC	3798

rivers

longitude	latitude	font size	rotation	font	pos.	river
13:12	51:33	6	-47	36	MC	Elbe
11:00	53:19	6	-30	36	MC	Elbe
09:50	48:26	6	27	36	MC	Donau
09:59	49:52	6	-60	36	MC	Main
07:53	50:09	6	-60	36	MC	Rhein

Fig. 8. Text files

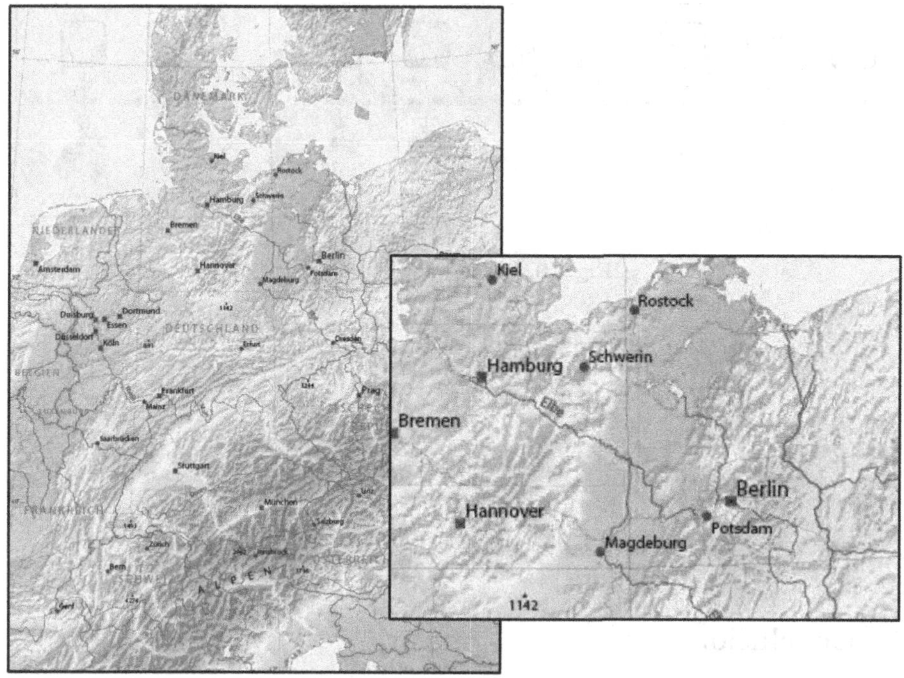

Fig. 9. Intermediate result

All the new text files have to be saved at the jABC folder. Then, using the psxy SIB, cities with more than 1 million inhabitants are assigned for example with a red square with a smaller black square inside. When all symbols are drawn, the command pstext plots all the text strings on the map. After this step you get a PostScript file with all the information you want. Now the map is almost ready and looks like the example shown in Figure 9.

3.4 Legend Key

The fourth part of the workflow generates a legend key of all the symbols and creates a scale bar using the pslegend service. For this part you have to put legend text files (e.g. legend_1.txt, legend_2.txt, legend_3.txt, legend_4.txt, legend_5.txt, legend_6.txt, legend_7.txt), the ocean_scale.cpt and the land.cpt into the jABC folder.

3.5 Final Map

At the last section the SIB ps2raster generates a raster of the PostScript file. The last step of the workflow is to render a PNG file of the raster and saves it in the jABC folder.

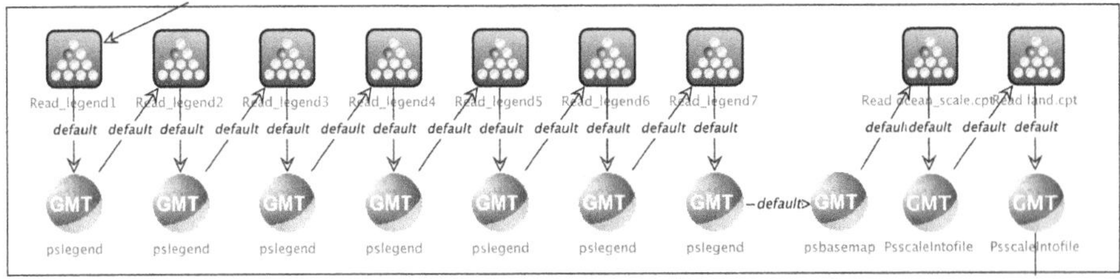

Fig. 10. Legend key (part 4)

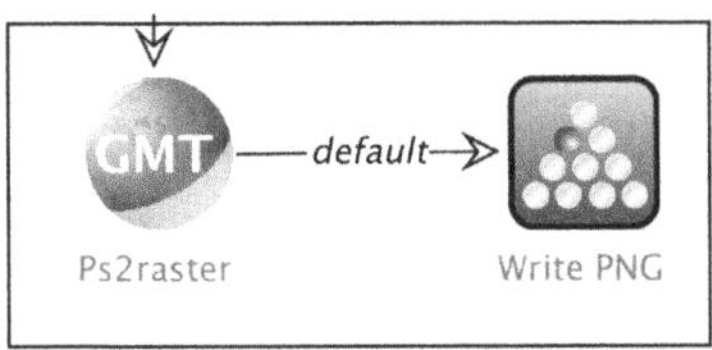

Fig. 11. Final map (part 5)

4 Conclusion

The goal of the workflow was to create a topographic map of a particular region in a simple way. For the example of Germany you could create a map very easily. For other countries or other areas, however, you have to change particular parameters of the workflow: At first the right part of the GLOBE DEM has to be chosen. The picture of the website http://www.ngdc.noaa.gov/mgg/topo/gltiles.html helps you finding the right part. Then you have to know where your area of interest is and configure the GMT SIBs accordingly. Also, if you change the area, you have to provide new text files about the cities, the heights, the rivers and the mountains as well. The headline of the legend key has to be changed, too.

Although this still requires some knowledge how the GMT services and commands work, and so the originally anticipated flexibility is not yet completely given, with the workflow you dont have to think about what GMT SIBs are needed to create a map. You just have to know where your area of interest is and where you have to change the parameters at the workflow. In the future it should be considered how this workflow could be more flexible without those changes.

This article is part of a larger evaluation [5], which aimed at illustrating the power of simplicity-oriented development [13] by validating the claim that process modeling can indeed be handed over to the domain experts by providing them with a graphical modeling framework [21] that covers low-level details in a service-oriented fashion [15], integrates high-level modeling in the overall development process in a way that user-level models become directly executable [14,11], and supports ad-hoc adaptations and evolution [10,12].

The project described in this article can be characterized as follows:

- Scientific domain: geoinformatics
- Number of models: 1
- Number of hierarchy levels: 1
- Total number of SIBs: 67
- SIB libraries used (cf. [8]): common-sibs (16), jeti-sibs (51)
- Service technologies used: jETI services

The geoinformatics part of this volume contains eight other articles on workflow applications in this domain [3,17,22,2,19,18,1,20]. Further geoinformatics workflow projects with the jABC have recently been started. Ongoing work is also exploring how to apply semantics-based (semi-) automatic workflow composition techniques (as provided by, e.g., [16]) to support the workflow design process, as described in [6,7,4] for the bioinformatics domain.

References

1. Hibbe, M.: Spotlocator Project Documentation. In: Lamprecht, A.-L., Margaria, T. (eds.) Process Design for Natural Scientists. CCIS, vol. 500, pp. 149–158. Springer, Heidelberg (2014)
2. Holler, R.: GraffDok: A Graffiti Documentation Application. In: Lamprecht, A.-L., Margaria, T. (eds.) Process Design for Natural Scientists. CCIS, vol. 500, pp. 235–247. Springer, Heidelberg (2014)
3. Kuntzsch, C.: Visualization of Data Transfer Paths. In: Lamprecht, A.-L., Margaria, T. (eds.) Process Design for Natural Scientists. CCIS, vol. 500, pp. 140–148. Springer, Heidelberg (2014)
4. Lamprecht, A.-L.: User-Level Workflow Design. LNCS, vol. 8311. Springer, Heidelberg (2013)
5. Lamprecht, A.-L., Margaria, T.: Scientific Workflows and XMDD. In: Lamprecht, A.-L., Margaria, T. (eds.) Process Design for Natural Scientists. CCIS, vol. 500, pp. 1–13. Springer, Heidelberg (2014)
6. Lamprecht, A.-L., Margaria, T., Steffen, B.: Bio-jETI: A framework for semantics-based service composition. BMC Bioinformatics 10(suppl. 10), S8 (2009)
7. Lamprecht, A.-L., Naujokat, S., Margaria, T., Steffen, B.: Semantics-based composition of EMBOSS services. Journal of Biomedical Semantics 2(suppl. 1), S5 (2011)
8. Lamprecht, A.-L., Wickert, A.: The Course's SIB Libraries. In: Lamprecht, A.-L., Margaria, T. (eds.) Process Design for Natural Scientists. CCIS, vol. 500, pp. 30–44. Springer, Heidelberg (2014)
9. Margaria, T., Nagel, R., Steffen, B.: jETI: A Tool for Remote Tool Integration. In: Halbwachs, N., Zuck, L.D. (eds.) TACAS 2005. LNCS, vol. 3440, pp. 557–562. Springer, Heidelberg (2005)

10. Margaria, T., Steffen, B.: Agile IT: Thinking in User-Centric Models. In: Margaria, T., Steffen, B. (eds.) ISoLA 2008. CCIS, vol. 17, pp. 490–502. Springer, Heidelberg (2009)
11. Margaria, T., Steffen, B.: Business Process Modelling in the jABC: The One-Thing-Approach. In: Cardoso, J., van der Aalst, W. (eds.) Handbook of Research on Business Process Modeling. IGI Global (2009)
12. Margaria, T., Steffen, B.: Continuous Model-Driven Engineering. IEEE Computer 42(10), 106–109 (2009)
13. Margaria, T., Steffen, B.: Simplicity as a Driver for Agile Innovation. Computer 43(6), 90–92 (2010)
14. Margaria, T., Steffen, B.: Service-Orientation: Conquering Complexity with XMDD. In: Hinchey, M., Coyle, L. (eds.) Conquering Complexity, pp. 217–236. Springer, London (2012)
15. Margaria, T., Steffen, B., Reitenspiess, M.: Service-Oriented Design: The Roots. In: Benatallah, B., Casati, F., Traverso, P. (eds.) ICSOC 2005. LNCS, vol. 3826, pp. 450–464. Springer, Heidelberg (2005)
16. Naujokat, S., Lamprecht, A.-L., Steffen, B.: Loose Programming with PROPHETS. In: de Lara, J., Zisman, A. (eds.) Fundamental Approaches to Software Engineering. LNCS, vol. 7212, pp. 94–98. Springer, Heidelberg (2012)
17. Noack, F.: CREADED: Coloured-Relief Application for Digital Elevation Data. In: Lamprecht, A.-L., Margaria, T. (eds.) Process Design for Natural Scientists. CCIS, vol. 500, pp. 182–195. Springer, Heidelberg (2014)
18. Respondeck, T.: A Workflow for Computing Potential Areas for Wind Turbines. In: Lamprecht, A.-L., Margaria, T. (eds.) Process Design for Natural Scientists. CCIS, vol. 500, pp. 196–211. Springer, Heidelberg (2014)
19. Scheele, L.: Location Analysis for Placing Artificial Reefs. In: Lamprecht, A.-L., Margaria, T. (eds.) Process Design for Natural Scientists. CCIS, vol. 500, pp. 212–224. Springer, Heidelberg (2014)
20. Sens, H.: Web-Based Map Generalization Tools Put to the Test. In: Lamprecht, A.-L., Margaria, T. (eds.) Process Design for Natural Scientists. CCIS, vol. 500, pp. 171–181. Springer, Heidelberg (2014)
21. Steffen, B., Margaria, T., Nagel, R., Jörges, S., Kubczak, C.: Model-Driven Development with the jABC. In: Bin, E., Ziv, A., Ur, S. (eds.) HVC 2006. LNCS, vol. 4383, pp. 92–108. Springer, Heidelberg (2007)
22. Teske, D.: Geocoder Accuracy Ranking. In: Lamprecht, A.-L., Margaria, T. (eds.) Process Design for Natural Scientists. CCIS, vol. 500, pp. 159–170. Springer, Heidelberg (2014)
23. Wessel, P.: The GMT Home Page, `http://gmt.soest.hawaii.edu` (Online; last accessed January 03, 2013)
24. Wikipedia. Topographic map — wikipedia, the free encyclopedia (2012), `http://en.wikipedia.org/w/index.php?title=Topographic_map&oldid=527445395` (Online; accessed January 4, 2013)

GraffDok — A Graffiti Documentation Application

Robin Holler

Potsdam University, Potsdam, D-14482, Germany
robin@wxyz.de

Abstract. GraffDok is an application helping to maintain an overview over sprayed images somewhere in a city. At the time of writing it aims at vandalism rather than at beautiful photographic graffiti in an underpass. Looking at hundreds of tags and scribbles on monuments, house walls, etc. it would be interesting to not only record them in writing but even make them accessible electronically, including images.

GraffDok's workflow is simple and only requires an EXIF-GPS-tagged photograph of a graffito. It automatically determines its location by using reverse geocoding with the given GPS-coordinates and the Gisgraphy WebService. While asking the user for some more meta data, GraffDok analyses the image in parallel with this and tries to detect fore- and background – before extracting the drawing lines and make them stand alone. The command line based tool ImageMagick is used here as well as for accessing EXIF data.

Any meta data is written to csv-files, which will stay easily accessible and can be integrated in TeX-files as well. The latter ones are converted to PDF at the end of the workflow, containing a table about all graffiti and a summary for each – including the generated characteristic graffiti pattern image.

Keywords: data acquisition, documentation, image analysis, image processing, geocoding, automation, automatization, graffiti, photography, LaTeX, meta data, ImageMagick, Gisgraphy.

1 Introduction: Workflow Scenario

GraffDok assumes there are lots of people out there carrying new smart mobile phones. They all have the possibility to capture their environment in photographs and upload them immediately to the www. So there's a nice big potential for crowd sourcing – not only for creating maps like OSM but for documentation too. At the moment GraffDok is still evolving and is working locally only but it is aiming at a large world wide database of graffiti.

First of all GraffDok is dealing with kinds of vandalism. But later on the beautiful graffiti will follow. That's the reason why the neutral word "documentation" lies within GraffDok's name and description: GraffDok can be used to create stats and even follow/locate a sprayer until he is arrested, but it does not

A.-L. Lamprecht et al. (Eds.): Process Design for Natural Scientists, CCIS 500, pp. 239–251, 2014.
DOI: 10.1007/978-3-662-45006-2_19

need to. There are some beautiful thoughts and purposes, e. g. a rating system for photogenic graffiti world wide.

In a wise foresight there will never be a big database with contributions from people all over the world until there is a quick and easy way to contribute. That's why this story starts with jABC: It may sound simple to stick picture and description together, creating a profile. But it requires great efforts to make this efficient, useful and thus sustainable. Any data must be complete and accurate. The images should be edited and saved as clean or even model like patterns – out of various photographs taken by mobile phone cameras! Only if all works out, it will be possible to search the database for graffiti by text and even by image.

Putting submission things in a standardized workflow seems therefor a good way to achieve entries of high quality only. It's always a good idea to take some time first, make some decisions about how to process the images best and then implement these thoughts in automatized processes. That way noone has to sit down and process all the images in editing software by sight. And yet there will be good results without significant deviations. There may be batch processing for images, but image processing is just one element of the process chain. With jABC one has not even to start diverse batch processing jobs. Just follow the entire workflow once it is created.

In future GraffDok will have to deal with creating a digital fingerprint of each graphic/pattern. Finding a way to express its characteristics as handy useful code, serving as findable marker in the database is not trivial, but necessary for searching by image. As a start GraffDok will concentrate on clean user submissions and image preprocessing. Establishing a large database with all that basic input will provide a solid foundation for further developments.

2 Service Analysis

GraffDok wants to add some readable and understandable geo information. That said it has to transform the coordinates into an address. The coordinates are given by the EXIF data attached to a (JPEG-)photograph out of a smart phone with GPS. So there's need for a (reverse) Geocoding Webservice. And there's a need for a tool able to read EXIF data and make them accessible, too.

There are many Webservices for geocoding. Google Maps can be used, for example. It's a simple service and most often it is as easy as creating a schematic URL containing latitude and longitude:

```
http://maps.googleapis.com/maps/api/geocode/xml?latlng=lat,long
```

would return an XML containing a lot of information to this point and local area. Most Geocoding Webservices are free to use and delivered valuable results while testing within jABC. In the end Gisgraphy [17] was implemented in the workflow as Geocoding WebService. Gisgraphy is not only free but based on an open source framework and offers its services via Java or REST API.

There are also a lot of tools able to read EXIF. There even is one, called exif [1]. But since we need an image processing tool as well: ImageMagick [3] is a powerful tool in terms of image processing and is not only able to process the images but will fetch all necessary EXIF data from an image, too. ImageMagick is most often used as command line tool without an graphical interface and is licensed under Apache 2.0.

Many graffiti images typically contain two classes: the surface in the background and the graffito itself in the foreground. In these cases the image analysis can be done by a nice bash script called fuzzythresh from Fred Weinhaus [26]. It is free for use in free apps as well as ImageMagick is. And it's fine for images with fore- and background typically revealing a bimodal shaped histogram.

Since GraffDok saves any meta data as csv-text-files and integrates these files in TeX-files, there's the need of an installed TeX distribution with enhancement by the LaTeX package csvsimple(.sty) [24]. Then it will be possible to import csv-files into TeX and finally form tables in PDF by running pdflatex on command line.

After all there shouldn't be any restrictions since all services are either free/libre software or free to use non-commercially. Moreover all important services should work independently from the platform in principal. But since GraffDok has evolved under an unix-like system (Ubuntu Linux) and did not use jETI yet, it may be possible that some code/paths have to be adjusted, e.g. to control some command line tools like ImageMagick by ExecuteCommand-SIBs. There is even little use of unix-tools like sed and cat, but it shouldn't be difficult to find an adequate replacement for Win and others.

3 Workflow Realization

The entire workflow is visible in figure 1: the four essential parts are framed by rounded rectangles.

The arrangement in the part on top shows when files are chosen and paths are defined, as well as where file names are extracted. There is a lot of interaction with the user since the program needs to get input first, most importantly a photograph of a graffito. As a result mainly common GUI SIBs are used here, except for one row of common basic SIBs dealing with strings and extraction of pattern.

So the first thing GraffDok does – after welcoming the user, of course – is to ask him for choosing the photograph. It should be a graffito detail, meaning a close framing without environment and concentrating on the motif: only the pattern on a certain surface. There is an option for a second wide angle image showing the area around the graffito. This second wide angle image will only be resized in further processing and could be added to the final graffito profile.

To keep it simple, GraffDok will make a suggestion for the working directory. By default the working directory is just derived from the selected image file path. Following the suggestion it will be build one level above. In other words: The image folder containing the original photograph would already lay inside

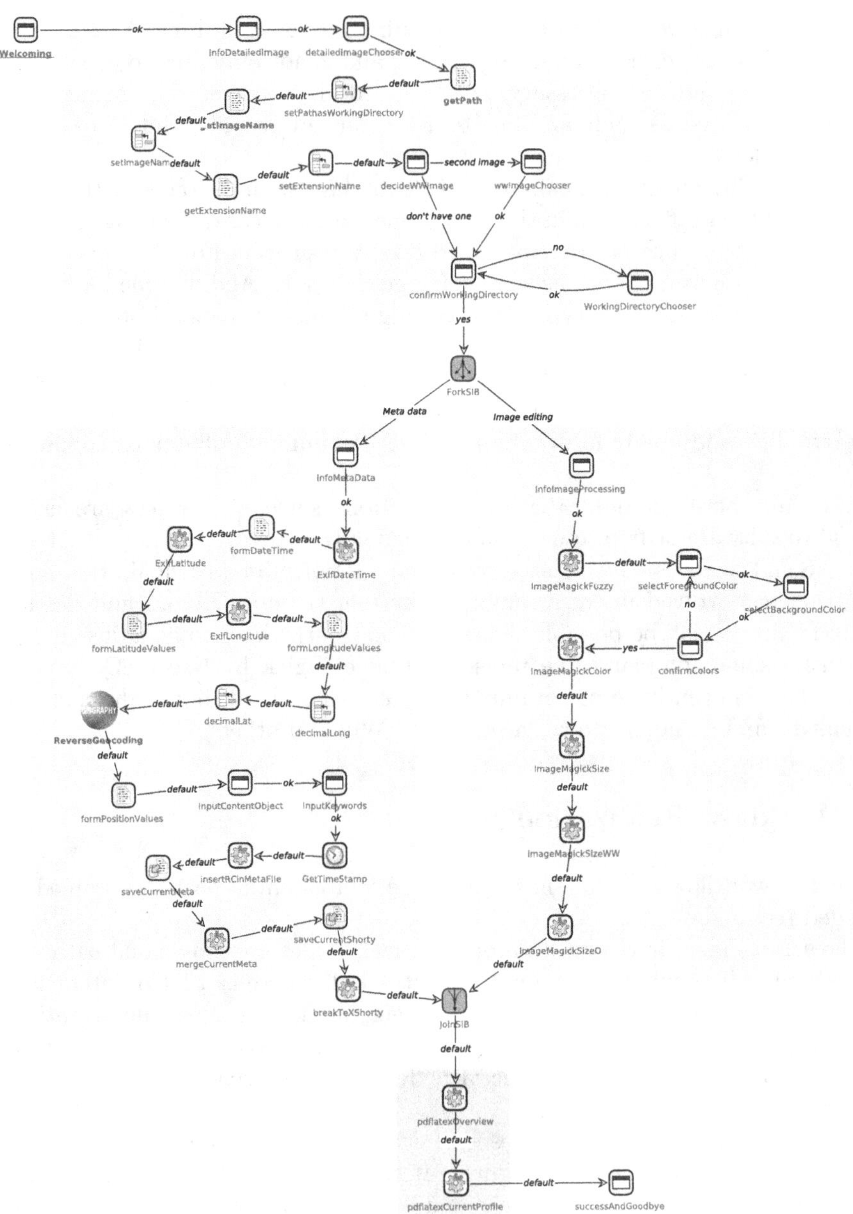

Fig. 1. The entire workflow devided in its four essential parts. Part on top: Choosing files, defining paths, file names, working directory. Middle left: Processing meta data and generating csv-/tex-files. Middle right: Processing images. Bottom part: Generating PDF documents (overview and current profile) including processed meta data as well as processed images.

the suggested working directory. Ideally the image folder is named "original" or similar since it will also serve as target folder for all further graffiti photographs.

But it's a user's decision to follow the suggestion. To make things work there have to be created two more folders inside the working directory. By default both should be created aside to the folder with original photographs. One called "Imagicks" will contain all processed images, the other one "MetaPDF" will save text-files and PDFs. Right in the working directory lies the fuzzythresh script which may create temporary files in there while working and iterating.

So the user implicitly gives the path of the suggested working directory by selecting the image of choice via file chooser. Technically a regular expression is used here to get the working directory out of the file path:

```
.*(?=/[\w]*/)
```

That expression takes any characters of a given file path until there is only one level of directory left. The last slash in a file path usually devides path from file name. So the latter one as well as the folder containing it, will both be cut off due to the positive lookbehind in the expression (lookbehind: second last slash, certain characters, last slash).

Example: From a chosen file path

```
~/jabc/GraffDok/original/IM0001.jpg
```

the working directory

```
~/jabc/GraffDok
```

would be derived.

That's what the common basic SIBs in the part on top of the workflow are for. In this case they are all using different but short and simple regular expressions, though it would be possible to use one complex regular expressions for all:

```
^(.*/)?(?:$|(.+?)(?:(\.[^.]*$)|$))
```

By using this expression for unix paths, one is able to address the target group by an index. The expression groups the string into the whole file path, the directory, the filename and finally a dot with extension.

By the way: the FileChooser is set to only show JPEG and TIFF in its dialog, assuming that these image formats are common and may hold the required EXIF data with the GPS coordinates. The limited choice is nice for finding files more quickly but can always be modified of course.

The middle left and right part will be processed in parallel. While the one on the right is all about image processing – consuming hardware power and time – the one on the left is processing meta data. This way the user is able to enter his descriptions while images are processed in the background.

As said the part on the right visualizes the image processing. The only interaction with the user is about which colors should be used in the processed image. Beside this interaction the acting of fuzzythresh and ImageMagick is controlled and initiated by ExecuteCommand-SIBs on command line.

Figure 2 shows, what a usual graffito photograph out of a mobile phone could look like. Of course the quality isn't splendid and without positive exposure correction most photographs will come out rather dark due to rather bright background surfaces in most cases, and the cam trying to expose it to a mid grey. But it should be sufficient to filter the pattern and its graphical characteristics.

Fig. 2. A sample photograph of a red harlekin face in Goettingen, Germany

With regard of the already addressed time to plan and create a good workflow, this is an important point. How to deal with various images differing in exposure/brightness, color, etc. without looking at each? There are questions on how to unify/preprocess and how to classify the images, to make the graffito class left.

In figure 2 a human eye has no problems with filtering the graffiti lines. But yet it could be visibly improved. And more important: It should be improved and made even clearer to make it contain only relevant information on the graffito itself. Then it will be easier or even possible to create a digital fingerprint – whatever it will look like in future.

In its current status GraffDok concentrates on emphasizing the characteristic of a pattern by using thresholds. ImageMagick offers many enhancements like simple global affecting filters for contrast and brightness or histogram stretching. Since the histograms of each color channel may be stretched differently the questions comes up, how important accurate colors are. A linear-stretch should avoid heavy color shifts. The command line would look like:

```
convert SDIM001.jpg -linear-stretch 1x1% linearStr.jpg
```

and as a result the pattern is visible more clearly. But first it's an overall global action on the image and second there are too many useless background information left. So one might try manual leveling to cut off this redundant information. To avoid hard edges one may may use sigmoidal contrast, too. The command lines would look like:

```
convert SDIM001.jpg -level 25%,40% leveled.jpg
convert SDIM001.jpg -sigmoidal-contrast 18%,30% sigmoidal.jpg
```

The results are quite promising and much better for extraction of this graffito pattern. But: the values to achieve these results have been found while trying and looking at the picture. In a common workflow with many diverse pictures this wouldn't be possible. The same intense value settings with such strong thresholding would make some other graffiti certainly disappear.

That's why there is only one choice: An analysis of the image first and a processing accordingly to the analysis afterwards. Fuzzythresh looks at the histogram and its typical bimodal shape due to fore- and background – before thresholding it to a binary black and white image. The latter one afterwards shows the foreground only in black while the rest is white (or inverse). One may read the description of the script author [26].

To make fuzzythresh run on a command line, type

```
. ./fuzzythresh SDIM001.jpg SDIM_fuzzy.jpg
```

Due to the calculated (iteratively and a bit slow) threshold at 34.8709% for this image, the result is fine. There's only the pattern left, but it is black. Since the pattern itself seems a lot more important than the lost color this should be okay. Sprayers will probably also switch colors, rather than using the same color for a certain tag all the time.

Since there is a possibility to assign colors to the resulting binary image in ImageMagick, this may compensate the loss of original color. It even may be nicer because of dealing with a smaller and more exact color pool in the database. Also, the original image and its colors always remain accessible through the graffito profile in the database.

Back to the workflow, this is how images will be processed: first step is the fuzzy script with image analysis, second is a user interaction about the coloring of the generated black and white image. Three common gui SIBs handle this interaction, two as input SIBs for entering fore- and background color and one to confirm the selection.

On command line ImageMagick simply needs fore- and background color as parameters (fg/hg):

```
convert graffito_bw.gif +level-colors fg,hg graffito_color.gif
```

Now sizing is the only thing left in image processing. Assuming that the final profile document will have fixed spaces of 500 px in width and height for its images, resizing will be done by reducing to 500 x 500 px after the longest side and filling white color where necessary:

```
convert fuzzy.jpg -resize 500x500 -size 500x500 xc:white
+swap -gravity center  -composite fuzzy_sizedwhite_500.jpg
```

With finishing the middle right part of the workflow there will be up to five new processed images. Both originals (detail and wide angle) will have copies in decreased size of 500 x 500 px. And the more important detail image is available in three more versions as clean binary pattern, as image in clean adapted colors and as final image in reduced size. Figure 3 shows the original images in /original/ while figure 4 shows the processed images in /Imagicks/.

Fig. 3. One detailed and one wide angle photograph as originals

Fig. 4. Five images processed from two original images – ready to be used in the profile

The middle left part of the workflow is dealing with the meta data of the captured graffito. As already stated these processes will be executed in parallel with the image processing of the middle right part.

First GraffDok uses ImageMagick on command line to read specific EXIF data from the input image, e.g. date and latitude/longitude. Since there most often have to be made adjustments in each returned value, there are ExtractPattern-SIBs in between the ExecuteCommand-SIBs. Afterwards two PutExpression-SIBs help transforming the notation of the coordinates from ddd mm' ss,ss" into ddd,dddddd for each: latitude and longitude. The reason for calculating to decimal values is the Webservice Gisgraphy, accepting only decimal values in the request query.

Since Gisgraphy not only returns few values but a list containing addresses in XML ordered by distance, one have to restrict the result to the one closest at the given coordinates. To extract all relevant information again an ExtractPattern-SIB is used.

To this point the middle left part of the workflow is processed really fast and without interaction to the user. However the following two InputDialog-SIBs will ask for the type/content of the graffito and the kind of object it was sprayed on. Then the user is also prompted to enter few keywords. Until no digital fingerprint works, these keywords are important to make the database searchable.

Since there are no hardware power consuming tasks to do in this part of the workflow, the submission of text by the user takes some time which is used to finish image processing in parallel.

All current processed and entered meta data is written in a simple comma-separated text file named currentMeta.csv. Each graffito and therefore each detailed photograph will be evaluated in this way. Each time all information is stored in a new line of a collecting csv-file named allMeta.csv.

ExecuteCommand is used to do some operations on text files. For example a carriage return is added to allMeta.csv. This will ensure writing in a new line with the current meta data. This is important because comma-separated text files won't work otherwise. So there are WriteTextFile-SIBs creating and writing current meta data in a csv-text-file and there are ExecuteCommand-SIBs for merging current data to allMeta.csv and to add line breaks.

The file allMeta.csv lays inside /MetaPDF/ and since it has only its headline and no entries by default, the headline shows what kind of information will be entered:

```
ID, date, content, object, city, stand name, street type, OSM,
 profile, keywords
```

Next to allMeta.csv inside /MetaPDF/ lays a lightweight TeX-file, staying unchanged but integrating the growing allMeta.csv:

```
\documentclass{article}
\usepackage[landscape]{geometry}
\geometry{hmargin=.1cm,vmargin=.4cm}
\usepackage[utf8]{inputenc}
\usepackage{csvsimple}

\begin{document}
\csvautotabular{allMeta.csv}
\end{document}
```

When the left and right part of the workflow are finished and join again, we'll have processed meta data written in text files (csv and tex) on the one hand, and we have processed clean and small images on the other hand. The little framed part to the end covers two final ExecuteCommand-SIBs. All processed text-files as well as the images are available to them now. So they can perform pdflatex on command line. As a result there will be two PDF documents: a table containing all meta data from each processed image (figure 5), and a profile showing meta data of the current image next to its characteristic pattern.

0_overview.pdf

Vorherige Nächste 1 (1 von 1) 100%

ID	date	content	object	city	stand name	street type	latitude	longitude	keywords
20120810-1523SDIM001	2012:05:05 13:17	face	public monument	Göttingen	Mühlenstraße	PEDESTRIAN	51 32 6 N	9 56 4 E	harlekin red laughing
20120810-1538SDIM001de	2012:05:05 13:17	scripture	private house	Göttingen	Mühlenstraße	PEDESTRIAN	51 32 6 N	9 56 4 E	RASH 60x20cm blue
20120810-1753201208-20	2012:05:05 15:08	fratze	sockel	Göttingen	Wilhelmsplatz	PEDESTRIAN	51 32 1 N	9 56 16 E	harlekin also laughing

Fig. 5. Generated overview-PDF, CVS integrated in TeX through csvsimple

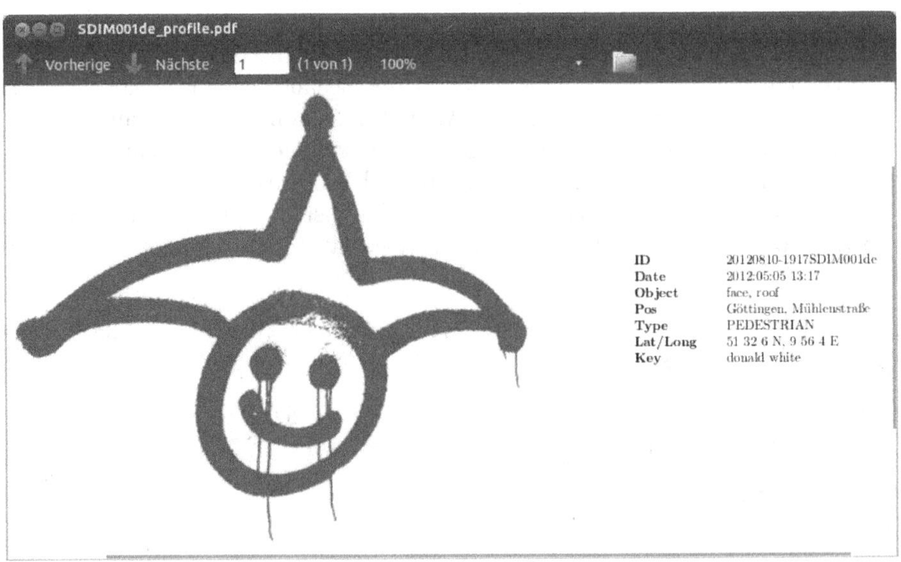

Fig. 6. Generated profile-PDF: graffito pattern next to current meta data

4 Conclusion

There are obvious advantages using GraffDok. The user still has to enter meta data each time he's processing a photograph and there's no way around human input or image description. But the user is guided, and all other things are done automatically, e. g. a growing table as graffiti overview. And these processes are even done in the time the user needs to enter the description.

So it is not a real one-click-application, but except for the image description it is! And as long as we take simple photographs with distinct graffiti lines on a surface, the graffiti are processed and extracted from their background very well. In some time it should be easy to create nice stats, for example in which area the most graffiti can be found. The choice of collecting data as csv should also be a benefit then, because csv-files are quite easy to handle with GNU R. Also, csv-files are in general easily editable in any editor or tab-based calculation software.

TeX may be a good choice, too. The layout is very simple yet. But TeX offers precise positioning and standardized outputs for more complex profile PDF-documents in future. With the help of csvsimple both, TeX and CSV, are quite usable in combination, while concentrating on a minimum.

Of course there is room for improvement in this first version of GraffDok. First of all there should be a multiple file input in future, allowing multiple descriptions at a time, maybe with thumbnails. At least in case somebody takes a lot of images it is for sure annoying to start from the beginning with every graffito.

Also the image processing only works fine with the most common type of graffiti: distinct lines on homogenous backgrounds. In this simple case thresholding works well enough. But to handle graffiti with different colors and mixed backgrounds, in other words: more classes, it will become necessary to do a more complex image classification. To stay with Open Source and to avoid too many different software, one may take GNU R for the stats as well as for the image classification, e. g. via random forests.

A digital fingerprint is hard to develop but would be greatly useful. It's a pity it will still take some time until one can capture a graffito and GraffDok tells immediately where this pattern was found elsewhere – without crawling databases by own sight or keywords. In terms of image recognition some free and open source frameworks for Augmented Reality may help. Especially those working markerless, recognizing any image without predefined binary markers/codes.

There are few more options to make this project even better. There are ways and tools like tth doing tex2html. By converting all TeX-Profiles into HTML-Websites and converting the overview to a website as well, one could make the database accessible to everyone via web. It would be easy to hyperlink from the overview to a profile or to OSM showing the waypoint.

And the whole bunch of visualizing stats may follow, e. g. spatial distribution. An interface/GUI for editing old entries would be nice, too. And a beautifully visualised comparison of entries – maybe telling, that there already was a similar graffito at a certain place, but maybe was cleaned and sprayed on again.

This article is part of a larger evaluation [7], which aimed at illustrating the power of simplicity-oriented development [14] by validating the claim that process modeling can indeed be handed over to the domain experts by providing them with a graphical modeling framework [23] that covers low-level details in a service-oriented fashion [16], integrates high-level modeling in the overall development process in a way that user-level models become directly executable [15,12], and supports ad-hoc adaptations and evolution [11,13].

The project described in this article can be characterized as follows:

- Scientific domain: geoinformatics
- Number of models: 1
- Number of hierarchy levels: 1
- Total number of SIBs: 46
- SIB libraries used (cf. [10]): common-sibs (45), gisgraphy-sibs (1)
- Service technologies used: REST web services

The geoinformatics part of this volume contains eight other articles on workflow applications in this domain [5,19,4,25,21,20,2,22]. Further geoinformatics workflow projects with the jABC have recently been started. Ongoing work is also exploring how to apply semantics-based (semi-) automatic workflow composition techniques (as provided by, e.g., [18]) to support the workflow design process, as described in [8,9,6] for the bioinformatics domain.

References

1. exif – the simple command line interface to libexif, an open source EXIF library written in C, `http://libexif.sourceforge.net/` (Online; last accessed January 20, 2013)
2. Hibbe, M.: Spotlocator Project Documentation. In: Lamprecht, A.-L., Margaria, T. (eds.) Process Design for Natural Scientists. CCIS, vol. 500, pp. 149–158. Springer, Heidelberg (2014)
3. ImageMagick Studio LLC. ImageMagick – open source software for editing images, `http://www.imagemagick.org/` (Online; last accessed January 20, 2013)
4. Kind, J.: Creation of Topographic Maps. In: Lamprecht, A.-L., Margaria, T. (eds.) Process Design for Natural Scientists. CCIS, vol. 500, pp. 225–234. Springer, Heidelberg (2014)
5. Kuntzsch, C.: Visualization of Data Transfer Paths. In: Lamprecht, A.-L., Margaria, T. (eds.) Process Design for Natural Scientists. CCIS, vol. 500, pp. 140–148. Springer, Heidelberg (2014)
6. Lamprecht, A.-L.: User-Level Workflow Design. LNCS, vol. 8311. Springer, Heidelberg (2013)
7. Lamprecht, A.-L., Margaria, T.: Scientific Workflows and XMDD. In: Lamprecht, A.-L., Margaria, T. (eds.) Process Design for Natural Scientists. CCIS, vol. 500, pp. 1–13. Springer, Heidelberg (2014)
8. Lamprecht, A.-L., Margaria, T., Steffen, B.: Bio-jETI: A framework for semantics-based service composition. BMC Bioinformatics 10(suppl. 10), S8 (2009)

9. Lamprecht, A.-L., Naujokat, S., Margaria, T., Steffen, B.: Semantics-based composition of EMBOSS services. Journal of Biomedical Semantics 2(suppl. 1), S5 (2011)
10. Lamprecht, A.-L., Wickert, A.: The Course's SIB Libraries. In: Lamprecht, A.-L., Margaria, T. (eds.) Process Design for Natural Scientists. CCIS, vol. 500, pp. 30–44. Springer, Heidelberg (2014)
11. Margaria, T., Steffen, B.: Agile IT: Thinking in User-Centric Models. In: Margaria, T., Steffen, B. (eds.) ISoLA 2008. CCIS, vol. 17, pp. 490–502. Springer, Heidelberg (2009)
12. Margaria, T., Steffen, B.: Business Process Modelling in the jABC: The One-Thing-Approach. In: Cardoso, J., van der Aalst, W. (eds.) Handbook of Research on Business Process Modeling. IGI Global (2009)
13. Margaria, T., Steffen, B.: Continuous Model-Driven Engineering. IEEE Computer 42(10), 106–109 (2009)
14. Margaria, P., Steffen, B.: Simplicity as a Driver for Agile Innovation. Computer 43(6), 90–92 (2010)
15. Margaria, T., Steffen, B.: Service-Orientation: Conquering Complexity with XMDD. In: Hinchey, M., Coyle, L. (eds.) Process Design for Natural Scientists, pp. 217–236. Springer, London (2012)
16. Margaria, T., Steffen, B., Reitenspiess, M.: Service-Oriented Design: The Roots. In: Benatallah, B., Casati, F., Traverso, P. (eds.) ICSOC 2005. LNCS, vol. 3826, pp. 450–464. Springer, Heidelberg (2005)
17. Masclet, D.: Gisgraphy project – open source framework offering geolocalisation and geocoding services, `http://www.gisgraphy.com/` (Online; last accessed January 20, 2013)
18. Naujokat, S., Lamprecht, A.-L., Steffen, B.: Loose Programming with PROPHETS. In: de Lara, J., Zisman, A. (eds.) Fundamental Approaches to Software Engineering. LNCS, vol. 7212, pp. 94–98. Springer, Heidelberg (2012)
19. Noack, F.: CREADED: Coloured-Relief Application for Digital Elevation Data. In: Lamprecht, A.-L., Margaria, T. (eds.) Process Design for Natural Scientists. CCIS, vol. 500, pp. 182–195. Springer, Heidelberg (2014)
20. Respondeck, T.: A Workflow for Computing Potential Areas for Wind Turbines. In: Lamprecht, A.-L., Margaria, T. (eds.) Process Design for Natural Scientists. CCIS, vol. 500, pp. 196–211. Springer, Heidelberg (2014)
21. Scheele, L.: Location Analysis for Placing Artificial Reefs. In: Lamprecht, A.-L., Margaria, T. (eds.) Process Design for Natural Scientists. CCIS, vol. 500, pp. 212–224. Springer, Heidelberg (2014)
22. Sens, H.: Web-Based Map Generalization Tools Put to the Test: a jABC Workflow. In: Lamprecht, A.-L., Margaria, T. (eds.) Process Design for Natural Scientists. CCIS, vol. 500, pp. 171–181. Springer, Heidelberg (2014)
23. Steffen, B., Margaria, T., Nagel, R., Jörges, S., Kubczak, C.: Model-Driven Development with the jABC. In: Bin, E., Ziv, A., Ur, S. (eds.) HVC 2006. LNCS, vol. 4383, pp. 92–108. Springer, Heidelberg (2007)
24. Sturm, T.F.: csvsimple – open source LaTeX package for processing of files with comma separated values, `http://www.ctan.org/tex-archive/macros/latex/contrib/csvsimple/` (Online; last accessed January 20, 2013)
25. Teske, D.: Geocoder Accuracy Ranking. In: Lamprecht, A.-L., Margaria, T. (eds.) Process Design for Natural Scientists. CCIS, vol. 500, pp. 159–170. Springer, Heidelberg (2014)
26. Weinhaus, F.: fuzzythresh script – bash script for automatically thresholding a two class image to binary black and white format using fuzzy c-means, free use in free software, `http://www.fmwconcepts.com/imagemagick/fuzzythresh/` (Online; last accessed January 20, 2013)

Author Index